Theories of Memory

THEORIES OF MEMORY

A READER

Edited by Michael Rossington and Anne Whitehead

Contributing editors:
Linda Anderson, Kate Chedgzoy,
Pablo Mukherjee and Jennifer Richards

THE JOHNS HOPKINS UNIVERSITY PRESS
BALTIMORE

First published in the United Kingdom by Edinburgh University Press, 2007
Published in the United States by the Johns Hopkins University Press, 2007
9 8 7 6 5 4 3 2 1

The Johns Hopkins University Press
2715 N. Charles Street
Baltimore, MD 21218-4363
www.press.jhu.edu

ISBN 10: 0-8018-8728-3 (cloth: alk. paper)
ISBN 13: 978-0-8018-8728-4

ISBN 10: 0-8018-8729-1 (pbk.: alk. paper)
ISBN 13: 978-0-8018-8729-1

Library of Congress Control Number: 2007921656

A catalog record for this book is available from the British Library.

CONTENTS

Part III: Identities

PREFACE

This volume has emerged out of the *MA in Literary Studies: Writing, Memory, Culture*, which is taught in the School of English Literature, Language and Linguistics at Newcastle University. We would like to acknowledge the contribution, first and foremost, of the many students who have taken the degree programme since it began in 2001, upon whom much of this material has been tried out in seminars. As well as expressing gratitude to our contributing editors for all their work, we would also like to thank other colleagues in the School of English who contributed in important ways to the volume: John Beck, Stacy Gillis, Gemma Robinson and Terry R. Wright, as well as other staff who have taught on the programme. The School of English has provided generous material assistance in its financial support for copyright fees and in awarding Tom Theobald a postgraduate bursary for his work on the volume. We owe particular thanks to Linda Anderson for her support and encouragement, to Tom Theobald for his invaluable technical expertise and to Rowena Bryson for her administrative assistance. We would finally like to thank Jackie Jones and the readers at Edinburgh University Press, who provided constructive and detailed feedback and suggestions.

Michael Rossington and Anne Whitehead

ACKNOWLEDGEMENTS

Grateful acknowledgement is made to the following sources for permission to reproduce material previously published elsewhere. Every effort has been made to trace the copyright holders, but if any have been inadvertently overlooked, the publisher will be pleased to make the necessary arrangements at the first opportunity.

Edith Hamilton and H. Cairns (eds) THE COLLECTED DIALOGUES OF PLATO, Princeton University Press, 1963, pp. 897, 496–7, 520. HAMILTON, EDITH; *PLATO* © 1961 Princeton University Press, 1989 renewed. Reprinted by permission of Princeton University Press.

Richard Sorabji (ed. and trans.), ARISTOTLE ON MEMORY, 2nd ed., Gerald Duckworth & Co. Ltd., 2004, pp. 47–60. ARISTOTLE ON MEMORY © 1972, 2004 by Richard Sorabji and originally published by Gerald Duckworth & Co. Ltd. Reprinted by permission of Gerald Duckworth & Co. Ltd.

Cicero, ON THE IDEAL ORATOR (DE ORATORE), trans, with introduction, notes, appendixes, glossary, and indexes by James M. May and Jakob Wisse, Oxford University Press, 2001, pp. 218–21. From CICERO: ON THE IDEAL ORATOR, translated by Jakob Wisse, copyright © 2001 by Oxford University Press, Inc. Used by permission of Oxford University Press, Inc.

[Cicero], AD C. HERENNIUM DE RATIONE DICENDI (RHETORICA AD HERENNIUM), trans. by Harry Caplan, Harvard University Press, 1954,

R. J. Hollingdale, Cambridge University Press, 1997, pp. 60–7, 260. Copyright © Cambridge University Press, reproduced with permission.

Henri Bergson, MATTER AND MEMORY, trans. Nancy Margaret Paul and W. Scott Palmer, New York, Zone Books, 1991, pp. 77–84. Copyright © 1988 Urzone, Inc. Reprinted by permission of Zone Books.

Sigmund Freud, 'A Note upon the "Mystic Writing-Pad"' [1925], in ON METAPSYCHOLOGY: THE THEORY OF PSYCHOANALYSIS, Vol. 11 of 'The Penguin Freud Library', trans. by James Strachey, ed. by Angela Richards, Penguin, 1991, pp. 429–34. Translation and Editorial Matter copyright © Angela Richards and the Institute of Psycho-Analysis, 1955, 1957, 1958, 1961, 1962, 1964. Additional Editorial Matter copyright © Angela Richards, 1984. Sigmund Freud © Copyrights, The Institute of Psycho-Analysis and The Hogarth Press for permission to quote from THE STANDARD EDITION OF THE COMPLETE PSYCHOLOGICAL WORKS OF SIGMUND FREUD translated and edited by James Strachey. Reprinted by permission of The Random House Group Ltd. U.S. rights quoted from Sigmund Freud, COLLECTED PAPERS, Volume 5, ed. by James Strachey. Published by Basic Books, a member of Perseus Books, L.L.C.

Walter Benjamin, 'On The Image of Proust' [1929], in SELECTED WRITINGS, Vol. 2, 1937–34, pp. 237–47. Reprinted by permission of the publisher from WALTER BENJAMIN: SELECTED WRITINGS, VOLUME 2, 1927–34, trans. by Rodney Livingstone and others, edited by Michael W. Jennings, Howard Eiland, and Gary Smith, Cambridge, Mass.: The Belknap Press of Harvard University Press, Copyright © 1999 by the President and Fellows of Harvard College. 'On the Image of Proust' from ILLUMINATIONS by Walter Benjamin, copyright © 1955 by Suhrkamp Verlag, Frankfurt a. M, English translation by Harry Zohn © 1968 and renewed 1996 by Harcourt, Inc., reprinted by permission of Harcourt, Inc. Originally published as Walter Benjamin, *Illuminationem: Ausgewählte Schriften* (Suhrkamp Verlag). Copyright © der »Schriften« 1955 by Suhrkamp Verlag, Frankfurt a. M.

Maurice Halbwachs, THE COLLECTIVE MEMORY [1950], trans. by Francis J. Ditter and Vida Yazdi Ditter, intro. by Mary Douglas, New York: Harper Colophon Books, 1980, pp. 78–84. Excerpt from THE COLLECTIVE MEMORY by MAURICE HALBWACHS and trans. by FRANCIS AND VIDA DITTER. Copyright 1950 by Presses Universitaires de France. English translation copyright © 1980 by Harper & Row, Publishers, Inc. Introduction copyright © 1980 by Mary Douglas. Reprinted by permission of HarperCollins Publishers.

Pierre Nora (trans. Marc Roudebush), 'Between Memory and History: "*Les Lieux de Mémoire*"', REPRESENTATIONS, Vol. 26, No. 1: 7–12. © 1989,

Marianne Hirsch and Valerie Smith, 'Feminism and Cultural Memory: An Introduction', in Marianne Hirsch and Valerie Smith, eds. SIGNS: JOURNAL OF WOMEN IN CULTURE AND SOCIETY 28.1 (2002), pp. 3–12. Copyright © 2002 by The University of Chicago. Reprinted by permission of The University of Chicago Press and the authors.

Annette Kuhn, FAMILY SECRETS: ACTS OF MEMORY AND IMAGINATION, London: Verso, 1999, pp. 1–5, 55–8. Copyright © Verso 1995, 1999. Reproduced with permission of the publishers.

Benedict Anderson, IMAGINED COMMUNITIES: REFLECTIONS ON THE ORIGIN AND SPREAD OF NATIONALISM, rev. ed., London and New York: Verso, 1991, pp. 187–89, 191–97, 201–206. Copyright © Benedict Anderson, 1983, 1991. Reproduced with permission of Verso Press.

Étienne Balibar, 'The Nation Form: History and Ideology', in Philomena Essed and David Theo Goldberg, eds, RACE CRITICAL THEORIES, pp. 220–30, copyright © Blackwell Publishers Ltd 2002. Editorial matter and organization copyright Philomena Essed and David Theo Goldberg 2002. Reprinted with permission of the publisher.

Paul Gilroy, THERE AIN'T NO BLACK IN THE UNION JACK, Routledge, 1992, pp. 43–6, 48–53, 62–5. Copyright © 1987 Paul Gilroy. Reprinted with permission of the Taylor and Francis Group.

Victor Burgin, IN/DIFFERENT SPACES: PLACE AND MEMORY IN VISUAL CULTURE, pp. 117–21, 128–37. Copyright © 1996, The Regents of the University of California. Used with permission.

Avtar Brah, CARTOGRAPHIES OF DIASPORA, Routledge, 1996, pp. 204–08. Copyright © 1996 Avtar Brah. Reprinted with permission of the Taylor and Francis Group.

Edward W. Said, OUT OF PLACE: A MEMOIR, London: Granta Books, 1999, pp. 3–12. Copyright © Edward W. Said, 1999. Reprinted with permission of the Wylie Agency.

ILLUSTRATIONS

INTRODUCTION

Michael Rossington and Anne Whitehead

And suddenly the memory returns. The taste was that of the little crumb of madeleine which on Sunday mornings at Combray (because on those mornings I did not go out before church-time), when I went to say good day to her in her bedroom, my aunt Léonie used to give me, dipping it first in her own cup of real or of lime-flower tea. The sight of the little madeleine had recalled nothing to my mind before I tasted it; perhaps because I had so often seen such things in the interval, without tasting them, on the trays in pastry-cooks' windows, that their image had dissociated itself from those Combray days to take its place among others more recent; perhaps because of those memories, so long abandoned and put out of mind, nothing now survived, everything was scattered; the forms of things, including that of the little scallop-shell of pastry, so richly sensual under its severe, religious folds were either obliterated or had been so long dormant as to have lost the power of expansion which would have allowed them to resume their place in my consciousness. But when from a long-distant past nothing subsists, after the people are dead, after the things are broken and scattered, still, alone, more fragile, but with more vitality, more unsubstantial, more persistent, more faithful, the smell and taste of things remain poised a long time, like souls, ready to remind us, waiting and hoping for their moment, amid the ruins of all the rest; and bear unfaltering, in the tiny and almost impalpable drop of their essence, the vast structure of recollection. (Proust, 2000: 58)

I

In her analytical account of memory, the philosopher Mary Warnock has commented that 'memory . . . inevitably brings in the physiological' (Warnock, 1987: 1). She argues persuasively that in addressing the question of what memory is, the obstacle of 'dualism', that is a philosophical belief that mind and body are separate, needs to be removed. Instead we need to recognise that according to the insights of psychology, physiology and other scientific disciplines, memory is a quality possessed by any organism, and may be defined as 'the capacity of a body or substance for manifesting effects of, or exhibiting behaviour dependent on, its previous state, behaviour or treatment' (*OED*, 6b). Most contemporary accounts of memory begin with the premise that it is not located in the mind of a human being or animal but is rather an aspect of the brain's behaviour which necessarily is both mental and physical at the same time. For Warnock, an extension of the *OED* definition of memory above is that it is '*that by the possession of which an animal learns from experience*' (Warnock, 1987: 6). But, one might argue, it is not only animals, including human ones, that so learn. In common contemporary usage, 'memory' may be understood as *any* mechanism through which such experiential learning takes place. The memory characteristic of a machine such as a computer by which data is stored that may be retrieved is sometimes called 'virtual'. And much remembering in everyday life is done by machines and therefore is virtual in this sense. Thus, at a basic level, it is possible to see how scientific and medical investigations of memory understand it in terms of traces in neurological networks and programmable functions (see Rose, 1998 and Sejnowski, 1998). Although in this Reader we have not had space to include extracts representative of such approaches, these ways of thinking and their ethical and cultural consequences are important to note at the outset.

An alternative way of thinking about memory is to consider its function in humans' consciousness of themselves as having distinct identities over time. That memory plays a significant role in personal identity has been examined rewardingly by contemporary philosophers (see, for example, Parfit, 1984). Such debates often refer back to John Locke's attempt at what might be styled a 'common-sense' definition in *An Essay Concerning Human Understanding* (1690): 'to find where *personal Identity* consists, we must consider what *Person* stands for; which, I think, is a thinking intelligent Being, that has reason and reflection, and can consider it self as it self, the same thinking thing in different times and places' (Locke, 1975: 335). Recent accounts, such as the following from David Wiggins, have both qualified and extended this definition in light of the physiological dimension of memory referred to above:

> The hospitalized amnesiac or Nijinksy even at the last stage of madness are the same man and the same person . . . Let us amend Locke, and say a person is any animal, the physical make-up of whose species constitutes

the species' typical members, thinking, intelligent beings, with reason and reflection, and typically enables them to consider themselves as themselves the same thinking things, in different times and places. Memory is not then irrelevant to personal identity, but the way it is relevant is simply that it is one highly important element among others in the account of what it is for a person to be still there, *alive*. It plays its part in determining the continuity principle for persons, as opposed to bodies or cadavers. (Wiggins, cited in Warnock, 1987: 74)

Medical research into the condition of amnesia (literally, the absence of memory) is one helpful way of reflecting on these issues. As Max Deutscher remarks, amnesia demonstrates that 'memory as retention of skills is different from the recollection of events' (Deutscher, 1998: 297) in that an amnesiac may know how to prepare a meal but not know when she last ate. The following account by an amnesiac patient, cited by Barbara Wilson, seems to illustrate Wiggins's point that while memory may be relevant to personal identity, it is possible to have a sense of identity without it:

> My memory limitations are not so much a problem any more. I don't mourn the loss of my memory as I can't remember what it used to be like. The condition has helped me to evolve, I think, into a different type of person . . . I have become more cerebral, my thinking more esoteric, and I am very comfortable with this. I think it suits my character. (Wilson, 1998: 133)

In clinical practice, Wilson comments that the 'use of computers as prosthetic memory aids' (Wilson, 1998: 130) is becoming increasingly common in the treatment of amnesia. The cultural and ethical consequences of the possibility of a prosthetic memory, that is an organism that, like any other, may be implanted (and therefore of a subject with memories that are not its own), have been explored in a cybercultural reading of the films *Blade Runner* and *Total Recall* (see Landsberg, 2000).

A characteristic of thinkers who have sought to undertake conceptual ground-clearing in relation to memory is their compulsive need to discriminate among its many meanings. From Aristotle's distinction between remembering and recollecting to Hegel's *Erinnerung* and *Gedächtnis* to the present, memory has proved itself too overwhelming a topic to be encompassed by a single definition. Warnock is again useful here. There are skills, responses or modes of behaviour that are learned by human beings, non-human animals and even machines which we may, in her phraseology, term '*habit memory*' (a locution also used by Henri Bergson) whereas, by contrast, '*conscious memory* consists of recalling or recollecting past experience' (Warnock, 1987: 9, my emphases). These definitions of 'habit memory' and 'conscious memory' are useful but even more so is her injunction for us to understand that they are not exclusive but in continual dialogue with one another:

> It is over-simple to think of memory as one 'faculty' which can be explained by one account. But it is not much better to think of it as two faculties. It is better to think in terms of a continuum, at one end of which is the mysterious phenomenon of consciousness. Somewhere along the line animals must begin to know what they are doing in remembering. There is a distinction to be drawn at the edges of the continuum between habit memory and conscious memory. But neither is irrelevant to the other. (Warnock, 1987: 14)

The sense registered here that conscious memory entails an awareness of what is being done in the act of remembering connects Aristotle and Locke.

While acknowledging that the extracts in this book are confined, largely, to Western (that is, European and Anglo-American) philosophical traditions, our endeavour has been to show the value of an albeit highly selective account of thinking about memory from the classical period to the present. Through a historical approach it is possible to identify, for example, a preoccupation with image-based theories of memory from Aristotle through Cicero and the mnemonic traditions outlined by Mary Carruthers and Frances Yates to Locke and Hume but also to note a definite break with such thinking in Hegel. Equally, one may discern the recourse to spatial metaphors in the *loci memoriae* examined by Yates, Locke's 'Storehouse', Hegel's 'pit' and Nora's 'lieux de mémoire'. One can identify in Hume's anxiety to separate memory from the imagination a heralding of 'Romantic' and 'Modern' explorations of the inter-relationship between creativity and memory in the autobiographically inspired work of Rousseau, Wordsworth and Proust and in Benjamin's literary criticism. In Marx and Nietzsche a critical engagement with nineteenth-century attitudes to history is advanced through regard to memory, of which forgetting is a crucial dimension. However, it would be mistaken to suggest that thinking about memory has undergone a chronological *development* over the centuries. Plato's influential contribution demonstrates the point that while each contribution is distinct and to some extent historically specific, there are commonalities of idiom. In *Phaedrus*, memory is understood as recollection, that is the revival of knowledge acquired before birth, an idea that seems to resonate with the profundity ascribed to certain kinds of memory in Hegel's definition of *Erinnerung*, Bergson's 'pure memory' and Proust's *mémoire involuntaire*, while in *Theaetetus*, the gift of Mnemosyne, the mother of the Greek Muses, is conceptualised as the imprinting of perceptions or ideas on a block of wax 'as we might stamp the impression of a seal ring', a notion of legibility present in Freud's meditation on the 'Mystic Writing-Pad'.

II

Raymond Williams's classic study *Keywords: A Vocabulary of Culture and Society* (1976) sought to identify and define a number of words central to the discussion and analysis of culture. Although the terms 'History', 'Myth',

'Tradition' and 'Unconscious' were included in the volume, the word 'Memory' was notably absent. However, the updated version edited by Tony Bennett et al., *New Keywords: A Revised Vocabulary of Culture and Society* (2005), includes an entry on 'Memory' by Bill Schwarz in addition to others on 'Holocaust', 'Heritage' and 'Time'. This shift both registers and makes visible the 'memory boom' that had occurred since the original publication. The factors contributing to the surge of interest in memory in the closing decade or so of the twentieth century were varied and complex. Postmodernism focused on the perception that it was no longer possible for the historical past to be retrieved, that the acceleration and commodification of history had resulted in amnesia or, at best, an ideologically motivated recuperation of the past. Developments in technology had led to a sophisticated engagement with and theorisation of virtual memory; simultaneous to this, many written and visual archives were being digitised and electronically stored. In the post-Cold War era, new archives were opening up and revealing memories previously unavailable while nations newly independent of the Soviet Union sought self-definition by negotiating often complex, conflicted and troubled pasts. As the century drew to a close, there was an increasing concern with how best to remember the traumatic instances that had punctuated its history – including, but not limited to, wars and genocides – and the vicissitudes of remembering and forgetting were painfully played out in the Truth and Reconciliation Commissions of South Africa, Guatemala and Chile. In the remainder of this section, it is our aim to outline in more detail other important contributing factors to the 'memory boom' of the 1990s: the emergence of key publications, the debates around False Memory Syndrome and developments in the academic fields of Holocaust studies, postcolonialism and poststructuralism. In the following section, we will briefly indicate the critical responses to memory studies that have emerged – most notably from Kerwin Lee Klein and Wulf Kansteiner – and then consider recent work by Avishai Margalit and Paul Ricoeur as an implicit riposte to such critiques.

One factor of undoubted importance to the emergence of memory as a key area of definition and debate was the publication of Yosef Yerushalmi's *Zakhor: Jewish History and Jewish Memory* (1982), followed closely by Pierre Nora's 'Between Memory and History', the introduction to his magisterial edited project *Les Lieux de Mémoire* (1984; trans. 1989). Both of these texts emerged out of a close engagement with the work of Maurice Halbwachs on collective memory and both of them opposed memory as a primitive and sacred form to modern historical consciousness. As many critics, including John Frow, have observed of Nora – and the same point can be made in relation to Yerushalmi – his work is characterised by a nostalgic and elegiac tone and too easy an opposition between memory and history, which implicitly positions memory as an anti-historical discourse. In spite, or perhaps because, of this, the work of Yerushalmi and Nora made a significant impact and reinvigorated Halbwachs's work on collective memory. Their publications were quickly followed by others

5

and formed a significant factor in the ensuing scholarly boom of memory studies.

Another contributing factor to the 'memory boom' lay in the debates surrounding False Memory Syndrome (FMS) in the early 1990s. These originated in 1993 with the False Memory Syndrome Foundation in Philadelphia, in which parents came together to protest against what they believed to be their grown daughters' false accusations of childhood sexual abuse. Ann Scott observes of the ensuing crisis: 'Memory – its reliability, its nature, its formation, its dissipation, its susceptibility to distortion – became an urgent matter at every level, from the intimately familial to the more public stage and ultimately the US courts' (Scott, 1996: xxvi). The proponents of FMS argued that the recovery of memory in therapy was not necessarily reliable, that although the adult women in therapy seemed to be accessing long repressed and buried memories, it may be the case that suggestion was at work. A high-profile defender of FMS was the psychologist Elizabeth Loftus. She called into question the mechanism of 'repression' – specifically, the idea that early traumatic experiences could be pushed into the unconscious and reside there for years, isolated from the rest of mental life (see Joslyn, Carlyn and Loftus, 1997) – and thereby cast into doubt the legacy of Sigmund Freud, for the notion of repression was most closely associated with his work. The debates around FMS raised crucial issues in relation to remembering and forgetting. How can 'repression' be disproved when it hinges on remembering a moment of forgetting? Is the 'truth' value of a memory to be judged by its relation to a past event, or by its meaning in the present for an individual? What is the evidentiary status of a memory, when it is of necessity based on a past that no longer exists? FMS also suggested that an entire event could be fabricated in the memory by suggestion; by implication, memory was no longer securely tied to the individual subjectivity. The boundaries of the self and of identity were revealed to be fragile and porous, for childhood memories, it seemed, could come as much from without as from within.

The debates surrounding FMS can be compared instructively to the work on memory that was emerging out of Holocaust studies in the early 1990s. The work on testimony that was produced by Shoshana Felman and Dori Laub was similarly troubled by questions of accuracy and authenticity. In *Testimony: Crises of Witnessing in Literature, Psychoanalysis and History* (1992), Laub gives the example of a woman survivor of Auschwitz who misremembers in her testimony the number of chimneys destroyed in the Auschwitz rebellion. For historians, this renders her testimony without value for it does not give an accurate representation of the past. For Laub, however, the woman's mistake makes her testimony more powerful, for it speaks of the incomprehensibility of witnessing *any* chimneys destroyed at Auschwitz (Felman and Laub, 1992: 59–63). At stake here are similar questions of narrative, truth and identity to those which characterised the debates around FMS. These issues surfaced most forcefully in Holocaust studies with the revelation in 1998 that Binjamin

Wilkomirski's celebrated autobiography of the camps, *Fragments: Memories of a Childhood, 1939–1948* (1996) was a 'fake'; its author was the Swiss Bruno Grosjean, who had never been confined in a concentration camp (for further discussion, see Lappin, 1999, and Maechler, 2000).

In Holocaust studies, the centrality of memory was emphasised in the first instance by survivors themselves. In his last work, *The Drowned and the Saved* (1988), Primo Levi devoted his opening chapter to discussing the vicissitudes of memory in relation to the event. Another survivor of Auschwitz, Charlotte Delbo, also opened her final work *Days and Memory* (1990) by examining the nature of her memories. For Delbo, the memory of Auschwitz is permanent and fixed: 'Auschwitz is so deeply etched in my memory that I cannot forget one moment of it' (Delbo, 1990: 2). In order to survive after Auschwitz, her memory has split into two: 'external memory' is connected with thinking processes and everyday normality, while 'deep memory' is 'the memory of the senses' which returns the survivor to the agony of the camps in an intense reliving of the experience. Memory is both foregrounded and problematised in the texts of Holocaust survivors, who remain profoundly troubled by a past which impinges upon and disturbs the present.

Following the work of survivors like Levi and Delbo, memory emerged as an important theoretical focus in the discourse of Holocaust studies. A strong interest in traumatic memory arose in the early 1990s, centred on Cathy Caruth's edited volume *Trauma: Explorations in Memory* (1995). Although the concept of trauma had a wide application across a range of historical events and academic disciplines, the Holocaust provided a limit case and was the focus for much work in this field. Caruth provided a model for thinking through the connections between the individual and collective historical experiences, such as war and genocide. In *The Holocaust: Theoretical Readings* (2003), Neil Levi and Michael Rothberg indicate that trauma studies was also concerned to address an unresolved past of 'intellectual complicity' in the Holocaust, in particular 'the very different complicities of such figures as Martin Heidegger and Paul de Man' (Levi and Rothberg, 2003: 16).[1] As the children of survivors reached adulthood, the question of whether the trauma of the Holocaust could be passed on to the next generation became a central focus, most notably in the work of Marianne Hirsch (1997). She coined the term 'postmemory' to describe the ways in which individuals can be haunted by a past that they have not experienced personally but which has somehow been 'transferred' to them, often unconsciously, by family members.[2] Although Hirsch largely confines her discussion to the intimate familial context, her work is also suggestive of a broader model for thinking through the ways in which we are affected by the traumas of recent history at a collective or cultural level.

Drawing on the work of Nora on collective memory, a distinct strand of Holocaust studies focused on how the event is remembered across different cultural contexts, and what political interests in the present can be served by memorialising the Nazi genocide. Most notable in this context was the publication of James E. Young's influential study of Holocaust memorials, *The Texture of Memory* (1993). Young argued that there was not a single Holocaust but that every nation remembers the event according to its own traditions, ideals and experiences. Drawing on Nora, Young viewed Holocaust memorials as 'sites of memory' which reflect the shifting meanings and political resonances of the Holocaust. The 1993 opening of the United States Holocaust Memorial Museum in Washington, DC focused particular attention on the American memorialisation of the Holocaust.[3] Peter Novick's *The Holocaust and Collective Memory* (2000) charted the history of the postwar response to the Holocaust in America and asked why and how this event, which took place in Europe, came to assume so central a place in American cultural consciousness. Both Novick and Young – like Nora before them – assumed that the nation played a central role in the operation and organisation of collective memory.

A further contributing factor to the surge of interest in memory in the 1990s was the academic discourse of postcolonial studies, which had enjoyed its own 'boom' in the previous decade.[4] At the heart of postcolonialism is the study of empires and how they continue to shape the present. Postcolonialism, then, with its focus on the continuing effects of the processes and systems of empire, has an inherent interest in temporality and the past. A key figure in the emergence of postcolonial studies was the Martiniquan psychiatrist and freedom fighter Frantz Fanon, who became a member of the central committee of the Algerian Front de Libération Nationale during the war of independence. In *The Wretched of the Earth* (1967), Fanon drew on his psychiatric work in order to trace a link between individual self-esteem and collective cultural or national esteem. He argued that feelings of shame, self-contempt and dignity are determined in large part by one's cultural position. In the final chapter of his study, 'Colonial War and Mental Disorders', Fanon addressed the theme of memory by including notes and dialogues from his psychiatric work at a hospital in Blida-Joinville. These powerfully and disturbingly reveal the ways in which memories of colonialism are played out as mental illness. Of key importance here, then, is the intersection of the individual and the collective in relation to memory, and the central role of the nation in defining identity – to the extent that Fanon offers a defence of violence as the necessary response to colonisation.

Gayatri Chakravorty Spivak and Homi K. Bhabha played a central role in the academic consolidation of postcolonial criticism. Spivak's critical appraisal of the Subaltern Studies historians in 'Subaltern Studies: Deconstructing Historiography' (1998) is particularly interesting in the context of memory studies. Subaltern Studies historians argue that their task is to recover the history of the Indian people, the non-elite narratives of colonial and post-colonial India. Spivak questions whether the subaltern (understood as the marginalised, dispossessed opposite of the cultural elite) can indeed speak for him or herself, or whether the subaltern is condemned to be known, represented and spoken for only by third parties. In relation to memory, first-person accounts of subaltern memory are the vital historical resource most often missing from the archive. Spivak is concerned that intellectuals in the West '[grant] to the oppressed either [a] very expressive subjectivity . . . or, instead, a total unrepresentability' (Spivak, 1998: 209). For her, subalterns leave a trace or 'subject-effect' in colonial narratives and documents (Spivak, 1998: 204); their discursive identities offer a way for us to remember those people who were neither very expressive nor entirely unrepresentable.

Homi Bhabha's work focuses on the trope of mimicry, which is itself a form of repetition or remembrance. He argues in *The Location of Culture* (1994) that there are two aspects of mimicry worth considering: mimicry as a practice encouraged by colonisers in an attempt to create an identity for colonised peoples – in which the coloniser requires colonial subjects to remember and repeat the norms of the occupying power – and mimicry as a signifier of ambivalence, through which the binary relationship of the coloniser and the colonised is undermined. Colonialism creates subjects who are 'almost the same but not quite' (Bhabha, 1994: 89) and in difference lies potential subversion and resistance. Bhabha's interest in ambivalent formulations of colonialism offers a celebratory vision of subalterns outmanoeuvring the colonisers, and provides a tentative model for non-violent anti-colonial agency. Spivak and Bhabha both draw on deconstruction in order to emphasise the complex discursive construction of political communities. For both writers, memory is central to postcolonialism and they draw out the ways in which personal and cultural memory can be used to analyse, and potentially to undermine or contest, the structures of empire.

The final context for the emergence of memory studies is poststructuralism. 'Poststructuralism' does not describe a coherent movement but is a way of identifying a number of critical thinkers who challenged critical orthodoxies and took up the position that identities do not relate to essences but are events in language. Closely related to conceptions of identity, memory formed one of the categories in literary studies that poststructuralism revisited and re-evaluated. Poststructuralist critics typically advanced not by directly propounding their ideas, but by drawing attention to the language of a particular piece of writing, tracing through their analysis its figurative and rhetorical gestures. Poststructuralism contributed to memory studies a series of sustained and close readings of founding literary and theoretical treatments of memory, which demonstrated that the text is a network of signifiers that necessarily fails to produce a final, definitive meaning.

Paul de Man taught on the literary studies programme at Yale University and exerted a considerable influence on Cathy Caruth and Shoshana Felman. One of the most influential essays by de Man is his 1979 reading of two passages by Jean-Jacques Rousseau: the conclusion of book II of the *Confessions* (1771) and the fourth reverie in *Reveries of a Solitary Walker* (1778). Both passages concern Rousseau's memory of an episode in his youth when he stole a ribbon and blamed a maidservant named Marion for the theft; his accusation led to her dismissal. De Man concludes that the point of Rousseau's act of memory is not what he confesses – the truth or otherwise of Marion's dismissal – but the very act of confession itself, both as a staging of the self and as the generation of a text.[5] Jacques Derrida's work displayed an ongoing fascination with Freud and, in particular, the suppressed or overlooked role of writing in the elaboration of psychoanalysis. In a famous early essay, 'Freud and the Scene of Writing' (1978), Derrida returned to Freud's 'Note upon the "Mystic Writing-Pad"' (1925) in order to unravel the significance of the metaphors of writing which pervade Freud's description of the unconscious. If the unconscious is a text – as Freud's writing implies – then Derrida argued that its contents, composed of interwoven traces, cannot be straightforwardly recovered; they are only accessible through supplementary modes of interpretation. In 'Nietzsche, Genealogy, History' (1977), Foucault returned to Nietzsche's concept of genealogy in order to draw out its implications for a critique of traditional historical discourse. Foucault contested the notion of history as tracing a development from origin to culmination; he argued that a 'genealogical analysis' could counter history by drawing out the discontinuity and instability at the heart of identity. The impact of poststructuralism on memory studies was felt primarily in its insistence, through close readings of a number of key eighteenth- and nineteenth-century texts, that meaning was unstable and undecidable and that the past could not be fully recuperated; the act of memory was therefore both compromised and necessarily incomplete.

III

The emergence of 'memory' as an influential area of study in the 1990s resulted from a complex convergence and intersection of academic discourses and disciplines. The first major critique of the 'memory boom' was Kerwin Lee Klein's essay 'On the Emergence of *Memory* in Historical Discourse' (2000). Here, Klein argues that 'memory' has assumed the role of a meta-theoretical trope and, in its current usage, refers both to individual psychologies and to cultural practices of remembering and their attendant material artefacts – including, but not limited to, archives, public monuments and museums. Discussions of collective memory, he argues, too readily accord to memory the status of a historical agent, so that 'we enter a new age in which archives remember and statues forget' (Klein, 2000: 136). It is important for an engaged political analysis, he points out, to remain attentive to *who* is doing the remembering and the forgetting. Although 'memory' is a leading term in cultural discourse, Klein argues that it is too often vague and undefined. More troubling to him than this, however, is the link between the rise of memory studies and identity politics, particularly in the context of post-1960s America. Memory appeals to us, he claims, because of the (often unstated) implication that it occupies a site of authenticity. In this sense, 'memory' currently serves as a therapeutic alternative to historical discourse. Memory is often opposed to the hegemony of history, and is associated with the articulations of ethno-racial groups; Klein accordingly warns us to be wary of 'the tendency to employ memory as the mode of discourse natural to the people without history' (Klein, 2000: 144).

Klein's critique was closely followed by Wulf Kansteiner's 'Finding Meaning in Memory: A Methodological Critique of Collective Memory Studies' (2002). Here, Kansteiner argues that memory studies have not done enough to establish a clear conceptual and methodological basis for collective memory processes. Like Klein, Kansteiner discerns a lack of precise definition in discussions of collective memory, so that the terminology of individual memory is too often extended and misapplied: 'Collectives are said to remember, to forget, and to repress the past; but this is done without any awareness that such language is at best metaphorical and at worst misleading about the phenomenon under study' (Kansteiner, 2002: 185). Collective memories have their own dynamics and processes for which we need appropriate methods of analysis. Kansteiner also echoes Klein in protesting that there is too much emphasis on the material artefact in discussions of collective memory. For Kansteiner, collective memory represents a complex process of cultural interaction and negotiation between three different historical agents: the visual and discursive objects of memory, memory makers and memory consumers. Although memory studies have drawn attention to the first two elements, they have consistently overlooked the role of the latter. Kansteiner finds this politically troubling, for it is precisely memory consumers who often read memorial artefacts against the grain of their intended meaning. For Kansteiner, then, memory studies need to shift their focus from the production of memory objects – which tends to emphasise the formation of a stable interpretative community – to their reception, which brings to light who actually identifies with these representations. Finally, Kansteiner also draws attention to the interrelation between memory studies and identity politics, pointing out that historically crises of memory have tended to coincide with crises of identity. Reflecting on the contributing factors to the current 'memory boom' – therapeutic controversies, high-profile judicial cases, post-Cold War ethnic conflicts – Kansteiner observes that, certainly in this instance, 'memory is valorized where identity is problematized' (Kansteiner, 2002: 184). His analysis provides a suggestive model for thinking through a history of memory. The current crisis of memory would then not be exceptional, but would correspond to earlier historical crises of identity; this mode of analysis could accordingly be extended to research into memory in the Romantic, Enlightenment and early-modern periods.

For Klein and Kansteiner, then, although memory studies represent a dynamic and impressive contribution to recent research in the humanities, they are nevertheless flawed by attendant problems of methodology and conceptualisation. More recent work has sought to move away from these critiques and to focus once again on the importance and necessity of memory work, particularly in the context of ethics. Paul Ricoeur's dense and difficult last work *Memory, History, Forgetting* (2004) is divided into three sections which each adopt different conceptual approaches: phenomenology for memory, epistemology for history and hermeneutics for forgetting. In the first section, Ricoeur seeks to explore who is the primary agent of remembering: the individual or the collective. His discussion reconciles the two positions by attributing memory to individuals but assuming that individuals are essentially relational. Individual and collective memories have a reciprocal relationship and Ricoeur does not prioritise one over the other. In relation to history, Ricoeur insists that memory, in the form of testimony, is its foundation or bedrock: 'We must not forget that everything starts not from the archives, but from testimony and that . . . we have nothing better than testimony, in the final analysis, to assure ourselves that something did happen in the past' (Ricoeur, 2004: 147). In the final section of his book, Ricoeur turns his attention to the question of forgetting which, he insists, is an integral and necessary part of remembering. Central to the ethics of memory is the relation between forgetting and forgiving. Ricoeur makes a distinction between forgetting in reserve – where a memory of the injury can still be called to mind – and total forgetting. Although it is not entirely clear which of the two Ricoeur prefers, Margalit observes of his analysis: 'I think he is willing to pay the price for forgiving in the soft currency of forgetting in reserve and not with the hard currency of total forgetfulness' (Margalit, 2005: 11). At the close of his work, then, Ricoeur leaves his reader suspended somewhere between amnesty and amnesia.

In *The Ethics of Memory* (2002), Avishai Margalit covers similar ground to Ricoeur. He starts by distinguishing the realm of ethics from that of morality. This is, in turn, founded on a distinction between two types of human relations: 'thick relations' which connect those with a shared past, and 'thin relations' which connect those who are strangers or remote to each other. Ethics regulates the ways in which we conduct our thick relations, while morality tells us how we should conduct our thin relations. Although the thick relations of family, nation and ethnic or religious groupings form the natural communities of memory, Margalit questions whether there are certain shared memories that should be held in mind by humanity as a moral community. The problem here, as Margalit points out, is that a single event – for example, the Holocaust – will not have the same meanings for different communities, while there will also be an inevitable bias, in deciding which events to remember, towards the First World. Margalit closes, like Ricoeur, by considering the relation between forgiving and forgetting. Like Ricoeur, he draws a distinction between two types of forgiveness: forgiveness as blotting out the sin and forgiveness as covering it up. He concludes, more decisively than Ricoeur, that 'forgiveness is based on disregarding the sin rather than forgetting it' (Margalit, 2002: 197). For both Ricoeur and Margalit, then, memory work is important in spite of, or perhaps because of, its inherent problems and difficulties. Both writers seek to elaborate in detail the processes of collective memory and to think through the relations between individual and collective remembering. What is particularly striking in both texts, however, and perhaps suggests a future direction for memory studies, is the emphasis on forgetting as an integral part of memory, and the attempt to think through the relationship between forgetting and forgiving – an important focus for both individuals and political communities, as we are confronted with the problems of how to live with, and move on from, violent, disruptive and traumatic histories.

IV

In *Theories of Memory: A Reader* we address a number of interrelated aims. We seek to provide a comprehensive survey of theories of memory from the classical period to the present day. We try to historicise the idea of memory by tracing theories in the field chronologically. We also aim to identify and foreground an important trend in contemporary theory, demonstrating the extent to which ideas of memory permeate the fields of literature and culture. With these objectives in mind, the volume is structured in three parts, which are in turn divided into sections as outlined below. Part I, 'Beginnings', introduces central positions in thinking about memory. The first section starts with classical viewpoints and also refers to the major studies by Mary Carruthers and Frances Yates in order to introduce important questions concerning the nature of memory and the relation between memory and text. The second section focuses on ideas of memory in the Enlightenment and Romantic periods. The final section introduces memory in key nineteenth- and early twentieth-century texts. All of the extracts in this section are in dialogue with material in the later parts. Part II, 'Positionings', develops the work in Part I by identifying major positions within recent and contemporary literary studies through which memory is defined and debated. Each of the approaches outlined in Part II – 'Collective Memory', 'Jewish Memory Discourse' and 'Trauma' – challenges or critiques orthodox thinking about memory. Part III, 'Identities', seeks to explore the role of memory in defining subjectivities. It draws on and extends Part II by focusing attention on the ways in which theoretical positionings have formed and informed the construction of identities at both individual and cultural levels. The section on 'Gender' explores the ethical and political issues surrounding memory and embodiment, while the sections 'Race/Nation' and 'Diaspora' highlight the importance of recent work that has addressed the relation between memory and location. In choosing the extracts for the sections, we seek to combine the classic accounts of memory with some more unexpected choices in order to broaden the scope of current memory studies in what we feel to be productive directions.

Each of the sections features an introduction that sets the ideas in their theoretical and historical context. The extracts are edited and introduced by a number of contributing editors who work within their own areas of specialism. We recommend that, in approaching the volume, readers consult the general introduction in the first instance to provide overall orientation, and then use the section introductions to guide their reading of the extracts. Each of the sections also contains suggestions for further reading in the area, so that readers will be able to find support and resources for specialising further. We have aimed, in compiling the volume, to provide an accessible and informative guide to the main positions and debates for those who are new to the area of memory studies. We have also sought, for those with more knowledge of the field, to collect the most important theoretical material in a single volume for the first time. Although we expect that the volume will primarily be of interest to those who are involved in historicising or theorising memory, we also anticipate that it will appeal to anyone who is interested in what is happening in literary theory now, its conception of itself and its dialogue with subjects (such as 'memory') which are not obviously its own. In the interests of maintaining coherence and focus, we decided from the outset to limit the extracts in the volume to theoretical writing that addresses memory, thereby omitting literary inclusions. This was an economy that we felt to be necessary, although we recognise that important theories of memory are inextricably embedded in versions of the literary, from Augustine through Rousseau to Proust and beyond. It is testimony to the vibrancy of memory studies that there were, necessarily, many extracts that we had to exclude reluctantly and we urge readers to follow the suggestions for further reading to encounter in full the energy and richness of this field.

NOTES

1. Heidegger was an advocate of Nazism; for more on this, see Collins (2000). After de Man's death, the Belgian scholar Ortwin de Graef uncovered wartime journalism that the former had published in a German-run newspaper during the occupation of Belgium. Of the 170 articles that were discovered, the most problematic was 'Jews in Contemporary Literature', published in *Le Soir* on 4 March 1941. For more on this, see Hamacher, Hertz and Keenan (1989).
2. The experiences of the second generation are movingly explored by Art Spiegelman in his *Maus* comic books. See Spiegelman (1987) and (1992).
3. See, for example, Flanzbaum (1999), Shandler (1999) and Mintz (2001).
4. We would like to thank Gemma Robinson for her generous contribution to this discussion of postcolonial studies.
5. For Felman's response to de Man's reading of Rousseau, see Felman and Laub (1992: 120–64).

REFERENCES AND FURTHER READING

Anderson, Benedict (1983; rev. edn 1991) *Imagined Communities: Reflections on the Origins and Spread of Nationalism*. London and New York: Verso.
Bal, Mieke, Jonathan Crewe and Leo Spitzer (eds) (1999) *Acts of Memory: Cultural Recall in the Present*. Hanover, NH, and London: University Press of New England.
Bennett, Tony, Lawrence Grossberg and Meaghan Morris (eds) (2005) *New Keywords: A Revised Vocabulary of Culture and Society*. Malden, MA: Blackwell.
Bhabha, Homi K. (1994) *The Location of Culture*. London and New York: Routledge.
Caruth, Cathy (ed.) (1995) *Trauma: Explorations in Memory*. Baltimore, MD, and London: Johns Hopkins University Press.
Collins, Jeff (2000) *Heidegger and the Nazis*. New York: Totem Books.
De Man, Paul (1979) 'Excuses (Confessions)', in *Allegories of Reading: Figural Language in Rousseau, Nietzsche, Rilke, and Proust*. New Haven, CT, and London: Yale University Press, pp. 278–302.
Delbo, Charlotte (1990) *Days and Memory*, trans. Rosette Lamont. Marlboro, VT: Marlboro Press.

Derrida, Jacques (1978) 'Freud and the Scene of Writing', in *Writing and Difference*, trans. Alan Bass. London: Routledge & Kegan Paul, pp. 246–91.

Deutscher, Max (1998) 'Memory', in Edward Craig (gen. ed.), Vol. 6 of *The Routledge Encyclopaedia of Philosophy*. London and New York: Routledge, pp. 296–300.

Draaisma, Douwe (2000) *Metaphors of Memory: A History of Ideas about the Mind*, trans. Paul Vincent. Cambridge: Cambridge University Press.

Fanon, Frantz (1967) *The Wretched of the Earth*, trans. Constance Farrington. Harmondsworth: Penguin.

Fara, Patricia and Karalyn Patterson (eds) (1998) *Memory*. Cambridge: Cambridge University Press.

Felman, Shoshana and Dori Laub (1992) *Testimony: Crises of Witnessing in Literature, Psychoanalysis and History*. New York and London: Routledge.

Flanzbaum, Hilene (ed.) (1999) *The Americanization of the Holocaust*. Baltimore, MD, and London: Johns Hopkins University Press.

Foucault, Michel (1977) 'Nietzsche, Genealogy, History', in D. F. Bouchard (ed.), *Language, Counter-Memory, Practice: Selected Essays and Interviews*. Ithaca, NY: Cornell University Press, pp. 139–64.

Gilroy, Paul (1993) *The Black Atlantic: Modernity and Double Consciousness*. London and New York: Verso.

Hamacher, Werner, Neil Hertz and Thomas Keenan (eds) (1989) *Responses: On Paul de Man's Wartime Journalism*. Lincoln, NE: University of Nebraska Press.

Hirsch, Marianne (1997) *Family Frames: Photography, Narrative and Postmemory*. Cambridge, MA and London: Harvard University Press.

Hodgkin, Katharine and Susannah Radstone (eds) (2003) *Contested Pasts: The Politics of Memory*. London: Routledge.

Joslyn, Susan, Linda Carlin and Elizabeth F. Loftus (1997) 'Remembering and Forgetting Sexual Abuse', *Memory*, 5(6): 703–24.

Kansteiner, Wulf (2002) 'Finding Meaning in Memory: A Methodological Critique of Memory Studies', *History and Theory*, 41: 179–97.

Klein, Kerwin Lee (2000) 'On the Emergence of *Memory* in Historical Discourse', *Representations*, 69: 127–50.

Krell, David Farrell (1990) *Of Memory, Reminiscence and Writing: On the Verge*. Bloomington, IM: Indiana University Press.

LaCapra, Dominick (2001) *Writing History, Writing Trauma*. Baltimore, MD and London: Johns Hopkins University Press.

Landsberg, Alison (2000) 'Prosthetic Memory: *Total Recall* and *Blade Runner*', in David Bell and Barbara M. Kennedy (eds), *The Cybercultures Reader*. London and New York: Routledge, pp. 191–201.

Lappin, Elena (1999) 'The Man with Two Heads', *Granta*, 66: 7–66.

Le Goff, Jacques (1992) *History and Memory*, trans. Steven Rendell and Elizabeth Clamon. New York: Columbia University Press.

Levi, Neil and Michael Rothberg (eds) (2003) *The Holocaust: Theoretical Readings*. Edinburgh: Edinburgh University Press.

Levi, Primo (1988) *The Drowned and the Saved*, trans. Raymond Rosenthal. London: Abacus.

Locke, John (1975) *An Essay Concerning Human Understanding*, ed. Peter H. Nidditch. Oxford: Clarendon Press.

Maechler, Stefan (2001) *The Wilkomirski Affair: A Study in Biographical Truth*, trans. John E. Woods. London: Picador.

Margalit, Avishai (2002) *The Ethics of Memory*. Cambridge, MA, and London: Harvard University Press.

—— (2005) 'Partial Recall', *Times Literary Supplement*, 30 September: 9–11.

Mintz, Alan (2001) *Popular Culture and the Shaping of Holocaust Memory in America*. Seattle, WA, and London: University of Washington Press.

Nora, Pierre (1989) 'Between Memory and History: *Les Lieux de Mémoire*', *Representations*, 26: 7–25.

Novick, Peter (2000) *The Holocaust and Collective Memory*. London: Bloomsbury.

Parfit, Derek (1984) *Reasons and Persons*, Part III: *Personal Identity*. Oxford: Oxford University Press.

Proust, Marcel ([1922] 2000) *Swann's Way*, trans. C. K. Scott Moncrieff. London: Penguin.

Radstone, Susannah (ed.) (2000) *Memory and Methodology*. Oxford and New York: Berg.

—— and Katharine Hodgkin (eds) (2003) *Regimes of Memory*. London: Routledge.

Ricoeur, Paul (2004) *Memory, History, Forgetting*, trans. Kathleen Blamey and David Pellauer. Chicago and London: University of Chicago Press.

Rose, Steven P. R. (1998) 'How Brains Make Memories', in Fara and Patterson, op. cit., pp. 134–61.

Samuel, Raphael (1996) *Theatres of Memory*, Vol 1: *Past and Present in Contemporary Culture*. London: Verso.

—— (1999) *Theatres of Memory*, Vol. 2: *Island Stories: Unravelling Britain*. London: Verso.

Schwarz, Bill (2005) 'Memory', in Tony Bennett, Lawrence Grossberg and Meaghan Morris (eds), *New Keywords: A Revised Vocabulary of Culture and Society*. Malden, MA: Blackwell, pp. 214–17.

Scott, Ann (1996) *Real Events Revisited: Fantasy, Memory and Psychoanalysis*. London: Virago.

Sejnowski, Terence (1998) 'Memory and Neural Networks', in Fara and Patterson, op. cit., pp. 162–81.

Shandler, Jeffrey (1999) *While America Watches: Televising the Holocaust*. New York and Oxford: Oxford University Press.

Sheringham, Michael (1993) 'The Otherness of Memory', in *French Autobiography: Devices and Desires: From Rousseau to Perec*. Oxford: Clarendon Press, pp. 288–326.

Spiegelman, Art (1987) *Maus I: A Survivor's Tale – My Father Bleeds History*. Harmondsworth: Penguin.

—— (1992) *Maus II: A Survivor's Tale – And Here My Troubles Began*. Harmondsworth: Penguin.

Spivak, Gayatri Chakravorty (1998) 'Subaltern Studies: Deconstructing Historiography', in *In Other Worlds: Essays in Cultural Politics*. New York and London: Routledge, pp. 197–221.

Warnock, Mary (1987) *Memory*. London and Boston: Faber.

Weinrich, Harald (2004) *Lethe: The Art and Critique of Forgetting*, trans. Steven Randall. Ithaca, NY, and London: Cornell University Press.

Wilkomirski, Binjamin (1996) *Fragments: Memories of a Childhood, 1939–1948*, trans. Carol Brown Janeway. London: Picador.

Williams, Raymond (1976) *Keywords: A Vocabulary of Culture and Society*. London: Fontana.

Wilson, Barbara A. (1998) 'When Memory Fails', in Fara and Patterson, op. cit., pp. 113–33.

Yerushalmi, Yosef Hayim (1982) *Zakhor: Jewish History and Jewish Memory*. Seattle, WA, and London: University of Washington Press.

Young, James E. (1993) *The Texture of Memory: Holocaust Memorials and Meaning*. New Haven, CT, and London: Yale University Press.

PART I
BEGINNINGS

SECTION I
CLASSICAL AND EARLY MODERN
IDEAS OF MEMORY

Edited by Jennifer Richards

INTRODUCTION

Jennifer Richards

Remembering has long been a venerated faculty, but the way in which it is valued and the reasons for this have changed radically over time. Memory is no longer recognised as an 'art' or 'craft'; it is no longer an essential component of school or university curricula. However, to ancient Greek philosophers, remembering and reasoning were interconnected activities, while to the Roman rhetoricians of the first century BC and AD, a good memory was 'the treasure-house of eloquence' (Quintilian, 1979: XI.ii.1). We can only marvel now at the formidable feats of memory which this craft produced in the Middle Ages and the Renaissance: the capacity to recite the whole of Virgil's *Aeneid* or entire books of the Bible in their original *or* a rearranged order (Carruthers and Ziolkowski, 2002: 5), or, say, the ability of Peter of Ravenna who could 'repeat from memory the whole of canon law, text and gloss . . . two hundred speeches and sayings of Cicero; three hundred sayings of the philosophers; twenty thousand legal points' (Yates, this volume, p. 61). Stranger still are the complex visual symbols that were deployed as memory aids (see Yates, this volume) and, furthermore, the medieval mindset that could find ethical value in the ability to recite long texts verbatim (Carruthers, this volume).

The conception of memory varies considerably from antiquity to early modernity: Plato (428–347 BC) argued that rhetorical training diminishes our capacity to remember, while the Roman rhetoricians, in contrast, developed the art that was to inform late medieval and Renaissance *Memoria*. However, two emphases are shared within these periods: first, the idea that 'memory' is an active process which is defined by the two activities of collection and recollection, of storing and retrieval; second, that these activities constitute the basis of knowing and understanding. A useful way of discerning differences within this tradition which are crucial for later developments is to distinguish between dialectical (or philosophical) and rhetorical memory. The source for dialectical memory is Greek moral philosophy, in particular Plato's dialogue *Phaedrus* and Aristotle's short treatise *De Memoria et Reminiscentia* (*On Memory and Recollection*), an appendix to *De Anima* (On the soul). In both texts recollection is understood as a way of thinking, an art of reasoning.

Plato's *Phaedrus* explores the relationship between rhetoric and dialectic, between persuasion and reasoning. Its argument is that only an education in philosophy, in the art of dialectic, represented here by the two-sided debate between 'Socrates' and 'Phaedrus', strengthens our memory. Or rather, only a philosophical education realises our innate capacity to reason and so to live moral lives. This capacity is described by Socrates as a 'memory' of the divine origins of our soul. According to Socrates, the philosopher understands how to use 'reminders' of this world properly. For example, when he sees a beautiful young man, like Phaedrus, he controls any lustful desire he may feel and dwells instead on what his physique recalls, the original idea of true beauty. The proper use of this reminder in turn inspires the philosopher to teach (or remind) the young man of this truth. This is contrasted with the rhetorical education offered to Phaedrus by the sophist 'Lysias', recalled at the opening of the dialogue, which represents the wrong way of remembering *and* thinking. Rhetorical training is dismissed by Socrates because the intentions of the rhetorician are distrusted: its teachers and practitioners are accused of aiming merely to satisfy personal desires and to attain political advantage. Worse still, their method of 'thinking' and communicating, which depends on rote-learning of speeches that follow a prearranged structure explicated in the technical handbooks, serves only to jog the memory. Rhetorical training depletes rather than nurtures 'memory' because it makes it dependent on props; it does not encourage the reasoning process that, in Socrates' view, is needed to realise (recall) our divinely-gifted capacity to reason.

Aristotle's *On Memory and Recollection* is also a study of dialectical memory, but its approach is rather different to Plato's; it is based more clearly on the observation of how the mind retrieves information. Important emphases in this study include Aristotle's understanding of the associative and visual character of memory. Every memory, he suggests, has a visual likeness and an affective quality, and this enables its recall. He also draws an important distinction between remembering and recollecting. Many animals can remember, he notes, but only humankind can both remember and 'recollect'. Recollection is a deliberate action; it is a 'search' entailing reflection on 'time' and the objects remembered through the orderly association of ideas and images. This process involves independent reasoning: the dialectician is not learning arguments off by heart; rather he is actively tracing patterns of argument *and* the process of their recall.

The source for rhetorical memory is the Roman handbooks on oratory of the first century BC and AD. Rhetoric or oratory is an art of persuasion; its practitioners rely on a good memory to recall the points of a case in the correct order, the arguments made by an antagonist in court so they can respond to them fully, and also their own speeches so that they appear extempore when delivered. In this tradition, memory is very clearly an art or craft, a series of learned techniques that can enhance natural ability. Its status as an art, and the importance of order to it, are underscored by the Roman orator **Marcus Tullius Cicero**, who recalls the story of its origins in *De oratore* (On the ideal orator) (55 BC). According to this story, Simonides of Ceos (*c.* 556–468 BC) was the sole survivor of a disaster, when guests at a banquet were killed by a collapsing roof. Simonides remembers where each guest sat, and he is thus able to identify the crushed bodies for burial. Reflecting on his natural skill he makes the discovery 'that order is what most brings light to our memory' (this volume, p. 40). This story is retold in rhetorical handbooks as a way of introducing the most important technique of rhetorical memory training, the 'place' system: this depends on the placing and ordering in an imagined space or 'background' in the mind the vivid symbols that represent the content to be remembered.

A detailed account of rhetorical memory and its place system is offered in *Rhetorica ad Herennium* (*Rhetoric to Herennius*) (*c.* 100 BC). The orator who wants to train his memory, we are told, must create a background for storing images, usually an architectural location such as a house; this enables the orderly retrieval of the images which are used to mark the objects or words to be remembered. These images should be vivid and remarkable so as to aid memory. To cite one example: the author of this manual explains how a prosecutor might keep in mind the details of a convoluted case involving a number of witnesses and accessories in which a defendant is accused of killing a man with poison in order to obtain an inheritance. He might do so by imagining the victim in bed with the defendant at the bedside 'holding in his right hand a cup, and in his left tablets, and on his fourth finger a ram's testicles' (this volume, p. 45). This last image is especially opaque, but to a Roman orator it vividly represents the presence of the witnesses (Latin, *testes*).

Rhetorica ad Herennium offers an orderly account of this mnemonic technique of storage and it provided the basis for the art's later development; for this reason it is included in this volume. However, readers may also want to consult Book XI.ii of Quintilian's *Institutio oratoria* (*On the training of the orator*) (*c.*AD 93), which usefully distinguishes between the process of recalling content (*Memoria rerum*), detailed in *Rhetorica ad Herennium*, and the rote-learning of speeches, the remembering of words (*Memoria verborum*) that is sometimes also described as 'grammatical memory' (Carruthers and Ziolkowski, 2002: 10). Rote-learning depends on the repeated reading of one's own writing as well as other texts, and it is compared by Quintilian 'to chewing the cud' (XI.ii.41). This method is recommended by Quintilian as useful training for boys who need to build a treasure-house of memories (knowledge) which they can draw upon to compose their speeches. However, it is of limited use to the orator who is preparing to speak in public since there is nothing less persuasive, Quintilian explains, than the impression that one is reeling off a speech verbatim. More useful to the orator is *Memoria rerum*, the recollection of the general matter of a speech and its order, both because this method is less time-consuming than rote-learning and because it endows the orator with a flexibility and quickness that enables him to deliver speeches as if they were extempore (XI.ii.44–7).

Memory training is central to educational curricula in the Middle Ages and the Renaissance, as the extracts from the critical work of **Mary Carruthers** and **Frances Yates** reproduced in this volume establish. With Jan M. Ziolkowski, Mary Carruthers has also edited an anthology of writings detailing medieval memory techniques, the introduction to which helpfully distinguishes between the *Memoria* of the early and later Middle Ages: between, on the one hand, the 'prayerful, ruminative contemplation of biblical texts' (*Memoria verborum*) in the early monastic tradition founded by Augustine of Hippo, John Cassian and Jerome and, on the other hand, the rhetorical techniques which favour the recollection of content (*Memoria rerum*). The techniques of rhetorical memory were re-introduced following reforms in the Church in the twelfth century which led to a revival of oratory, and which were supported by the wider dissemination of technical handbooks like *Rhetorica ad Herennium* (Carruthers and Ziolkowski, 2002: 17–23).

The extract from Carruthers's study represented in this volume explores the early monastic tradition of *Memoria* as an art of reading, which was informed mainly by the techniques recommended by Quintilian for the memorising of texts – their rereading, copying out and annotation and recitation – and which was conceived as a process of rumination and digestion. What is so fascinating and surprising about this form of *Memoria* is that it constitutes both an 'art' *and* a way of being in the world, a way of organising the 'self' and of managing the relationship between 'self' and others. The early medieval *Memoria* informed a conception of reading as 'tropological'; this is reading which turns 'the text onto and into one's self' (this volume, p. 51). Originality and imagination are of less value than a good memory, which enables a reader to internalise another's work. The reader has to 'digest' what they are reading, placing it so securely in their memory that they effectively become its 'new author' (this volume, p. 54). Whereas we consider such assimilation unethical, an example of 'plagiarism' or the theft of intellectual property, in the monasteries of the Middle Ages it was conceived rather as an ethical dialogue between memories (this volume, p. 54), the sharing and preservation of communal wisdom. This is to be contrasted with the return to rhetorical memory in the late Middle Ages and Renaissance, the imaginative and often humorous techniques of which are described and illustrated by Frances Yates. Medieval and Renaissance manuals repeated and expanded on the variety of 'backgrounds' for the rhetorical place system – a quiet space such as an unfrequented church, visual alphabets, the spheres of the universe. Both the use of backgrounds and of striking images (for example, the black teeth and snaky hair of Envy) to help recall the virtues and vices in a moral universe represent the overlap between the late medieval and early Renaissance *Memoria*. But there are also important differences in the Renaissance, as suggested by Yates: the laicisation and popularisation of memory schemes, as well as a new conception of their practical use (this volume, p. 62).

REFERENCES AND FURTHER READING

Augustine, Saint (1961) 'Book X', in *Confessions*, trans. R. S. Pine-Coffin. London: Penguin, pp. 207–52.

Carruthers, Mary and Jan M. Ziolkowski (eds) (2002) *The Medieval Craft of Memory: An Anthology of Texts and Pictures*. Philadelphia: University of Pennsylvania Press.

Coleman, Janet (1992) *Ancient and Medieval Memories: Studies in the Reconstruction of the Past*. Cambridge and New York: Cambridge University Press.

Derrida, Jacques (1981) 'Plato's Pharmacy', in *Dissemination*, trans. Barbara Johnson. Chicago: University of Chicago Press, pp. 61–171.

Goody, Jack and Ian Watt (1968) *Literacy in Traditional Society*. Cambridge: Cambridge University Press.

Quintilian (1979) *The Institutio Oratoria of Quintilian*, trans. H. E. Butler. Cambridge, MA: Harvard University Press; London: William Heinemann.

Streuver, Nancy S. (2004) 'Rhetoric: Time, Memory, Memoir', in Walter Jost and Wendy Olmsted (eds), *Companion to Rhetoric and Rhetorical Criticism*. Oxford: Blackwell, pp. 425–41.

<h1 style="text-align:center">1.1</h1>

PLATO: *FROM* THEAETETUS *AND* PHAEDRUS

SOCRATES: Imagine, then, for the sake of argument, that our minds contain a block of wax, which in this or that individual may be larger or smaller, and composed of wax that is comparatively pure or muddy, and harder in some, softer in others, and sometimes of just the right consistency.

THEAETETUS: Very well.

SOCRATES: Let us call it the gift of the Muses' mother, Memory, and say that whenever we wish to remember something we see or hear or conceive in our own minds, we hold this wax under the perceptions or ideas and imprint them on it as we might stamp the impression of a seal ring. Whatever is so imprinted we remember and know so long as the image remains; whatever is rubbed out or has not succeeded in leaving an impression we have forgotten and do not know.

PHAEDRUS 249B–250C

SOCRATES: For only the soul that has beheld truth may enter into this our human form – seeing that man must needs understand the language of forms, passing from a plurality of perceptions to a unity gathered together by reasoning – and such understanding is a recollection of those things which our

Source: Plato, *Theaetetus*, 191c–191e, *Phaedrus*, 249d–250e, and *Phaedrus*, 274c–275b, in E. Hamilton and H. Cairns (eds), *The Collected Dialogues of Plato* (Princeton, NJ: Princeton University Press, 1963), pp. 897, 496–7, 520.

souls beheld aforetime as they journeyed with their god, looking down upon the things which now we suppose to be, and gazing up to that which truly is.

Therefore is it meet and right that the soul of the philosopher alone should recover her wings, for she, so far as may be, is ever near in memory to those things a god's nearness whereunto makes him truly god. Wherefore if a man makes right use of such means of remembrance, and ever approaches to the full vision of the perfect mysteries, he and he alone becomes truly perfect. Standing aside from the busy doings of mankind, and drawing nigh to the divine, he is rebuked by the multitude as being out of his wits, for they know not that he is possessed by a deity.

Mark therefore the sum and substance of all our discourse touching the fourth sort of madness – to wit, that this is the best of all forms of divine possession, both in itself and in its sources, both for him that has it and for him that shares therein – and when he that loves beauty is touched by such madness he is called a lover. Such a one, as soon as he beholds the beauty of this world, is reminded of true beauty, and his wings begin to grow; then is he fain to lift his wings and fly upward; yet he has not the power, but inasmuch as he gazes upward like a bird, and cares nothing for the world beneath, men charge it upon him that he is demented.

Now, as we have said, every human soul has, by reason of her nature had contemplation of true being; else would she never have entered into this human creature; but to be put in mind thereof by things here is not easy for every soul. Some, when they had the vision, had it but for a moment; some when they had fallen to earth consorted unhappily with such as led them to deeds of unrighteousness, wherefore they forgot the holy objects of their vision. Few indeed are left that can still remember much, but when these discern some likeness of the things yonder, they are amazed, and no longer masters of themselves, and know not what is come upon them by reason of their perception being dim.

Now in the earthly likenesses of justice and temperance and all other prized possessions of the soul there dwells no luster; nay, so dull are the organs wherewith men approach their images that hardly can a few behold that which is imaged, but with beauty it is otherwise. Beauty it was ours to see in all its brightness in those days when, amidst that happy company, we beheld with our eyes that blessed vision, ourselves in the train of Zeus, others following some other god; then were we all initiated into that mystery which is rightly accounted blessed beyond all others; whole and unblemished were we that did celebrate it, untouched by the evils that awaited us in days to come; whole and unblemished likewise, free from all alloy, steadfast and blissful were the spectacles on which we gazed in the moment of final revelation; pure was the light that shone around us, and pure were we, without taint of that prison house which now we are encompassed withal, and call a body, fast bound therein as an oyster in its shell.

PHAEDRUS 274C–275B

SOCRATES: The story is that in the region of Naucratis in Egypt there dwelt one of the old gods of the country, the god to whom the bird called Ibis is sacred, his own name being Theuth. He it was that invented number and calculation, geometry and astronomy, not to speak of draughts and dice, and above all writing. Now the king of the whole country at that time was Thamus, who dwelt in the great city of Upper Egypt which the Greeks call Egyptian Thebes, while Thamus they call Ammon. To him came Theuth, and revealed his arts, saying that they ought to be passed on to the Egyptians in general. Thamus asked what was the use of them all, and when Theuth explained, he condemned what he thought the bad points and praised what he thought the good. On each art, we are told, Thamus had plenty of views both for and against; it would take too long to give them in detail. But when it came to writing Theuth said, 'Here, O king, is a branch of learning that will make the people of Egypt wiser and improve their memories; my discovery provides a recipe for memory and wisdom.' But the king answered and said, 'O man full of arts, to one it is given to create the things of art, and to another to judge what measure of harm and of profit they have for those that shall employ them. And so it is that you, by reason of your tender regard for the writing that is your offspring, have declared the very opposite of its true effect. If men learn this, it will implant forgetfulness in their souls; they will cease to exercise memory because they rely on that which is written, calling things to remembrance no longer from within themselves, but by means of external marks. What you have discovered is a recipe not for memory, but for reminder. And it is no true wisdom that you offer your disciples, but only its semblance, for by telling them of many things without teaching them you will make them seem to know much, while for the most part they know nothing, and as men filled, not with wisdom, but with the conceit of wisdom, they will be a burden to their fellows.'

1.2

ARISTOTLE: DE MEMORIA ET REMINISCENTIA

CHAPTER ONE

Programme

449ᵇ4 In discussing memory and remembering, it is necessary to say what they are, and how their occurrence is to be explained, and to which part of the soul this affection, and recollecting, belong. For it is not the same people who are good at remembering and at recollecting. Rather, for the most part, slow people are better at remembering, while those who are quick and learn well are better at recollecting.

First main topic. The object of memory. This is the past, not the future or present, nor what is present as an object of perception or theorizing. But after perception or theorizing is over, one can remember, and in doing so, will remember the fact of having perceived or theorized.

449ᵃ9 First, then, one must consider what sort of things the objects of memory are, for this often leads people astray. For it is not possible to remember the future, which is instead an object of judgment and prediction. (There might even be a predictive science, as some people say divination is.) Nor is memory of the present; rather, perception is, for by perception we know neither the

Source: Aristotle, 'De Memoria et Reminiscentia', in *Aristotle on Memory*, trans., with inter-pretative summaries, Richard Sorabji, 2nd edn (London: Duckworth, 2004), pp. 47–60.

future nor the past, but only the present. But memory is of the past. No one would say he was remembering what was present, when it was present, e.g. this white thing when he was seeing it; nor would he say he was remembering the object of his theorizing when he was in the act of theorizing and thinking. Rather he says simply that he is perceiving the one, and exercising scientific knowledge of the other. But when a person possesses scientific knowledge and perception without actually exercizing them, under these conditions he remembers in the one case that he learned or theorized, in the other that he heard, or saw, or something of the kind. For whenever someone is actively engaged in remembering, he always says in his soul in this way that he heard, or perceived, or thought this before.

Conclusions. Memory is not identical with, but subsequent to, perception and conception. It is a state or affection connected with these. Only those animals which can perceive the time-lapse can remember.

449^{b}24 Therefore memory is not perception or conception, but a state or affection connected with one of these, when time has elapsed. There is no memory of the present at the present, as has been said. But perception is of the present, prediction of the future, and memory of the past. And this is why all memory involves time. So only animals which perceive time remember, and they do so by means of that with which they perceive.

Second main topic. To what part of the soul does memory belong? Two reasons why it belongs to the perceptual part. (a) It involves cognizing time. Time must be cognized in the same way as magnitude and change, since these are three interrelated continua. We know, then, from our discussion of cognizing magnitude that the cognition will be by means of images. (b) Memory also involves cognizing the thing remembered. And this too is done by means of images. Any connexion between memory and the intellect is merely incidental.

449^{b}30 An account has already been given of imagination in the discussion of the soul, and it is not possible to think without an image. For the same effect occurs in thinking as in drawing a diagram. For in the latter case, though we do not make any use of the fact that the size of the triangle is determinate, we none the less draw it with a determinate size. And similarly someone who is thinking, even if he is not thinking of something with a size, places something with a size before his eyes, but thinks of it not as having a size. If its nature is that of things which have a size, but not a determinate one, he places before his eyes something with a determinate size, but thinks of it simply as having size. Now the reason why it is not possible to think of anything without continuity, nor of things not in time without time, is another story. But it is necessary that magnitude and change should be known by the same means as time. And an image is an affection belonging to the common sense. So it is apparent that knowledge of these is due to the primary perceptive part. Memory, even the memory of objects of thought, is not without an image. So memory will belong to thought in virtue of an incidental association, but in its own right to the primary perceptive part.

Corollaries. But for this, memory would not belong to animals lower than man, and perhaps to no mortal animals. Even as it is, it does not belong to those animals which lack perception of time.

450ª15 And this is why some other animals too have memory, and not only men and those animals that have judgment or intelligence. But if memory were one of the thinking parts, not many of the other animals would have it, and perhaps no mortal animals would, since even as it is, they do not all have memory, because they do not all have perception of time. For, as we said before, when someone is actively engaged in memory, he perceives in addition that he saw this, or heard it, or learned it earlier; and earlier and later are in time.

Summary

450ª22 It is apparent, then, to which part of the soul memory belongs, namely the same part as that to which imagination belongs. And it is the objects of imagination that are remembered in their own right, whereas things that are not grasped without imagination are remembered in virtue of an incidental association.

Third main topic. An impasse. Why it arises. Memory involves an image in the soul, which is among other things a sort of imprint in the body of a former sense-image. (A suitable surface is needed in the body to take the quasi-imprint.)

450ᵇ25 One might be puzzled how, when the affection is present but the thing is absent, what is not present is ever remembered. For it is clear that one must think of the affection, which is produced by means of perception in the soul and in that part of the body which contains the soul, as being like a sort of picture, the having of which we say is memory. For the change that occurs marks in a sort of imprint, as it were, of the sense-image, as people do who seal things with signet rings.

450ª32 (And this is also why memory does not occur in those who are subject to a lot of movement, because of some trouble or because of their time of life, just as if the change and the seal were falling on running water. In others, because of wearing down, as in the old parts of buildings, and because of the hardness of what receives the affection, the imprint is not produced. And this is why the very young and the old have poor memory, since they are in a state of flux, the former because they are growing, the latter because they are wasting away. Similarly the very quick and the very slow are also obviously neither of them good at remembering. For the former are too fluid, the latter too hard. Therefore with the former the image does not remain in the soul, while with the latter it does not take hold.)

The impasse. What it is. How by contemplating and perceiving this image does one remember something quite distinct from it?

450ᵇ11 But then, if this is the sort of thing that happens with memory, does one remember this affection, or the thing from which it was produced? For if the former, we would remember nothing absent; but if the latter, how is it that while perceiving the affection we remember the absent thing which we are not perceiving? And if it is like an imprint or drawing in us, why should the perception of this be the memory of a different thing, rather than of the affection itself? For one who is exercising his memory contemplates this affection and perceives this. How therefore will he remember what is not present? For at that rate one could also see and hear what is not present.

Solution. One contemplates the image as being of, i.e. as being a copy of, something distinct.

450ᵇ20 Or is there a way in which this is possible and happens? For the figure drawn on a panel is both a figure and a copy, and while being one and the same, it is both, even though the being of the two is not the same. And one can contemplate it both as a figure and as a copy. In the same way one must also conceive the image in us to be something in its own right and to be of another thing. In so far, then, as it is something in its own right, it is an object of contemplation or an image. But in so far as it is of another thing, it is a sort of copy and a reminder. So again when the change connected with the other thing is active, if the soul perceives the image as something in its own right, it appears to come to one as a thought or image. But if one contemplates the image as being of another thing, and (just as in the case of the drawing) as a copy, and as of Coriscus, when one hasn't seen Coriscus, then (not only in the case of the drawing is the experience of so contemplating it different from when one contemplates it as a drawn figure; but also) in the case of the soul, the one image occurs simply as a thought, the other, because it is a copy (as in the case of the drawing), is a reminder.

Corollaries of this solution. The possibility of regarding, or not regarding, one's image as a copy helps to explain four phenomena. (a) Doubt as to whether one has memory. (b) Suddenly switching to remembering. (c) Wrongly supposing one has memory. (d) Memorizing.

451ᵃ2 And for this reason, when changes like this are produced in our soul as a result of former perception, we sometimes do not know whether this is happening in accordance with the previous perception, and are in doubt whether it is memory or not.

451ᵃ5 At other times it happens that we have a thought and recollect that we heard or saw something earlier. This happens when one changes from contemplating the image as the thing that it is to contemplating it as being of something else.

451ᵃ8 The contrary also happens, as it did to Antipheron of Oreus and other mad people. For they used to speak of their images as things that had occurred and as if they were remembering them. This happens whenever someone contemplates what is not a copy as if it were.

451ᵃ12 Exercizes safeguard memory by reminding one. And this is nothing other than contemplating something frequently as a copy and not as a thing in its own right.

Retrospect

451ᵃ14 Now, it has been said what memory and remembering are, namely the having of an image regarded as a copy of that of which it is an image, and to which part in us memory belongs, namely the primary perceptive part and that with which we perceive time.

CHAPTER TWO

First main topic. What recollection is not. Recollection is not the recovery of memory, for no memory need have preceded. Admittedly recollection may be the recovery of scientific knowledge, perception, etc., and so perception or the acquisition of scientific knowledge must have preceded. But it does not follow that memory must have preceded, for perception and the acquisition of scientific knowledge do not presuppose prior memory, nor incorporate within themselves the acquisition of memory, nor are they immediately followed by remembering.

Recollection is not the acquisition of memory. For remembering, followed by memory, can precede any act of recollection.

Recollection cannot even be defined simply as the recovery of scientific knowledge, perception, etc., if we want to distinguish it from relearning.

451ᵃ18 It remains to speak about recollecting. First, then, one must take as being the case all that is true in the essays. For recollection is neither the recovery nor the acquisition of memory. For when someone first learns or experiences something, he does not recover any memory, since none has preceded. Nor does he acquire memory from the start, for once the state or affection has been produced within a person, then there is memory. So memory is not produced within someone at the same time that the experience is being produced within him. Further, at the indivisible and final instant when the experience has first been produced within, although the affection and scientific knowledge are already present in the person who had the experience (if one should call the state or affection scientific knowledge – and nothing prevents us also remembering in virtue of an incidental association some of the objects of our scientific knowledge), none the less remembering itself, does not occur until time has elapsed. For a person remembers now what he saw or experienced earlier. He does not now remember what he experienced now.

451ᵃ31 Further, it is apparent that a person can remember from the start, once he has perceived or experienced something, without having just now recollected it. But when he recovers previously held scientific knowledge, or perception, or that of which we were earlier saying that the state connected with it is memory, this is, and is the time of, recollecting one of the things mentioned. (When one does remember, it results that memory follows.)

451ᵇ6 Nor indeed do these things in all circumstances yield recollection when they are reinstated in a man who had them before. Rather, in some circumstances they do, in others they do not. For the same man can learn and discover the same thing twice. So recollecting must differ from these cases, and it must be that people recollect when a principle is within them over and above the principle by which they learn.

Second main topic. Prerequisites and method of recollection. Prerequisites: images are naturally fitted to occur in a certain order, and will do so, if not of necessity, then by habit.

451ᵇ10 Acts of recollection happen because one change is of a nature to occur after another. If the changes follow each other of necessity, clearly a person who undergoes the earlier change will always undergo the later one. But if they follow each other not of necessity but by habit, then for the most part a person will undergo the later one. It can happen that by undergoing certain changes once a person is more habituated than he is by undergoing other changes many times. And this is why after seeing some things once, we remember better than we do after seeing other things many times.

Method: sometimes one takes a short cut, and chooses a starting-point which (because it is similar, opposite, or neighbouring) will lead one straight to the thing one wishes to recollect. The image corresponding to such a starting-point comes next to, or overlaps with, or is the same as, the image of the thing to be recollected. But for the most part, one has to pass through other images first, before one reaches the image of the penultimate item in the series. Even so, the method of recollecting is the same as when one takes a short cut, if one considers how each item in the series is related to its successor.

451ᵇ16 Whenever we recollect, then, we undergo one of the earlier changes, until we undergo the one after which the change in question habitually occurs.

451ᵇ18 And this is exactly why we hunt for the successor, starting in our thoughts from the present or from something else, and from something similar, or opposite, or neighbouring. By this means recollection occurs. For the changes connected with these things in some cases are the same, in others are together, and in others include a part, so that the remainder which one underwent after that part is small.

451ᵇ22 Sometimes, then, people search in this way. But also when they do not search in this way they recollect, whenever the change in question occurs after another one. And for the most part it is after the occurrence of other changes like those we spoke of that the change in question occurs. There is no need to consider how we remember what is distant, but only what is neighbouring, for clearly the method is the same. (I mean the successor, not having searched in advance, and not having recollected.) For the changes follow each other by habit, one after another.

Method (cont.). The importance of getting a starting-point.

451ᵇ29 And thus whenever someone wishes to recollect, he will do the following. He will seek to get a starting-point for a change after which will be the change in question. And this is why recollections occur quickest and best from a starting-point. For as the things are related to each other in succession, so also are the changes. And whatever has some order, as things in mathematics do, is easily remembered. Other things are remembered badly and with difficulty.

Recollecting and relearning distinguished in light of the above. He who recollects can move on to what follows the starting-point without the help of someone else.

452ᵃ4 And recollecting differs from relearning in that a person will be able somehow to move on by himself to what follows the starting-point. When he cannot, but depends on someone else, he no longer remembers. Often a person is unable to recollect, at a given moment, but when he searches he can, and he finds what is sought. This occurs when he excites many changes, until he excites a change of a sort on which the thing will follow. For remembering is the presence within of the power which excites the changes, and this in such a way that the man moves of himself and because of changes that he possesses, as has been said.

The importance of starting-points (resumed).

452ᵃ12 But one should get a starting-point. And this is why people are thought sometimes to recollect starting from places. The reason is that people go quickly from one thing to another, e.g. from milk to white, from white to air, and from this to fluid, from which one remembers autumn, the season one is seeking.

The middle member of a triplet makes a good starting-point. If unsuccessful with the first triplet, one should skip on to the middle member of the next triplet.

452ᵃ17 In general in every case the middle also looks like a starting-point. For if no sooner, a person will remember when he comes to this, or else he will no longer remember from any position, as for example if someone were to think of the things denoted by A B Γ Δ E Z H Θ. For if he has not remembered at Θ, he will remember at Z for from here he can move in either direction to H or to E. But if he was not seeking one of these, after going to Γ he will remember, if he is searching for Δ or B, or if he is not, he will remember after going to A. And so in all cases.

The possibility just mentioned of moving to alternative destinations from the same starting-point explains why from a given starting-point one sometimes remembers and sometimes does not. Habit may divert one to the wrong destination. Alternatively, so may similarity. The method of recollecting has now been described.

452ᵃ24 The reason why one sometimes remembers and sometimes does not, starting from the same position, is that it is possible to move to more than one point from the same starting-point, e.g. from Γ to Z or Δ. So if a man is moved through something old, he moves instead to something to which he is more habituated. For habit is already like nature. (And this is why what we think of frequently we recollect quickly. For just as by nature one thing is after another, so also in the activity. And frequency creates nature.)

452ᵃ30 But just as among natural events there occur also ones contrary to nature and the result of luck, still more is this so among events that are due to habit, seeing that nature does not belong to these in the same way. So a person is sometimes moved to one place and at other times differently, especially when something draws him away elsewhere from the one place. For this reason also when we have to remember a name, if we know a similar one, we blunder onto that.

Recollecting, then, happens in this way.

Third main topic. Estimating time-lapses. Remembering involves estimating time-lapses. Different time-lapses, like different spatial magnitudes, are represented by differing small scale models in one's thought.

452^b7 But the main thing is that one must know the time, either in units of measurement or indeterminately. Assume there is something with which a person distinguishes more and less time. Probably it is in the same way as he distinguishes magnitudes. For a person thinks of things large and distant not through stretching out his thought there, as some people say one stretches sight (for even if the things do not exist, he can think of them in the same way), but by means of a change which is in proportion. For there are in the thought similar shapes and changes. How, then, when someone is thinking of larger things, will the fact that he is thinking of them differ from the fact of thinking of smaller things? For everything within is smaller and in proportion to what is without.

452^b15 Perhaps just as one can receive in oneself something distinct but in proportion to the forms, so also in the case of the distances. It is then, as though, if a person undergoes the change AB, BE, he constructs ΓΔ. For the changes AΓ and ΓΔ are in proportion. Why, then, does he construct ΓΔ rather than ZH? Is it that as AΓ is to AB, so is Θ to I? So one undergoes these latter changes simultaneously. But if someone wishes to think of ZH, he thinks in the same way of BE, but instead of the changes Θ, I, he thinks of the changes K, Λ. For these latter are related as is ZA to BA.

Estimating time-lapses (cont.). The image of the thing remembered and the image representing the time-lapse must occur together. One must not wrongly suppose one's image is of a certain thing. One need not know the time-lapse in standard units of measurement.

452^b23 Whenever, then, the change connected with the thing and that connected with the time occur together, then one is exercising memory. But if a person thinks he is doing this, when he is not, then he thinks he is remembering. For nothing prevents him from being deceived and thinking he is remembering when he is not. However, when exercising his memory a person cannot think he is not doing so and fail to notice that he is remembering. For this turned out to be what remembering was. But if the change connected with the thing occurs without that connected with the time, or the latter without the former, one does not remember.

452^b29 The change connected with the time is of two sorts. For sometimes a person does not remember the time in units of measurement, e.g. that he did something or other the day before yesterday; but sometimes also he does remember the time this way. None the less, he remembers, even if it be not in units of measurement. And people are in the habit of saying that they remember but don't know when, whenever they do not know the amount of time in units of measurement.

Fourth main topic. Recollecting and remembering. Differences between the two. Recollecting is too like reasoning to belong to animals lower than man.

453ᵃ4 Now, it has been said in what precedes that it is not the same people who are good at remembering and at recollecting. Recollecting differs from remembering not only in respect of the time, but in that many other animals share in remembering, while of the known animals one may say that none other than man shares in recollecting. The explanation is that recollecting is, as it were, a sort of reasoning. For in recollecting, a man reasons that he formerly saw, or heard, or had some such experience, and recollecting is, as it were, a sort of search. And this kind of search is an attribute only of animals which also have the deliberating part. For indeed deliberation is a sort of reasoning.

Fifth main topic. Recollection involves the body. Evidence of its physiological character: some people become upset when they fail to recollect, and succeed in recollecting after giving up, which needs to be explained by saying that they have set up motion in an organ, and, once set up, the motion will not stop, until what is sought returns.

453ᵃ14 The following is a sign that the affection is something to do with the body, and that recollection is a search in something bodily for an image. It upsets some people when they are unable to recollect in spite of applying their thought hard, and when they are no longer trying, they recollect none the less. This happens most to melancholic people. For images move them most. The reason for recollecting not being under their control is that just as it is no longer in people's power to stop something when they throw it, so also he who is recollecting and hunting moves a bodily thing in which the affection resides. The people who get upset most are those who happen to have fluid around the perceptive region. For once moved, the fluid is not easily stopped until what is sought returns and the movement takes a straight course.

That a motion, once set up, may be hard to stop explains various other phenomena.

453ᵃ26 And this is also why, when cases of anger and of fear set something moving, they are not halted, even though the people set up counter-movements in turn, but rather the anger and fear make counter-movements in the original direction. And the affection is like names and tunes and sayings, when one such has come to be very much on someone's lips. For after the people have stopped, and without their wishing such a thing, it comes to them to sing it or say it again.

Further evidence of the physiological character of recollection. Defects in memory can be traced to physiological conditions.

453ᵃ31 Those also whose upper parts are especially large and those who are dwarf-like have poorer memories than their opposites because they have a great weight resting on the perceptive part, and neither from the start are the changes able to persist within such people and avoid being dispersed, nor during recollecting does the movement easily take a straight course. The extremely young and the very old have poor memory because of the movement in them. For the one group is wasting away, the other growing rapidly. Further, children at any rate are also dwarf-like until late in their youth.

Retrospect

453^b7 Now, it has been stated what is the nature of memory and remembering, and what it is in the soul that animals remember with, and what recollecting is, and in what manner it occurs, and through what causes.

1.3

CICERO: *FROM* ON THE IDEAL ORATOR (DE ORATORE)

MEMORY

'You now have my views on the discovery and arrangement of our material. I shall add a few words about memory, in order to lighten Crassus' work and to leave him nothing else to discuss but the methods for imparting distinction to these things.'[1] 'Go right ahead,' said Crassus, 'for I am happy to observe that you have now been revealed as a master of the theory, at last unveiled and stripped of the cover of your feigned ignorance. And it is very convenient that you leave little or nothing to me, and I am much obliged.' 'As for this question, how much I have left for you to do,' said Antonius, 'that will now be up to you to decide. If you choose to deal with the matter honestly, I am leaving everything to you. But if you want to feign ignorance, then you will have to consider how to satisfy our friends here.

'But, to return to the subject,' he continued, 'I do not have the great intellectual abilities that Themistocles had, which could make me prefer an art of forgetting to one of remembering. And I am thankful to Simonides of Ceos, who is said to have been the first to introduce the art of memory. According to this story, Simonides was dining at Crannon in Thessaly at the house of Scopas, a rich nobleman. When he had finished singing the poem that he had composed in Scopas' honor, in which he had written much about Castor and Pollux for

Source: Cicero, *On the Ideal Orator (De oratore)*, trans., with introduction, notes, appendixes, glossary and indexes, by James M. May and Jakob Wisse (New York, Oxford: Oxford University Press, 2001), pp. 218–21.

the sake of embellishment, as poets do, Scopas reacted with excessive stinginess. He told him that he would pay him only half the agreed fee for this poem; if he liked, he could ask for the rest from his friends the Tyndarides,[2] who had received half the praise.[3] A little later, the story goes on, Simonides received a message to go outside: two young men were standing at the door, who were urgently asking for him. He got up and went outside, but saw no one. In the meantime, precisely while he was gone, the room where Scopas was giving his banquet collapsed, and Scopas, together with his relatives, was buried under the fallen roof and died. When their families wanted to arrange their funeral, but could not possibly distinguish them because they had been completely crushed, it was reportedly Simonides who, from his recollection of the place where each of them had been reclining at table, identified every one of them for burial. Prompted by this experience, he is then said to have made the discovery that order is what most brings light to our memory. And he concluded that those who would like to employ this part of their abilities should choose localities, then form mental images of the things they wanted to store in their memory, and place these in the localities. In this way, the order of the localities would preserve the order of the things, while the images would represent the things themselves; and we would use the localities like a wax tablet, and the representations like the letters written on it.[4]

'What need is there for me to mention the benefit that the memory offers to the orator, its great usefulness and its great power? That you can retain what you learned when accepting a case, as well as what you have thought out yourself about it? That you can have all of your thoughts fixed in your mind, and your entire supply of words neatly arranged? That you can listen in such a way to your client who instructs you about the case, or to your opponent whom you will have to answer, that what they say is not just poured into your ears, but seems inscribed into your mind? Accordingly, only those with a powerful memory know what they are going to say, how far they will pursue it, how they will say it, which points they have already answered and which still remain. Such people also remember much of the material they have used in the past in other cases, and much that they have heard others use. Now I do acknowledge that nature is the chief source of this asset, as it is of everything that I have been talking about before. But it is true of the whole art of speaking (or perhaps it is only a shadow and semblance of an art),[5] that its function is not to produce or create from scratch what is nowhere present in our own natural abilities, but to rear and develop what has already been born and created within us. Yet, there is barely anyone whose memory is so keen that he can retain the order of all words and thoughts without arranging his material and representing it by symbols; nor anyone, really, whose memory is so dull that practicing this system on a regular basis will not help him at all.

'Indeed, as Simonides wisely observed – or whoever it was who discovered this – , the things best pictured by our minds are those that have been conveyed and imprinted on them by one of the senses. Now the keenest of all our senses is the sense of sight. Therefore, things perceived by our hearing or during our thought processes can be most easily grasped by the mind, if they are also conveyed to our minds through the mediation of the eyes. In this way, as he saw, invisible objects that are inaccessible to the judgement of sight are represented by a kind of figure,[6] an image, a shape, so that things we can scarcely take hold of by thinking may be grasped, so to speak, by looking at them. But these concrete forms, just like everything that falls under the faculty of sight, must be located somewhere; for a concrete object without a locality is inconceivable. Consequently (for I don't want to talk too much or be obtrusive while the subject is so well known and common), the localities we use must be numerous, clearly visible, and at moderate intervals, while our images should be lively, sharp, and conspicuous, with the potential to present themselves quickly and to strike the mind. Practice, the starting point for developing a habit, will provide the requisite skill. Particularly useful ways of practicing are[7] forming representations by changes and by transformations of words into similar ones with different endings, or by the substitution of the part for the whole, and giving shape to a complete thought by an image consisting of a single word,[8] – all this according to the systematic approach of a consummate painter, who keeps the different localities distinct from each other by employing a variety of shapes.[9] Memorization of words, which is less necessary for us, is characterized by a greater variety of images. After all, there are many words that serve as joints connecting the limbs of our language,[10] and it is impossible to find shapes that resemble these. For them, we must mold images for constant use. Memorization of content, however, is the proper business of the orator. This is where we can use representation by separate, well-placed persons and objects, so that we can apprehend thoughts by means of images, and their order by means of the localities.

And it is not true, as lazy people always say, that the memory is overwhelmed by the weight of the images, and that they even obscure what our natural memory could have grasped by itself. I myself have met eminent people with almost superhuman memories, Charmadas in Athens and in Asia Metrodorus of Scepsis (who is said to be still alive); and both said that they recorded what they wanted to remember by means of images in the localities that they had chosen, just as if they were writing them out by means of letters on a wax tablet. Hence, if someone does not have a natural faculty of memory, this practice cannot be used to unearth one, but if one is latent, the practice should be used to make it grow.

Notes

1. By 'imparting distinction' (*exornentur*, cf. *ornatus*), Antonius refers to the theory of style [. . .].
2. I.e., the Sons of Tyndareos, a common way of referring to Castor and Pollux.
3. Some poets who wrote so-called lyric poetry, i.e., poetry sung to musical accompaniment (which flourished ca. 650–450 BC), used myths to illustrate the points made in the poems. Castor and Pollux were probably mentioned by Simonides

because his poem celebrated Scopas' victory in a boxing contest (Pollux being known as a boxer; cf. Quintilion 11.2.11). The reaction here ascribed to Scopas, however, suggests that the precise relevance of such myths, which has often vexed modern scholarship (especially in the case of Pindar), was perhaps even unclear to contemporaries (see also Cicero's phrase, 'for the sake of embellishment').

4. This description of the system can be so brief because it was known to the others present and to Cicero's readers [. . .]. The comparison to writing was traditional.

5. Antonius' observation about nature versus art in the case of memory is interrupted by an analogous observation on the art of speaking in general [. . .]

6. This unexpected word, 'figure' (*conformatio*), seems chosen in order to suggest a similarity between the formation of mental images in memorizing and the formation of figures of speech [. . .]

7. 'Particularly useful ways of practicing are' is not in the transmitted Latin text, but something like this seems required to complete the sense.

8. The interpretation of this sentence is difficult. Cicero seems to suggest that practicing the representation and reshaping of words by means of certain tropes and figures of speech will enhance the ability to find visual representations useful for memorizing (see . . . 'figure,' with note 6). Four types seem to be indicated: mere change of endings (*mensa*, 'table,' can be an image for *mensis*, 'month'), 'transformation' (*immutatio*), i.e., change of endings involving metonymy [. . .], synecdoche [. . .], and metaphor [. . .].

9. Cicero seems to imply that a painter indicates spatial dimensions by the way the painted objects stand out from each other. The point may be that we should exercise ourselves in the choice of suitably various and striking images, so that when we place them in the 'localities' in our mind, everything will still be easy to distinguish.

10. 'Limbs' translates *membra*, which is also the term for 'clauses'; the words serving as 'joints' are conjunctions, prepositions, etc., nowadays often called function words (as distinct from content words).

1.4

[CICERO]: *FROM* AD HERENNIUM

XVI. Now let me turn to the treasure-house of the ideas supplied by Invention, to the guardian of all the parts of rhetoric, the Memory.[1]

The question whether memory has some artificial quality, or comes entirely from nature, we shall have another, more favourable, opportunity to discuss. At present I shall accept as proved that in this matter art and method are of great importance, and shall treat the subject accordingly. For my part, I am satisfied that there is an art of memory – the grounds of my belief I shall explain elsewhere.[2] For the present I shall disclose what sort of thing memory is.

There are, then, two kinds of memory: one natural, and the other the product of art. The natural memory is that memory which is imbedded in our minds, born simultaneously with thought. The artificial memory is that memory which is strengthened by a kind of training and system of discipline. But just as in everything else the merit of natural excellence often rivals acquired learning, and art, in its turn, reinforces and develops the natural advantages,[3] so does it happen in this instance. The natural memory, if a person is endowed with an exceptional one, is often like this artificial memory, and this artificial memory, in its turn, retains and develops the natural advantages by a method of discipline. Thus the natural memory must be strengthened by discipline so as to become exceptional, and, on the other hand, this memory provided by discipline requires natural ability. It is neither more nor less true in this instance than in

Source: [Cicero], *Ad C. Herennium De Ratione Dicendi (Rhetorica Ad Herennium)*, trans. by Harry Caplan (London: William Heinemann Ltd.; Cambridge, MA: Harvard University Press, 1954), pp. 205–25.

the other arts that science thrives by the aid of innate ability, and nature by the aid of the rules of art. The training here offered will therefore also be useful to those who by nature have a good memory, as you will yourself soon come to understand.[4] But even if these, relying on their natural talent, did not need our help, we should still be justified in wishing to aid the less well-endowed. Now I shall discuss the artificial memory.

The artificial memory includes backgrounds and images. By backgrounds I mean such scenes as are naturally or artificially set off on a small scale, complete and conspicuous, so that we can grasp and embrace them easily by the natural memory – for example, a house, an intercolumnar space, a recess, an arch, or the like. An image is, as it were, a figure, mark, or portrait of the object we wish to remember; for example, if we wish to recall a horse, a lion, or an eagle, we must place its image in a definite background. Now I shall show what kind of backgrounds we should invent and how we should discover the images and set them therein.

XVII. Those who know the letters of the alphabet can thereby write out what is dictated to them and read aloud what they have written. Likewise, those who have learned mnemonics can set in backgrounds what they have heard, and from these backgrounds deliver it by memory. For the backgrounds are very much like wax tablets[5] or papyrus, the images like the letters, the arrangement and dis-position of the images like the script, and the delivery is like the reading. We should therefore, if we desire to memorize a large number of items, equip ourselves with a large number of backgrounds, so that in these we may set a large number of images. I likewise think it obligatory to have these backgrounds in a series, so that we may never by confusion in their order be prevented from following the images – proceeding from any background we wish, whatsoever its place in the series, and whether we go forwards or backwards – nor from delivering orally what has been committed to the backgrounds.

XVIII. For example, if we should see a great number of our acquaintances standing in a certain order, it would not make any difference to us whether we should tell their names beginning with the person standing at the head of the line or at the foot or in the middle. So with respect to the backgrounds. If these have been arranged in order, the result will be that, reminded by the images, we can repeat orally what we have committed to the backgrounds, proceeding in either direction from any background we please. That is why it also seems best to arrange the backgrounds in a series.

We shall need to study with special care the backgrounds we have adopted so that they may cling lastingly in our memory, for the images, like letters, are effaced when we make no use of them, but the backgrounds, like wax tablets, should abide. And that we may by no chance err in the number of backgrounds, each fifth background should be marked. For example, if in the fifth we should set a golden hand, and in the tenth some acquaintance whose first name is Decimus, it will then be easy to station like marks in each successive fifth background.

XIX. Again, it will be more advantageous to obtain backgrounds in a deserted than in a populous region, because the crowding and passing to and fro of people confuse and weaken the impress of the images, while solitude keeps their outlines sharp. Further, backgrounds differing in form and nature must be secured, so that, thus distinguished, they may be clearly visible; for if a person has adopted many intercolumnar spaces, their resemblance to one another will so confuse him that he will no longer know what he has set in each background. And these backgrounds ought to be of moderate size and medium extent, for when excessively large they render the images vague, and when too small often seem incapable of receiving an arrangement of images. Then the backgrounds ought to be neither too bright nor too dim, so that the shadows may not obscure the images nor the lustre make them glitter. I believe that the intervals between backgrounds should be of moderate extent, approximately thirty feet; for, like the external eye, so the inner eye of thought is less powerful when you have moved the object of sight too near or too far away.

Although it is easy for a person with a relatively large experience to equip himself with as many and as suitable backgrounds as he may desire, even a person who believes that he finds no store of backgrounds that are good enough, may succeed in fashioning as many such as he wishes. For the imagination can embrace any region whatsoever and in it at will fashion and construct the setting of some background. Hence, if we are not content with our ready-made supply of backgrounds, we may in our imagination create a region for ourselves and obtain a most serviceable distribution of appropriate backgrounds.

On the subject of backgrounds enough has been said; let me now turn to the theory of images.

XX. Since, then, images must resemble objects, we ought ourselves to choose from all objects likenesses for our use. Hence likenesses are bound to be of two kinds, one of subject-matter,[6] the other of words. Likenesses of matter are formed when we enlist images that present a general view of the matter with which we are dealing; likenesses of words are established when the record of each single noun or appellative is kept by an image.

Often we encompass the record of an entire matter by one notation, a single image. For example, the prosecutor has said that the defendant killed a man by poison, has charged that the motive for the crime was an inheritance, and declared that there are many witnesses and accessories to this act. If in order to facilitate our defence we wish to remember this first point, we shall in our first background form an image of the whole matter. We shall picture the man in question as lying ill in bed, if we know his person. If we do not know him, we shall yet take some one to be our invalid, but not a man of the lowest class, so that he may come to mind at once. And we shall place the defendant at the bedside, holding in his right hand a cup, and in his left tablets, and on the fourth finger[7] a ram's testicles. In this way we can record the man who was poisoned, the inheritance, and the witnesses. In like fashion we shall set the other counts of the charge in backgrounds successively, following their order, and whenever we wish to remember a point, by properly arranging the patterns of the backgrounds[8] and carefully imprinting the images, we shall easily succeed in calling back to mind what we wish.

XXI. When we wish to represent by images the likenesses of words, we shall be undertaking a greater task and exercising our ingenuity the more. This we ought to effect in the following way:

Iam domum itionem reges Atridae parant.[9]

'And now their home-coming the kings, the sons of Atreus, are making ready.'

If we wish to remember this verse, in our first background we should put Domitius, raising hands to heaven while he is lashed by the Marcii Reges[10] – that will represent 'Iam domum itionem reges' ('And now their home-coming the kings,'); in the second background, Aesopus and Cimber,[11] being dressed as for the rôles of Agamemnon and Menelaüs in *Iphigenia* – that will represent 'Atridae parent' ('the sons of Atreus, are making ready'). By this method all the words will be represented. But such an arrangement of images succeeds only if we use our notation to stimulate the natural memory, so that we first go over a given verse twice or three times to ourselves and then represent the words by means of images. In this way art will supplement nature. For neither by itself will be strong enough, though we must note that theory and technique are much the more reliable. I should not hesitate to demonstrate this in detail, did I not fear that, once having departed from my plan, I should not so well preserve the clear conciseness of my instruction.

Now, since in normal cases some images are strong and sharp and suitable for awakening recollection, and others so weak and feeble as hardly to succeed in stimulating memory, we must therefore consider the cause of these differences, so that, by knowing the cause, we may know which images to avoid and which to seek.

XXII. Now nature herself teaches us what we should do. When we see in everyday life things that are petty, ordinary, and banal, we generally fail to remember them, because the mind is not being stirred by anything novel or marvellous. But if we see or hear something exceptionally base, dishonourable, extraordinary, great, unbelievable, or laughable, that we are likely to remember a long time. Accordingly, things immediate to our eye or ear we commonly forget; incidents of our childhood we often remember best.[12] Nor could this be so for any other reason than that ordinary things easily slip from the memory while the striking and novel stay longer in mind. A sunrise, the sun's course, a sunset, are marvellous to no one because they occur daily.[13] But solar eclipses are a source of wonder because they occur seldom, and indeed are more marvellous than lunar eclipses, because these are more frequent. Thus nature shows that she is not aroused by the common, ordinary event, but is moved by a new or striking occurrence. Let art, then, imitate nature,[14] find what she desires, and follow as she directs. For in invention nature is never last, education never first; rather the beginnings of things arise from natural talent, and the ends are reached by discipline.

We ought, then, to set up images of a kind that can adhere longest in the memory. And we shall do so if we establish likenesses as striking as possible; if we set up images that are not many or vague, but doing something; if we assign to them exceptional beauty or singular ugliness; if we dress some of them with crowns or purple cloaks, for example, so that the likeness may be more distinct to us; or if we somehow disfigure them, as by introducing one stained with blood or soiled with mud or smeared with red paint, so that its form is more striking, or by assigning certain comic effects to our images, for that, too, will ensure our remembering them more readily. The things we easily remember when they are real we likewise remember without difficulty when they are figments, if they have been carefully delineated. But this will be essential – again and again to run over rapidly in the mind all the original backgrounds in order to refresh the images.

XXIII. I know that most of the Greeks who have written on the memory[15] have taken the course of listing images that correspond to a great many words, so that persons who wished to learn these images by heart would have them ready without expending effort on a search for them. I disapprove of their method on several grounds. First, among the innumerable multitude of words it is ridiculous to collect images for a thousand. How meagre is the value these can have, when out of the infinite store of words we shall need to remember now one, and now another? Secondly, why do we wish to rob anybody of his initiative, so that, to save him from making any search himself, we deliver to him everything searched out and ready? Then again, one person is more struck by one likeness, and another more by another. Often in fact when we declare that some one form resembles another, we fail to receive universal assent, because things seem different to different persons. The same is true with respect to images: one that is well-defined to us appears relatively inconspicuous to others. Everybody, therefore, should in equipping himself with images suit his own convenience. Finally, it is the instructor's duty to teach the proper method of search in each case, and, for the sake of greater clarity, to add in illustration some one or two examples of its kind, but not all. For instance, when I discuss the search for Introductions, I give a method of search and do not draught a thousand kinds of Introductions. The same procedure I believe should be followed with respect to images.

XXIV. Now, lest you should perchance regard the memorizing of words either as too difficult or as of too little use, and so rest content with the memorizing of matter, as being easier and more useful, I must advise you why I do not disapprove of memorizing words. I believe that they who wish to do easy things without trouble and toil must previously have been trained in more difficult things. Nor have I included memorization of words to enable us to get verse by rote, but rather as an exercise whereby to strengthen that other kind of memory, the memory of matter, which is of practical use. Thus we may without effort pass from this difficult training to ease in that other memory. In every discipline artistic theory is of little avail without unremitting exercise, but especially in mnemonics theory is almost valueless unless made good by industry, devotion, toil, and care. You can make sure that you have as many backgrounds as possible and that these conform as much as possible to the rules; in placing the images you should exercise every day. While an engrossing preoccupation may often distract us from our other pursuits, from this activity nothing whatever can divert us. Indeed there is never a moment when we do not wish to commit something to memory, and we wish it most of all when our attention is held by business of special importance. So, since a ready memory is a useful thing, you see clearly with what great pains we must strive to acquire so useful a faculty. Once you know its uses you will be able to appreciate this advice. To exhort you further in the matter of memory is not my intention, for I should appear either to have lacked confidence in your zeal or to have discussed the subject less fully than it demands.

I shall next discuss the fifth part of rhetoric. You might rehearse in your mind each of the first four divisions, and – what is especially necessary – fortify your knowledge of them with exercise.

NOTES

1. On ancient mnemonics see Helga Hajdu, *Das mnemotechnische Schrifttum des Mittelalters* (Vienna, Amsterdam, and Leipzig, 1936), pp. 11–33, and L. A. Post, *Class. Weekly* 25 (1932). 105–10; on Memory in oral literature, J. A. Notopoulos, *Trans. Am. Philol. Assn.* 69 (1938). 465–93. The rhetorical interest in *memoria* appears early, among the sophists, who valued its uses in the learning of common places and for improvisation. Our author's mnemonic system is the oldest extant. Whether such pictorial methods were widely used by the orators we do not know, but the theory persists to this day. See also Longinus, in Spengel-Hammer 1 (2). 197–206; Cicero, *De Oratore* 2. 85. 350–88. 360; and esp. Quintilian's historical and critical treatment, 11. 2 .1–51.
2. Whether our author ever published such an explanation we do not know.
3. For the commonplace *cf.* Isocrates, *Adv. Soph.* 14 ff., *Antid.* 189 ff.; Plato, *Phaedrus* 269 D; Cicero, *Pro Archia* 7. 15, *Tusc. Disp.* 2. 13, Crassus in *De Oratore* 1. 25. 113 ff.; Horace, *Ars Poet.* 408–11; the comic (?) poet Simylus, in *Stobaeus*, 4. 18 a 4; Longinus, *De Sublim.* 36. 4; Quintilian, 2. 19. 1 ff., and (on Delivery) 11. 3. 11 ff.; and for its application to *memoria* Antonius in Cicero, *De oratore* 2. 88. 360, and Longinus, in Spengel-Hammer 1 (2). 204.
4. *Cf.* XXII below.
5. *Cf.* 'the table of my memory,' Shakespeare, *Hamlet* 1. 5. 98. For the analogy with wax *cf.* Socrates in Plato, *Theaet.* 191 CD; Cicero, *Part. Orat.* 6. 26, and in *De Oratore* 2. 88. 360, Charmadas (*fl.* 107 BC) and Metrodorus (born *c.*150 BC); and the seal-ring in Aristotle, *De Mem. et Recollect.* 450 ab. *Cf.* also, in Theophrastus, *De Sens.* 51–2, Democritus' theory that in vision the air is moulded like wax, and see the interpretation of this passage by Paul Friedländer, *Die platonischen Schriften* (Berlin and Leipzig, 1930), p. 448, note 1.
6. Thus *memoria* embraces the speaker's command of his material as well as of the words.
7. According to Macrobius, *Sat.* 7. 13. 7–8, the anatomists spoke of a nerve which extends from the heart to the fourth finger of the left hand (the *digitus medicinalis*),

where it interlaces into the other nerves of that finger; the finger was therefore ringed, as with a crown. *Testiculi* suggests *testes* (witnesses). Of the scrotum of the ram purses were made; thus the money used for bribing the witnesses may perhaps also be suggested.

8. At 3. xvi. 29 above *formae* is used to describe the images.

9. An iambic senarius, whether our author's own creation or from a tragedy by an unknown author (the *Iphigenia* mentioned below?) is uncertain. Note that here the play is upon the form of the word, not its meaning, and that no special provision is made for the adverb *iam*. Quintilian, 11. 2. 25, doubts the efficacy of symbols to record a series of connected words: 'I do not mention the fact that some things, certainly conjunctions, for example, cannot be represented by images.'

10. The scene is doubtless our author's own creation. Rex was the name of one of the most distinguished families of the Marcian *gens*; the Domitian (of plebeian origin) was likewise a celebrated *gens*.

11. Clodius Aesopus (a friend of Cicero) was the greatest tragic actor of the first half of the first century BC; Cimber, mentioned only here, was no doubt also a favourite of the day. See Otto Ribbeck, *Die römische Tragödie im Zeitalter der Republik* (Leipzig, 1875), pp. 674–6.

12. *Cf.* Jerome, *Apol. adv. libr. Rufini* 1. 30.

13. *Cf.* Lucretius 2.1037–8: 'So wondrous would this sight have been. Yet, wearied as all are with satiety of seeing, how truly no one now deigns to gaze up at the bright quarters of heaven!'

14. The idea is a commonplace in a variety of schools of thought: e.g., Democritus, fragm. 154, in Diels-Kranz, *Die Fragmente der Vorsokratiker*, 6th ed., 2. 173, and Lucretius 5. 1102, 1354, 1361 ff., 1379; Aristotle, *Physica* 2. 2 (194 a) and 2. 8 (199 a), *Meteor.* 4. 3 (381 b), *De mundo* 5 (396 b, in Diels-Kranz 1. 153); Theophrastus, *De Caus. Plant.* 2. 18. 2; Dionysius Halic., *Isaeus*, ch. 16; Seneca, *Epist.* 65. 3; Marcus Aurelius, *Medit.* 11. 10; Plotinus, *Enn.* 5. 8. 1; Cicero, *Orator* 18. 58; Quintilian, 8. 3. 71; Dante, *Inferno* 11. 97 ff.

15. Precisely who these predecessors were we do not know.

1.5

MARY J. CARRUTHERS: *FROM* THE BOOK OF MEMORY: A STUDY IN MEDIEVAL CULTURE

Perhaps no advice is as common in medieval writing on the subject, and yet so foreign, when one thinks about it, to the habits of modern scholarship as this notion of 'making one's own' what one reads in someone else's work. 'Efficere tibi illas familiares,' Augustine's admonition to 'Francesco,' does not mean 'familiar' in quite the modern sense. *Familiar* is rather a synonym of *domesticare*, that is, to make something familiar by making it a part of your own experience. This adaptation process allows for a tampering with the original text that a modern scholar would (and does) find quite intolerable, for it violates most of our notions concerning 'accuracy,' 'objective scholarship,' and 'the integrity of the text.' Modern scholars learn all they can about a text, making sure they know the meaning of every word in it. So did medieval scholars; that was what *lectio* was for. But a modern scholar is concerned primarily with getting the text 'objectively right,' treating it as an ultimate and sole authority. We are taught to 'legitimate' our reading (by which we mean our interpretation or understanding) solely by the text; we see ourselves as its servants, and although both the possibility and the utility of such absolute objectivity have been called into question many times during this century, this attitude remains a potent assumption in scholarly debate, even for those most wedded to reader-response theories.

Source: Mary J. Carruthers, *The Book of Memory: A Study of Memory in Medieval Culture* (Cambridge: Cambridge University Press, 1990), pp. 164–70, 327–9.

But the medieval scholar's relationship to his texts is quite different from modern 'objectivity.' Reading is to be digested, to be ruminated, like a cow chewing her cud, or like a bee making honey from the nectar of flowers. Reading is memorized with the aid of *murmur*, mouthing the words subvocally as one turns the text over in one's memory; both Quintilian and Martianus Capella stress how murmur accompanies meditation. It is this movement of the mouth that established rumination as a basic metaphor for memorial activities.[1] The process familiarizes a text to a medieval scholar, in a way like that by which human beings may be said to 'familiarize' their food. It is both physiological and psychological, and it changes both the food and its consumer. Gregory the Great writes, 'We ought to transform what we read into our very selves, so that when our mind is stirred by what it hears, our life may concur by practicing what has been heard.'[2] Hugh of St Victor writes of walking through the forest ('silva') of Scripture, 'whose ideas [*sententias*] like so many sweetest fruits, we pick as we read and chew [*ruminamus*] as we consider them.'[3]

The various stages of the reading process are succinctly described at the end of Hugh of St Victor's Chronicle preface [. . .]. All exegesis emphasized that understanding was grounded in a thorough knowledge of the *littera*, and for this one had to know grammar, rhetoric, history, and all the other disciplines that give information, the work of *lectio*. But one takes all of that and builds upon it during meditation; this phase of reading is ethical in its nature, or 'tropological' (turning the text onto and into one's self) as Hugh defines it. I think one might best begin to understand the concept of 'levels' in exegesis as 'stages' of a continuous action, and the 'four-fold way' (or three-fold, as the case may be) as a useful mnemonic for readers, reminding them of how to complete the entire reading process. 'Littera' and 'allegoria' (grammar and typological history) are the work of *lectio* and are essentially informative about a text; tropology and anagogy are the activities of digestive meditation and constitute the ethical activity of making one's reading one's own.

The ruminant image is basic to understanding what was involved in *memoria* as well as *meditatio*, the two being understood as the agent and its activity. Though monastic theology developed the idea of meditation in terms of prayer and psalmody its basis in the functions of memory continued to be emphasized. *Ruminatio* is an image of regurgitation, quite literally intended; the memory is a stomach, the stored texts are the sweet-smelling cud originally drawn from the meadows of books (or lecture), they are chewed in the palate. Gregory the Great says that in Scripture 'venter mens dicitur,' thereby adding *venter* to *cor* as a synonym for memory in Scripture.[4] Six centuries later, Hugh of St Victor, discussing *memoria* in *Didascalicon*, says that it is imperative to replicate frequently the matter one has memorized and placed in the 'arcula' of one's memory, and 'to recall it from the stomach of memory to the palate.'[5]

Composition is also spoken of as *ruminatio*. In one of his sermons, Augustine says that he has not prepared formally but desires that he be allowed to ruminate upon the day's Scriptural reading.[6] Another example, the most famous of all, is in Bede's account of the English poet, Caedmon, who changed ('convertebat') what he learned by hearing in *lectio,* or sermons, into sweetest poetry by recollecting it within himself ('rememorandum rerum') and ruminating like a clean animal ('quasi mundum animal ruminendo').[7] Caedmon's rumination occurs at night, the optimal time for such activity; the fact that he was a cowherd may be coincidental to the story, but Bede emphasizes it so much that one suspects he thought the detail significant in the context. Philip West has suggested that his profession suits his ruminative activities; perhaps the ancient link between poets and ruminative animals, found in many cultures, has some connection with the rumination of composition.

Metaphors which use digestive activities are so powerful and tenacious that 'digestion' should be considered another basic functional model for the complementary activities of reading and composition, collection and recollection. Unlike the heart, no medical tradition seems to have placed any of the sensory-processing functions in the stomach, but 'the stomach of memory' as a metaphoric model had a long run. Milton, his biographers agree, mentally composed a store of verses each day, which he then dictated to a secretary. John Aubrey comments that while Milton had a good natural memory, 'I believe that his excellent method of thinking and disposing did much to help his memory,' a clear reference to the kind of training, disciplined practice, and deliberate design ('disposing') that had always been features of classical memory-training. And Milton's anonymous biographer, speaking also of his mental composition, remarks that if the poet's secretary were late, 'he would complain, saying he wanted to be milked.'[8]

Likening the products of mental rumination to those of digestion led to some excellent comedy; one thinks at once of Rabelais and of Chaucer's Summoner's Tale. But the metaphor was also realized seriously. There is a remarkably graphic statement of it in the *Regula monachorum* ascribed to Jerome, though composed probably in the twelfth century. The writer speaks of the various stomach rumblings, belchings, and flatulence that accompany the nightly gathering of the monks in prayer. But, he continues, as a famous pastor has said, just as smoke drives out bees, so ructation caused by indigestion drives away the inspiration of the Holy Spirit. Belching and farting, however, are caused by the preparation and digestion of food. 'Wherefore, as a belch bursts forth from the stomach according to the quality of the food, and the significance [to health] of a *flatus* is according either to the sweetness or stench of its odor, so the cogitations of the inner man bring forth words, and *from the abundance of the heart the mouth speaks* (Lk. 6:45). The just man, eating, fills his soul. And when he is replete with sacred doctrine, from the good treasury of his memory he brings forth those things which are good.'[9] No comment is needed on this text, so very odd and even irreligious to us, except to observe that I can think of few more cogent statements of the curious consequences deriving from ancient and medieval notions of the soul's embodiment than this serious, pious linking of the sweetness of prayer and of the stomach. Though the immediate notion of the Spirit as a breath or wind ('flatus') is Biblical, moderns, accustomed to thinking of this trope as a mere figure of speech, would never make the connection this medieval writer did. It stems from exactly the psychosomatic assumptions that directed medical writers to prescribe foot-soaking, head-washing, and chewing coriander to improve memory, sweetness of the mouth and stomach being evidently as necessary to the healthy production of memory as a stress-free body (with relaxed feet and a non-itching scalp) is to productive concentration.

The monastic custom of reading during meals is described in some texts as an explicit literalizing of the metaphor of consuming a book as one consumes food. A late *Regula* for women adapted from the writings of St Jerome makes the connection clear: there should be reading during meals 'so that while the body is fattened [*saginatur*] with food, the mind should be filled [*saturetur*] with reading.'[10] Benedict's *Rule* says that 'while the brothers are eating they should not lack in reading';[11] the contemporaneous (sixth century) *Regula magistri* gives the reason why in words much like those of the later rule I just quoted. Every brother who has learned his letters should take his turn reading during meals, 'so that there should never be a lack of restoration for the body nor of divine food, for as Scripture says, man does not live by bread alone but in every word of the Lord, so that in two ways the Brothers may be repaired, when they chew with their mouths and are filled up through their ears.'[12] The Rule for women continues by characterizing how each sister should follow the reading. With absorbed, intent mind ('mens sobria intenta sit') she should actively, emotionally enter into the reading. She sighs anxiously when, in prophecy or historical narrative, the word of God shows enmity to the wicked. She is filled with great joy when the favor of the Lord is shown to the good. 'Words do not resound, but sighs; not laughter and derision but tears.'[13] This last comment is a reformation of one of Jerome's dicta, that 'the preacher should arouse wailing rather than applause,'[14] itself an idea that accords with the advice given by Quintilian and others that an orator must above all arouse the emotions of his audience. This *Rule* admonishes against laughter because, like applause, derision is associated in the writer's mind with detachment and disengagement from the material, tears with the opposite; the state of being 'engaged with' and 'totally absorbed in' the text (as I would translate the adjectives *sobria* and *intenta*) is necessary for its proper digestion.

Commentary on the two moments in Scripture (Ezekiel 3:3 and Revelation 10:9–11) in which a prophet is given a book to eat that is sweet as honey in the mouth underlines the need to consume one's reading.[15] 'Therefore we devour and digest the book, when we read the words of God,' says Hugo de Folieto in the twelfth century. 'Many indeed read, but from their reading they remain ignorant . . . but others devour and digest the holy books and are not ignorant because their memory does not let go of the rules for life whose meaning it can grasp.'[16] And Jerome, commenting on the Ezekiel text, says 'when by assiduous meditation we truly may have stored the book of the Lord in the treasury of our memory, we fill our belly in a spiritual sense, and our bowels are filled, that we may have with the Apostle the bowels of mercy (Coloss. 3:12), and that belly is filled concerning which Jeremias said: 'My bowels, my bowels! I am pained at my very heart' (Jer. 4:19).'[17]

Biblical study provides a model for other literary study. In the same part of the second dialogue in *Secretum* we looked at earlier, Augustine says that one needs a store of precepts from one's reading, in order to guard against sudden emotion and passion – anger for instance. Yes, replies 'Francesco,' he has found much good on this matter not only in philosophers but in poets as well. And he proceeds to give an interpretive reading of *Aeneid* I, 52–7, the description of Aeolus in the cave of the winds:

> As I carefully study every word, I have heard with my ears the fury, the rage, the roar of the winds; I have heard the trembling of the mountain and the din. Notice how well it all applies to the tempest of anger . . . I have heard the king, sitting on his high place, his sceptre grasped in his hand, subduing, binding in chains, and imprisoning those rebel blasts.[18]

And he demonstrates his interpretation by appealing to the last line of the description, 'mollitque animos et temperat iras' (I. 57); this, says Petrarch, shows that this passage can refer to the mind when it is vexed by anger.

Augustine praises the meaning which 'Francesco' has found hidden in the poet's words, which are so copious and familiar in his memory. For, 'whether Virgil himself meant this while he wrote, or whether, entirely remote from any such consideration, he wished only to describe a maritime storm in these verses and nothing else,'[19] the lesson which 'Francesco' has derived concerning anger is truthful and well-said. Extraordinary as this opinion is to a scholar brought up on notions of the inviolate authority of the text, we should not assume on the other hand that Petrarch's words, in the mouth of his revered mentor, indicate only an extreme subjectivity. Virgil's words remain significant themselves as the subject of the disciplines associated with *lectio*, and a source of wisdom and experience (via memory) for anyone who cares to read and remember them. The focus for Petrarch at this point is rather what the individual reader makes of those words, and that focus is not scientific but ethical.

Virgil's words having been devoured (or one might say 'harvested'), digested, and familiarized by 'Francesco' through *meditatio*, have now become *his* words as they cue the representational processes of his recollection. It is as though at this point the student of the text, having digested it by re-experiencing it in memory, has become not its interpreter, but its new author, or re-author. Petrarch has re-spoken Virgil; 're-written Virgil' we would say, with strong disapproval. But the re-writing which is acknowledged in what both Augustine and 'Francesco' say, is seen as a good not for Virgil's text, which is irrelevant at this point except as it has occasioned Petrarch's remembrance, but for 'Francesco's' moral life.[20]

Hugh of St Victor's preface to the *Chronica* [. . .] gives usefully succinct definitions of the three 'levels' of Biblical exegesis which indicate quite clearly which belong to the activity of *lectio* and which to *meditatio*. *Littera* is the subject of grammatical and rhetorical study; *historia* is the foreshadowing relationship of one event in the Bible to another, and is what is often also called *allegoria*. After these disciplines comes *tropologia* (which is more like what we think of as 'allegorical'); it is what the text means to us when we turn its words, like a mirror, upon ourselves, how we understand it when we have domesticated it and made it our own, and that is the special activity of memorative *meditatio*, the 'culmination' of *lectio* but bound by none of its rules, a free play of the recollecting mind. 'Holy Scripture,' wrote Gregory the Great, quoting Augustine, 'presents a kind of mirror to the eyes of the mind, that our inner face may be seen in it. There truly we learn our own ugliness, there our own beauty.'[21] As we do this, the text's initial sweetness may well turn to indigestion and pain, as it did for St John, but such *dolor* is to be welcomed. For, as Hugo de Folieto comments on Revelation 10:11, 'He certainly suffers pain in his stomach who feels affliction of mind. For this can be understood because, while the word of God may begin by being sweet in the mouth of our heart, before long the *animus* grows bitter in doubt against itself.' And he quotes Gregory, 'We devour the book when with eager desire we clothe ourselves with the words of life.'[22]

The psychology of the memory phantasm provides the rationale for the ethical value of the reading method which Petrarch describes. A properly-made phantasm is both a 'likeness' (*simulacrum*) and one's 'gut-level response' to it (*intentio*), and it is an emotional process that causes change in the body. The insistently physical matrix of the whole memorative process accounts for Petrarch's slow, detailed refashioning of Virgil's description. The active agency of the reader, 'discutiens,' 'breaking up' or 'shattering' (one could even translate 'deconstructing') each single word as he recreates the scene in his memory, is emphasized: 'Ego autem audivi . . . audivi . . . audivi.' He re-hears, re-sees, re-feels, experiences and re-experiences. In this way, Virgil's words are embodied in Petrarch's recollection as an experience of tumult and calm that is more physiological (emotional, passionate) than 'mental,' in our sense. Desire underlies the whole experience, changing from turmoil through anger to repose.[23] The re-created reading becomes useful precisely because in the heat of passion Petrarch's emotions replay that process of change, for he can remember what right action *feels* like. That is not a rational decision process, but one of desire and will guided through the process of change by remembered habit, 'firma facilitas' or *hexis*.

[. . .] [T]he medieval understanding of the complete process of reading does not observe in the same way the basic distinction we make between 'what I read in a book' and 'my experience.' This discussion by Petrarch, I think, makes clear why, for 'what I read in a book' *is* 'my experience,' and I make it mine by incorporating it (and we should understand the word 'incorporate' quite literally) in my memory. One remembers the boast of Chaucer's eagle in *The*

House of Fame that he can so palpably represent 'skiles' to his students that they can 'shake hem by the biles' (*HF*, II, 869–70), the avian manner of making them one's dear friends.

In this way, reading a book extends the process whereby one memory engages another in a continuing dialogue that approaches Plato's ideal (expressed in *Phaedrus*) of two living minds engaged in learning. Medieval reading is conceived to be not a 'hermeneutical circle' (which implies mere solipsism) but more like a 'hermeneutical dialogue' between two memories, that in the text being made very much present as it is familiarized to that of the reader. Isidore of Seville, we remember, in words echoed notably by John of Salisbury, says that written letters recall through the windows of our eyes the voices of those who are not present to us (and one thinks too of that evocative medieval phrase, 'voces paginarum,' 'the voices of the pages').[24] So long as the reader, in meditation (which is best performed in a *murmur* or low voice), reads attentively, that other member of the dialogue is in no danger of being lost, the other voice will sound through the written letters. Perhaps it is not inappropriate to recall again, having just spoken of Petrarch, the Greek verb, *ànagignósko*, 'to read,' but literally 'to know again' or 'remember.'

NOTES

1. See Leclercq, *Love of Learning*, p. 73, who cites a number of writers. *Ruminare* was used metaphorically to mean 'meditate' in pagan writing also; the earliest citation in the *Ox. Lat. Dict.* is third century, B.C. (s.v. *rumino*). Quintilian, though he does not actually use the verb, says that meditation (by which he means memorizing) is like rechewing one's food (*Inst.*, XI, 2, 41). See also Philip West, 'Rumination in Bede's Account of Caedmon.'
2. *Moralia in Job*, I, 33 (*PL* 75, 542C) 'In nobismetipsis namque debemus transformare quod legimus; ut cum per auditum se animus excitat, ad operandum quod audierit vita concurrat.'
3. *Didascalicon*, V, 5: 'cuius sententias quasi fructus quosdam dulcissimos legendo carpimus, tractando ruminamus'; Buttimer, p. 103, lines 26–7. Notice Hugh's use of the gerundive form of *tractare*, in a context similar to that in which Ockham also uses it [. . .]. It seems to be a scholastic use, 'tracting' for the process of making 'tracts' by mentally collating extracts during meditational composition (recall the account of Thomas Aquinas's composing habits [. . .]). On the genre called *tractatus*, see Kristeller, 'The Scholar and His Public' in *Medieval Aspects of Renaissance Learning*, esp. pp. 4–12.
4. *Cura pastoralis*, III, 12 (*PL* 77, 69).
5. *Didascalicon*, III, 11; 'hoc etiam saepe replicare et de ventre memoriae ad palatum revocare necesse est'; Buttimer, p. 61, lines 1–2. The quote from Gregory is found in *PL* 77, 69B.
6. *Sermones*, 352, 1 (*PL* 39, 1550): 'Unde cum sermonem ad vestram Charitatem non praepararemus, hinc nobis esse tractandum Domino imperante cognovimus. Volebamus enim hodierna die vos in ruminatione permittere, scientes quam abundantes epulas ceperitis.'
7. *Historia Ecclesiastica*, IV, 24. Philip West has discussed this passage and its context in the monastic traditions of *ruminatio* in 'Rumination in Bede's Account of Caedmon.'
8. See Darbishire (ed.), *The Early Lives of Milton*; my thanks to James Thorpe of the Huntington Library for bringing this material to my attention.

9. *Regula monachorum*, cap. 14 (*PL 30*, 365B): 'Ad orationem nocte consurgenti non indigestio cibi ructum faciat, sed inanitas. Nam quidam vir inter pastores eximius: sicut fumus, inquit, fugat apes, sic indigesta ructatio avertit Spiritus sancti charismata. Ructus autem dicitur proprie digestio cibi, et concoctarum escarum in ventum efflatio. Quomodo ergo juxta qualitatem ciborum de stomacho ructus erumpit, et vel boni, vel mali odoris flatus indicium est, ita interioris hominis cogitationes verba proferunt, et *ex abundantia cordis os loquitur* (Lk. 6:45). Justus comedens replet animam suam. Cumque sacris doctrinis fuerit satiatus, de boni cordis thesauro profert ea quae bona sunt.' This passage was cited by West, p. 220, note 11, from the 1984 reprinted edition, in which it is on column 353D.

10. *PL 30*, 435C: 'ut dum corpus saginatur cibo, saturetur anima lectione.'

11. *Regula Benedicta*, cap. 38 (*PL 66*, 601–602): 'Mensis fratrum edentium lectio deesse non debet.'

12. *Regula magistri*, cap. 24 (p. 217): 'ut nunquam desit carnali refectioni et aeca [= esca] divina, sicut dicit Scriptura, non in solo pane vivit homo sed in omni verbo domini, ut dupliciter Fratres reficiant, cum ore manducant et auribus saginantur.'

13. *PL 30*, 435C–D: 'Tunc uniuscujusque mens sobria intenta sit dulcedini verbi Dei, suspiret anxia, cum propheticus aut historicus sermo Dei saevitiam monstrat in pravos. Gaudio repleatur immenso, cum benignita Dei annuntiatur in bonos . . . Non resonent verba, sed gemitus: non risus et cachinnus, sed lacrymae.'

14. *Epist.*, 52. 8 (*PL 22*, 534): 'Docente te in Ecclesia, non clamor populi, sed gemitus suscitetur. Lacrymae auditorum, laudes tuae sint.' See Riché, *Education and Culture*, pp. 82–83.

15. The two accounts differ in one important particular, which the commentators noted. In Ezekiel, the prophet is presented with a roll and 'written therein lamentations, and mourning, and woe'; he is commanded 'Son of man, cause thy belly to eat, and fill thy bowels with this roll that I give thee. Then did I eat it; and it was in my mouth as honey for sweetness.' At that moment, he receives his commission to prophecy. In Revelation, the angel tells the prophet that the 'little book' will be sweet in the mouth but bitter in his belly; 'And I took the little book out of the angel's hand and ate it up; and it was in my mouth sweet as honey: and as soon as I had eaten it, my belly was bitter.'

16. *De claustro anime*, IV, 33 (*PL 176*, 1171D): 'Librum ergo devoramus et comedimus, dum verba Dei legimus. Multi enim legunt, et ab ipsa lectione jejuni sunt . . . [alii] sanctum librum devorant, et comedunt, et jejuni non sunt, quia praecepta vitae quae sensus capere potuit, memoria non amisit.'

17. *Commentarium in Ezechielem*, I, 3 (*PL 25*, 35D): 'Quando vero assidua meditatione in memoriae thesauro librum Domini condiderimus, impletur spiritualiter venter noster, et saturantur viscera, ut habeamus cum apostolo Paulo viscera misericordiae, et impleatur ille venter, de quo Jeremias loquitur: *Ventrem meum, ventrem meum ego doleo: et sensus cordis mei conturbant me* (Jer. 4:19).'

18. 'Ego autem, singula verba discutiens, audivi indignationem, audivi luctamen, audivi tempestates sonoras, audivi murmur ac fremitum . . . Audivi rursum regem in arce sedentem, audivi sceptrum tenentem, audivi prementem et vinclis ac carcere frenantem'; *Prose*, p. 124.

19. 'Sive enim id Virgilius ipse sensit, dum scriberet, sive ab omni tali consideratione remotissimus, maritimam his versibus et nil aliud describere voluit tempestatem'; *Prose*, p. 124.

20. R. W. Southern has written of John of Salisbury 'patiently picking over the literary deposit of the past. The names of Lucan, Macrobius, Martianus Capella, Ovid, Cicero, follow each other in his pages with a fine impartiality, each in turn pointing a doctrine or adorning a sentence. Once the nectar had been extracted, John of Salisbury passed on like a bee to another flower, diligently, unemotionally, not stopping to consider whether it was a cowslip or a clover, so long as it gave up its treasure'; *Medieval Humanism*, p. 126. I would disagree with Southern's adverb

'unemotionally' (for a memory cannot be stored without an emotion), but otherwise he precisely describes the attitude of a medieval scholar towards his sources. As he also writes of twelfth-century authors, they looked backward to the past 'only for the quite practical purpose of equipping themselves to look forward' prudently. In this passage from his *Secretum*, Petrarch, devoted textual scholar though he was, shows himself, *as an interpreter of texts*, to share John of Salisbury's attitude. Here again one can distinctly see the difference between the activities of *lectio*, or textual commentation and scholarship, and *meditatio*, the application of reading to individual moral life.

21. *Moralia in Job*, II, I (*PL 75*, 553D): 'Scriptura sacramentis oculis quasi quoddam speculum opponitur, ut interna nostra facies in ipsa videatur. Ibi etenim foeda, ibi pulchra nostra cognoscimus.' He is quoting 'ad res' Augustine, *In Psalmo 103*, ser. 1, n. 4. On the activities of *lectio* and *meditatio* in monastic textual study, see Leclercq, esp. pp. 15–17.

22. *De claustro anime*, IV, c. 33 (*PL 176*, 1172A): 'Ventrem quippe doluit, qui mentis afflictionem sensit. Sed sciendum est quia, cum sermo Dei in ore cordis dulcis esse coeperit, hujus procul dubio contra semetipsum animus amarescit.' From Gregory he quotes, 'Librum devoramus cum verba vitae cum aviditate sumimus' (1171C).

23. Since the will acts from desire, a total loss of desire would also mean a loss of free will. This idea belongs in the category of 'essential' Augustine, but it is best defined in *De trinitate*. The fullest literary expression of it is the whole *Divine Comedy*, but perhaps one moment especially captures it. At the end of *Purgatorio*, Dante finds himself able to do whatever he desires because his will is completely good; however he has not, one should notice, been *purged* of desire. 'Take henceforth thy pleasure for guide,' Virgil tells him; 'Free, upright and whole is thy will and it were a fault not to act on its bidding' (*Purgatorio*, 27, 131, 140–41).

24. Balogh, 'Voces Paginarum,' lists several variants of this phrase, including 'sonus litterarum' (Ambrose), 'vox antiqua chartarum' (Cassiodorus); Paulus Diaconus wrote that 'pagina canit,' 'the page sings' or 'chants,' perhaps an allusion to the murmur of memorative meditation.

FRANCES A. YATES: *FROM* THE ART OF MEMORY

The *Oratoriae artis epitome* by Jacobus Publicius was printed at Venice in 1482;[1] the rhetoric has attached to it, as an appendix, an *Ars memorativa*. This beautiful little printed book will surely, we may expect, take us out into a new world, the world of the revived interest in classical rhetoric of the advancing Renaissance. But is Publicius so very modern? The position of his memory section at the end of the rhetoric reminds us of the position of the memory section in the thirteenth-century *Fiore di Rettorica*, at the end and detachable. And the mystical introduction to the *Ars memorativa* is somewhat reminiscent of thirteenth-century mystical rhetorics of the Boncompagno type.

If the keenness of the mind is lost, so Publicius informs us in this introduction, through being enclosed within these earthly confines, the following 'new precepts' will help towards its release. The 'new precepts' are the rules for places and images. Publicius's interpretation of these includes the construction of '*ficta loca*', or imaginary places, which are none other than the spheres of the universe – the spheres of the elements, planets, fixed stars, and higher spheres – topped by 'Paradisus', all of which is shown on a diagram [Fig. 1]. In his rules for images which begin 'Simple and spiritual intentions slip easily from the memory unless joined to a corporeal similitude' he follows Thomas Aquinas. He dwells on the 'Ad Herennian' strikingness demanded of memory images, that they should have ridiculous movements, amazing gestures, or be filled with overpowering sadness or severity.[2] Unhappy Envy as described by

---

Source: Frances A. Yates, *The Art of Memory* (1966; London: Pimlico, 1992), pp. 117–27, 387–8.

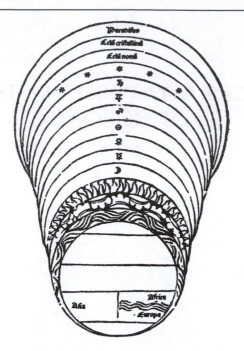

Fig. 1   The Spheres of the Universe as a Memory System. From J. Publicius,
Oratoriae artis epitome, 1482.

Ovid with her livid complexion, black teeth, and snaky hair, is a good example
of what a memory image should be.

Far from introducing us to a modern world of revived classical rhetoric,
Publicius's memory section seems rather to transport us back into a Dantesque
world in which Hell, Purgatory, and Paradise are remembered on the spheres
of the universe, a Giottesque world with its sharpened expressiveness of virtue
and vice memory figures. To use Ovid's Envy as a moving memory image from
the poets is not a surprising new classical feature but belongs into the earlier
memory tradition as interpreted by Albertus Magnus. In short, this first printed
memory treatise is not a symptom of the revival of the classical art of memory
as part of the Renaissance revival of rhetoric; it comes straight out of the
medieval tradition.

It is significant that this work, which looks so Renaissance and Italianate in
its printed form, was known to an English monk many years before it was
printed. A manuscript in the British Museum which Volkmann discovered was
written in 1460 by Thomas Swatwell, probably a monk of Durham; it is a copy
of the *Ars oratoria* of Jacobus Publicius.[3] The English monk has carefully
transcribed the memory section, ingeniously developing some of Publicius's
fantasies in the quietness of his cloister.[4]

Nevertheless, the times are changing, the humanists are gaining a better understanding of the civilization of classical antiquity; classical texts are circulating in

printed editions. The student of rhetoric now has many more texts at his disposal than those First and Second Rhetorics on which the alliance of the artificial memory with Prudence had been built. In 1416, Poggio Bracciolini had discovered a complete text of Quintilian's *Institutio oratoria* which had its *editio princeps* at Rome in 1470, soon followed by other editions. [. . .] [O]f the three Latin sources for the classical art of memory, it is Quintilian who gives the clearest account of the art as a mnemotechnic. In Quintilian the art could now be studied as a lay mnemotechnic, quite divorced from the associations which had grown up around the 'Ad Herennian' rules in their progress through the Middle Ages. And the way would be open for an enterprising person to teach the art of memory in a new way, as a success technique. The ancients, who knew everything, knew how to train the memory, and the man with a trained memory has an advantage over others which will help him get on in a competitive world. There will be a demand for the artificial memory of the ancients as now better understood. An enterprising person saw an opportunity here and seized it. His name was Peter of Ravenna.

The *Phoenix, sive artificiosa memoria* (first edition at Venice in 1491) by Peter of Ravenna became the most universally known of all the memory text books. It went through many editions in many countries,[5] was translated,[6] included in the popular general knowledge hand-book by Gregor Reisch,[7] copied by enthusiasts from the printed editions.[8] Peter was a tremendous self-advertiser which helped to boost his methods, but his fame as a memory teacher was probably largely due to the fact that he brought the mnemotechnic out into the lay world. People who wanted an art of memory to help them practically, and not in order to remember Hell, could turn to the *Phoenix* of Peter of Ravenna.

Peter gives practical advice. When discussing the rule that memory *loci* are to be formed in quiet places he says that the best type of building to use is an unfrequented church. He describes how he goes round the church he has chosen three or four times, committing the places in it to memory. He chooses his first place near the door; the next, five or six feet further in; and so on. As a young man he started with one hundred thousand memorized places, but he has added many more since then. On his travels, he does not cease to make new places in some monastery or church, remembering through them histories, or fables, or Lenten sermons. His memory of the Scriptures, of canon law, and many other matters is based on this method. He can repeat from memory the whole of the canon law, text and gloss (he was a jurist trained at Padua); two hundred speeches or sayings of Cicero; three hundred sayings of the philosophers; twenty thousand legal points.[9] Peter probably was one of those people with very good natural memories who had so drilled themselves in the classical technique that they really could perform astonishing feats of memory. I think that one can definitely see an influence of Quintilian in Peter's account of his vast number of places, for it is Quintilian alone, of the classical sources who says that one may form memory places when on journeys.

On images, Peter makes use of the classical principle that memory images should if possible resemble people we know. He gives the name of a lady, Juniper of Pistoia, who was dear to him when young and whose image he finds stimulates his memory! Possibly this may have something to do with Peter's variation on the classical lawsuit image. To remember that a will is not valid without seven witnesses, says Peter, we may form an image of a scene in which 'the testator is making his will in the presence of two witnesses, and then a girl tears up the will'.[10] As with the classical lawsuit image, we are baffled as to why such an image, even if Juniper is the destructive girl, should help Peter remember his simple point about witnesses.

Peter laicised and popularised memory and emphasised the purely mnemo-technical side. Nevertheless there is a good deal of unexplained confusion and curious detail in Peter's mnemonics, indicating that he is not altogether detached from the medieval tradition. His books become absorbed in the general memory tradition as it rolls on its way. Most subsequent writers on memory mention him, not excluding Romberch, the Dominican, who cites 'Petrus Ravennatis' as an authority as well as Tullius and Quintilian, or Thomas Aquinas and Petrarch.

I do not attempt to survey here the whole tribe of the printed memory treatises. [. . .] Some treatises teach what I shall hereafter call 'the straight mnemotechnic', perhaps better understood after the recovery of Quintilian. In many, the mnemotechnic is closely entangled with surviving influences of the medieval uses of the art. In some there are traces of infiltration of medieval forms of magic memory, such as the *Ars notoria*, into the art.[11] In some there are influences from the Renaissance Hermetic and occult transformation of the art [. . .].

But it is important that we should look here more particularly at what memory treatises by Dominicans were like in the sixteenth century, since the main strand, descending from the scholastic emphasis on memory, is in my opinion the most important strand in the history of the subject. The Dominicans were naturally at the centre of this tradition, and in Johannes Romberch, a German, and Cosmas Rossellius, a Florentine, we have two Dominicans who wrote books on memory, small in format but packed with detail, apparently intended to make the Dominican art of memory generally known. Romberch says that his book will be useful to theologians, preachers, confessors, jurists, advocates, doctors, philosophers, professors of the liberal arts, and ambassadors. Rossellius makes a similar statement. Romberch's book was published near the beginning of the sixteenth century; Rossellius's near its end. Together they span the century, as influential memory teachers who are frequently quoted. In fact, Publicius, Peter of Ravenna, Romberch, and Rossellius may be said to be the leading names amongst writers on memory.

The *Congestorium artificiose memorie* (1520)[12] of Johannes Romberch is well named, for it is a strange congestion of memory material. Romberch knows all the three classical sources, not only *Ad Herennium* but also Cicero's

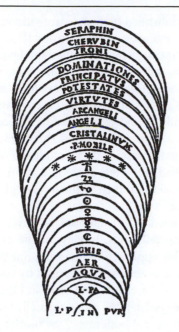

*Fig. 2   The Spheres of the Universe as a Memory System. From J. Romberch,
Congestorium artificiose memorie, ed. of 1533.*

De oratore and Quintilian. By his frequent citation of the name of Petrarch,[13] he absorbs the poet into the Dominican memory tradition; Peter of Ravenna and others are also drawn into the congestion. But his basis is Thomas Aquinas, whose formulations, both in the *Summa* and in the Aristotle commentary, he quotes on nearly every other page.

The book is in four parts; the first introductory, the second on places, the third on images; the fourth part outlines an encyclopedic memory system.

Romberch envisages three different types of place systems, as all belonging to artificial memory.

The first type uses the cosmos as a place system, as illustrated in his diagram [Fig. 2]. Here we see the spheres of the elements, of the planets, of the fixed stars, and above them the celestial spheres and those of the nine orders of angels. What are we to remember on these cosmic orders? Marked on the lower part of the diagram we see the letters 'L.PA; L.P; PVR; IN'. These stand for the places of Paradise, of the Earthly Paradise, of Purgatory, and of Hell.[14] In Romberch's view, remembering places such as these belongs to artificial memory. He calls such realms 'imaginary places' [*ficta loca*]. For the invisible things of Paradise we are to form places in memory in which we put the choirs of angels, the seats of the blessed, Patriarchs, Prophets, Apostles, Martyrs. The same is to be done for Purgatory and Hell, which are 'common places' or inclusive places, which are to be ordered into many particular places, to be remembered in order with inscriptions on them. The places of Hell contain images of sinners being punished in them in accordance with the nature of their sins, as explained in the memorized inscriptions.[15]

This type of artificial memory may be called the Dantesque type, not because the Dominican treatise is influenced by the *Divine Comedy*, but because Dante was influenced by such an interpretation of artificial memory [. . .].

As another type of place system, Romberch envisages using the signs of the zodiac as giving an easily memorized order of places. He gives the name of Metrodorus of Scepsis as the authority on this.[16] He found the information about the zodiacal memory system of Metrodorus of Scepsis in Cicero's *De oratore* and in Quintilian. He adds that, if a more extended star-order for memory is needed, it is useful to turn to the images given by Hyginus of all the constellations of the sky.[17]

He does not state what kind of material he envisages as being memorized on the images of the constellations. In view of the predominantly theological and didactic nature of his approach to memory, one might guess that the constellation order as a place system was to be used by preachers for remembering the order of their sermons on virtues and vices in Heaven and Hell.

His third type of place system is the more normally mnemotechnical method of memorizing real places on real buildings,[18] as on the abbey and its associated buildings illustrated by a cut. The images which he is using on places in this building are those of 'memory objects' of the type already referred to. Here we are on the ground of 'the straight mnemotechnic' and from the instructions about memorising places in buildings given in this part of the book, the reader could have learned the use of the art as a straight mnemotechnic, of the more mechanical type described by Quintilian. Though even here there are curious and non-classical elaborations about 'alphabetical orders'. It helps to have lists of animals, birds, names, arranged in alphabetical order to use with this system.

Amongst Romberch's additions to the place rules, is one which is not original to him; Peter of Ravenna gives it and it may go back much earlier. A memory *locus* which is to contain a memory image must not be larger than a man can reach;[19] this is illustrated by a cut of a human image on a *locus* [Fig. 3], reaching upwards and sideways to demonstrate the right proportions of the *locus* in relation to the image. This rule grows out of the artistic feeling for space, lighting, distance, in memory in the classical place rules, of which we earlier suggested an influence on Giotto's painted *loci*. It evidently applies to human images, not to memory objects as images, and may imply a similar kind of interpretation of the place rules (that is to make the images placed in regular orders stand out from their backgrounds).

On images,[20] Romberch retails the classical rules on striking images with many elaborations and with much quotation from Thomas on corporeal similitudes. As usual the memory images are not illustrated nor are they very clearly described. We have to construct our own from the rules.

There are however some illustrations in this section of the book but they are 'visual alphabets'. Visual alphabets are ways of representing letters of the

*Fig. 3   Human Image on a Memory Locus. From Romberch,
Congestorium artificiose memorie, ed. of 1533.*

alphabet by images. These are formed in various ways; for example with pictures of objects whose shape resemble letters of the alphabet, as compasses or a ladder for A; or a hoe for N. Another way is through pictures of animals or birds arranged in the order of the first letter of their names, as A for *Anser*, goose, B for *Bubo*, owl. Visual alphabets are very common in the memory treatises and they almost certainly come out of an old tradition. Boncompagno speaks of an 'imaginary alphabet' which is to be used for remembering names.[21] Such alphabets are frequently described in the manuscript treatises. Publicius's is the first printed treatise to illustrate them;[22] thereafter they are a normal feature of most printed memory treatises. Volkmann has reproduced a number of them from various treatises,[23] but without discussing what their origin may be or for what purposes they were intended to be used.

The visual alphabet probably comes out of endeavours to understand *Ad Herennium* on how proficients in artificial memory write in images in their memories. According to the general principles of artificial memory we should put everything that we want to fix in memory into an image. Applied to the letters of the alphabet, this would mean that they are better remembered if put into images. The notion as worked out in the visual alphabets is of infantile simplicity, like teaching a child to remember C through the picture of a Cat. Rossellius, apparently in perfect seriousness, suggests that we should remember the word AER through the images of an Ass, an Elephant, and a Rhinoceros![24]

A variation on the visual alphabet, suggested, I believe, by the words of *Ad Herennium* on remembering a number of our acquaintances standing in a row, is formed by arranging persons known to the practitioner of artificial memory in alphabetical order of their names. Peter of Ravenna gives a splendid example of this method in use when he states that to remember the word ET he visualises

Eusebius standing in front of Thomas; and he has only to move Eusebius back behind Thomas to remember the word TE![25]

The visual alphabets illustrated in the memory treatises, were I believe, intended to be used for making inscriptions in memory. In fact, this can be proved from the example illustrated in the third part of Romberch's book of a memory image covered with inscriptions in visual alphabets. This is one of the very rare cases in which a memory image is illustrated; and the image turns out to be the familiar figure of old Grammatica, the first of the liberal arts, with some of her familiar attributes, the scalpel and the ladder. She is here not only the well-known personification of the liberal art of Grammar, but a memory image being used to remember material about grammar through inscriptions on her. The inscription across her chest and the images near or on her are derived from Romberch's visual alphabets, both the 'objects' ones and the 'birds' one which he is using in combination. He explains that he is memorizing in this way the answer to the question as to whether Grammar is a common or a particular science; the reply involves the use of the terms *predicatio*, *applicatio*, *continentia*.[26] *Predicatio* is memorized by the bird beginning with a P (a *Pica* or pie) which she holds, and its associated objects from the object alphabet. *Applicatio* is remembered by the Aquila[27] and associated objects on her arm. *Continentia* is remembered by the inscription on her chest in the 'objects' alphabet [. . .].

Though devoid of aesthetic charm, Romberch's Grammar is of importance to the student of artificial memory. She proves the point that personifications, such as the familiar figures of the liberal arts, when reflected in memory, become memory images. And that inscriptions are to be made in memory on such figures for memorizing material about the subject of the personification. The principle exemplified in Romberch's Grammar could be applied to all other personifications, such as those of the virtues and vices, when used as memory images. [. . .] The images themselves recall the memory of the 'things' and the inscriptions memorized on them are 'memory for words' about the 'things'. Or so I would suggest.

Romberch's Grammar, here undoubtedly being used as a memory image, shows the method in action, with the added refinement that the inscriptions are made (so it is supposed) more memorable by being made not in ordinary writing, but in images for the letters from visual alphabets.

NOTES

1. Second edition, Venice, 1485.
2. Ed. of Venice, 1485, Sig. G 8 *recto*. Cf. Rossi, *Clavis*, p. 38.
3. B. M. Additional 28,805; cf. Volkmann, pp. 145 ff.
4. One of the English monk's memory diagrams (reproduced by Volkmann, P1. 145) is probably magical.
5. Amongst these are those of Bologna, 1492; Cologne, 1506, 1608; Venice, 1526, 1533; Vienna, 1541, 1600; Vicenza, 1600.
6. The English translation is by Robert Copland, *The Art of Memory that is otherwise called the Phoenix*, London, *circa* 1548. [. . .]

7. Gregor Reisch, *Margarita philosophica*, first edition 1496, many later editions. Peter of Ravenna's art of memory is in Lib. III, Tract. II, cap. XXIII.

8. Cf. Rossi, *Clavis*, p. 27, note. To the manuscript copies of Ravenna's work mentioned by Rossi may be added those in Vat. Lat. 5347 f. 60, and in Paris, Lat. 8747, f. 1.

9. Petrus Tommai (Peter of Ravenna), *Foenix*, ed. of Venice, 1491, sigs. b iii–b iv.

10. *Ibid.* sig. c iii *recto*.

11. Possible examples of this are Jodocus Weczdorff, *Ars memorandi nova secretissima, circa*, 1600, and Nicolas Simon aus Weida, *Ludus artificialis oblivionis*, Leipzig, 1510. Frontispieces and diagrams from these heavily magical works are reproduced by Volkmann, Pls. 168–71.

12. I use the edition of Venice, 1533. Romberch may be more agreeably studied in Lodovico Dolce's Italian translation [. . .].

13. Romberch, pp. 2 *verso*, 12 *verso*, 14 *recto*, 20 *recto*, 26 *verso* etc.

14. *Ibid.*, pp. 17 *recto* ff., 31 *recto* ff.

15. *Ibid.*, pp. 18 *recto* and *verso*. [. . .]

16. *Ibid.*, pp. 25 *recto* ff.

17. *Ibid.*, p. 33 *verso*.

18. *Ibid.*, pp. 35 *recto* ff.

19. *Ibid.*, p. 28 *verso*.

20. *Ibid.*, pp. 39 *verso* ff.

21. Boncompagno, *Rhetorica novissima, ed. cit.*, p. 278, 'De alphabeto imaginario'.

22. Publicius's 'objects' alphabet, on which one of Romberch's is based, is reproduced by Volkmann, Pl. 146.

23. Volkmann, Pls. 146–7, 150–1, 179–88, 194, 198. Another device was to form images for numbers from objects; examples from Romberch, Rossellius, Porta, are reproduced by Volkmann, Pls. 183–5, 188, 194.

24. Cosmas Rossellius, *Thesaurus artificiosae memoriae*, Venice, 1579, p. 119 *verso*.

25. Petrus Tommai (Peter of Ravenna) *Foenix, ed. cit.*, sig. c i *recto*.

26. Romberch, pp. 82 *verso*–83 *recto*.

27. If Romberch had stuck to his own 'birds' alphabet, the A bird should have been an *Anser* [. . .]; but the text [p. 83 *recto*] states that the bird on Grammar's arm is an *Aquila*.

SECTION 2
ENLIGHTENMENT AND ROMANTIC MEMORY

Edited by Michael Rossington

INTRODUCTION

Michael Rossington

In a profound and wide-ranging discussion of the implications of Romantic uses of memory for history and individual identity, Frances Ferguson scrutinises the debt owed to **John Locke** who identified 'the importance of memory for anchoring a sense of individual continuity over time' (Ferguson, 1996: 509). As well as its legacy to the eighteenth century and beyond, Locke's conception of memory has parallels with classical and medieval accounts, as is evident in 'Of Retention' reproduced here from the fourth edition of *An Essay Concerning Human Understanding* (1700), which incorporates modifications to this chapter made in the second edition of 1694 (the *Essay* was first published in 1690). In addition to deploying the language of imprinting and impressions familiar since Plato, memory appears to be conceived of by Locke as a place, 'the Store-house of our *Ideas*', which functions as a means to mental safe-keeping, 'a Repository, to lay up those *Ideas*, which at another time [the narrow Mind of Man] might have use of' (this volume, p. 75). Moreover, memory is promoted as necessary to any creature of intellect: 'where it is wanting, all the rest of our Faculties are in a great measure useless' (p. 77). However, as he argued in his treatise *Some Thoughts Concerning Education* (1693), a merely mechanistic approach to the cultivation of memory, such as forcing young children to learn languages by rote, is likely to be counter-productive: 'strength of Memory is owing to an happy Constitution, and not to any habitual Improvement got by Exercise' (Locke, 1989: 232). Instead of mind-numbing 'memorising', Locke advocates an alternative, virtuous end to training the young in this art:

[I]t may do well, to give them something every day to remember; but something still, that is in it self worth the remembring, and what you would never have out of Mind, whenever you call, or they themselves search for it. This will oblige them often to turn their Thoughts inwards, than which you cannot wish them a better intellectual habit. (Locke, 1989: 233–4)

The mind's faculty for retaining ideas and reviving them again after they have disappeared is one dimension of memory. But Locke is making a further and novel point about mental self-consciousness: 'the Mind has a Power, in many cases, to revive Perceptions, which it has once had, with this additional Perception annexed to them, that it has had them before' (this volume, p. 75) Such an account of the mind's awareness of its own power to revive ideas and perceptions it has stored up looks forward to Wordsworth's concept of 'spots of time' in Book XI of *The Prelude* (1805). Moreover in the following sentence Locke recasts memory such that it is less a place than a function of the mind: 'And in this Sense it is, that our *Ideas* are said to be in our Memories, when indeed, they are actually no where, but only there is an ability in the Mind, when it will, to revive them again; and as it were paint them anew on it self' (this volume, pp. 75–6). A consequence of this conception of memory for a sense of selfhood is that Locke, in Ferguson's words, 'freed individuals from having to repeat the same actions continually and introduced them instead to a vision of their own possible progress and development' (Ferguson, 1996: 509).

Distinctive in the treatment of memory in *A Treatise of Human Nature* (1739–40) by **David Hume** is the repeated pairing of the term with 'imagination'. On the one hand, Hume seeks to distinguish between the properties of these two faculties, on the other to draw attention to what, to him, is their perilous proximity (noted by Aristotle who asserted that memory belongs to the same part of the soul as imagination (this volume, p. 30)). Whereas in the first extract, 'Of the ideas of the memory and imagination', Hume posits that ideas of the memory are more *vivid* representations of copied impressions than those of the imagination, in the second, 'Of the impressions of the senses and memory', which begins with the sceptical claim that the ultimate cause of impressions is impossible to know, Hume probes further the contrast between these two faculties, concluding that 'the difference betwixt [memory] and the imagination lies in [memory's] superior force and vivacity.' This reiteration of the claim made in the first extract that the ideas of the memory are 'more *strong* and *lively* than those of the fancy', that is more faithful (in the sense of historically accurate) to their source than the imagination, is, however, subject to qualification: 'an idea of the memory, by losing its force and vivacity, may degenerate to such a degree, as to be taken for an idea of the imagination; so on the other hand an idea of the imagination may acquire such a force and vivacity, as to pass for an idea of the memory, and counterfeit its effects on the belief and

71

judgment' (this volume, p. 82). Such is the uneasy relationship between memory and imagination that the ideas of imagination may thus, in certain circumstances, come to supplant those of memory in their greater force and vividness. Such circumstances include 'the case of liars' (this volume, p. 83), says Hume, sounding like Plato in his description of poets. That memory and imagination may feed one another is evident in Hume's scepticism towards conventional ideas of selfhood in a later section, 'Of personal identity', not included here. Hume sounds markedly contemporary in his refusal to accept a commonsense notion that human selves are stable and coherent. In a celebrated passage, he declares: 'I may venture to affirm of the rest of mankind, that they are nothing but a bundle or collection of different perceptions, which succeed each other with inconceivable rapidity, and are in a perpetual flux and movement' (Hume, 2000: 165). For Hume, then, our imagination gives us the illusion of there being a unity in our different perceptions over time. And memory contributes to this (illusory) sense of continuity that goes to make up our (false) idea of unified selfhood: 'having once acquir'd this notion of causation from the memory, we can extend the same chain of causes, and consequently the identity of our persons beyond our memory, and can comprehend times, and circumstances, and actions, which we have entirely forgot, but suppose in general to have existed' (Hume, 2000: 171). Hume's *Treatise* thus points to a willingness to admit an essential discontinuity in human experience which the imagination in collaboration with memory seeks to overcome. In these ways, Hume's ideas about memory look forward to the difficulty of 'knowing' the past, of articulating the grounds of its impact upon the present, registered in such autobiographical works as Wordsworth's *Prelude* and in poststructuralist and psychoanalytical treatments of memory.

The final extract in this section is from **Georg Wilhelm Friedrich Hegel**'s *Philosophy of Mind*, the third part of his *Encyclopaedia* (1830). Stephen Houlgate characterises this work thus:

> [u]nlike Descartes and Locke, Hegel is not doing epistemology in the *Philosophy of [Mind]* and is not primarily concerned with determining how we can know objects in the world. He is doing ontology and seeking to understand what the basic activities of the mind *are*.
>
> Each activity of the mind discussed by Hegel is to be understood as a form of subjective freedom . . . those treated later exhibit greater freedom than those treated earlier, and Hegel's account as a whole thus shows how human subjectivity progressively emancipates itself from nature. (Houlgate, 1998: 255)

Sub-section (γγ), 'Memory' (*Gedächtnis*), included here, follows (αα) 'Recollection' (*Erinnerung*) and (ββ) 'Imagination' (*Einbildungskraft*) in a section entitled (β) 'Representation (or Mental Idea)' (*Vorstellung*). Like Aristotle, Hegel differentiates memory from recollection, but in his own idiom. In *Erinnerung* the intelligence is described as 'this night-like mine or pit in which is stored a world of infinitely many images and representations, yet without being in consciousness' (Hegel, 1971: 204). *Erinnerung* is therefore in no ordinary sense 'recollection', as Michael Inwood explains:

> Hegel takes *Erinnerung* to be, not primarily recollection, but the internalization of a sensory INTUITION as an image (*Bild*); the image is abstracted from the concrete spatio-temporal position of the intuition, and given a place in the intelligence (which has its own subjective space and time). But the image is fleeting, and passes out of consciousness. The imagination is thus needed to revive or reproduce the image. (Inwood, 1992: 188)

While Hume saw memory and imagination as contesting faculties, Hegel's theory of memory enlists imagination to rescue images from the 'night-like mine or pit'. *Einbildungskraft* is defined progressively as 'reproductive', 'associative' and 'creative' (*Phantasie*), this last a state in which the mind 'freely combines and subsumes these stores [of images and ideas belonging to it] in obedience with its peculiar tenor' (Hegel, 1971: 209). In *Gedächtnis*, the final stage of *Vorstellung*, memory is considered under three headings: 'retentive', 'reproductive' and 'mechanical'. It is worth noting in the account of 'reproductive' memory Hegel's contempt for the precedence given to images over names in classically based mnemonics: 'The recent attempts – already, as they deserved, forgotten – to rehabilitate the Mnemonic of the ancients, consist in transforming names into images, and thus again deposing memory to the level of imagination' (this volume, p. 86). In its highest form, the 'mechanical', it is *Gedächtnis* 'which makes the transition to the highest capacity of the thinking intellect' (de Man, 1996: 101): 'Memory is . . . the passage into the function of *thought*, which no longer has a *meaning*, i.e. its objectivity is no longer severed from the subjective, and its inwardness does not need to go outside for its existence' (this volume, p. 88). This ultimate state of *Gedächtnis*, in which we 'freely abstract from meaning, hold a series of purely meaningless signs in our mind and thereby become conscious of ourselves as "abstract subjectivity"' (Houlgate, 1998: 255) is captured, for Hegel, in the satisfying etymological kinship in the German language between *Gedächtnis* and *Gedanke*. Inwood's gloss is helpful here: 'the past participle of *denken* ("to think") is *gedacht* ("(having been) thought") so that *Gedächtnis* has the flavour of "having-been-thoughtness"' (Inwood, 1992: 188). Hegel's consideration of memory has been considered influential within 'poststructuralism' (Derrida, Krell), literary theory (de Man), and psychoanalysis (Mills).

References and Further Reading

Biro, John (1993) 'Hume's New Science of the Mind', in David Fate Norton (ed.), *The Cambridge Companion to Hume*. Cambridge: Cambridge University Press, pp. 33–64.

Clingham, Greg (2002) *Johnson, Writing, and Memory*. Cambridge: Cambridge University Press.

De Man, Paul (1996) 'Sign and Symbol in Hegel's *Aesthetics*', in Andrzej Warminski (ed.), *Aesthetic Ideology*. Minneapolis, MN, and London: University of Minnesota Press, pp. 91–104.

Derrida, Jacques ([1968] 1982) 'The Pit and the Pyramid: Introduction to Hegel's Semiology', in *Margins of Philosophy*, trans. with additional notes Alan Bass. Brighton: Harvester Press, pp. 69–108.

—— (1986) *Memoires for Paul de Man*, trans. Cecile Lindsay, Jonathan Culler and Eduardo Cadava. New York: Columbia University Press.

Ferguson, Frances (1996) 'Romantic Memory', *Studies in Romanticism*, 35: pp. 509–33.

Hegel, Georg Wilhelm Friedrich (1971) *Philosophy of Mind*, Being Part Three of *The Encyclopaedia of the Philosophical Sciences* (1830), trans. by William Wallace, together with the Zusatze in Boumann's Text (1845), trans. by A. V. Miller, Foreword J. N. Findlay. Oxford: Clarendon Press.

Houlgate, Stephen (ed.) (1998) *The Hegel Reader*. Oxford: Blackwell.

Hume, David (2000) *A Treatise of Human Nature*, eds David Fate Norton and Mary J. Norton, intro. David Fate Norton, 'Oxford Philosophical Texts'. Oxford: Oxford University Press.

Inwood, Michael (1992) '[M]emory, Recollection and Imagination', in *A Hegel Dictionary*. Oxford: Blackwell, pp. 186–8.

Krell, David Farrell (1990) 'Of Pits and Pyramids: Hegel on Memory, Remembrance and Writing', in *Of Memory, Reminiscence, and Writing: On the Verge*. Bloomington, IN: Indiana University Press, pp. 205–39.

Locke, John (1975) *An Essay Concerning Human Understanding*, ed. Peter H. Nidditch. Oxford: Clarendon Press.

—— (1989) *Some Thoughts Concerning Education*, eds John W. and Jean S. Yolton. Oxford: Clarendon Press.

Mills, Jon (2002) *The Unconscious Abyss: Hegel's Anticipation of Psychoanalysis*. Albany, NY: State University of New York Press.

Sutton, John (1998) 'John Locke and the Neurophilosophy of Self', in *Philosophy and Memory Traces: Descartes to Connectionism*. Cambridge: Cambridge University Press, pp. 157–76.

Warnock, Mary (1987) *Memory*. London: Faber.

JOHN LOCKE: *FROM* AN ESSAY CONCERNING HUMAN UNDERSTANDING

OF RETENTION

§ 1. The next Faculty of the Mind, whereby it makes a farther Progress towards Knowledge, is that which I call *Retention*, or the keeping of those simple *Ideas*, which from Sensation or Reflection it hath received. This is done two ways. First, by keeping the *Idea*, which is brought into it, for some time actually in view, which is called *Contemplation*.

§ 2. The other way of Retention is the Power to revive again in our Minds those *Ideas*, which after imprinting have disappeared, or have been as it were laid aside out of Sight: And thus we do, when we conceive Heat or Light, Yellow or Sweet, the Object being removed. This is *Memory*, which is as it were the Store-house of our *Ideas*. For the narrow Mind of Man, not being capable of having many *Ideas* under View and Consideration at once, it was necessary to have a Repository, to lay up those *Ideas*, which at another time it might have use of. But our *Ideas* being nothing, but actual Perceptions in the Mind, which cease to be any thing, when there is no perception of them, this *laying up* of our *Ideas* in the Repository of the Memory, signifies no more but this, that the Mind has a Power, in many cases, to revive Perceptions, which it has once had, with this additional Perception annexed to them, that it has had them before. And in this Sense it is, that our *Ideas* are said to be in our Memories, when indeed, they are actually no where, but only there is an ability in the Mind, when it will,

Source: John Locke, *An Essay Concerning Human Understanding* [1700; first published in 1690], ed. Peter H. Nidditch (Oxford: Clarendon Press, 1975), pp. 149–55.

to revive them again; and as it were paint them anew on it self, though some with more, some with less difficulty; some more lively, and others more obscurely. And thus it is, by the Assistance of this Faculty, that we are said to have all those *Ideas* in our Understandings, which though we do not actually contemplate, yet we can bring in sight, and make appear again, and be the Objects of our Thoughts, without the help of those sensible Qualities, which first imprinted them there.

§ 3. *Attention* and *Repetition help* much to the fixing any *Ideas* in *the Memory*: But those, which naturally at first make the deepest, and most lasting Impression, are those, which are accompanied with *Pleasure* or *Pain*. The great Business of the Senses, being to make us take notice of what hurts, or advantages the Body, it is wisely ordered by Nature (as has been shewn) that Pain should accompany the Reception of several *Ideas*; which supplying the Place of Consideration and Reasoning in Children, and acting quicker than Consideration in grown Men, makes both the Young and Old avoid painful Objects, with that haste, which is necessary for their Preservation; and in both settles in the Memory a caution for the Future.

§ 4. Concerning the several *degrees* of lasting, wherewith *Ideas* are imprinted on the *Memory*, we may observe, That some of them have been produced in the Understanding, by an Object affecting the Senses once only, and no more than once: Others, that have more than once offer'd themselves to the Senses, have yet been little taken notice of; the Mind, either heedless, as in Children, or otherwise employ'd, as in Men, intent only on one thing, not setting the stamp deep into it self. And in some, where they are set on with care and repeated impressions, either through the temper of the Body, or some other default, the Memory is very weak: In all these cases, *Ideas* in the Mind quickly fade, and often vanish quite out of the Understanding, leaving no more footsteps or remaining Characters of themselves, than Shadows do flying over Fields of Corn; and the Mind is as void of them, as if they never had been there.

§ 5. Thus many of those *Ideas*, which were produced in the Minds of Children, in the beginning of their Sensation (some of which, perhaps, as of some Pleasures and Pains, were before they were born, and others in their Infancy) if in the future Course of their Lives, they are not repeated again, are quite lost, without the least glimpse remaining of them. This may be observed in those, who by some Mischance have lost their sight, when they were very Young; in whom the *Ideas* of Colours, having been but slightly taken notice of, and ceasing to be repeated, do quite wear out; so that some years after, there is no more Notion, nor Memory of Colours left in their Minds, than in those of People born blind. The Memory in some Men, 'tis true, is very tenacious, even to a Miracle: But yet there seems to be a constant decay of all our *Ideas*, even of those which are struck deepest, and in Minds the most retentive; so that if they be not sometimes renewed by repeated Exercise of the Senses, or Reflection on those kind of Objects, which at first occasioned them, the Print wears out, and at last there remains nothing to be seen. Thus the *Ideas*, as well as Children, of our Youth, often die before us: And our Minds represent to us those Tombs, to which we are approaching; where though the Brass and Marble remain, yet the Inscriptions are effaced by time, and the Imagery moulders away. *The Pictures drawn in our Minds, are laid in fading Colours*; and if not sometimes refreshed, vanish and disappear. How much the Constitution of our Bodies, and the make of our animal Spirits, are concerned in this; and whether the Temper of the Brain make this difference, that in some it retains the Characters drawn on it like Marble, in others like Free-stone, and in others little better than Sand, I shall not here enquire, though it may seem probable, that the Constitution of the Body does sometimes influence the Memory; since we oftentimes find a Disease quite strip the Mind of all its *Ideas*, and the flames of a Fever, in a few days, calcine all those Images to dust and confusion, which seem'd to be as lasting, as if graved in Marble.

§ 6. But concerning the *Ideas* themselves, it is easie to remark, That those that are *oftenest refreshed* (amongst which are those that are conveyed into the Mind by more ways than one) by a frequent return of the Objects or Actions that produce them, *fix themselves best in the Memory*, and remain clearest and longest there; and therefore those, which are of the original Qualities of Bodies, *viz. Solidity, Extension, Figure, Motion*, and *Rest*, and those that almost constantly affect our Bodies, as *Heat* and *Cold*; and those which are the Affections of all kinds of Beings, as *Existence, Duration*, and *Number*, which almost every Object that affects our Senses, every Thought which imploys our Minds, bring along with them: These, I say, and the like *Ideas*, are seldom quite lost, whilst the Mind retains any *Ideas* at all.

§ 7. In this secondary Perception, as I may so call it, or viewing again the *Ideas*, that are lodg'd *in the Memory, the Mind is oftentimes more than barely passive*, the appearance of those dormant Pictures, depending sometimes on the Will. The Mind very often sets it self on work in search of some hidden *Idea*, and turns, as it were, the Eye of the Soul upon it; though sometimes too they start up in our Minds of their own accord, and offer themselves to the Understanding; and very often are rouzed and tumbled out of their dark Cells, into open Day-light, by some turbulent and tempestuous Passion; our Affections bringing *Ideas* to our Memory, which had otherwise lain quiet and unregarded. This farther is to be observed, concerning *Ideas* lodg'd in the Memory, and upon occasion revived by the Mind, that they are not only (as the Word *revive* imports) none of them new ones; but also that the Mind takes notice of them, as of a former Impression, and renews its acquaintance with them, as with *Ideas* it had known before. So that though *Ideas* formerly imprinted are not all constantly in view, yet in remembrance they are constantly known to be such, as have been formerly imprinted, *i.e.* in view, and taken notice of before by the Understanding.

§ 8. *Memory*, in an intellectual Creature, is necessary in the next degree to Perception. It is of so great moment, that where it is wanting, all the rest of our Faculties are in a great measure useless: And we in our Thoughts, Reasonings, and Knowledge, could not proceed beyond present Objects, were it not for the assistance of our Memories, wherein there may be *two defects*.

First, That it *loses the Idea* quite, and so far it produces perfect Ignorance. For since we can know nothing farther, than we have the *Idea* of it, when that is gone, we are in perfect *ignorance*.

Secondly, That it moves slowly, and *retrieves not the Ideas*, that it has, and are laid up in store, *quick enough* to serve the Mind upon occasions. This, if it be to a great degree, is *Stupidity*; and he, who through this default in his Memory, has not the *Ideas*, that are really preserved there, ready at hand, when need and occasion calls for them, were almost as good be without them quite, since they serve him to little purpose. The dull Man, who loses the opportunity, whilst he is seeking in his Mind for those *Ideas*, that should serve his turn, is not much more happy in his Knowledge, than one that is perfectly ignorant. 'Tis the business therefore of the Memory to furnish to the Mind those dormant *Ideas*, which it has present occasion for, and in the having them ready at hand on all occasions, consists that which we call *Invention*, *Fancy*, and quickness of Parts.

§ 9. These are defects, we may observe, in the Memory of one Man compared with another. There is another defect, which we may conceive to be in the memory of Man in general, compared with some superiour created intellectual Beings, which in this faculty may so far excel Man, that they may have constantly in view the whole Scene of all their former actions, wherein no one of the thoughts they have ever had, may slip out of their sight. The omniscience of God, who knows all things past, present, and to come, and to whom the thoughts of Men's hearts always lie open, may satisfie us of the possibility of this. For who can doubt, but God may communicate to those glorious Spirits, his immediate Attendants, any of his Perfections, in what proportion he pleases, as far as created finite Beings can be capable. 'Tis reported of that prodigy of Parts, Monsieur *Pascal*, that, till the decay of his health had impaired his memory, he forgot nothing of what he had done, read, or thought in any part of his rational Age. This is a privilege so little known to most Men, that it seems almost incredible to those, who, after the ordinary way, measure all others by themselves: But yet, when considered, may help us to enlarge our thoughts towards greater Perfections of it in superior ranks of Spirits. For this of Mr. *Pascal* was still with the narrowness, that humane Minds are confin'd to here, of having great variety of *Ideas* only by succession, not all at once: Whereas the several degrees of Angels may probably have larger views, and some of them be endowed with capacities able to retain together, and constantly set before them, as in one Picture, all their past knowledge at once. This, we may conceive, would be no small advantage to the knowledge of a thinking Man; if all his past thoughts, and reasonings could be always present to him. And therefore we may suppose it one of those ways, wherein the knowledge of separate Spirits may exceedingly surpass ours.

§ 10. This faculty of laying up, and retaining the *Ideas*, that are brought into the Mind, several *other Animals* seem to have, to a great degree, as well as Man.

For to pass by other Instances, Birds learning of Tunes, and the endeavours one may observe in them, to hit the Notes right, put it past doubt with me, that they have Perception and retain *Ideas* in their Memories, and use them for Patterns. For it seems to me impossible that they should endeavour to conform their Voices to Notes (as 'tis plain they do) of which they had no *Ideas*. For though I should grant Sound may mechanically cause a certain motion of the animal Spirits, in the Brains of those Birds, whilst the Tune is actually playing; and that motion may be continued on to the Muscles of the Wings, and so the Bird mechanically be driven away by certain noises, because this may tend to the Birds Preservation: yet that can never be supposed a Reason, why it should cause mechanically, either whilst the Tune was playing, much less after it has ceased, such a motion in the Organs of the Bird's Voice, as should conform it to the Notes of a foreign Sound, which imitation can be of no use to the Bird's Preservation. But which is more, it cannot with any appearance of Reason, be supposed (much less proved) that Birds, without Sense and Memory, can approach their Notes, nearer and nearer by degrees, to a Tune play'd yesterday; which if they have no *Idea* of in their Memory, is now no-where, nor can be a Pattern for them to imitate, or which any repeated Essays can bring them nearer to. Since there is no reason why the sound of a Pipe should leave traces in their Brains, which not at first, but by their after-endeavours, should produce the like Sounds; and why the Sounds they make themselves, should not make traces which they should follow, as well as those of the Pipe, is impossible to conceive.

DAVID HUME: *FROM* A TREATISE OF HUMAN NATURE

OF THE IDEAS OF THE MEMORY AND IMAGINATION

1. We find by experience, that when any impression has been present with the mind, it again makes its appearance there as an idea; and this it may do after two different ways: Either when in its new appearance it retains a considerable degree of its first vivacity, and is somewhat intermediate betwixt an impression and an idea; or when it entirely loses that vivacity, and is a perfect idea.[1] The faculty, by which we repeat our impressions in the first manner, is call'd the MEMORY, and the other the IMAGINATION. 'Tis evident at first sight, that the ideas of the memory are much more lively and strong than those of the imagination, and that the former faculty paints its objects in more distinct colours, than any which are employ'd by the latter. When we remember any past event, the idea of it flows in upon the mind in a forcible manner; whereas in the imagination the perception is faint and languid, and cannot without difficulty be preserv'd by the mind steady and uniform for any considerable time. Here then is a sensible difference betwixt one species of ideas and another. But of this more fully hereafter.[2]

2. There is another difference betwixt these two kinds of ideas, which is no less evident, namely that tho' neither the ideas of the memory nor imagination, neither the lively nor faint ideas can make their appearance in the mind,

Source: David Hume, *A Treatise of Human Nature* [1739–40], ed. by David Fate Norton and Mary J. Norton (Oxford: Oxford University Press, 2000), pp. 11–13, 59–61 (Book I, Part I, Section 3; Book I, Part III, Section 5), pp. 428, 450–1.

unless their correspondent impressions have gone before to prepare the way for them, yet the imagination is not restrain'd to the same order and form with the original impressions;[3] while the memory is in a manner ty'd down in that respect, without any power of variation.

3. 'Tis evident, that the memory preserves the original form, in which its objects[4] were presented, and that wherever we depart from it in recollecting any thing, it proceeds from some defect or imperfection in that faculty. An historian may, perhaps, for the more convenient carrying on of his narration, relate an event before another, to which it was in fact posterior; but then he takes notice of this disorder, if he be exact; and by that means replaces the idea in its due position. 'Tis the same case in our recollection of those places and persons, with which we were formerly acquainted. The chief exercise of the memory is not to preserve the simple ideas, but their order and position. In short, this principle[5] is supported by such a number of common and vulgar phænomena, that we may spare ourselves the trouble of insisting on it any farther.

4. The same evidence follows us in our second principle, *of the liberty of the imagination to transpose and change its ideas*. The fables we meet with in poems and romances put this entirely out of question.[6] Nature there is totally confounded, and nothing mention'd but winged horses, fiery dragons, and monstrous giants. Nor will this liberty of the fancy[7] appear strange, when we consider, that all our ideas are copy'd from our impressions, and that there are not any two impressions which are perfectly inseparable.[8] Not to mention, that this is an evident consequence of the division of ideas into simple and complex.[9] Wherever the imagination perceives a difference among ideas, it can easily produce a separation.

OF THE IMPRESSIONS OF THE SENSES AND MEMORY

1. In this kind of reasoning, then, from causation, we employ materials, which are of a mix'd and heterogeneous nature, and which, however connected, are yet essentially different from each other. All our arguments concerning causes and effects consist both of an impression of the memory or senses, and of the idea of that existence, which produces the object of the impression, or is produc'd by it.[1] Here therefore we have three things to explain, viz. *First*, The original impression. *Secondly*, The transition to the idea of the connected cause or effect. *Thirdly*, The nature and qualities of that idea.

2. As to those *impressions*, which arise from the *senses*, their ultimate cause is, in my opinion, perfectly inexplicable by human reason, and 'twill always be impossible to decide with certainty, whether they arise immediately from the object,[2] or are produc'd by the creative power of the mind,[3] or are deriv'd from the author of our being.[4] Nor is such a question any way material to our present purpose. We may draw inferences from the coherence of our perceptions, whether they be true or false; whether they represent nature justly, or be mere illusions of the senses.[5]

3. When we search for the characteristic, which distinguishes the *memory* from the imagination, we must immediately perceive, that it cannot lie in the simple ideas it presents to us; since both these faculties borrow their simple ideas from the impressions, and can never go beyond these original perceptions. These faculties are as little distinguish'd from each other by the arrangement of their complex ideas. For tho' it be a peculiar property of the memory to preserve the original order and position of its ideas, while the imagination transposes and changes them, as it pleases; yet this difference is not sufficient to distinguish them in their operation, or make us know the one from the other; it being impossible to recal the past impressions, in order to compare them with our present ideas, and see whether their arrangement be exactly similar. Since therefore the memory is known, neither by the order of its *complex* ideas, nor the nature of its *simple* ones; it follows, that the difference betwixt it and the imagination lies in its superior force and vivacity. A man may indulge his fancy in feigning any past scene of adventures;[6] nor wou'd there be any possibility of distinguishing this from a remembrance of a like kind, were not the ideas of the imagination fainter and more obscure.

4. It frequently happens, that when two men have been engag'd in any scene of action, the one shall remember it much better than the other, and shall have all the difficulty in the world to make his companion recollect it. He runs over several circumstances in vain; mentions the time, the place, the company, what was said, what was done on all sides; till at last he hits on some lucky circumstance, that revives the whole, and gives his friend a perfect memory of every thing. Here the person that forgets receives at first all the ideas from the discourse of the other, with the same circumstances of time and place; tho' he considers them as mere fictions of the imagination. But as soon as the circumstance is mention'd, that touches the memory, the very same ideas now appear in a new light, and have, in a manner, a different feeling from what they had before. Without any other alteration, beside that of the feeling, they become immediately ideas of the memory,[7] and are assented to.

5. Since, therefore, the imagination can represent all the same objects that the memory can offer to us, and since those faculties are only distinguish'd by the different *feeling* of the ideas they present, it may be proper to consider what is the nature of that feeling. And here I believe every one will readily agree with me, that the ideas of the memory are more *strong* and *lively* than those of the fancy. A painter, who intended to represent a passion or emotion of any kind, wou'd endeavour to get a sight of a person actuated by a like emotion, in order to enliven his ideas, and give them a force and vivacity superior to what is found in those, which are mere fictions of the imagination. The more recent this memory is, the clearer is the idea; and when after a long interval he wou'd return to the contemplation of his object, he always finds its idea to be much decay'd,[8] if not wholly

obliterated. We are frequently in doubt concerning the ideas of the memory, as they become very weak and feeble; and are at a loss to determine whether any image proceeds from the fancy or the memory, when it is not drawn in such lively colours as distinguish that latter faculty. I think I remember such an event, says one; but am not sure. A long tract of time has almost worn it out of my memory, and leaves me uncertain whether or not it be the pure offspring of my fancy.

6. And as an idea of the memory, by losing its force and vivacity, may degenerate to such a degree, as to be taken for an idea of the imagination; so on the other hand an idea of the imagination may acquire such a force and vivacity, as to pass for an idea of the memory, and counterfeit its effects on the belief and judgment. This is noted in the case of liars; who by the frequent repetition of their lies, come at last to believe and remember them, as realities; custom and habit having in this case, as in many others, the same influence on the mind as nature, and infixing the idea with equal force and vigour.

7. Thus it appears, that the *belief* or *assent*, which always attends the memory and senses, is nothing but the vivacity of those perceptions they present; and that this alone distinguishes them from the imagination. To believe is in this case to feel an immediate impression of the senses, or a repetition of that impression in the memory. 'Tis merely the force and liveliness of the perception, which constitutes the first act of the judgment,[9] and lays the foundation of that reasoning, which we build upon it, when we trace the relation of cause and effect.

Notes

Book 1 Part 1 Sect. 3: Of the ideas of the memory and imagination

If an impression reappears in the mind after an absence, it does so either as an idea of the *memory* or an idea of the *imagination*. Ideas of the memory more or less replicate both the form and order of the impressions they copy, especially the form of simple impressions, and they retain some of the force or intensity of their originals. In comparison with ideas of the memory, ideas of the imagination are weaker representations of the impressions they copy. In addition, because the imagination is free to transform and reorder its elements, and thus produce new complex ideas, the ideas of the imagination often depart from the form and the order of the impressions they copy.

1. *perfect idea*] an idea that has no force or vivacity.
2. Part 3. Sect. 5 [Hume's note]. See 1.3.5. 3–6 (below).
3. *yet the imagination . . . impressions*] In so far as ideas appear to represent a sequence of events or a spatial arrangement, the imagination can reorder them in any way it wishes. We can even imagine, for example, that the events of last Tuesday came after those of last Wednesday, or that the sun rises in the west.
4. *objects*] The *objects* of the memory (and of the imagination) are ideas.
5. *this principle*] The principle is that 'the memory preserves the original form, in which its objects were presented'.
6. *The fables . . . question*] The fables illustrate and confirm the second principle.
7. *fancy*] imagination. Hume often uses *fancy* and *imagination* interchangeably.

8. *and that . . . inseparable*] Although Hume does not here say so, the principle that each of our impressions is completely separable from every other impression is of central importance to many arguments found in the *Treatise*.
9. *Not to mention . . . complex*] Given that complex ideas are made up of simple ones, themselves derived from simple impressions, it follows (1) that the mind (the imagination) can manipulate ideas, and (2) that complex ideas may be broken down into their constituent parts.

Book 1 Part 3 Sect. 5. Of the impressions of the senses and memory

The three component parts or elements of our reasonings concerning cause and effect are an original impression, an idea, and a transition or inference from the impression to that idea. Hume notes that it is impossible for us to account for our original impressions of sensation. We do not know if these arise from objects, from some creative power of our own minds, or from actions of the deity. Nor does it matter. Whatever the source of these impressions, we can make inferences as a result of the coherent patterns which they are found to have. We are then reminded that the perceptions of memory are more forceful or livelier than those of the imagination. The perceptions of memory generally *feel* different from those of the imagination. From this fact it appears that the belief which accompanies the senses and memory is nothing more than the force or liveliness of the perceptions they present to us.

1. *produc'd by it*] Note that Hume's account of causal reasoning is intended to explain inferences from effects to causes as well as from causes to effects.
2. *they arise . . . object*] This is the position taken by the many philosophers (Locke, for example) who suppose our impressions of sensation are caused by external objects.
3. *produc'd by . . . mind*] This possibility is suggested by Descartes in *Meditations* 3.
4. *deriv'd from . . . being*] Hume puts in very general terms the view of Malebranche and the Occasionalists. Malebranche lays out the three possibilities mentioned by Hume, but distinguishes two senses in which (what Hume calls) impressions of sensation could be said to derive from the Diety: either 'God has produced them in us while creating the soul or produces them every time we think about a given object' or else (as Malebranche went on to argue) 'the soul is joined to a completely perfect being that contains all . . . the ideas of created beings' (*The Search After Truth* 3.2.1.2; see also 3.2.6; and *Elucidations* 6, 10, 15).
5. *We may . . . senses*] Hume argues that, whatever may be the source of our impressions of sensation (a question that cannot be answered with certainty), the manner or order in which these impressions present themselves enables us to make causal inferences.
6. *feigning . . . adventures*] Feigning here is conscious invention.
7. *they become . . . memory*] The ideas come to have, that is, a greater force and vivacity, or intensity, than they had when they were considered fabrications of the imagination.
8. *much decay'd*] Hobbes had defined memory as 'decaying sense'. See *Leviathan* 1.2; see also Locke, *Essay* 2.10.4–5.
9. *first act . . . judgment*] Belief, understood as an act of assent, was widely taken to be the first act of the judgement. Hume offers a revised manner of understanding that act.

2.3

GEORG WILHELM FRIEDRICH HEGEL: *FROM* PHILOSOPHY OF MIND, BEING PART THREE OF THE ENCYCLOPAEDIA OF THE PHILOSOPHICAL SCIENCES

MEMORY[1]

§ 461

Under the shape of memory the course of intelligence passes through the same inwardizing (recollecting) functions, as regards the intuition of the *word*, as representation in general does in dealing with the first immediate intuition [. . .]. (1) Making its own the synthesis achieved in the sign, intelligence, by this inwardizing (memorizing) elevates the *single* synthesis to a universal, i.e. permanent, synthesis, in which name and meaning are for it objectively united, and renders the intuition (which the name originally is) a representation. Thus the import (connotation) and sign, being identified, form one representation: the representation in its inwardness is rendered concrete and gets existence for its import: all this being the work of memory which retains names (retentive Memory).

Zusatz. We shall consider memory under the three forms of:

1. the memory which retains names (retentive memory);
2. reproductive memory;
3. mechanical memory.

Source: Georg Wilhelm Friedrich Hegel, *Philosophy of Mind.* Being Part Three of *The Encyclopaedia of the Philosophical Sciences* (1830), trans. William Wallace, together with the Zusätze Additions in Boumann's text (1845), trans. A. V. Miller, Foreword J. N. Findlay (Oxford: Clarendon Press, 1971), pp. 219–23.

Of primary importance here, therefore, is the retention of the meaning of names, of our ability to remember the ideas objectively linked to language-signs. Thus when we hear or see a word from a foreign language, its meaning becomes present to our mind; but it does not follow that the converse is true, that we can produce for our ideas the corresponding word-signs in that language. We learn to speak and write a language later than we understand it.

§ 462

The name is thus the thing so far as it exists and counts in the ideational realm. (2) In the name, *Reproductive* memory has and recognizes the thing, and with the thing it has the name, apart from intuition and image. The name, as giving an *existence* to the content in intelligence, is the externality of intelligence to itself; and the inwardizing or recollection of the name, i.e. of an intuition of intellectual origin, is at the same time a self-externalization to which intelligence reduces itself on its own ground. The association of the particular names lies in the meaning of the features sensitive, representative, or cogitant – series of which the intelligence traverses as it feels, represents, or thinks.

Given the name lion, we need neither the actual vision of the animal, nor its image even: the name alone, if we *understand* it, is the unimaged simple representation. We *think* in names.

The recent attempts – already, as they deserved, forgotten – to rehabilitate the Mnemonic of the ancients, consist in transforming names into images, and thus again deposing memory to the level of imagination. The place of the power of memory is taken by a permanent tableau of a series of images, fixed in the imagination, to which is then attached the series of ideas forming the composition to be learned by rote. Considering the heterogeneity between the import of these ideas and those permanent images, and the speed with which the attachment has to be made, the attachment cannot be made otherwise than by shallow, silly, and utterly accidental links. Not merely is the mind put to the torture of being worried by idiotic stuff, but what is thus learnt by rote is just as quickly forgotten, seeing that the same tableau is used for getting by rote every other series of ideas, and so those previously attached to it are effaced. What is mnemonically impressed is not like what is retained in memory really got by heart, i.e. strictly produced from within outwards, from the deep pit of the ego, and thus recited, but is, so to speak, read off the tableau of fancy. – Mnemonic is connected with the common prepossession about memory, in comparison with fancy and imagination; as if the latter were a higher and more intellectual activity than memory. On the contrary, memory has ceased to deal with an image derived from intuition – the immediate and incomplete mode of intelligence; it has rather to do with an object which is the product of intelligence itself – such a *without-book*[2] as remains locked up in the *within-book*[3] of intelligence, and is, within intelligence, only its outward and existing side.

Zusatz. The word as *sounded* vanishes in *time*; the latter thus demonstrates itself in the former to be an *abstract*, that is to say, merely *destructive*, negativity. The true, concrete negativity of the language-sign is *intelligence*, since by this the sign is changed from something outward to something inward and as thus transformed is preserved. Words thus attain an existence animated by thought. This existence is absolutely necessary to our thoughts. We only know our thoughts, only have definite, actual thoughts, when we give them the form of objectivity, of a being distinct from our inwardness, and therefore the shape of externality, and of an externality, too, that at the same time bears the stamp of the highest inwardness. The articulated sound, the *word*, is alone such an inward externality. To want to think without words as Mesmer once attempted is, therefore, a manifestly irrational procedure which, as Mesmer himself admitted, almost drove him insane. But it is also ridiculous to regard as a defect of thought and a misfortune, the fact that it is tied to a word; for although the common opinion is that it is just the *ineffable* that is the most excellent, yet this opinion, cherished by conceit, is unfounded, since what is ineffable is, in truth, only something obscure, fermenting, something which gains clarity only when it is able to put itself into words. Accordingly, the word gives to thoughts their highest and truest existence. Of course, one can also indulge in a mass of verbiage, yet fail to grasp the matter in hand. But then what is at fault is not the word, but a defective, vague, superficial thinking. Just as the true *thought* is the very thing itself, so too is the *word* when it is employed by genuine thinking. Intelligence, therefore, in filling itself with the word, receives into itself the nature of the thing. But this reception has, at the same time, the meaning that intelligence thereby takes on the nature of a *thing* and to such a degree that subjectivity, in its distinction from the thing, becomes quite empty, a mindless container of words, that is, a mechanical memory. In this way the profusion of remembered words can, so to speak, switch round to become the extreme alienation of intelligence. The more familiar I become with the meaning of the word, the more, therefore, that this becomes united with my inwardness, the more can the objectivity, and hence the definiteness, of meaning, vanish and consequently the more can memory itself, and with it also the words, become something bereft of mind.

§ 463

(3) As the interconnection of the names lies in the meaning, the conjunction of their meaning with the reality as names is still an (external) synthesis; and intelligence in this its externality has not made a complete and simple return into self. But intelligence is the universal – the single plain truth of its particular self-divestments; and its consummated appropriation of them abolishes that distinction between meaning and name. This supreme inwardizing of representation is the supreme self-divestment of intelligence, in which it renders itself the mere *being*, the universal space of names as such, i.e. of meaningless words. The ego, which is this abstract being, is, because subjectivity, at the same time the power over the different names – the link which, having nothing in itself, fixes in itself series of them and keeps them in stable order. So far as they merely *are*, and intelligence is here itself this *being* of theirs, its power is a merely abstract subjectivity – memory; which, on account of the complete externality

in which the members of such series stand to one another, and because it is itself this externality (subjective though that be), is called mechanical [. . .].

A composition is, as we know, not thoroughly conned by rote, until one attaches no meaning to the words. The recitation of what has been thus got by heart is therefore of course accentless. The correct accent, if it is introduced, suggests the meaning: but this introduction of the signification of an idea disturbs the mechanical nexus and therefore easily throws out the reciter. The faculty of conning by rote series of words, with no principle governing their succession, or which are separately meaningless, for example, a series of proper names, is so supremely marvellous, because it is the very essence of mind to have its wits about it; whereas in this case the mind is estranged in itself, and its action is like machinery. But it is only as uniting subjectivity with objectivity that the mind has its wits about it. Whereas in the case before us, after it has in intuition been at first so external as to pick up its facts ready made, and in representation inwardizes or recollects this datum and makes it its own – it proceeds as memory to make itself external in itself, so that what is its own assumes the guise of something found. Thus one of the two dynamic factors of thought, viz. objectivity, is here put in intelligence itself as a quality of it. – It is only a step further to treat memory as mechanical – the act implying no intelligence – in which case it is only justified by its uses, its indispensability perhaps for other purposes and functions of mind. But by so doing we overlook the proper signification it has in the mind.

§ 464

If it is to be the fact and true objectivity, the mere name as an existent requires something else – to be interpreted by the representing intellect. Now in the shape of mechanical memory, intelligence is at once that external objectivity and the meaning. In this way intelligence is explicitly made an *existence* of this identity, i.e. it is explicitly active as such an identity which as reason it is implicitly. Memory is in this manner the passage into the function of *thought*, which no longer has a *meaning*, i.e. its objectivity is no longer severed from the subjective, and its inwardness does not need to go outside for its existence.

The German language has etymologically assigned memory (*Gedächtnis*), of which it has become a foregone conclusion to speak contemptuously, the high position of direct kindred with thought (*Gedanke*). – It is not matter of chance that the young have a better memory than the old, nor is their memory solely exercised for the sake of utility. The young have a good memory because they have not yet reached the stage of reflection; their memory is exercised with or without design so as to level the ground of their inner life to pure being or to pure space in which the fact, the implicit content, may reign and unfold itself with no antithesis to a subjective inwardness. Genuine ability is in youth generally combined with a good memory. But empirical statements of this sort help little towards a knowledge of what memory intrinsically is. To comprehend the position and meaning of memory and to understand its organic interconnection with thought is one of the hardest points, and hitherto one quite unregarded in the theory of mind. Memory *qua* memory is itself the merely *external* mode, or merely *existential* aspect of thought, and thus needs a complementary element. The passage from it to thought is to our view or implicitly the identity of reason with this existential mode: an identity from which it follows that reason only exists in a subject, and as the function of that subject. Thus active reason is *Thinking*.

NOTES

1. Gedächtnis.
2. Auswendiges.
3. Inwendiges.

SECTION 3
MEMORY AND LATE MODERNITY

Edited by Michael Rossington and Anne Whitehead

INTRODUCTION

Michael Rossington and Anne Whitehead

The extracts in this section are examples of engagements with memory in the work of key 'late modern' thinkers frequently invoked in contemporary critical theory.

The 'immediate pressure of events' (Marx, 1973: 143) which occasioned **Karl Marx**'s essay, *The Eighteenth Brumaire of Louis Bonaparte* (1852), was the *coup d'état* in Paris of 2 December 1851. The essay's mocking title marks this event as a repetition – 'the second edition of the eighteenth Brumaire!' (this volume, p. 97) – by reference to Napoleon I's coup of 9 November 1799 (that is, 18 Brumaire of Year VIII in the French Revolutionary calendar). In the essay's well-known opening passage, included here, Marx exposes a moment of apparent political agency as a hollow toying with historical memory. In 1851, the borrowing of the dress of a remembered moment of historical crisis – the first Napoleon's assumption of power – turns out to be not just illusory but perilous: 'As long as the French were engaged in revolution, they could not free themselves of the memory of Napoleon' (this volume, p. 99). Contrasting his analysis of the coup with those of Hugo and Proudhon in his Preface to the second edition (1869), Marx comments: 'I show how . . . the *class struggle* in France created circumstances and conditions which allowed a mediocre and grotesque individual to play the hero's role' (Marx, 1973: 144). The political crisis in its high theatricality is legible, through his critique, as a masquerade enabled by the very forces which prevent genuine change. For this reason Marx advocates a turning against memory: 'The social revolution of the nineteenth century can only create its poetry from the future, not from the past' (this volume, p. 99). For some (e.g. Derrida, 1994), however, the acknowledgement of spectral hauntings remains a prominent feature of the economy of Marx's writings.

Friedrich Nietzsche's 'On the Uses and Disadvantages of History for Life' (1874), the second of his *Untimely Meditations*, may be seen as a continuation of that suspicion of historical sensibility that is the concern of Marx's essay. But Nietzsche sees the blindness to which attention to the past may lead as necessary rather than culpable. In the first section of the essay, included here, happiness is defined as 'the ability to forget or, expressed in more scholarly fashion, the capacity to feel *unhistorically* during its duration' (this volume, p. 103). For Nietzsche a dialectical tension between memory and forgetting, or past and future, is essential for what he terms 'life': *the unhistorical and the historical are necessary in equal measure for the health of an individual, of a people, and of a culture*' (p. 104). That this tension takes the form of an agonistic struggle, often described in violent language, is most evident in the third species of history after the *monumental* and the *antiquarian* defined in the second and third sections of the essay (not included here). This *critical* mode is necessary, for 'If he is to live, man must possess and from time to time employ the strength to break up and dissolve a part of the past' (Nietzsche, 1997: 75). Nietzsche's notion that such rupture is productive – 'an attempt to give oneself as it were *a posteriori*, a past in which one would like to originate in opposition to that in which one did originate' (Nietzsche, 1997: 76) – may be seen to anticipate, as Paul Hamilton has pointed out, the libertarian reappropriation or 'tiger's leap into the past' advocated in Walter Benjamin's 'Theses on the Philosophy of History' (Benjamin, 1973: 263; Hamilton, 2003: 94–101).

The next extract in this section is from **Henri Bergson**'s *Matter and Memory* (1896). In this work, Bergson sought to overcome the dualism between representation and matter that prevailed in contemporary thinking about perception. He argued that the term 'memory' is not singular, but rather combines two different kinds of memories. The first is 'habit memory', which consists in obtaining certain automatic behaviour by means of repetition and which coincides with the acquisition of sensori-motor mechanisms. The second is 'pure memory', which refers to the survival of personal memories in the unconscious. Although we are accustomed to thinking in terms of dualistic extremes, Bergson argues that most forms of remembering combine these two kinds of memories: referring to the mnemonic systems dating back to classical times, for example, he suggests that their methods foreground 'pure memory' precisely in order to put it in the service of 'habit memory'. Bergson was a cousin by marriage of Marcel Proust and his work left its traces on the latter's distinction between 'voluntary memory' and 'involuntary memory'. The Bergsonian influence on Proust did not escape the attention of Benjamin, who argued in 'On Some Motifs in Baudelaire' that Proust's *Remembrance of Things Past* puts 'Bergson's theory of experience to the test' (Benjamin, 1973: 159). Benjamin himself notably found the Bergsonian-Proustian model of memory wanting in its particular emphasis on the individual. He observed: 'Where there is experience in the strict sense of the word, certain contents of the individual past combine with material of the collective past' (Benjamin, 1973: 161). Benjamin's critique finds its echo in the work of Maurice Halbwachs. Initially a student of Bergson at the Lycée Henri IV in Paris, Halbwachs subsequently turned from individualistic Bergsonian philosophy to Durkheimian sociology. Nevertheless, Bergson's influence can still be discerned in Halbwachs' theories of collective memory (represented in Part II, Section 4), which still leave some trace to individual psychology.

Sigmund Freud's 'A Note upon the "Mystic Writing-Pad" ' (1925) is a short but fascinating account of the memory process. In the piece, Freud seeks to elaborate his notion of the unconscious by returning to and rewriting classical accounts of memory which deploy the metaphor of inscription. Freud is not happy with the notion of memory as writing on paper, which leaves a permanent trace, for it suggests the model of an endlessly proliferating archive. The model of writing on a blackboard or a wax tablet, where the inscription can be erased, also seems inadequate to describe memory, however, for it means that the mind retains no lasting record of the past. Freud turns for a solution to the 'Mystic Writing Pad', for it provides a model in which there are two separate but interrelated layers or levels: the celluloid covering sheet from which the writing vanishes once it is lifted, and the wax slab beneath which retains the permanent trace of what was written, an inscription which is legible in certain lights. For Freud, these two layers correspond with the conscious mind, which forms no permanent traces, and the unconscious, which stores a more permanent record that appears or is visible to us at certain times. Freud's essay, concerned with the processes of writing, rewriting and erasure, itself rewrites, writes over, the traces of the classical conception of memory outlined by thinkers such as Plato and Aristotle. It is, in turn, rewritten or reinscribed by Jacques Derrida in his famous analysis of the 'Mystic Writing Pad' in *Writing and Difference*. Freud's model thus takes on a performative force which extends beyond the analytical, so that the essay itself is an act at once of inscription and reinscription, of writing and erasure, of remembering and forgetting.

Reflections on memory pervade the writings of **Walter Benjamin**. As well as 'On Some Motifs in Baudelaire', from the innovative cultural history of *The Arcades Project* through the personal recollections of 'A Berlin Chronicle' to the attempt to invigorate contemporary political discourse in 'Theses', Benjamin's sophisticated meditations on remembering may be seen as in dialogue with Marx, Nietzsche, Bergson and Freud. Such is the concentration of 'On the Image of Proust' (1929), included here, that in writing about Proust, Hannah Arendt remarked that Benjamin may be seen to be 'speaking about himself' (Benjamin, 1973: 7). The celebrated definitions of *mémoire voluntaire* and *mémoire involuntaire* in *Remembrance of Things Past* are revised by Benjamin at the start of this essay into a nuanced account of the mutuality of recollection and forgetting. Furthermore, memory is advanced as integral to textuality.

Through the Latin root of the word 'text' (*textum*, meaning 'web'), Proust's writing is found to be underpinned by 'memory's strict regulations for weaving' in which '[o]nly the *actus purus* of recollection itself, not the author or the plot, constitutes the unity of the text' (this volume, p. 120). This metaphor of the web is repeated in the closing part of the essay in the analogy of involuntary remembrance to the weight of a fishing net. Proust's famous attention to the 'tenacity' with which 'memories are preserved by the sense of smell' is likened by Benjamin to 'the sense of weight experienced by someone who casts his nets into the sea of the *temps perdu*. And his sentences are the entire muscular activity of the intelligible body; they contain the whole enormous effort to raise this catch' (this volume, p. 128). Benjamin's metaphors of how Proust's language retrieves the past may thus be seen to be notably physical, almost organic in character, and in this respect echo preoccupations with materiality in the extracts from Marx, Nietzsche, Bergson and Freud.

REFERENCES AND FURTHER READING

Benjamin Walter (1973) *Illuminations*, trans. Harry Zohn, ed. and intro. Hannah Arendt. London: Fontana.

—— (1999) 'A Berlin Chronicle', trans. Edmund Jephcott, in Michael W. Jennings, Howard Eiland and Gary Smith (eds), *Selected Writings*, Vol. 2, 1927–34, trans. Rodney Livingstone and others. Cambridge, MA, and London: Harvard University Press, pp. 595–637.

—— (1999) *The Arcades Project*, trans. Howard Eiland and Kevin McLaughlin, prepared on the basis of the German volume, ed. Rolf Tiedemann. Cambridge, MA: Harvard University Press.

—— (1999) 'On the Image of Proust', trans. Harry Zohn, in *Selected Writings*, Vol. 2, op. cit., 237–47.

Bergson, Henri (1988) *Matter and Memory*, trans. Nancy Margaret Paul and W. Scott Palmer. New York: Zone Books.

Buck-Morss, Susan (1989) 'Historical Nature: Ruin', in *The Dialectics of Seeing: Walter Benjamin and the Arcades Project*. Cambridge, MA, and London: MIT Press, pp. 159–204.

Derrida, Jacques ([1966] 1978) 'Freud and the Scene of Writing', in *Writing and Difference*, trans. Alan Bass. London and New York: Routledge, pp. 246–91.

—— (1994) *Specters of Marx: The State of the Debt, the Work of Mourning, and the New International*, trans. Peggy Kamuf. New York: Routledge.

Foucault, Michel ([1971] 1977) 'Nietzsche, Genealogy, History', in Donald F. Bouchard (ed.), *Language, Counter-Memory, Practice: Selected Essays and Interviews*, trans. Donald F. Bouchard and Sherry Simon. Ithaca, NY: Cornell University Press, pp. 139–64.

Hamilton, Paul (2003) *Historicism*, 2nd edn. London and New York: Routledge.

Krell, David Farrell (1990) *Of Memory, Reminiscence, and Writing: On the Verge*. Bloomington, IN: Indiana University Press.

Leslie, Esther (2000) *Walter Benjamin: Overpowering Conformism*. London: Pluto Press.

Ley Roff, Sarah (2004) 'Benjamin and Psychoanalysis', in David S. Ferris (ed.), *The Cambridge Companion to Walter Benjamin*. Cambridge: Cambridge University Press, pp. 115–33.

Marx, Karl (1973) *The Eighteenth Brumaire of Louis Bonaparte*, trans. Ben Fowkes, in David Fernbach (ed. and intro.), *Surveys from Exile: Political Writings*, Vol. 2. Harmondsworth and London: Penguin and New Left Review, pp. 146–249.

Nietzsche, Friedrich (1994) *On the Genealogy of Morality*, trans. Carol Diethe, ed. Keith Ansell-Pearson. Cambridge: Cambridge University Press.

—— (1997) *Untimely Meditations*, trans. R. J. Hollingdale, ed. Daniel Breazeale. Cambridge: Cambridge University Press.

Said, Edward W. (1984), 'On Repetition', in *The World, the Text, and the Critic*. London: Faber, pp. 111–25.

KARL MARX: *FROM* THE EIGHTEENTH BRUMAIRE OF LOUIS BONAPARTE

Hegel remarks somewhere that all the great events and characters of world history occur, so to speak, twice.[1] He forgot to add: the first time as tragedy, the second as farce. Caussidière in place of Danton, Louis Blanc in place of Robespierre, the Montagne of 1848–51 in place of the Montagne of 1793–5, the Nephew in place of the Uncle.[2] And we can perceive the same caricature in the circumstances surrounding the second edition of the eighteenth Brumaire![3]

Men make their own history, but not of their own free will; not under circumstances they themselves have chosen but under the given and inherited circumstances with which they are directly confronted. The tradition of the dead generations weighs like a nightmare on the minds of the living. And, just when they appear to be engaged in the revolutionary transformation of themselves and their material surroundings, in the creation of something which does not yet exist, precisely in such epochs of revolutionary crisis they timidly conjure up the spirits of the past to help them; they borrow their names, slogans and costumes so as to stage the new world-historical scene in this venerable disguise and borrowed language. Luther put on the mask of the apostle Paul; the Revolution of 1789–1814 draped itself alternately as the Roman republic and the Roman empire; and the revolution of 1848 knew no better than to parody at some points 1789 and at others the revolutionary traditions of 1793–5. In the same way, the beginner who has learned a new language always retranslates

Source: Karl Marx, *The Eighteenth Brumaire of Louis Bonaparte* [1852], trans. Ben Fowkes, in *Surveys from Exile: Political Writings*, Vol. 2, ed. and intro. David Fernbach (Harmondsworth and London: Penguin and New Left Review, 1973), pp. 146–50.

it into his mother tongue: he can only be said to have appropriated the spirit of the new language and to be able to express himself in it freely when he can manipulate it without reference to the old, and when he forgets his original language while using the new one.

If we reflect on this process of world-historical necromancy, we see at once a salient distinction. Camille Desmoulins, Danton, Robespierre, Saint-Just and Napoleon, the heroes of the old French Revolution, as well as its parties and masses, accomplished the task of their epoch, which was the emancipation and establishment of modern *bourgeois* society, in Roman costume and with Roman slogans. The first revolutionaries smashed the feudal basis to pieces and struck off the feudal heads which had grown on it. Then came Napoleon. Within France he created the conditions which first made possible the development of free competition, the exploitation of the land by small peasant property, and the application of the unleashed productive power of the nation's industries. Beyond the borders of France he swept away feudal institutions so far as this was necessary for the provision on the European continent of an appropriate modern environment for the bourgeois society in France. Once the new social formation had been established, the antediluvian colossi disappeared along with the resurrected imitations of Rome – imitations of Brutus, Gracchus, Publicola, the tribunes, the senators, and Caesar himself. Bourgeois society in its sober reality had created its true interpreters and spokesmen in such people as Say,[4] Cousin,[5] Royer-Collard,[6] Benjamin Constant[7] and Guizot. The real leaders of the bourgeois army sat behind office desks while the fathead Louis XVIII served as the bourgeoisie's political head. Bourgeois society was no longer aware that the ghosts of Rome had watched over its cradle, since it was wholly absorbed in the production of wealth and the peaceful struggle of economic competition. But unheroic as bourgeois society is, it still required heroism, self-sacrifice, terror, civil war, and battles in which whole nations were engaged, to bring it into the world. And its gladiators found in the stern classical traditions of the Roman republic the ideals, art forms and self-deceptions they needed in order to hide from themselves the limited bourgeois content of their struggles and to maintain their enthusiasm at the high level appropriate to great historical tragedy. A century earlier, in the same way but at a different stage of development, Cromwell and the English people had borrowed for their bourgeois revolution the language, passions and illusions of the Old Testament. When the actual goal had been reached, when the bourgeois transformation of English society had been accomplished, Locke drove out Habakkuk.

In these revolutions, then, the resurrection of the dead served to exalt the new struggles, rather than to parody the old, to exaggerate the given task in the imagination, rather than to flee from solving it in reality, and to recover the spirit of the revolution, rather than to set its ghost walking again.

For it was only the ghost of the old revolution which walked in the years from 1848 to 1851, from Marrast, the *républicain en gants jaunes*[8] who disguised himself as old Bailly,[9] right down to the adventurer who is now hiding his commonplace and repulsive countenance beneath the iron death-mask of Napoleon.

An entire people thought it had provided itself with a more powerful motive force by means of a revolution; instead, it suddenly found itself plunged back into an already dead epoch. It was impossible to mistake this relapse into the past, for the old dates arose again, along with the old chronology, the old names, the old edicts, long abandoned to the erudition of the antiquaries, and the old minions of the law, apparently long decayed. The nation might well appear to itself to be in the same situation as that mad Englishman in Bedlam, who thought he was living in the time of the pharaohs. He moaned every day about the hard work he had to perform as a gold-digger in the Ethiopian mines, immured in his subterranean prison, by the exiguous light of a lamp fixed on his own head. The overseer of the slaves stood behind him with a long whip, and at the exits was a motley assembly of barbarian mercenaries, who had no common language and therefore understood neither the forced labourers in the mines nor each other. 'And I, a freeborn Briton,' sighed the mad Englishman, 'must bear all this to make gold for the old pharaohs.' 'To pay the debts of the Bonaparte family,' sighed the French nation. As long as he was in his right mind, the Englishman could not free himself of the obsession of making gold. As long as the French were engaged in revolution, they could not free themselves of the memory of Napoleon. The election of 10 December 1848[10] proved this. They yearned to return from the dangers of revolution to the fleshpots of Egypt, and 2 December 1851 was the answer. They have not merely acquired a caricature of the old Napoleon, they have the old Napoleon himself, in the caricature form he had to take in the middle of the nineteenth century.

The social revolution of the nineteenth century can only create its poetry from the future, not from the past. It cannot begin its own work until it has sloughed off all its superstitious regard for the past. Earlier revolutions have needed world-historical reminiscences to deaden their awareness of their own content. In order to arrive at its own content the revolution of the nineteenth century must let the dead bury their dead. Previously the phrase transcended the content; here the content transcends the phrase.

The February revolution was a surprise attack, it took the old society *unawares*. The people proclaimed this unexpected *coup de main*[11] to be an historic deed, the opening of a new epoch. On 2 December the February revolution was conjured away by the sleight of hand of a cardsharper. It is no longer the monarchy that appears to have been overthrown but the liberal concessions extracted from it by a century of struggle. Instead of *society* conquering a new content for itself, it only seems that the *state* has returned to its most ancient form, the unashamedly simple rule of the military sabre and the clerical cowl. The answer to the *coup de main* of February 1848 was the *coup de tête*[12] of December 1851. Easy come, easy go! However, the intervening period has not gone unused. Between 1848 and 1851 French society, using an abbreviated because revolutionary method, caught up on the studies and experiences which would in the normal or, so to speak, textbook course of development have had to precede the February revolution if it were to do more than merely shatter the surface. Society now appears to have fallen back behind its starting-point; but in reality it must first create the revolutionary starting-point, i.e. the situation, relations, and conditions necessary for the modern revolution to become serious.

Bourgeois revolutions, such as those of the eighteenth century, storm quickly from success to success. They outdo each other in dramatic effects; men and things seem set in sparkling diamonds and each day's spirit is ecstatic. But they are short-lived; they soon reach their apogee, and society has to undergo a long period of regret until it has learned to assimilate soberly the achievements of its period of storm and stress. Proletarian revolutions, however, such as those of the nineteenth century, constantly engage in self-criticism, and in repeated inter-ruptions of their own course. They return to what has apparently already been accomplished in order to begin the task again; with merciless thoroughness they mock the inadequate, weak and wretched aspects of their first attempts; they seem to throw their opponent to the ground only to see him draw new strength from the earth and rise again before them, more colossal than ever; they shrink back again and again before the indeterminate immensity of their own goals, until the situation is created in which any retreat is impossible, and the conditions themselves cry out:

Hic Rhodus, hic salta! Here is the rose, dance here![13]

NOTES

1. It is doubtful whether Hegel ever wrote these words. This theme, which Marx elaborates on in the ensuing paragraphs, is an expansion of a number of hints thrown out by Engels in his letter to Marx of 3 December 1851. See *MESC*, p. 62: 'It really seems as if old Hegel in his grave were acting as World Spirit and directing history, ordaining most conscientiously that it should all be unrolled twice over, once as a great tragedy and once as a wretched farce.'
2. Louis Bonaparte was the nephew of Napoleon I.
3. Napoleon I's *coup d'état* against the Directory took place on 9 November 1799, i.e. on 18 Brumaire of the year VIII by the revolutionary calendar. Marx therefore described Louis Bonaparte's coup of 2 December 1851 as the second edition of the eighteenth Brumaire.
4. Jean-Baptiste Say was a French economist, who popularized the doctrines of Adam Smith in the early nineteenth century.
5. Victor Cousin was a French philosopher, appointed Minister of Education in Thiers's short-lived cabinet of 1840. He endeavoured to combine the ideas of Descartes, Hume and Kant into a system he himself described as 'eclecticism'.
6. Pierre-Paul Royer-Collard was a political theorist and politician under the Restoration and the July monarchy. He supported constitutional monarchy as, quite explicitly, the organ of bourgeois rule.
7. Benjamin Constant was a liberal writer and politician, a leading figure in the Opposition of the 1820s to the rule of Charles X and the ultras.
8. Yellow-gloved republican.
9. Jean-Sylvain Bailly was a leader of the liberal and constitutionalist bourgeoisie in the first French revolution; guillotined in 1793.

10. On 10 December 1848 Louis Bonaparte was elected President of the French Republic by a large majority.
11. Surprise attack.
12. Impulsive act.
13. The Latin phrase comes from one of Aesop's fables. It is the reply made to a boaster who claimed he had once made an immense leap in Rhodes: 'Rhodes is here. Leap here and now.' But the German phrase, '*Hier ist die Rose, hier tanze!*' (here is the rose, dance here), is Hegel's variant, in the Preface to the *Philosophy of Right*. The Greek '*Rhodos*' can mean both Rhodes and rose.

FRIEDRICH NIETZSCHE: *FROM* ON THE USES AND DISADVANTAGES OF HISTORY FOR LIFE

1

Consider the cattle, grazing as they pass you by: they do not know what is meant by yesterday or today, they leap about, eat, rest, digest, leap about again, and so from morn till night and from day to day, fettered to the moment and its pleasure or displeasure, and thus neither melancholy nor bored. This is a hard sight for man to see; for, though he thinks himself better than the animals because he is human, he cannot help envying them their happiness – what they have, a life neither bored nor painful, is precisely what he wants, yet he cannot have it because he refuses to be like an animal. A human being may well ask an animal: 'Why do you not speak to me of your happiness but only stand and gaze at me?' The animal would like to answer, and say: 'The reason is I always forget what I was going to say' – but then he forgot this answer too, and stayed silent: so that the human being was left wondering.

But he also wonders at himself, that he cannot learn to forget but clings relentlessly to the past: however far and fast he may run, this chain runs with him. And it is a matter for wonder: a moment, now here and then gone, nothing before it came, again nothing after it has gone, nonetheless returns as a ghost and disturbs the peace of a later moment. A leaf flutters from the scroll of time, floats away – and suddenly floats back again and falls into the man's lap. Then

Source: Friedrich Nietzsche, 'On the Uses and Disadvantages of History for Life' [1874], in *Untimely Meditations*, ed. Daniel Breazale, trans. R. J. Hollingdale (Cambridge: Cambridge University Press, 1997), pp. 60–7, 260.

the man says 'I remember' and envies the animal, who at once forgets and for whom every moment really dies, sinks back into night and fog and is extinguished for ever. Thus the animal lives *unhistorically*: for it is contained in the present, like a number without any awkward fraction left over; it does not know how to dissimulate, it conceals nothing and at every instant appears wholly as what it is; it can therefore never be anything but honest. Man, on the other hand, braces himself against the great and ever greater pressure of what is past: it pushes him down or bends him sideways, it encumbers his steps as a dark, invisible burden which he can sometimes appear to disown and which in traffic with his fellow men he is only too glad to disown, so as to excite their envy. That is why it affects him like a vision of a lost paradise to see the herds grazing or, in closer proximity to him, a child which, having as yet nothing of the past to shake off, plays in blissful blindness between the hedges of past and future. Yet its play must be disturbed; all too soon it will be called out of its state of forgetfulness. Then it will learn to understand the phrase 'it was': that password which gives conflict, suffering and satiety access to man so as to remind him what his existence fundamentally is – an imperfect tense that can never become a perfect one. If death at last brings the desired forgetting, by that act it at the same time extinguishes the present and all existence and therewith sets the seal on the knowledge that existence is only an uninterrupted has-been, a thing that lives by negating, consuming and contradicting itself.

If happiness, if reaching out for new happiness, is in any sense what fetters living creatures to life and makes them go on living, then perhaps no philosopher is more justified than the Cynic: for the happiness of the animal, as the perfect Cynic, is the living proof of the rightness of Cynicism. The smallest happiness, if only it is present uninterruptedly and makes happy, is incomparably more happiness than the greatest happiness that comes only as an episode, as it were a piece of waywardness or folly, in a continuum of joy-lessness, desire and privation. In the case of the smallest or of the greatest happiness, however, it is always the same thing that makes happiness happiness: the ability to forget or, expressed in more scholarly fashion, the capacity to feel *unhistorically* during its duration. He who cannot sink down on the threshold of the moment and forget all the past, who cannot stand balanced like a goddess of victory without growing dizzy and afraid, will never know what happiness is – worse, he will never do anything to make others happy. Imagine the extremest possible example of a man who did not possess the power of forgetting at all and who was thus condemned to see everywhere a state of becoming: such a man would no longer believe in his own being, would no longer believe in himself, would see everything flowing asunder in moving points and would lose himself in this stream of becoming: like a true pupil of Heraclitus, he would in the end hardly dare to raise his finger.[1] Forgetting is essential to action of any kind, just as not only light but darkness too is essential for the life of everything organic. A man who wanted to feel historically through and through would be like one forcibly deprived of sleep, or an animal that had to live only by rumination and ever repeated rumination. Thus: it is possible to live almost without memory, and to live happily moreover, as the animal demonstrates; but it is altogether impossible to *live* at all without forgetting. Or, to express my theme even more simply: *there is a degree of sleeplessness, of rumination, of the historical sense, which is harmful and ultimately fatal to the living thing, whether this living thing be a man or a people or a culture.*

To determine this degree, and therewith the boundary at which the past has to be forgotten if it is not to become the gravedigger of the present, one would have to know exactly how great the *plastic power* of a man, a people, a culture is: I mean by plastic power the capacity to develop out of oneself in one's own way, to transform and incorporate into oneself what is past and foreign, to heal wounds, to replace what has been lost, to recreate broken moulds. There are people who possess so little of this power that they can perish from a single experience, from a single painful event, often and especially from a single subtle piece of injustice, like a man bleeding to death from a scratch; on the other hand, there are those who are so little affected by the worst and most dreadful disasters, and even by their own wicked acts, that they are able to feel tolerably well and be in possession of a kind of clear conscience even in the midst of them or at any rate very soon afterwards. The stronger the innermost roots of a man's nature, the more readily will he be able to assimilate and appropriate the things of the past; and the most powerful and tremendous nature would be characterized by the fact that it would know no boundary at all at which the historical sense began to overwhelm it; it would draw to itself and incorporate into itself all the past, its own and that most foreign to it, and as it were transform it into blood. That which such a nature cannot subdue it knows how to forget; it no longer exists, the horizon is rounded and closed, and there is nothing left to suggest there are people, passions, teachings, goals lying beyond it. And this is a universal law: a living thing can be healthy, strong and fruitful only when bounded by a horizon; if it is incapable of drawing a horizon around itself, and at the same time too self-centred to enclose its own view within that of another, it will pine away slowly or hasten to its timely end. Cheerfulness, the good conscience, the joyful deed, confidence in the future – all of them depend, in the case of the individual as of a nation, on the existence of a line dividing the bright and discernible from the unilluminable and dark; on one's being just as able to forget at the right time as to remember at the right time; on the possession of a powerful instinct for sensing when it is necessary to feel historically and when unhistorically. This, precisely, is the proposition the reader is invited to meditate upon: *the unhistorical and the historical are necessarily in equal measure for the health of an individual, of a people and of a culture.*

First of all, there is an observation that everyone must have made: a man's historical sense and knowledge can be very limited, his horizon as narrow as that of a dweller in the Alps, all his judgments may involve injustice and he may falsely suppose that all his experiences are original to him – yet in spite of this injustice and error he will nonetheless stand there in superlative health and vigour, a joy to all who see him; while close beside him a man far more just and instructed than he sickens and collapses because the lines of his horizon are always restlessly changing, because he can no longer extricate himself from the delicate net of his judiciousness and truth for a simple act of will and desire. On the other hand we have observed the animal, which is quite unhistorical, and dwells within a horizon reduced almost to a point, and yet lives in a certain degree of happiness, or at least without boredom and dissimulation; we shall thus have to account the capacity to feel to a certain degree unhistorically as being more vital and more fundamental, inasmuch as it constitutes the foundation upon which alone anything sound, healthy and great, anything truly human, can grow. The unhistorical is like an atmosphere within which alone life can germinate and with the destruction of which it must vanish. It is true that only by imposing limits on this unhistorical element by thinking, reflecting, comparing, distinguishing, drawing conclusions, only through the appearance within that encompassing cloud of a vivid flash of light – thus only through the power of employing the past for the purposes of life and of again introducing into history that which has been done and is gone – did man become man: but with an excess of history man again ceases to exist, and without that envelope of the unhistorical he would never have begun or dared to begin. What deed would man be capable of if he had not first entered into that vaporous region of the unhistorical? Or, to desert this imagery and illustrate by example: imagine a man seized by a vehement passion, for a woman or for a great idea: how different the world has become to him! Looking behind him he seems to himself as though blind, listening around him he hears only a dull, meaningless noise; whatever he does perceive, however, he perceives as he has never perceived before – all is so palpable, close, highly coloured, resounding, as though he apprehended it with all his senses at once. All his valuations are altered and disvalued; there are so many things he is no longer capable of evaluating at all because he can hardly feel them any more: he asks himself why he was for so long the fool of the phrases and opinions of others; he is amazed that his memory revolves unwearyingly in a circle and yet is too weak and weary to take even a single leap out of this circle. It is the condition in which one is the least capable of being just; narrow-minded, ungrateful to the past, blind to dangers, deaf to warnings, one is a little vortex of life in a dead sea of darkness and oblivion: and yet this condition – unhistorical, anti-historical through and through – is the womb not only of the unjust but of every just deed too; and no painter will paint his picture, no general achieve his victory, no people attain its freedom without having first desired and striven for it in an unhistorical condition such as that described. As he who acts is, in Goethe's words, always without a conscience,[2] so is he also always without knowledge; he forgets most things so as to do one thing, he is unjust towards what lies behind him, and he recognizes the rights only of that which is now to come into being and no other rights whatever. Thus he who acts loves his deed infinitely more than it deserves to be loved: and the finest deeds take place in such a superabundance of love that, even if their worth were incalculable in other respects, they must still be unworthy of this love.

If, in a sufficient number of cases, one could scent out and retrospectively breathe this unhistorical atmosphere within which every great historical event has taken place, he might, as a percipient being, raise himself to a *suprahistorical* vantage point such as Niebuhr once described as the possible outcome of historical reflection. 'History, grasped clearly and in detail', he says, 'is useful in one way at least: it enables us to recognize how unaware even the greatest and highest spirits of our human race have been of the chance nature of the form assumed by the eyes through which they see and through which they compel everyone to see – compel, that is, because the intensity of their consciousness is exceptionally great. He who has not grasped this quite definitely and in many instances will be subjugated by the appearance of a powerful spirit who brings to a given form the most impassioned commitment.' We may use the word 'suprahistorical' because the viewer from this vantage point could no longer feel any temptation to go on living or to take part in history; he would have recognized the essential condition of all happenings – this blindness and injustice in the soul of him who acts; he would, indeed, be cured for ever of taking history too seriously, for he would have learned from all men and all experiences, whether among Greeks or Turks, from a single hour of the first or of the nineteenth century, to answer his own question as to how or to what end life is lived. If you ask your acquaintances if they would like to relive the past ten or twenty years, you will easily discover which of them is prepared for this suprahistorical standpoint: they will all answer No, to be sure, but they will have different reasons for answering No. Some may perhaps be consoling themselves: 'but the next twenty will be better'; they are those of whom David Hume says mockingly:

> And from the dregs of life hope to receive
> What the first sprightly running could not give.[3]

Let us call them historical men; looking to the past impels them towards the future and fires their courage to go on living and their hope that what they want will still happen, that happiness lies behind the hill they are advancing towards. These historical men believe that the meaning of existence will come more and more to light in the course of its *process*, and they glance behind them only so that, from the process so far, they can learn to understand the present and to desire the future more vehemently; they have no idea that, despite their pre-occupation with history, they in fact think and act unhistorically, or that their occupation with history stands in the service, not of pure knowledge, but of life.

But our question can also be answered differently. Again with a No – but with a No for a different reason: with the No of the suprahistorical man, who sees no salvation in the process and for whom, rather, the world is complete and reaches its finality at each and every moment. What could ten more years teach that the past ten were unable to teach!

Whether the sense of this teaching is happiness or resignation or virtue or atonement, suprahistorical men have never been able to agree; but, in opposition to all historical modes of regarding the past, they are unanimous in the proposition: the past and the present are one, that is to say, with all their diversity identical in all that is typical and, as the omnipresence of imperishable types, a motionless structure of a value that cannot alter and a significance that is always the same. Just as the hundreds of different languages correspond to the same typically unchanging needs of man, so that he who understood these needs would be unable to learn anything new from any of these languages, so the suprahistorical thinker beholds the history of nations and of individuals from within, clairvoyantly divining the original meaning of the various hiero-glyphics and gradually even coming wearily to avoid the endless stream of new signs: for how should the unending superfluity of events not reduce him to satiety, over-satiety and finally to nausea! So that perhaps the boldest of them is at last ready to say to his heart, with Giacomo Leopardi:

> Nothing lives that is worthy
> Thy agitation, and the earth deserves not a sigh.
> Our being is pain and boredom and the world is dirt – nothing more.
> Be calm.[4]

But let us leave the suprahistorical men to their nausea and their wisdom: today let us rejoice for once in our unwisdom and, as believers in deeds and progress and as honourers of the process, give ourselves a holiday. Our valuation of the historical may be only an occidental prejudice: but let us at least make progress within this prejudice and not stand still! Let us at least learn better how to employ history for the purpose of *life*! Then we will gladly acknowledge that the suprahistorical outlook possesses more wisdom than we do, provided we can only be sure that we possess more life: for then our unwisdom will at any rate have more future than their wisdom will. And in order to leave no doubt as to the meaning of this antithesis of life and wisdom, I shall employ an ancient, tried-and-tested procedure and straightway propound a number of theses.

A historical phenomenon, known clearly and completely and resolved into a phenomenon of knowledge, is, for him who has perceived it, dead: for he has recognized in it the delusion, the injustice, the blind passion, and in general the whole earthly and darkening horizon of this phenomenon, and has thereby also understood its power in history. This power has now lost its hold over him insofar as he is a man of knowledge: but perhaps it has not done so insofar as he is a man involved in life.

History become pure, sovereign science would be for mankind a sort of conclusion of life and a settling of accounts with it. The study of history is something salutary and fruitful for the future only as the attendant of a mighty new current of life, of an evolving culture for example, that is to say only when it is dominated and directed by a higher force and does not itself dominate and direct.

Insofar as it stands in the service of life, history stands in the service of an unhistorical power, and, thus subordinate, it can and should never become a pure science such as, for instance, mathematics is. The question of the degree to which life requires the service of history at all, however, is one of the supreme questions and concerns in regard to the health of a man, a people or a culture. For when it attains a certain degree of excess, life crumbles and degenerates, and through this degeneration history itself finally degenerates too.

NOTES

1. *like a true pupil . . . finger*: An allusion to Cratylus, a sophist who, according to Aristotle (*Metaphysics*, IV.1010a.12), concluded that since truth could neither be known nor spoken, he would not speak at all, but 'only move his finger.'
2. *As who acts . . . without a conscience*: Goethe, *Maxims and Reflections*, no. 251.
3. '*And from . . . could not give*': Though cited by Hume in Part X of *Dialogues on Natural Religion* (1779), this verse (which Nietzsche quotes in English) is actually from John Dryden's play *Aurengzebe* (1675), Act IV, scene 1.
4. '*Nothing lives . . . Be calm*': From Leopardi's poem 'A se stesso' ('To Himself'), cited by Nietzsche in German translation.

HENRI BERGSON: *FROM* MATTER AND MEMORY

We have said that the body, placed between the objects which act upon it and those which it influences, is only a conductor, the office of which is to receive movements and to transmit them (when it does not arrest them) to certain motor mechanisms, determined if the action is reflex, chosen if the action is voluntary. Everything, then, must happen as if an independent memory gathered images as they successively occur along the course of time; and as if our body, together with its surroundings, was never more than one among these images, the last is that which we obtain at any moment by making an instantaneous section in the general stream of becoming. In this section our body occupies the center. The things which surround it act upon it, and it reacts upon them. Its reactions are more or less complex, more or less varied, according to the number and nature of the apparatus which experience has set up within it. Therefore, in the form of motor contrivances, and of motor contrivances only, it can store up the action of the past. Whence it results that past images, properly so called, must be otherwise preserved; and we may formulate this first hypothesis:

I. *The past survives under two distinct forms: first, in motor mechanisms; secondly, in independent recollections.*

But then the practical, and, consequently, the usual function of memory, the utilizing of past experience for present action – recognition, in short – must take

Source: Henri Bergson, *Matter and Memory*, trans. N. M. Paul and W. Scott Palmer (New York: Zone Books, 1991), pp. 77–84.

place in two different ways. Sometimes it lies in the action itself and in the automatic setting in motion of a mechanism adapted to the circumstances; at other times it implies an effort of the mind which seeks in the past, in order to apply them to the present, those representations which are best able to enter into the present situation. Whence our second proposition:

II. *The recognition of a present object is effected by movements when it proceeds from the object, by representations when it issues from the subject.*

[. . .] [A]lready we may speak of the body as an ever advancing boundary between the future and the past, as a pointed end, which our past is continually driving forward into our future. Whereas my body, taken at a single moment, is but a conductor interposed between the objects which influence it and those on which it acts, it is, nevertheless, when replaced in the flux of time, always situated at the very point where my past expires in a deed. And, consequently, those particular images, which I call cerebral mechanisms, terminate at each successive moment the series of my past representations, being the extreme prolongation of those representations into the present, their link with the real, that is, with action. Sever that link – and you do not necessarily destroy the past image, but you deprive it of all means of acting upon the real and, consequently [. . .] of being realized. It is in this sense, and in this sense only, that an injury to the brain can abolish any part of memory. Hence our third, and last, proposition:

III. *We pass, by imperceptible stages, from recollections strung out along the course of time to the movements which indicate their nascent or possible action in space. Lesions of the brain may affect these movements, but not these recollections.*

We have now to see whether experience verifies these three propositions.

I. *The two forms of memory.* I study a lesson, and in order to learn it by heart I read it a first time, accentuating every line; I then repeat it a certain number of times. At each repetition there is progress; the words are more and more linked together and at last make a continuous whole. When that moment comes, it is said that I know my lesson by heart, that it is imprinted on my memory.

I consider now how the lesson has been learned, and picture to myself the successive phases of the process. Each successive reading then recurs to me with its own individuality; I can see it again with the circumstances which attended it then and still form its setting. It is distinguished from those which preceded or followed it by the place which it occupied in time; in short, each reading stands out in my mind as a definite event in my history. Again it will be said that these images are recollections, that they are imprinted on my memory. The same words, then, are used in both cases. Do they mean the same thing?

The memory of the lesson, which is remembered in the sense of learned by heart, has *all* the marks of a habit. Like a habit, it is acquired by the repetition of the same effort. Like a habit, it demands first a decomposition and then a recomposition of the whole action. Lastly, like every habitual bodily exercise, it is stored up in a mechanism which is set in motion as a whole by an initial impulse, in a closed system of automatic movements which succeed each other in the same order and, together, take the same length of time.

The memory of each successive reading, on the contrary, the second or the third for instance, has *none* of the marks of a habit. Its image was necessarily imprinted at once on the memory, since the other readings form, by their very definition, other recollections. It is like an event in my life; its essence is to bear a date, and, consequently, to be unable to occur again. All that later readings can add to it will only alter its original nature; though my effort to recall this image becomes more and more easy as I repeat it, the image, regarded in itself, was necessarily at the outset what it always will be.

It may be urged that these two recollections, that of the reading and that of the lesson, differ only as the less from the more, and that the images successively developed by each repetition overlie each other, so that the lesson once learned is but the composite image in which all readings are blended. And I quite agree that each of the successive readings differs from the preceding mainly in the fact that the lesson is better known. But it is no less certain that each of them, considered as a new reading and not as a lesson better known, is entirely sufficient to itself, subsists exactly as it occurred, and constitutes with all its concomitant perceptions an original moment of my history. We may even go further and aver that consciousness reveals to us a profound difference, a difference in kind, between the two sorts of recollection. The memory of a given reading is a representation and only a representation; it is embraced in an intuition of the mind which I may lengthen or shorten at will; I assign to it any duration I please; there is nothing to prevent my grasping the whole of it instantaneously, as in one picture. On the contrary, the memory of the lesson I have learned, even if I repeat this lesson only mentally, requires a definite time, the time necessary to develop one by one, were it only in imagination, all the articulatory movements that are necessary: it is no longer a representation; it is an action. And, in fact, the lesson once learned bears upon it no mark which betrays its origin and classes it in the past; it is part of my present, exactly like my habit of walking or of writing; it is lived and acted, rather than represented: I might believe it innate, if I did not choose to recall at the same time, as so many representations, the successive readings by means of which I learned it. Therefore, these representations are independent of it, and, just as they preceded the lesson as I now possess and know it, so that lesson once learned can do without them.

Following to the end this fundamental distinction, we are confronted by two different memories theoretically independent. The first records, in the form of memory-images, all the events of our daily life as they occur in time; it neglects no detail; it leaves to each fact, to each gesture, its place and date. Regardless of utility or of practical application, it stores up the past by the mere necessity of its own nature. By this memory is made possible the intelligent, or rather intellectual, recognition of perception already experienced; in it we take refuge every time that, in the search for a particular image, we remount the slope of our past. But every perception is prolonged into a nascent action; and while the images are taking their place and order in this memory, the movements which continue them modify the organism and create in the body new dispositions toward action. Thus is gradually formed an experience of an entirely different order, which accumulates within the body, a series of mechanisms wound up and ready, with reactions to external stimuli ever more numerous and more varied and answers ready prepared to an ever growing number of possible solicitations. We become conscious of these mechanisms as they come into play; this consciousness of a whole past of efforts stored up in the present is indeed also a memory, but a memory profoundly different from the first, always bent upon action, seated in the present and looking only to the future. It has retained from the past only the intelligently coordinated movements which represent the accumulated efforts of the past; it recovers those past efforts, not in the memory-images which recall them, but in the definite order and systematic character with which the actual movements take place. In truth it no longer *represents* our past to us, it *acts* it; and if it still deserves the name of memory, it is not because it conserves bygone images, but because it prolongs their useful effect into the present moment.

Of these two memories, of which the one *imagines* and the other *repeats*, the second may supply the place of the first and even sometimes be mistaken for it. When a dog welcomes his master, barking and wagging his tail, he certainly recognizes him; but does this recognition imply the evocation of a past image and the comparison of that image with the present perception? Does it not rather consist in the animal's consciousness of a certain special attitude adopted by his body, an attitude which has been gradually built up by his familiar relations with his master, and which the mere perception of his master now calls forth in him mechanically? We must not go too far; even in the animal it is possible that vague images of the past overflow into the present perception; we can even conceive that its entire past is virtually indicated in its consciousness; but this past does not interest the animal enough to detach it from the fascinating present, and its recognition must be rather lived than thought. To call up the past in the form of an image, we must be able to withdraw ourselves from the action of the moment, we must have the power to value the useless, we must have the will to dream. Man alone is capable of such an effort. But even in him the past to which he returns is fugitive, ever on the point of escaping him, as though his backward turning memory were thwarted by the other, more natural, memory, of which the forward movement bears him on to action and to life.

When psychologists talk of recollection as of a fold in a material, as of an impress graven deeper by repetition, they forget that the immense majority of our memories bear upon events and details of our life of which the essence is to have a date, and, consequently, to be incapable of being repeated. The memories which we acquire voluntarily by repetition are rare and exceptional. On the contrary, the recording, by memory, of facts and images unique in their kind takes place at every moment of duration. But inasmuch as *learned* memories are more useful, they are more remarked. And as the acquisition of these memories by a repetition of the same effort resembles the well-known process of habit, we prefer to set this kind of memory in the foreground, to erect it into the model memory, and to see in spontaneous recollection only the same phenomenon in a nascent state, the beginning of a lesson learned by heart. But how can we overlook the radical difference between that which must be built up by repetition and that which is essentially incapable of being repeated? Spontaneous recollection is perfect from the outset; time can add nothing to its image without disfiguring it; it retains in memory its place and date. On the contrary, a learned recollection passes out of time in the measure that the lesson is better known; it becomes more and more impersonal, more and more foreign to our past life. Repetition, therefore, in no sense effects the conversion of the first into the last; its office is merely to utilize more and more the movements by which the first was continued, in order to organize them together and, by setting up a mechanism, to create a bodily habit. Indeed, this habit could be called a remembrance were it not that I remember that I have acquired it, and I remember its acquisition only because I appeal to that memory which is spontaneous, which dates events and records them but once. Of the two memories, then, which we have just distinguished, the first appears to be memory par excellence. The second, that generally studied by psychologists, is *habit interpreted by memory* rather than memory itself.

3.4

SIGMUND FREUD: A NOTE UPON THE 'MYSTIC WRITING-PAD'

If I distrust my memory – neurotics, as we know, do so to a remarkable extent, but normal people have every reason for doing so as well – I am able to supplement and guarantee its working by making a note in writing. In that case the surface upon which this note is preserved, the pocket-book or sheet of paper, is as it were a materialized portion of my mnemic apparatus, which I otherwise carry about with me invisible. I have only to bear in mind the place where this 'memory' has been deposited and I can then 'reproduce' it at any time I like, with the certainty that it will have remained unaltered and so have escaped the possible distortions to which it might have been subjected in my actual memory.

If I want to make full use of this technique for improving my mnemic function, I find that there are two different procedures open to me. On the one hand, I can choose a writing-surface which will preserve intact any note made upon it for an indefinite length of time – for instance, a sheet of paper which I can write upon in ink. I am then in possession of a 'permanent memory-trace'. The disadvantage of this procedure is that the receptive capacity of the writing-surface is soon exhausted. The sheet is filled with writing, there is no room on it for any more notes, and I find myself obliged to bring another sheet into use, that has not been written on. Moreover, the advantage of this procedure, the fact that it provides a 'permanent trace', may lose its value for me if after a time

Source: Sigmund Freud, 'A Note upon the "Mystic Writing-Pad"' [1925], in *On Metapsychology: The Theory of Psychoanalysis*, Vol. 11 of 'The Penguin Freud Library', trans. James Strachey, ed. Angela Richards (Harmondsworth: Penguin, 1991), pp. 429–34.

the note ceases to interest me and I no longer want to 'retain it in my memory'. The alternative procedure avoids both of these disadvantages. If, for instance, I write with a piece of chalk on a slate, I have a receptive surface which retains its receptive capacity for an unlimited time and the notes upon which can be destroyed as soon as they cease to interest me, without any need for throwing away the writing surface itself. Here the disadvantage is that I cannot preserve a permanent trace. If I want to put some fresh notes on the slate, I must first wipe out the ones which cover it. Thus an unlimited receptive capacity and a retention of permanent traces seem to be mutually exclusive properties in the apparatus which we use as substitutes for our memory: either the receptive surface must be renewed or the note must be destroyed.

All the forms of auxiliary apparatus which we have invented for the improvement or intensification of our sensory functions are built on the same model as the sense organs themselves or portions of them: for instance, spectacles, photographic cameras, trumpets.[1] Measured by this standard, devices to aid our memory seem particularly imperfect, since our mental apparatus accomplishes precisely what they cannot: it has an unlimited receptive capacity for new perceptions and nevertheless lays down permanent – even though not unalterable – memory traces of them. As long ago as in 1900 I gave expression in *The Interpretation of Dreams*[2] to a suspicion that this unusual capacity was to be divided between two different systems (or organs of the mental apparatus). According to this view, we possess a system *Pcpt.-Cs.*, which receives perceptions but retains no permanent trace of them, so that it can react like a clean sheet to every new perception; while the permanent traces of the excitations which have been received are preserved in 'mnemic systems' lying behind the perceptual system. Later, in *Beyond the Pleasure Principle* (1920),[3] I added a remark to the effect that the inexplicable phenomenon of consciousness arises in the perceptual system *instead of* the permanent traces.

Now some time ago there came upon the market, under the name of the 'Mystic Writing-Pad', a small contrivance that promises to perform more than the sheet of paper or the slate. It claims to be nothing more than a writing-tablet from which notes can be erased by an easy movement of the hand. But if it is examined more closely it will be found that its construction shows a remarkable agreement with my hypothetical structure of our perceptual apparatus and that it can in fact provide both an ever-ready receptive surface and permanent traces of the notes that have been made upon it.

The Mystic Pad is a slab of dark brown resin or wax with a paper edging; over the slab is laid a thin transparent sheet, the top end of which is firmly secured to the slab while its bottom end rests on it without being fixed to it. This transparent sheet is the more interesting part of the little device. It itself consists of two layers, which can be detached from each other except at their two ends. The upper layer is a transparent piece of celluloid; the lower layer is made of thin translucent waxed paper. When the apparatus is not in use, the lower surface of the waxed paper adheres lightly to the upper surface of the wax slab.

To make use of the Mystic Pad, one writes upon the celluloid portion of the covering-sheet which rests on the wax slab. For this purpose no pencil or chalk is necessary, since the writing does not depend on material being deposited on the receptive surface. It is a return to the ancient method of writing on tablets of clay or wax: a pointed stilus scratches the surface, the depressions upon which constitute the 'writing'. In the case of the Mystic Pad this scratching is not effected directly, but through the medium of the covering-sheet. At the points which the stilus touches, it presses the lower surface of the waxed paper on to the wax slab, and the grooves are visible as dark writing upon the otherwise smooth whitish-grey surface of the celluloid. If one wishes to destroy what has been written, all that is necessary is to raise the double covering-sheet from the wax slab by a light pull, starting from the free lower end.[4] The close contact between the waxed paper and the wax slab at the places which have been scratched (upon which the visibility of the writing depended) is thus brought to an end and it does not recur when the two surfaces come together once more. The Mystic Pad is now clear of writing and ready to receive fresh notes.

The small imperfections of the contrivance have, of course, no importance for us, since we are only concerned with its approximation to the structure of the perceptual apparatus of the mind.

If, while the Mystic Pad has writing on it, we cautiously raise the celluloid from the waxed paper, we can see the writing just as clearly on the surface of the latter, and the question may arise why there should be any necessity for the celluloid portion of the cover. Experiment will then show that the thin paper would be very easily crumpled or torn if one were to write directly upon it with the stilus. The layer of celluloid thus acts as a protective sheath for the waxed paper, to keep off injurious effects from without. The celluloid is a 'protective shield against stimuli'; the layer which actually receives the stimuli is the paper. I may at this point recall that in *Beyond the Pleasure Principle* [p. 298 ff.] I showed that the perceptual apparatus of our mind consists of two layers, of an external protective shield against stimuli whose task it is to diminish the strength of excitations coming in, and of a surface behind it which receives the stimuli, namely the system *Pcpt.-Cs.*

The analogy would not be of much value if it could not be pursued further than this. If we lift the entire covering-sheet – both the celluloid and the waxed paper – off the wax slab, the writing vanishes and, as I have already remarked, does not reappear again. The surface of the Mystic Pad is clear of writing and once more capable of receiving impressions. But it is easy to discover that the permanent trace of what was written is retained upon the wax slab itself and is legible in suitable lights. Thus the Pad provides not only a receptive surface that can be used over and over again, like a slate, but also permanent traces of what has been written, like an ordinary paper pad: it solves the problem of combining the two functions *by dividing them between two separate but interrelated component parts or systems*. But this is precisely the way in which, according to the hypothesis which I mentioned just now, our mental apparatus performs its perceptual function. The layer which receives the stimuli – the system *Pcpt.-Cs.* – forms no permanent traces; the foundations of memory come about in other, adjoining, systems.

We need not be disturbed by the fact that in the Mystic Pad no use is made of the permanent traces of the notes that have been received; it is enough that they are present. There must come a point at which the analogy between an auxiliary apparatus of this kind and the organ which is its prototype will cease to apply. It is true, too, that once the writing has been erased, the Mystic Pad cannot 'reproduce' it from within; it would be a mystic pad indeed if, like our memory, it could accomplish that. None the less, I do not think it is too far-fetched to compare the celluloid and waxed paper cover with the system *Pcpt.-Cs.* and its protective shield, the wax slab with the unconscious behind them, and the appearance and disappearance of the writing with the flickering-up and passing-away of consciousness in the process of perception.

But I must admit that I am inclined to press the comparison still further. On the Mystic Pad the writing vanishes every time the close contact is broken between the paper which receives the stimulus and the wax slab which preserves the impression. This agrees with a notion which I have long had about the method by which the perceptual apparatus of our mind functions, but which I have hitherto kept to myself.[5] My theory was that cathectic innervations are sent out and withdrawn in rapid periodic impulses from within into the completely pervious system *Pcpt.-Cs.* So long as that system is cathected in this manner, it receives perceptions (which are accompanied by consciousness) and passes the excitation on to the unconscious mnemic sytems; but as soon as the cathexis is withdrawn, consciousness is extinguished and the functioning of the system comes to a standstill.[6] It is as though the unconscious stretches out feelers, through the medium of the system *Pcpt.-Cs.*, towards the external world and hastily withdraws them as soon as they have sampled the excitations coming from it. Thus the interruptions, which in the case of the Mystic Pad have an external origin, were attributed by my hypothesis to the discontinuity in the current of innervation; and the actual breaking of contact which occurs in the Mystic Pad was replaced in my theory by the periodic non-excitability of the perceptual system. I further had a suspicion that this discontinuous method of functioning of the system *Pcpt.-Cs.* lies at the bottom of the origin of the concept of time.[7]

If we imagine one hand writing upon the surface of the Mystic Writing-Pad while another periodically raises its covering-sheet from the wax slab, we shall have a concrete representation of the way in which I tried to picture the functioning of the perceptual apparatus of our mind.

NOTES

1. This notion is expanded in Chapter III of *Civilization and its Discontents* (1930), Penguin Freud Library (P.F.L.), **12**, 276–7.

2. P.F.L., **4**, 689. As Freud mentions in *Beyond the Pleasure Principle* (1920), P.F L., **11**, 296, this distinction had already been drawn by Breuer in his theoretical section of *Studies on Hysteria* (1895), P.F.L., **3**, 263 *n*.
3. P.F.L, **11**, 296–7.
4. The method by which the covering-sheet is detached from the wax slab is slightly different in the current form of the device; but this does not affect the principle.
5. It had in fact been mentioned in *Beyond the Pleasure Principle*, P.F.L, **11**, 299. The notion reappears at the end of the paper on 'Negation' (1925), P.F.L, **11**, 440–1. It is already present in embryo at the end of Section 19 of Part 1 of the 'Project' of 1895.
6. This is in accordance with the 'principle of the insusceptibility to excitation of uncathected systems', which is discussed in an Editor's footnote to the metapsychological paper on dreams (1917), P.F.L, **11**, 234–5.
7. This also had been suggested in *Beyond the Pleasure Principle*, P.F.L, **11**, 300, and hinted at earlier, in 'The Unconscious' (1915), P.F.L, **11**, 191 ff. It is restated in 'Negation' (1925), P.F.L, **11**, 440–1, where, however, Freud attributes the sending out of feelers to the ego.

3.5

WALTER BENJAMIN: ON THE IMAGE OF PROUST

I

The thirteen volumes of Marcel Proust's *A la recherche du temps perdu* are the result of an unconstruable synthesis in which the absorption of a mystic, the art of a prose writer, the verve of a satirist, the erudition of a scholar, and the self-consciousness of a monomaniac have combined in an autobiographical work. It has rightly been said that all great works of literature establish a genre or dissolve one – that they are, in other words, special cases. Among these cases, this is one of the most unfathomable. From its structure, which is at once fiction, autobiography, and commentary, to the syntax of boundless sentences (the Nile of language, which here overflows and fructifies the plains of truth), everything transcends the norm. The first revealing observation that strikes one is that this great special case of literature at the same time constitutes its greatest achievement in recent decades. The conditions under which it was created were extremely unhealthy: an unusual malady, extraordinary wealth, and an abnormal gift. This is not a model life in every respect, but everything about it is exemplary. The outstanding literary achievement of our time is assigned a place at the heart of the impossible, at the center – and also at the point of indifference – of all dangers, and it marks this great realization of a 'lifework' as the last for a long time. The image of Proust is the highest physiognomic

Source: Walter Benjamin, 'On the Image of Proust' [1929], in *Selected Writings*, Vol. 2, 1927–1934, trans. Rodney Livingstone and others, eds. Michael W. Jennings, Howard Eiland and Gary Smith (Cambridge, MA: Harvard University Press, 1999), pp. 237–47.

expression which the irresistibly growing discrepancy between literature and life was able to assume. This is the lesson which justifies the attempt to evoke this image.

We know that in his work Proust described not a life as it actually was [*wie es gewesen ist*] but a life as it was remembered by the one who had lived it. Yet even this statement is imprecise and far too crude. For the important thing to the remembering author is not what he experienced, but the weaving of his memory, the Penelope work of recollection [*Eingedenken*]. Or should one call it, rather, a Penelope work of forgetting? Is not the involuntary recollection, Proust's *mémoire involontaire*, much closer to forgetting than what is usually called memory? And is not this work of spontaneous recollection, in which remembrance is the woof and forgetting the warp, a counterpart to Penelope's work rather than its likeness? For here the day unravels what the night has woven. When we awake each morning, we hold in our hands, usually weakly and loosely, but a few fringes of the carpet of lived existence, as woven into us by forgetting. However, with our purposeful activity and, even more, our purposive remembering, each day unravels the web, the ornaments of forgetting. This is why Proust finally turned his days into nights, devoting all his hours to undisturbed work in his darkened room with artificial illumination, so that none of those intricate arabesques might escape him.

The Latin word *textum* means 'web.' No one's text is more of a web or more tightly woven than that of Marcel Proust; to him nothing was tight or durable enough. From his publisher Gallimard we know that Proust's proofreading habits were the despair of typesetters. The galleys always came back covered with writing to the edge of the page, but not a single misprint had been corrected; all available space had been used for fresh text. Thus, the laws of remembrance were operative even within the confines of the work. For an experienced event is finite – at any rate, confined to one sphere of experience; a remembered event is infinite, because it is merely a key to everything that happened before it and after it. There is yet another sense in which memory issues strict regulations for weaving. Only the *actus purus* of remembrance itself, not the author or the plot, constitutes the unity of the text. One may even say that the intermittences of author and plot are only the reverse of the continuum of memory, the figure on the back side of the carpet. This is what Proust meant, and this is how he must be understood, when he said that he would prefer to see his entire work printed in one volume in two columns and without any paragraphs.

What was it that Proust sought so frenetically? What was at the bottom of these infinite efforts? Can we say that all lives, works, and deeds that matter were never anything but the undisturbed unfolding of the most banal, most fleeting, most sentimental, weakest hour in the life of the one to whom they pertain? When Proust in a well-known passage described the hour that was most his own, he did it in such a way that everyone can find it in his own existence. We might almost call it an everyday hour; it comes with the night, a lost twittering of birds, or a breath drawn at the sill of an open window. And there is no telling what encounters would be in store for us if we were less inclined to give in to sleep. Proust did not give in to sleep. And yet – or, rather, precisely for this reason – Jean Cocteau was able to say in a beautiful essay that the intonation of Proust's voice obeyed the laws of night and honey. By submitting to these laws, Proust conquered the hopeless sadness within him (what he once called 'l'imperfection incurable dans l'essence même du présent'),[1] and from the honeycombs of memory he built a house for the swarm of his thoughts. Cocteau recognized what really should be the major concern of all readers of Proust. He recognized Proust's blind, senseless, obsessive quest for happiness. It shone from his eyes; they were not happy, but in them lay happiness, just as it lies in gambling or in love. Nor is it hard to say why this heart-stopping, explosive will to happiness which pervades Proust's writings is so seldom comprehended by his readers. In many places Proust himself made it easy for them to view this oeuvre, too, from the time-tested, comfortable perspective of resignation, heroism, asceticism. After all, nothing makes more sense to the model pupils of life than the notion that a great achievement is the fruit of toil, misery, and disappointment. The idea that happiness could have a share in beauty would be too much of a good thing, something that their *ressentiment* would never get over.

There is a dual will to happiness, a dialectics of happiness: a hymnic form as well as an elegiac form. The one is the unheard-of, the unprecedented, the height of bliss; the other, the eternal repetition, the eternal restoration of the original, first happiness. It is this elegiac idea of happiness – it could also be called Eleatic – which for Proust transforms existence into a preserve of memory. To it he sacrificed in his life friends and companionship, in his works plot, unity of characters, the flow of the narration, the play of the imagination. Max Unold, one of Proust's more discerning readers, fastened on the 'boredom' thus created in Proust's writings and likened it to 'idle stories.' 'Proust managed to make the idle story interesting. He says: "Imagine, dear reader: yesterday I was dunking a bit of cake in my tea when it occurred to me that as a child I had spent some time in the country." For this he takes eighty pages, and it is so fascinating that you think you are no longer the listener but the daydreamer himself.' In such stories – 'all ordinary dreams turn into idle stories as soon as one tells them to someone' – Unold has discovered the bridge to the dream. No synthetic interpretation of Proust can disregard it. Enough inconspicuous gates lead into it – Proust's frenetic study, his impassioned cult of similarity. The true signs of its hegemony do not become obvious where he unexpectedly and startlingly uncovers similarities in actions, physiognomies, or speech rnannerisms. The similarity of one thing to another which we are used to, which occupies us in a wakeful state, reflects only vaguely the deeper similarity of the dream world in which everything that happens appears not in identical but in similar guise, opaquely similar to itself. Children know a symbol of this world: the stocking which has the structure of this dream world when, rolled up in the laundry hamper, it is a 'bag' and a 'present' at the same time. And just as children do not tire of quickly changing the bag and its contents into a third thing – namely, a stocking – Proust could not get his fill of emptying the dummy, his self, at one stroke in order to keep garnering that third thing, the image which satisfied his curiosity – indeed, assuaged his homesickness. He lay on his bed racked with homesickness, homesick for the world distorted in the state of similarity, a world in which the true surrealist face of existence breaks through. To this world belongs what happens in Proust, as well as the deliberate and fastidious way in which it appears. It is never isolated, rhetorical, or visionary; carefully heralded and securely supported, it bears a fragile, precious reality: the image. It detaches itself from the structure of Proust's sentences just as that summer day at Balbec – old, immemorial, mummified – emerged from the lace curtains under Françoise's hands.

II

We do not always proclaim loudly the most important thing we have to say. Nor do we always privately share it with those closest to us, our intimate friends, those who have been most devotedly ready to receive our confession. If it is true that not only people but also ages have such a chaste – that is, such a devious and frivolous – way of communicating what is most their own to a passing acquaintance, then the nineteenth century did not reveal itself to Zola or Anatole France, but to the young Proust, the insignificant snob, the playboy and socialite who snatched in passing the most astounding confidences from a declining age as if from another bone-weary Swann. It took Proust to make the nineteenth century ripe for memoirs. What before him had been a period devoid of tension now became a force field in which later writers aroused multifarious currents. Nor is it accidental that the most significant work of this kind was written by an author who was personally close to Proust as admirer and friend: the memoirs of the princesse de Clermont-Tonnerre. And the very title of her book, *Au temps des équipages*, would have been unthinkable prior to Proust. This book is the echo which softly answers Proust's ambiguous, loving, challenging call from the Faubourg Saint-Germain. In addition, this melodious performance is shot through with direct and indirect references to Proust in its tenor and its characters, which include him and some of his favorite objects of study from the Ritz. There is no denying, of course, that this puts us in a very feudal milieu, and, with phenomena like Robert de Montesquiou, whom the princesse de Clermont-Tonnerre depicts masterfully, in a very special one at that. But this is true of Proust as well, and in his writings, as we know, Montesquiou has a counterpart. All this would not be worth discussing, especially since the question of models would be secondary and unimportant for Germany, if German criticism were not so fond of taking the easy way out. Above all, it could not resist the opportunity to descend to the level of the lending-library crowd. Hack critics were tempted to draw conclusions about the author from the snobbish milieu of his writings, to characterize Proust's works as an internal affair of the French, a literary supplement to the *Almanach de Gotha*.[2] It is obvious, though, that the problems of Proust's characters are those of a satiated society. But there is not one that would be identical with those of the author, which are subversive. To reduce this to a formula, it was to be Proust's aim to construe the entire structure of high society as a physiology of chatter. In the treasury of its prejudices and maxims, there is not one that is not annihilated by his dangerous comic treatment. It is not the least of Léon Pierre-Quint's many services to Proust that he was the first to point this out. 'When humorous works are mentioned,' he wrote, 'one usually thinks of short, amusing books in illustrated jackets. One forgets about *Don Quixote*, *Pantagruel*, and *Gil Blas* – fat, ungainly tomes in small print.' The subversive side of Proust's work appears most convincingly in this context. Here, though, it is less humor than comedy that is the real source of his power; his laughter does not toss the world up but flings it down – at the risk that it will be smashed to pieces, which will then make him burst into tears. And unity of family, unity of personality, of sexual morality and class honor, are indeed smashed to bits. The pretensions of the bourgeoisie are shattered by laughter. Their retreat and reassimilation by the aristocracy is the sociological theme of the work.

Proust did not tire of the training which moving in aristocratic circles required. Assiduously and without much constraint, he conditioned his personality, making it as impenetrable and resourceful, as submissive and difficult, as it had to be for the sake of his mission. Later on, this mystification and fussiness became so much a part of him that his letters sometimes constitute whole systems of parentheses, and not just in the grammatical sense – letters which despite their infinitely ingenious, flexible composition occasionally call to mind that legendary example of epistolary art: 'My dear Madam, I just noticed that I forgot my cane at your house yesterday; please be good enough to give it to the bearer of this letter. P.S. Kindly pardon me for disturbing you; I just found my cane.' Proust was most resourceful in creating complications. Once, late at night, he dropped in on the princesse de Clermont-Tonnerre and made his staying dependent on someone's bringing him his medicine from his house. He sent a valet for it, giving him a lengthy description of the neighborhood and of the house. Finally he said: 'You cannot miss it. It is the only window on the boulevard Haussmann in which there is still a light burning!' Everything but the house number! Anyone who has tried to get the address of a brothel in a strange city and has received the most long-winded directions, everything but the name of the street and the house number, will understand what is meant here and what the connection is with Proust's love of ceremony, his admiration for Saint-Simon, and, last but not least, his intransigent Frenchness. Isn't it the quintessence of experience to find out how very difficult it is to learn many things which apparently could be told in very few words? It is simply that such words are part of an argot established along lines of caste and class and unintelligible to outsiders. No wonder the secret language of the salons excited Proust. When he later embarked on his merciless depiction of the *petit clan*, the Courvoisiers, and the 'esprit d'Oriane,' he had already – through his association with the Bibescos – become conversant with the improvisations of a code language to which we too have now been introduced.

In his years of life in the salons, Proust developed not only the vice of flattery to an eminent – one is tempted to say, to a theological – degree, but the vice of curiosity as well. We detect in him the reflection of the laughter which like a flash fire curls the lips of the Foolish Virgins represented on the intrados of many of the cathedrals which Proust loved. It is the smile of curiosity. Was it curiosity that made him such a great parodist? If so, we would know how to evaluate the term 'parodist' in this context. Not very highly. For though it does justice to his abysmal malice, it skirts the bitterness, savagery, and grimness of the magnificent pieces which he wrote in the style of Balzac, Flaubert, Sainte-Beuve, Henri de Régnier, the Goncourts, Michelet, Renan, and his favorite Saint-Simon, and which are collected in the volume *Pastiches et mélanges*.[3] The mimicry of a man of curiosity is the brilliant device of these essays, as it is also a feature of his entire creativity, in which his passion for vegetative life cannot be taken seriously enough. Ortega y Gasset was the first to draw attention to the vegetative existence of Proust's characters, which are planted so firmly in their social habitat, influenced by the position of the sun of aristocratic favor, stirred by the wind that blows from Guermantes or Méséglise, and inextricably enmeshed in the thicket of their fate. This is the environment that gave rise to the poet's mimicry. Proust's most accurate, most conclusive insights fasten on their objects the way insects fasten on leaves, blossoms, branches, betraying nothing of their existence until a leap, a beating of wings, a vault, show the startled observer that some incalculable individual life has imperceptibly crept into an alien world. 'The metaphor, however unexpected,' says Pierre-Quint, 'forms itself quite close to the thought.'

The true reader of Proust is constantly jarred by small frights. In the use of metaphor, he finds the precipitate of the same mimicry which must have struck him as this spirit's struggle for survival under the leafy canopy of society. At this point we must say something about the close and fructifying interpenetration of these two vices, curiosity and flattery. There is a revealing passage in the writings of the princesse de Clermont-Tonnerre: 'And finally we cannot suppress the fact that Proust became intoxicated by the study of domestic servants – whether it be that an element which he encountered nowhere else intrigued his investigative faculties or that he envied servants their greater opportunities for observing the intimate details of things that aroused his interest. In any case, domestic servants in their various embodiments and types were his passion.' In the exotic shadings of a Jupien, a Monsieur Aimé, a Célestine Albalat, their ranks extend from Françoise – a figure with the coarse, angular features of Saint Martha that seems to be straight out of a book of hours – to those grooms and *chasseurs* who are paid for loafing rather than working. And perhaps the greatest concentration of this connoisseur of ceremonies was reserved for the depiction of these lower ranks. Who can tell how much servant curiosity became part of Proust's flattery, how much servant flattery became mixed with his curiosity, and where this artful copy of the role of the servant on the heights of the social scale had its limits? Proust presented such a copy, and he could not help doing so, for, as he once admitted, *voir* and *désirer imiter* were one and the same thing to him. This attitude, which was both sovereign and obsequious, has been preserved by Maurice Barrès in the most apposite words that have ever been written about Proust: 'Un poète persan dans une loge de portière.'[4]

There was something of the detective in Proust's curiosity. The upper ten thousand were to him a clan of criminals, a band of conspirators beyond compare: the *camorra* of consumers.[5] It excludes from its world everything that has a part in production, or at least demands that this part be gracefully and bashfully concealed behind the kind of manner that is sported by the polished professionals of consumption. Proust's analysis of snobbery, which is far more important than his apotheosis of art, constitutes the apogee of his criticism of society. For the attitude of the snob is nothing but the consistent, organized, steely view of life from the chemically pure standpoint of the consumer. And because even the remotest as well as the most primitive memory of nature's productive forces was to be banished from this satanic fairyland, Proust found an inverted relationship more serviceable than a normal one, even in love. But the pure consumer is the pure exploiter – logically and theoretically – and in Proust he is this in the full concreteness of his actual historical existence. He is concrete because he is impenetrable and elusive. Proust describes a class which is everywhere pledged to camouflage its material basis and which for this very reason is attached to a feudalism lacking any intrinsic economic significance but all the more serviceable as a mask of the upper middle class. This disillusioned, merciless deglamorizer of the ego, of love, of morals – for this is how Proust liked to view himself – turns his whole limitless art into a veil for this one most vital mystery of his class: the economic aspect. It is not as if he thereby serves his class; he is merely ahead of it. That which this class experiences begins to become comprehensible only with Proust. Yet much of the greatness of this work will remain inaccessible or undiscovered until this class has revealed its most pronounced features in the final struggle.

III

In the 1800s there was an inn by the name of 'Au Temps Perdu' at Grenoble; I do not know whether it still exists. In Proust, too, we are guests who enter through a door underneath a suspended sign that sways in the breeze, a door behind which eternity and rapture await us. Ramón Fernandez rightly distinguished between a *thème de l'éternité* and a *thème du temps* in Proust. But Proust's eternity is by no means a platonic or a utopian one; it is rapturous. Therefore, if 'time reveals a new and hitherto unknown kind of eternity to anyone who becomes engrossed in its passing,' this certainly does not enable an individual to approach 'the higher regions which a Plato or Spinoza reached with one beat of the wings.' It is true that in Proust we find rudiments of an enduring idealism, but it is not these elements which determine the greatness of his work. The eternity which Proust opens to view is intertwined time, not boundless time. His true interest is in the passage of time in its most real – that is, intertwined – form, and this passage nowhere holds sway more openly than in remembrance within and aging without. To follow the counterpoint of aging and remembering means to penetrate to the heart of Proust's world, to the universe of intertwining. It is the world in a state of similarity, and in it the *correspondances* rule; the Romantics were the first to comprehend them and Baudelaire embraced them most fervently, but Proust was the only one who managed to reveal them in our lived life. This is the work of *la mémoire involontaire*, the rejuvenating force which is a match for the inexorable process of aging. When that which has been is reflected in the dewy fresh 'instant,' a painful shock of rejuvenation pulls it together once more as irresistibly as the Guermantes Way and Swann's Way become intertwined for Proust when, in the thirteenth volume, he roams about the Combray area for the last time and discovers the intermingling of the roads. In an instant the landscape turns about like a gust of wind. 'Ah! que le monde est grand à la clarté des lampes! / Aux yeux du souvenir que le monde est petit!'[6] Proust has brought off the monstrous feat of letting the whole world age a lifetime in an instant. But this very concentration, in which things that normally just fade and slumber are consumed in a flash, is called rejuvenation. *A la Recherche du temps perdu* is the constant attempt to charge an entire lifetime with the utmost mental awareness. Proust's method is actualization, not reflection. He is filled with the insight that none of us has time to live the true dramas of the life that we are destined for. This is what ages us – this and nothing else. The wrinkles and creases in our faces are the registration of the great passions, vices, insights that called on us; but we, the masters, were not home.

Since the spiritual exercises of Loyola, Western literature has scarcely seen a more radical attempt at self-absorption. Proust's writing, too, has as its center a solitude which pulls the world down into its vortex with the force of a maelstrom. And the overloud and inconceivably hollow chatter which comes roaring out of Proust's novels is the sound of society plunging into the abyss of this solitude. Proust's invectives against friendship have their place here. It was a matter of perceiving the silence at the bottom of this crater, whose eyes are the quietest and most absorbing. What is manifested irritatingly and capriciously in so many anecdotes is the combination of an unparalleled intensity of conversation with an unsurpassable aloofness from one's interlocutor. There has never been anyone else with Proust's ability to show us things; Proust's pointing finger is unequaled. But there is another gesture in friendly togetherness, in conversation: physical contact. To no one is this gesture more alien than to Proust. He cannot touch his reader, either; he couldn't do this for anything in the world. If one wanted to group literature around these poles, dividing it into the deictic kind and the touching kind, the core of the former would be the work of Proust;

the core of the latter, the work of Péguy.[7] This is basically what Fernandez has formulated so well: 'Depth, or rather intensity, is always on his side, never on that of his interlocutor.' This is demonstrated brilliantly and with a touch of cynicism in Proust's literary criticism, the most significant document of which is an essay that came into being on the high level of his fame and the low level of his deathbed: 'À propos de Baudelaire.' The essay is jesuitical in its acquiescence in his own maladies, immoderate in the garrulousness of a man who is resting, frightening in the indifference of a man marked by death who wants to speak out once more, no matter on what subject. What inspired Proust here in the face of death also shaped him in his intercourse with his contemporaries: an alternation of sarcasm and tenderness which was so spasmodic and harsh that its recipients threatened to break down in exhaustion.

The provocative, unsteady quality of the man affects even the reader of his works. Suffice it to recall the endless succession of 'soit que . . .' [whether it be . . .'] by means of which an action is shown – exhaustively, depressingly – in the light of the countless motives upon which it may have been based. Yet these paratactic flights reveal the point at which weakness and genius coincide in Proust: the intellectual renunciation, the tested skepticism with which he approached things. After the self-satisfied inwardness of Romanticism, Proust came along – determined, as Jacques Rivière puts it, not to give the least credence to the 'Sirènes intérieures' ['internal Sirens']. 'Proust approaches experience without the slightest metaphysical interest, without the slightest penchant for construction, without the slightest tendency to console.' Nothing is truer than that. And thus the basic feature of this work, too, which Proust kept proclaiming as having been planned, is anything but the result of construction. But it is as planned as the lines on the palm of our hand or the arrangement of the stamen in a calyx. Completely worn out, Proust, that aged child, fell back on the bosom of nature – not to suckle from it, but to dream to its heartbeat. One must picture him in this state of weakness to understand how felicitously Jacques Rivière interpreted the weakness when he wrote: 'Marcel Proust died of the same inexperience which permitted him to write his works. He died of ignorance of the world, and because he did not know how to change the conditions of his life which had begun to crush him. He died because he did not know how to make a fire or open a window.' And, to be sure, of his neurasthenic asthma.

The doctors were powerless in the face of this malady; not so the writer, who very systematically placed it in his service. To begin with the most external aspect, he was a perfect stage director of his illness. For months he connected, with devastating irony, the image of an admirer who had sent him flowers with their odor, which he found unbearable. Depending on the ups and downs of his malady he alarmed his friends, who dreaded and longed for the moment when the writer would suddenly appear in their drawing rooms long after midnight – 'brisé de fatigue' and for just five minutes, as he said – only to stay till the gray of dawn, too tired to get out of his chair or interrupt his conversation. Even as a writer of letters he extracted the most singular effects from his ailment. 'The wheezing of my breath is drowning out the sounds of my pen and of a bath which is being drawn on the floor below.' But that is not all, nor is the fact that his sickness removed him from fashionable living. This asthma became part of his art – if indeed his art did not create it. Proust's syntax rhythmically, step by step, enacts his fear of suffocating. And his ironic, philosophical, didactic reflections invariably are the deep breath with which he shakes off the crushing weight of memories. On a larger scale, however, the threatening, suffocating crisis was death, which he was constantly aware of, most of all while he was writing. This is how death confronted Proust, and long before his illness assumed critical dimensions – not as a hypochondriacal whim, but as a 'réalité nouvelle,' that new reality whose reflections on things and people are the marks of aging. A physiology of style would take us into the innermost core of this creativeness. No one who knows with what great tenacity memories are preserved by the sense of smell – but by smells that are not at all in the memory – will be able to call Proust's sensitivity to smells accidental. To be sure, most memories that we search for come to us as images of faces. Even the free-floating forms of *la mémoire involontaire* are still in large part isolated – though enigmatically present – images of faces. For this very reason, anyone who wishes to surrender knowingly to the innermost sway of this work must place himself in a special stratum – the bottommost – of this involuntary remembrance, a stratum in which the materials of memory no longer appear singly, as images, but tell us about a whole, amorphously and formlessly, indefinitely and weightily, in the same way the weight of the fishing net tells a fisherman about his catch. Smell – this is the sense of weight experienced by someone who casts his nets into the sea of the *temps perdu*. And his sentences are the entire muscular activity of the intelligible body; they contain the whole enormous effort to raise this catch.

For the rest, the closeness of the symbiosis between this particular creativity and this particular illness is demonstrated most clearly by the fact that in Proust there never was a breakthrough of that heroic defiance with which other creative people have risen up against their infirmities. And therefore one can say, from another point of view, that so close a complicity with life and the course of the world as Proust's would inevitably have led to ordinary, indolent contentment on any basis but that of such great and constant suffering. As it was, however, this illness was destined to have its place in the great work process – a place assigned to it by a furor devoid of desires or regrets. For the second time, there arose a scaffold like the one on which Michelangelo, his head thrown back, painted the Creation on the ceiling of the Sistine Chapel: the sickbed on which Marcel Proust held aloft the countless pages covered with his handwriting, dedicating them to the creation of his microcosm.

Published in *Die literarische Welt*, June – July 1929; revised 1934. *Gesammelte Schriften*, II, 310–324. Translated by Harry Zohn.

NOTES

1. 'The incurable imperfection in the very essence of the present.'
2. The *Almanach de Gotha* is a journal that chronicles the social activities of the French aristocracy.
3. Henri de Régnier (1864–1936) was a prominent French poet. Ernest Renan (1823–92) was a French philosopher, historian, and scholar of religion. Louis de Rouvroy, duc de Saint-Simon (1675–1755), was a soldier, statesman, and writer, whose *Mémoires* depict the French court under Louis XIV and Louis XV.
4. Maurice Barrès (1862–1923) was a French writer and politician whose individualism and nationalism were influential in the early twentieth century. The phrase translates: 'A Persian poet in a porter's lodge.'
5. The *camorra* was a secret Italian criminal society that arose in Naples in the nineteenth century.
6. 'Ah! How big the world is by lamplight, / But how small in the eyes of memory!' Charles Baudelaire, 'Le Voyage.'
7. Charles Péguy (1873–1914) was a French poet and philosopher whose work brought together Christianity, socialism, and French nationalism.

PART II
POSITIONINGS

SECTION 4
COLLECTIVE MEMORY

Edited by Michael Rossington

INTRODUCTION

Michael Rossington

Within the disciplines of sociology, history and cultural theory, the phrase 'collective memory' proposes that practices of remembrance are shaped and reinforced by the societies and cultures in which they occur. It needs to be acknowledged immediately that the view that memory-practices are 'schooled' and that the faculty of memory has an ethical function within the polity is nothing new. These ideas are central to classical, medieval and early modern European thought, as has been demonstrated in Part I, Section 1. However, the twentieth-century and contemporary preoccupation with 'cultural' as opposed to, or in dialogue with, 'individual' memory may be seen as a response to some influential late nineteenth- and early twentieth-century literary, philosophical and psychological expositions of the nature of recollection. Wordsworth's auto-biographical poem, *The Prelude*, Proust's *Remembrance of Things Past*, the philosophy of Henri Bergson, Freud's psychoanalysis, profoundly attentive though they are to the behaviour and influence of groups, have often been read in such a way as to encourage a view of recollection as a solitary act. By contrast, ways of remembering and giving significance to what is remembered are, in the extracts in this section, seen to be fostered and shared by family, religion, class, the media and other sources of the creation of group identities, referred to by Pierre Bourdieu as 'habitus' or 'systems of dispositions' (Bourdieu, 1984: 6). In these accounts, then, 'individual' turns out to be inseparable from 'collective' remembrance. Moreover, collective memory occupies an important function, distinct from history, in conceiving of a society's past.

The career of **Maurice Halbwachs** (1877–1945), in its transition from pupil of Bergson to protégé of Émile Durkheim and his nephew Marcel Mauss, marks out a disciplinary shift from the cognitive preoccupations of philosophy and psychology to the cultural concerns of sociology and anthropology. In introducing Halbwachs' work on memory, Mary Douglas defines this move by remarking that time in the work of Durkheim and Mauss is presented 'not as an intuition, but as a social construct' (Halbwachs, 1980: 6). In his first major work on the social structures of remembrance, *Les cadres sociaux de la mémoire* (1925), Halbwachs argued that, 'The individual calls recollections to mind by relying on the frameworks of social memory' (Halbwachs, 1992: 182). His later work, *La Mémoire collective* (1950), from which the extract below is taken, was prepared in his last years and published posthumously (he was deported from France during the Second World War and died in Buchenwald). In it, he explores the collective and multiple aspect of the frameworks of social memory and contrasts such frameworks with the singular principle of 'history': 'History can be represented as the universal memory of the human species. But there is no universal memory. Every collective memory requires the support of a group delimited in space and time' (this volume, p. 143). As is demonstrated in the two further extracts in this section, Halbwachs' work is important as a context for recent thinking about commemoration and public memory. He attends to the *milieux* in which remembering takes place, and to those aspects of time – loosely described under the rubric of 'tradition' – which History ignores, 'when nothing apparently happens, when life is content with repetition in a somewhat different, but essentially unaltered, form without rupture or upheaval' (Halbwachs, 1980: 85).

The extracts from the essay, 'Between Memory and History: *Les Lieux de Mémoire*' by the French historian, **Pierre Nora**, extend and refine Halbwachs' argument that there is a distinction between the understanding of time in collective memory and history. Nora's essay functions as a 'theoretical introduction' (Nora, 1989: 25) to a multi-volume collaborative project directed by him on the national memory of France, *Les Lieux de Mémoire* (1984–92), selections from which are published in two complementary English translations undertaken by American publishers (Nora, 1996–98 and Nora, 2001–). Nora's essay begins with 'the disappearance of peasant culture, that quintessential repository of memory' and its supplanting in post-industrialised France by what he describes as '"the acceleration of history"', inaugurated by the State and French historiography itself in the nineteenth and twentieth centuries (this volume, pp. 144–5). *Lieux de Mémoire* 'originate with the sense that there is no spontaneous memory, that we must deliberately create archives, maintain anniversaries, organize celebrations . . . because such activities no longer occur naturally'. Sites of memory, then, testify to a residual compulsion to commemorate within a 'fallen' – that is, secularised and amnesiac – modern world, hence his poetical description of them as, 'no longer quite life, not yet death, like shells on the shore when the sea of living memory has receded' (this volume, p. 149). In addition to its acknowledged debt to Halbwachs, Nora's essay may be located in other contexts too. First, as part of an investigation of national identity it may be seen usefully, as Lawrence D. Kritzman suggests, alongside the concept of 'the "imaginary communities" binding national memory' in the work of Benedict Anderson, included in Part III, Section 8 (Nora, 1996–98: I, ix). Secondly, it is an innovative historiographical enterprise which critiques prevailing models of French national history-writing. In this regard, Nora's reference to a formative childhood awareness of his own distinctive Frenchness seems relevant:

> When I was not yet ten years old, the war started, with the stunning spectacle of national collapse and the humiliation of foreign occupation. And since I was Jewish, I experienced exclusion, pursuit, the discovery of solidarities as unforeseen as the betrayals, and refuge with the Maquis in the Vercors. It was an adventure inscribed in the flesh of memory, sufficient to make you different from all other French children of your age. (Nora, 2001: vii)

Thirdly, the concept of *Lieux de Mémoire* is indebted explicitly to the exploration of the significance of *loci memoriae*, or 'memory places' in medieval thought in Yates' *The Art of Memory*, included in Part I, Section 1 (Nora, 1989: 25). Finally, the principles underlying Nora's project may be brought into dialogue with the role of memory in Walter Benjamin's radical critique of history as well as with the contemplation of time more generally in Benjamin's work (see Part I, Section 3). Benjamin's reflections on the sadness of *acedia* (in 'Theses on the Philosophy of History'), for example, come to mind in the nostalgic resonance of the concept of *Lieux de Mémoire* which has prompted Kritzman to comment that 'Nora's new reading of history uncovers the symptomology of a certain French *fin de siècle* melancholia' (Nora, 1996–98: I, xiii). Nora's theories have been important to recent assessments of Holocaust memorials (e.g. Young, 1993) and to literary studies of remembering (e.g. Clingham, 2002).

However, Nora has been challenged for overlooking uncomfortable aspects of Frenchness and the French past within his project. Perry Anderson, for example, has sharply criticized his enterprise as 'the erudition of patriotic appeasement', arguing that 'the entire imperial history of the country . . . becomes a *non-lieu* at the bar of these bland recollections . . . What are the *lieux de mémoire* that fail to include Dien Bien Phu? [Dien Bien Phu is the site, in Vietnam, of a battle fought against the Viets by the French in 1954]' (Anderson, 2004b: 10). In this regard, it is worth noting that the excavation of a site of colonial memory, Port Arthur in Tasmania, has been undertaken rewardingly by **John Frow** (Frow, 2000). Frow's essay which concludes this section (Frow, 1997), begins with a summary (not included here) of Nora's 'Between Memory and History' before criticising his association of memory with immediacy, organicism and the sacred. Like Anderson, Frow takes issue with what he sees as the elegiac character of Nora's memorialising project. Instead, Frow advocates a method which recognises that 'script and print have been of paramount importance in shaping memory and thought' (Frow, 1997:

243). Using Mary J. Carruthers's work on medieval mnemotechnics in support (see Part I, Section 1), he argues that, 'it is only by working out the implications of "writing" . . . for memory that we can avoid the nostalgic essentialism that affirms the reality of an origin by proclaiming its loss' (this volume, pp. 151–2). In another part of the essay not included here, Frow develops his argument with reference to recent controversies over recovered memories of childhood sexual abuse (so-called 'False Memory Syndrome') and to memoirs of the Holocaust. His essay ends with a meditation on an open-ended project, *Je me souviens* (1978), by the novelist Georges Perec, at the close of which the reader is invited to add to the author's list of shared memories. Frow sees Perec's book as constructing a 'domain of public memory' (Frow, 1997: 244). In this domain, the relationship between 'public history' and 'private memory' elaborated in the sociological and historical work on 'collective memory' by Halbwachs and Nora is reconceived through the explicit invocation of a textual practice in which the reader is asked to participate. The case for seeing 'collective memory', then, as, at root, a dimension of literary, or literary-cultural, studies is thereby advanced.

REFERENCES AND FURTHER READING

Anderson, Perry (2004a) 'Dégringolade', *London Review of Books*, 2 September, pp. 3–9.

—— (2004b) 'Union Sucrée', *London Review of Books*, 23 September, pp. 10–16.

Assmann, Jan ([1988] 1995) 'Collective Memory and Cultural Identity', trans. John Czaplicka, *New German Critique*, 65: 125–33.

Bourdieu, Pierre (1984) *Distinction: A Social Critique of the Judgement of Taste*, trans. Richard Nice. London: Routledge & Kegan Paul.

Clingham, Greg (2002) *Johnson, Writing, and Memory*. Cambridge: Cambridge University Press.

Connerton, Paul (1989) *How Societies Remember*. Cambridge: Cambridge University Press.

Davis, Natalie Zemon and Randolph Starn (eds) (1989) 'Memory and Counter-Memory', Special Issue, *Representations*, 26.

Frow, John (1997) '*Toute la mémoire du monde*: Repetition and Forgetting', in *Time and Commodity Culture: Essays in Cultural Theory and Postmodernity*. Oxford: Clarendon Press, pp. 218–46.

—— (2000) 'In the Penal Colony', in Michael Rossington and Anne Whitehead (eds), *Between the Psyche and the Polis: Refiguring History in Literature and Theory*. Aldershot and Burlington, VT: Ashgate, pp. 123–42.

Funkenstein, Amos (1989) 'Collective Memory and Historical Consciousness', *History and Memory*, 1(1): 5–26.

Halbwachs, Maurice ([1950] 1980) *The Collective Memory*, trans. Francis J. Ditter, Jr, and Vida Yazdi Ditter, intro. Mary Douglas. New York: Harper & Row.

—— (1992) *On Collective Memory*, ed., trans. and intro. Lewis A. Coser. Chicago and London: University of Chicago Press.

Kansteiner, Wulf (2002) 'Finding Meaning in Memory: A Methodological Critique of Collective Memory Studies', *History and Theory*, 41: 179–97.

Nora, Pierre ([1984] 1997) 'Entre Mémoire et Histoire: La problématique des lieux', in *Les Lieux de Mémoire*, Vol. 1. Paris: Éditions Gallimard, pp. 23–43.

—— (1989) 'Between Memory and History: *Les Lieux de Mémoire*', trans. Marc Roudebush, *Representations*, 26: 7–25.

Nora, Pierre (1996) 'From *Lieux de mémoire* to Realms of Memory' and 'General Introduction: Between Memory and History', in *Realms of Memory: Rethinking the French Past*, English Language Edition, ed. and Foreword Lawrence D. Kritzman, trans. Arthur Goldhammer, 3 vols. New York: Columbia University Press, 1996–8, I , xv–xxiv, pp. 1–20.

—— (2001) 'General Introduction', trans. Richard C. Holbrook, *Rethinking France: Les Lieux de Mémoire*, Vol. 1: The State, trans. Mary Trouille. Chicago and London: University of Chicago Press, pp. vii–xxii.

Novick, Peter (1999) *The Holocaust and Collective Memory: The American Experience*. London: Bloomsbury.

Samuel, Raphael (1994, 1998) *Theatres of Memory*, 2 vols. London: Verso.

Sennett, Richard (1998) 'Disturbing Memories', in Patricia Fara and Karalyn Patterson (eds), *Memory*. Cambridge: Cambridge University Press, pp. 10–26.

Wertsch, James V. (2002) *Voices of Collective Remembering*. Cambridge: Cambridge University Press.

Wood, Nancy (1999) *Vectors of Memory: Legacies of Trauma in Postwar Europe*. Oxford: Berg.

Young, James E. (1993) *The Texture of Memory: Holocaust Memorials and Meaning*. New Haven, CT and London: Yale University Press.

Zelizer, Barbie (1992) *Covering the Body: The Kennedy Assassination, the Media, and the Shaping of Collective Memory*. Chicago: University of Chicago Press.

MAURICE HALBWACHS: *FROM* THE COLLECTIVE MEMORY

The Ultimate Opposition Between Collective Memory and History

The collective memory is not the same as formal history, and 'historical memory' is a rather unfortunate expression because it connects two terms opposed in more than one aspect. [. . .] Undoubtedly, history is a collection of the most notable facts in the memory of man. But past events read about in books and taught and learned in schools are selected, combined, and evaluated in accord with necessities and rules not imposed on the groups that had through time guarded them as a living trust. General history starts only when tradition ends and the social memory is fading or breaking up. So long as a remembrance continues to exist, it is useless to set it down in writing or otherwise fix it in memory. Likewise the need to write the history of a period, a society, or even a person is only aroused when the subject is already too distant in the past to allow for the testimony of those who preserve some remembrance of it. The memory of a sequence of events may no longer have the support of a group: the memory of involvement in the events or of enduring their consequences, of participating in them or receiving a firsthand account from participants and witnesses, may become scattered among various individuals, lost amid new groups for whom these facts no longer have interest because the events are definitely external to them. When this occurs, the only means of preserving such remembrances is to write them down in a coherent narrative, for the writings

---

Source: Maurice Halbwachs, *The Collective Memory* [1950], trans. Francis J. Ditter, Jr and Vida Yazdi Ditter, intro. Mary Douglas (New York: Harper Colophon Books, 1980), pp. 78–84.

remain even though the thought and the spoken word die. If a memory exists only when the remembering subject, individual or group, feels that it goes back to its remembrances in a continuous movement, how could history ever be a memory, since there is a break in continuity between the society reading this history and the group in the past who acted in or witnessed the events?

Of course, one purpose of history might just be to bridge the gap between past and present, restoring this ruptured continuity. But how can currents of collective thought whose impetus lies in the past be re-created, when we can grasp only the present? Through detailed study historians can recover and bring to light facts of varying importance believed to be definitely lost, especially if they have the good fortune to discover unpublished memoirs. Nevertheless, when the *Mémoires de Saint-Simon*, for example, were published at the beginning of the nineteenth century, could it be said that French society of 1830 regained contact, a living and direct contact, with the end of the seventeenth century and the time of the Regency? What passed from these memoirs into the basic histories, which have a readership sufficiently widespread to really influence collective opinions? The only effect of such publications is to make us understand how distant we are from those who are doing the writing and being described. The barriers separating us from such a period are not overcome by scattered individuals merely devoting much time and effort to such reading. The study of history in this sense is reserved only for a few specialists. Even were there a group devoted to reading the *Mémoires de Saint-Simon*, it would be much too small to affect public opinion.

History wanting to keep very close to factual details must become erudite, and erudition is the affair of only a very small minority. By contrast, if history is restricted to preserving the image of the past still having a place in the contemporary collective memory, then it retains only what remains of interest to present-day society – that is, very little.

Collective memory differs from history in at least two respects. It is a current of continuous thought whose continuity is not at all artificial, for it retains from the past only what still lives or is capable of living in the consciousness of the groups keeping the memory alive. By definition it does not exceed the boundaries of this group. When a given period ceases to interest the subsequent period, the same group has not forgotten a part of its past, because, in reality, there are two successive groups, one following the other. History divides the sequence of centuries into periods, just as the content of a tragedy is divided into several acts. But in a play the same plot is carried from one act to another and the same characters remain true to form to the end, their feelings and emotions developing in an unbroken movement. History, however, gives the impression that everything – the interplay of interests, general orientations, modes of studying men and events, traditions, and perspectives on the future – is transformed from one period to another. The apparent persistence of the same groups merely reflects the persistence of external distinctions resulting from places, names, and the general character of societies. But the men composing the same group in two successive periods are like two tree stumps that touch at their extremities but do not form one plant because they are not otherwise connected.

Of course, reason sufficient to partition the succession of generations at any given moment is not immediately evident, because the number of births hardly varies from year to year. Society is like a thread that is made from a series of animal or vegetable fibers intertwined at regular intervals; or, rather, it resembles the cloth made from weaving these threads together. The sections of a cotton or silk fabric correspond to the end of a motif or design. Is it the same for the sequence of generations?

Situated external to and above groups, history readily introduces into the stream of facts simple demarcations fixed once and for all. In doing so, history not merely obeys a didactic need for schematization. Each period is apparently considered a whole, independent for the most part of those preceding and following, and having some task – good, bad, or indifferent – to accomplish. Young and old, regardless of age, are encompassed within the same perspective so long as this task has not yet been completed, so long as certain national, political, or religious situations have not yet realized their full implications. As soon as this task is finished and a new one proposed or imposed, ensuing generations start down a new slope, so to speak. Some people were left behind on the opposite side of the mountain, having never made it up. But the young, who hurry as if fearful of missing the boat, sweep along a portion of the older adults. By contrast, those who are located at the beginning of either slope down, even if they are very near the crest, do not see each other any better and they remain as ignorant of one another as they would be were they further down on their respective slope. The farther they are located down their respective slope, the farther they are placed into the past or what is no longer the past; or, alternatively, the more distant they are from one another on the sinuous line of time.

Some parts of this portrait are accurate. Viewed as a whole from afar and, especially, viewed from without by the spectator who never belonged to the groups he observes, the facts may allow such an arrangement into successive and distinct configurations, each period having a beginning, middle, and end. But just as history is interested in differences and contrasts, and highlights the diverse features of a group by concentrating them in an individual, it similarly attributes to an interval of a few years changes that in reality took much longer. Another period of society might conceivably begin on the day after an event had disrupted, partially destroyed, and transformed its structure. But only later, when the new society had already engendered new resources and pushed on to other goals, would this fact be noticed. The historian cannot take these demarcations seriously. He cannot imagine them to have been noted by those who lived during the years so demarcated, in the manner of the character in the farce who exclaims, 'Today the Hundred Years War begins!' A war or revolution may create a great chasm between two generations, as if an intermediate generation had just disappeared. In such a case, who can be sure that, on the day after, the youth of society will not be primarily concerned, as the old will be, with erasing any traces of that rupture, reconciling separated generations and maintaining, in spite of everything, continuity of social evolution? Society must live. Even when institutions are radically transformed, and especially then, the best means of making them take root is to buttress them with everything transferable from tradition. Then, on the day after the crisis, everyone affirms that they must begin again at the point of interruption, that they must pick up the pieces and carry on. Sometimes nothing is considered changed, for the thread of continuity has been retied. Although soon rejected, such an illusion allows transition to the new phase without any feeling that the collective memory has been interrupted.

In reality, the continuous development of the collective memory is marked not, as is history, by clearly etched demarcations but only by irregular and uncertain boundaries. The present (understood as extending over a certain duration that is of interest to contemporary society) is not contrasted to the past in the way two neighboring historical periods are distinguished. Rather, the past no longer exists, whereas, for the historian, the two periods have equivalent reality. The memory of a society extends as far as the memory of the groups composing it. Neither ill will nor indifference causes it to forget so many past events and personages. Instead, the groups keeping these remembrances fade away. Were the duration of human life doubled or tripled, the scope of the collective memory as measured in units of time would be more extensive. Nevertheless, such an enlarged memory might well lack richer content if so much tradition were to hinder its evolution. Similarly, were human life shorter, a collective memory covering a lesser duration might never grow impoverished because change might accelerate a society 'unburdened' in this way. In any case, since social memory erodes at the edges as individual members, especially older ones, become isolated or die, it is constantly transformed along with the group itself. Stating when a collective remembrance has disappeared and whether it has definitely left group consciousness is difficult, especially since its recovery only requires its preservation in some limited portion of the social body.

HISTORY, RECORD OF EVENTS; COLLECTIVE MEMORY, DEPOSITORY OF TRADITION

In effect, there are several collective memories. This is the second characteristic distinguishing the collective memory from history. History is unitary, and it can be said that there is only one history. Let me explain what I mean. Of course, we can distinguish the history of France, Germany, Italy, the history of a certain period, region, or city, and even that of an individual. Sometimes historical work is even reproached for its excessive specialization and fanatic desire for detailed study that neglects the whole and in some manner takes the part for the whole. But let us consider this matter more closely. The historian justifies these detailed studies by believing that detail added to detail will form a whole that can in turn be added to other wholes; in the total record resulting from all these successive summations, no fact will be subordinated to any other fact, since every fact is as interesting as any other and merits as much to be brought forth and recorded. Now the historian can make such judgments because he is not located within the viewpoint of any genuine and living groups of past or present. In contrast to the historian, these groups are far from affording equal significance to events, places, and periods that have not affected them equally. But the historian certainly means to be objective and impartial. Even when writing the history of his own country, he tries to synthesize a set of facts comparable with some other set, such as the history of another country, so as to avoid any break in continuity. Thus, in the total record of European history, the comparison of the various national viewpoints on the facts is never found; what is found, rather, is the sequence and totality of the facts such as they are, not for a certain country or a certain group but independent of any group judgment. The very divisions that separate countries are historical facts of the same value as any others in such a record. All, then, is on the same level. The historical world is like an ocean fed by the many partial histories. Not surprisingly, many historians in every period since the beginning of historical writing have considered writing universal histories. Such is the natural orientation of the historical mind. Such is the fatal course along which every historian would be swept were he not restricted to the framework of more limited works by either modesty or short-windedness.

Of course, the muse of history is Clio. History can be represented as the universal memory of the human species. But there is no universal memory. Every collective memory requires the support of a group delimited in space and time. The totality of past events can be put together in a single record only by separating them from the memory of the groups who preserved them and by severing the bonds that held them close to the psychological life of the social milieus where they occurred, while retaining only the group's chronological and spatial outline of them. This procedure no longer entails restoring them to lifelike reality, but requires relocating them within the frameworks with which history organizes events. These frameworks are external to these groups and define them by mutual contrast. That is, history is interested primarily in differences and disregards the resemblances without which there would have been no memory, since the only facts remembered are those having the common trait of belonging to the same consciousness. Despite the variety of times and places, history reduces events to seemingly comparable terms, allowing their interrelation as variations on one or several themes. Only in this way does it manage to give us a summary vision of the past, gathering into a moment and symbolizing in a few abrupt changes or in certain stages undergone by a people or individual, a slow collective evolution. In this way it presents us a unique and total image of the past.

PIERRE NORA: *FROM* BETWEEN MEMORY AND HISTORY: *LES LIEUX DE MÉMOIRE*

The acceleration of history: let us try to gauge the significance, beyond metaphor, of this phrase. An increasingly rapid slippage of the present into a historical past that is gone for good, a general perception that anything and everything may disappear – these indicate a rupture of equilibrium. The remnants of experience still lived in the warmth of tradition, in the silence of custom, in the repetition of the ancestral, have been displaced under the pressure of a fundamentally historical sensibility. Self-consciousness emerges under the sign of that which has already happened, as the fulfillment of something always already begun. We speak so much of memory because there is so little of it left.

Our interest in *lieux de mémoire* where memory crystallizes and secretes itself has occurred at a particular historical moment, a turning point where consciousness of a break with the past is bound up with the sense that memory has been torn – but torn in such a way as to pose the problem of the embodiment of memory in certain sites where a sense of historical continuity persists. There are *lieux de mémoire*, sites of memory, because there are no longer *milieux de mémoire*, real environments of memory.

Consider, for example, the irrevocable break marked by the disappearance of peasant culture, that quintessential repository of collective memory whose recent vogue as an object of historical study coincided with the apogee of industrial growth. Such a fundamental collapse of memory is but one familiar

Source: Pierre Nora, 'Between Memory and History: *Les Lieux de Mémoire*', trans. Marc Roudebush, in *Representations*, No. 26, Special Issue: Memory and Counter-Memory (Spring 1989), pp. 7–12.

example of a movement toward democratization and mass culture on a global scale. Among the new nations, independence has swept into history societies newly awakened from their ethnological slumbers by colonial violation. Similarly, a process of interior decolonization has affected ethnic minorities, families, and groups that until now have possessed reserves of memory but little or no historical capital. We have seen the end of societies that had long assured the transmission and conservation of collectively remembered values, whether through churches or schools, the family or the state; the end too of ideologies that prepared a smooth passage from the past to the future or that had indicated what the future should keep from the past – whether for reaction, progress, or even revolution. Indeed, we have seen the tremendous dilation of our very mode of historical perception, which, with the help of the media, has substituted for a memory entwined in the intimacy of a collective heritage the ephemeral film of current events.

The 'acceleration of history,' then, confronts us with the brutal realization of the difference between real memory – social and unviolated, exemplified in but also retained as the secret of so-called primitive or archaic societies – and history, which is how our hopelessly forgetful modern societies, propelled by change, organize the past. On the one hand, we find an integrated, dictatorial memory – unself-conscious, commanding, all-powerful, spontaneously actualizing, a memory without a past that ceaselessly reinvents tradition, linking the history of its ancestors to the undifferentiated time of heroes, origins, and myth – and on the other hand, our memory, nothing more in fact than sifted and sorted historical traces. The gulf between the two has deepened in modern times with the growing belief in a right, a capacity, and even a duty to change. Today, this distance has been stretched to its convulsive limit.

This conquest and eradication of memory by history has had the effect of a revelation, as if an ancient bond of identity had been broken and something had ended that we had experienced as self-evident – the equation of memory and history. The fact that only one word exists in French to designate both lived history and the intellectual operation that renders it intelligible (distinguished in German by *Geschichte and Historie*) is a weakness of the language that has often been remarked; still, it delivers a profound truth: the process that is carrying us forward and our representation of that process are of the same kind. If we were able to live within memory, we would not have needed to consecrate *lieux de mémoire* in its name. Each gesture, down to the most everyday, would be experienced as the ritual repetition of a timeless practice in a primordial identification of act and meaning. With the appearance of the trace, of mediation, of distance, we are not in the realm of true memory but of history. We can think, for an example, of the Jews of the diaspora, bound in daily devotion to the rituals of tradition, who as 'peoples of memory' found little use for historians until their forced exposure to the modern world.

Memory and history, far from being synonymous, appear now to be in fundamental opposition. Memory is life, borne by living societies founded in its name. It remains in permanent evolution, open to the dialectic of remembering and forgetting, unconscious of its successive deformations, vulnerable to manipulation and appropriation, susceptible to being long dormant and peri- odically revived. History, on the other hand, is the reconstruction, always problematic and incomplete, of what is no longer. Memory is a perpetually actual phenomenon, a bond tying us to the eternal present; history is a repre- sentation of the past. Memory, insofar as it is affective and magical, only accommodates those facts that suit it; it nourishes recollections that may be out of focus or telescopic, global or detached, particular or symbolic – responsive to each avenue of conveyance or phenomenal screen, to every censorship or projection. History, because it is an intellectual and secular production, calls for analysis and criticism. Memory installs remembrance within the sacred; history, always prosaic, releases it again. Memory is blind to all but the group it binds – which is to say, as Maurice Halbwachs has said, that there are as many memories as there are groups, that memory is by nature multiple and yet specific; collective, plural, and yet individual. History, on the other hand, belongs to everyone and to no one, whence its claim to universal authority. Memory takes root in the concrete, in spaces, gestures, images, and objects; history binds itself strictly to temporal continuities, to progressions and to relations between things. Memory is absolute, while history can only conceive the relative.

At the heart of history is a critical discourse that is antithetical to spontaneous memory. History is perpetually suspicious of memory, and its true mission is to suppress and destroy it. At the horizon of historical societies, at the limits of the completely historicized world, there would occur a permanent secularization. History's goal and ambition is not to exalt but to annihilate what has in reality taken place. A generalized critical history would no doubt preserve some museums, some medallions and monuments – that is to say, the materials necessary for its work – but it would empty them of what, to us, would make them *lieux de mémoire*. In the end, a society living wholly under the sign of history could not, any more than could a traditional society, conceive such sites for anchoring its memory.

Perhaps the most tangible sign of the split between history and memory has been the emergence of a history of history, the awakening, quite recent in France, of a historiographical consciousness. History, especially the history of national development, has constituted the oldest of our collective traditions: our quint- essential *milieu de mémoire*. From the chroniclers of the Middle Ages to today's practitioners of 'total' history, the entire tradition has developed as the controlled exercise and automatic deepening of memory, the reconstitution of a past without lacunae or faults. No doubt, none of the great historians, since Froissart, had the sense that he was representing only a particular memory. Commynes did not think he was fashioning a merely dynastic memory, La Popelinière merely a French memory, Bossuet a Christian and monarchical memory, Voltaire the memory of the progress of humankind, Michelet exclusively the 'people's' memory, and Lavisse solely the memory of the nation. On the contrary, each historian was convinced that his task consisted in establishing a more positive, all-encompassing, and explicative memory. History's procurement, in the last century, of scientific methodology has only intensified the effort to establish critically a 'true' memory. Every great historical revision has sought to enlarge the basis for collective memory.

In a country such as France the history of history cannot be an innocent operation; it amounts to the internal subversion of memory-history by critical history. Every history is by nature critical, and all historians have sought to denounce the hypocritical mythologies of their predecessors. But something fundamentally unsettling happens when history begins to write its own history. A historiographical anxiety arises when history assigns itself the task of tracing alien impulses within itself and discovers that it is the victim of memories which it has sought to master. Where history has not taken on the strong formative and didactic role that it has assumed in France, the history of history is less laden with polemical content. In the United States, for example, a country of plural memories and diverse traditions, historiography is more pragmatic. Different interpretations of the Revolution or of the Civil War do not threaten the American tradition because, in some sense, no such thing exists – or if it does, it is not primarily a historical construction. In France, on the other hand, historiography is iconoclastic and irreverent. It seizes upon the most clearly defined objections of tradition – a key battle, like Bouvines; a canonical manual, like the *Petit Lavisse* – in order to dismantle their mechanisms and analyze the conditions of their development. It operates primarily by introducing doubt, by running a knife between the tree of memory and the bark of history. That we study the historiography of the French Revolution, that we reconstitute its myths and interpretations, implies that we no longer unquestioningly identify with its heritage. To interrogate a tradition, venerable though it may be, is no longer to pass it on intact. Moreover, the history of history does not restrict itself to addressing the most sacred objects of our national tradition. By questioning its own traditional structure, its own conceptual and material resources, its operating procedures and social means of distribution, the entire discipline of history has entered its historiographical age, consummating its dissociation from memory – which in turn has become a possible object of history.

It once seemed as though a tradition of memory, through the concepts of history and the nation, had crystallized in the synthesis of the Third Republic. Adopting a broad chronology, between Augustin Thierry's *Lettres sur l'histoire de France* (1827) and Charles Seignobos's *Histoire sincère de la nation française* (1933), the relationships between history, memory, and the nation were characterized as more than natural currency: they were shown to involve a reciprocal circularity, a symbiosis at every level – scientific and pedagogical, theoretical and practical. This national definition of the present imperiously demanded justification through the illumination of the past. It was, however, a present that had been weakened by revolutionary trauma and the call for a general reevaluation of the monarchical past, and it was weakened further by the defeat of 1870, which rendered only more urgent, in the belated competition with German science and pedagogy – the real victors at Sadowa – the development of a severe documentary erudition for the scholarly transmission of memory. The tone of national responsibility assigned to the historian – half preacher, half soldier – is unequalled, for example, in the first editorial of the *Revue historique* (1876) in which Gabriel Monod foresaw a 'slow scientific, methodical, and collective investigation' conducted in a 'secret and secure manner for the greatness of the fatherland as well as for mankind.' Reading this text, and a hundred others like it, one wonders how the notion that positivist history was not cumulative could ever have gained credibility. On the contrary, in the teleological perspective of the nation the political, the military, the biographical, and the diplomatic all were to be considered pillars of continuity. The defeat of Agincourt, the dagger of Ravaillac, the day of the Dupes, the additional clauses of the treaty of Westphalia – each required scrupulous accounting. The most incisive erudition thus served to add or take away some detail from the monumental edifice that was the nation. The nation's memory was held to be powerfully unified; no more discontinuity existed between our Greco-Roman cradle and the colonies of the Third Republic than between the high erudition that annexed new territories to the nation's heritage and the schoolbooks that professed its dogma. The holy nation thus acquired a holy history; through the nation our memory continued to rest upon a sacred foundation.

To see how this particular synthesis came apart under the pressure of a new secularizing force would be to show how, during the crisis of the 1930s in France, the coupling of state and nation was gradually replaced by the coupling of state and society – and how, at the same time and for the same reasons, history was transformed, spectacularly, from the tradition of memory it had become into the self-knowledge of society. As such, history was able to highlight many kinds of memory, even turn itself into a laboratory of past mentalities; but in disclaiming its national identity, it also abandoned its claim to bearing coherent meaning and consequently lost its pedagogical authority to transmit values. The definition of the nation was no longer the issue, and peace, prosperity, and the reduction of its power have since accomplished the rest. With the advent of society in place of the nation, legitimation by the past and therefore by history yields to legitimation by the future. One can only acknowledge and venerate the past and serve the nation; the future, however, can be prepared for: thus the three terms regain their autonomy. No longer a cause, the nation has become a given; history is now a social science, memory a purely private phenomenon. The memory-nation was thus the last incarnation of the unification of memory and history.

The study of *lieux de mémoires*, then, lies at the intersection of two developments that in France today give it meaning: one a purely historiographical movement, the reflexive turning of history upon itself, the other a movement that is, properly speaking, historical: the end of a tradition of memory. The moment of *lieux de mémoire* occurs at the same time that an immense and intimate fund of memory disappears, surviving only as a reconstituted object beneath the gaze of critical history. This period sees, on the one hand, the decisive deepening of historical study and, on the other hand, a heritage consolidated. The critical principle follows an internal dynamic: our intellectual, political, historical frameworks are exhausted but remain powerful enough not to leave us indifferent; whatever vitality they retain impresses us only in their most spectacular symbols. Combined, these two movements send us at once to history's most elementary tools and to the most symbolic objects of our memory: to the archives as well as to the tricolor; to the libraries, dictionaries, and museums as well as to commemorations, celebrations, the Pantheon, and the Arc de Triomphe; to the *Dictionnaire Larousse* as well as to the Wall of the Fédérés where the last defenders of the Paris commune were massacred in 1870.

These *lieux de mémoire* are fundamentally remains, the ultimate embodiments of a memorial consciousness that has barely survived in a historical age that calls out for memory because it has abandoned it. They make their appearance by virtue of the deritualization of our world – producing, manifesting, establishing, constructing, decreeing, and maintaining by artifice and by will a society deeply absorbed in its own transformation and renewal, one that inherently values the new over the ancient, the young over the old, the future over the past. Museums, archives, cemeteries, festivals, anniversaries, treaties, depositions, monuments, sanctuaries, fraternal orders – these are the boundary stones of another age, illusions of eternity. It is the nostalgic dimension of these devotional institutions that makes them seem beleaguered and cold – they mark the rituals of a society without ritual; integral particularities in a society that levels particularity; signs of distinction and of group membership in a society that tends to recognize individuals only as identical and equal.

Lieux de mémoire originate with the sense that there is no spontaneous memory, that we must deliberately create archives, maintain anniversaries, organize celebrations, pronounce eulogies, and notarize bills because such activities no longer occur naturally. The defense, by certain minorities, of a privileged memory that has retreated to jealously protected enclaves in this sense intensely illuminates the truth of *lieux de mémoire* – that without commemorative vigilance, history would soon sweep them away. We buttress our identities upon such bastions, but if what they defended were not threatened, there would be no need to build them. Conversely, if the memories that they enclosed were to be set free they would be useless; if history did not besiege memory, deforming and transforming it, penetrating and petrifying it, there would be no *lieux de mémoire*. Indeed, it is this very push and pull that produces *lieux de mémoire* – moments of history torn away from the movement of history, then returned; no longer quite life, not yet death, like shells on the shore when the sea of living memory has receded.

JOHN FROW: *FROM TOUTE LA MÉMOIRE DU MONDE*: REPETITION AND FORGETTING

I have summarized Nora's argument at some length because it corresponds very precisely and very richly to that form of sociological thinking about modernity that Georg Stauth and Bryan Turner call 'nostalgic'. By this they mean the structuring of sociological thought by a series of contradictions between a realm of authenticity and fullness of being, and the actually existing 'forms of human association'[1] – a contradiction often projected on to a quasi-historical axis as that between modern and traditional societies.

The importance of memory within this paradigm lies not just in the privileged access it gives to this lost world, but in the immediacy with which it evokes it into presence. I mean 'immediacy' here in all of the following senses: memory is thought of as partaking of spirituality independent of the materiality of the sign; it is unstructured by social technologies of learning or recall; it is incapable of reflexivity (it cannot take itself as an object), and its mode of apprehension is thus rooted in the 'inherent self-knowledge' and the 'unstudied reflexes' of the body; it is organically related to its community and partakes of the continuity of tradition – a historical time without rupture or conflict, and without any but the most naturalized modes of transmission, above all that of the story, which 'embeds [an event] in the life of the storyteller in order to pass it on as experience to those listening';[2] this is to say – using Walter Benjamin's categories – that it is a function of deeply embedded experience (*Erfahrung*)

Source: John Frow, '*Toute la mémoire du monde*: Repetition and Forgetting', in *Time and Commodity Culture: Essays in Cultural Theory and Postmodernity* (Oxford: Oxford University Press, 1997), pp. 222–9.

rather than of more or less conscious perception (*Erlebnis*);[3] it is thus – following Benjamin's overlay of Freud's account of memory traces on to Proust's distinction – essentially *mémoire involontaire* rather than *mémoire volontaire*;[4] finally, this memory is *auratic*: it is no accident that much of the vocabulary Nora uses to describe it – that of piety, of ritual, of the relation to the ancestors – is religious, and evokes a continuity of passage between the living and the dead.[5]

This whole manner of thinking of collective memory and of its relation to auto-biographical memory is surely no longer tenable. It is not a useful tool for conceptualizing the social organization of memory; it provides no mechanism for identifying its 'technological' underpinnings; and it cannot account for the materiality of signs and of the representational forms by which memory is structured.

The question of an alternative conception of memory that I want to formulate is this: how can memory be thought as *tekhnè*, as mediation, as writing?

I find a clear statement of the theoretical issues involved in this formulation in Mary Carruthers's work on medieval memory systems (to which I shall return shortly in discussing archival models of memory). Writing against Walter Ong's argument that the invention of print both furthered and depended upon 'a profound reorientation within the human spirit which made it possible to think of all the possessions of the mind, that is, of knowledge and of expression, in terms more committed to space than those of earlier times',[6] and his belief that this movement is closely paralleled by the spatially diagrammed taxonomies of Agricola's and Ramus's place-logics, she refuses the qualitative distinctions he draws between pre- and post-Gutenberg, aural and visual cultures, cultures of the image and of the word, oral cultures of memory and literate cultures of spatialized information storage.[7] The salient fact she points to in medieval thought is that it draws no distinction in kind 'between writing on the memory and writing on some other surface'.[8] Rather than being an external support or implement in relation to memory, the activity of writing is a kind of memorization itself, or at least is intimately bound up with it. Thus, on the one hand, 'the symbolic representations that we call writing are no more than cues or triggers for the memorial "representations". . . upon which human cognition is based'; and, on the other, 'anything that encodes information in order to stimulate the memory to store or retrieve information is "writing", whether it be alphabet, hieroglyph, ideogram, American Indian picture writing, or Inca knot-writing' (pp. 31–2). From the very beginning medieval educators 'had as visual and spatial an idea of *locus* as any Ramist had, which they inherited continuously from antiquity, and indeed that concern for the lay-out of memory governed much in medieval education designed to aid the mind in forming and maintaining heuristic formats that are both spatial and visualizable' (p. 32); medieval mnemotechnic systems *are* a form of writing, and – this is my extrapolation from this argument – it is only by working out the implications of 'writing' (in these senses) for memory that we can avoid the nostalgic essentialism that affirms the reality of an origin by proclaiming its loss.

Let me propose two figures through which to imagine the order and ordering of memory.

The first is a series of versions of the archive (the information storage system), which I summarize in the image of the Bibliothèque Nationale as Resnais films it in his 1957 feature *Toute la mémoire du monde* (a movie that exists for me only as I remember it across a gap of more than twenty years). The camera pans endlessly across the stacks, the storage rooms, the out-of-the-way depositories filled with an infinity of useless and forgotten print; beneath a reedy and distorted voice-over (saying what?) this waste of human memory unfolds its delirium of repetition, its 'leagues of insensate cacophony'.[9] . . . And in a dream embedded within Borges's story 'The Secret Miracle', the librarian of the Clementine library says: ' "God is in one of the letters of one of the pages of one of the 400,000 volumes of the Clementine. My fathers and the fathers of my fathers have sought after that letter. I've gone blind looking for it".'[10]

The logic of the archive is a logic of the inscription (or deposit) and the storage of information in systematically articulated space, and of ready retrieval on the basis of that articulation. The moments of inscription/deposit and of storage correspond to the two major metaphors through which European culture has conceptualized memory over the last two and a half millennia: the metaphor of the surface of inscription, traditionally a wax writing tablet (*tabula rasa*); and that of the *thesaurus* (the storehouse, and its metonyms: the aviary, the storage bin, and the box or cluster of boxes). Both metaphors suppose a direct relation between space and mental categories (Henry Roediger, mapping the history of these metaphors, writes that in each of them 'memories or memory traces are considered to be discrete objects stored in particular locations in the mind space');[11] and both suppose the physical reality of memory traces. Thus for Aristotle the metaphor of storage is a quite literal one: sense perceptions are coded as mental images (*phantasmata*) which are physically inscribed – like the imprint of a signet ring on wax – in distinct sites (*topoi*) in the brain.[12] There is an indexical linkage between the vanished past and its persistent material vestiges in the present. This model, as Mary Carruthers argues, continues to hold sway right through the Middle Ages. The metaphor of writing on wax tablets (a metaphor that captures both the stability and the instability of inscriptions)

> shows that the ancients and their mediaeval heirs thought that each 'bit' of knowledge was remembered in a particular place in the memory, which it occupied as a letter occupies space on a writing surface. The words *topos*, *sedes*, and *locus*, used in writings on logic and rhetoric as well as on mnemonics, refer fundamentally to physical locations in the brain, which are made accessible by means of an ordering system that functions somewhat like a cross between the routing systems used by programs to

store, retrieve, merge, and distinguish the information in a computer's 'memory', and postal addresses or library shelf-marks.[13]

I think it is fair to say that a version of this conception is still the predominant metaphor in contemporary cognitive psychology, although it is now based more explicitly in the model of the electronic storage and random-access retrieval of coded information.[14] I identify the following problems with the model: first, its realism (its assumption that the past is accessible only because of its physical persistence as trace); second, its intentionalism (its assumption that meanings taken up are the repetition of meanings laid down); third, its inability to account for forgetting other than as a fault or as decay or as a random failure of access.[15] It is a model of memory to which forgetting is merely incidental.

Borges's story 'Funes the Memorious' tells of the remembered encounter between the narrator and a young man who, after an accident that leaves him crippled, wakens into a present which is almost intolerable in its brightness and in the vividness and detail of his memory:

> He remembered the shapes of the clouds in the south at dawn on the 30th of April of 1882, and he could compare them in his recollection with the marbled grain in the design of a leather-bound book which he had seen only once, and with the lines in the spray which an oar raised in the Rio Negro on the eve of the battle of the Quebracho.[16]

His memory corresponds fully, in other words, to the infinity of his lived perceptions. But what he knows, therefore, and all he can know, is particulars. Even that impossible idiom imagined by Locke in which each individual object has its own name would be too general for Funes, since he 'not only remembered every leaf on every tree of every wood, but even every one of the times he had perceived or imagined it' (p. 103). He 'could continuously make out the tranquil advances of corruption, of caries, of fatigue. He noted the progress of death, of moisture. He was the solitary and lucid spectator of a multiform world which was instantaneously and almost intolerably exact' (p. 104). But he is almost incapable of simple generalities, and – like Luria's mnemonist, who could remember at a glance extended passages of text, but, unable to sift the significant from the insignificant, had immense difficulty understanding them[17] – Funes, the narrator suspects, 'was not very capable of thought. To think is to forget a difference, to generalize, to abstract. In the overly replete world of Funes there was nothing but details, almost contiguous details' (ibid.).

'Funes'– 'a long metaphor of insomnia', Borges called it[18] – is thus also a kind of allegory of the metaphor of memory as storage. But it is from Borges's stories, from the *structure* of these stories, that I take my second figure of memory.

This second figure is far less easy to cast in a visual form. It is predicated on the non-existence of the past, with the consequence that memory, rather than being the repetition of the physical traces of the past, is a construction of it under conditions and constraints determined by the present. My figure, then, is that of the logic of textuality:[19] a logic of an autonomous narrative order and necessity which takes the form of structural symmetry and the reversibility of time.[20] In Borges's stories this logic is manifested in a number of recurrent motifs: that of the *symmetry* (the reversibility) between duellists, between hero and traitor, between detective and criminal, and the spatial symmetries and mirror-images that organize the stories' *mise-en-scène*; the motif of the *labyrinth* (spatial, textual, or conceptual – the concept of infinity, or that of the *mise-en-abyme*), a structure which is at once fully determined and yet, because of its complexity, necessarily indeterminate; and the motif of *destiny*, the 'future as irrevocable as the past',[21] the textual time which is always-already written but also, because it is endlessly repeated, always reversible. Such a logic of textuality is of course in no way restricted to Borges's stories. In one way or another it is common to all texts, both 'fictional' and 'non-fictional': Borges's stories merely have the merit of making it explicit, sometimes as an object of parody or critique.

Reversibility is here opposed to *retrieval*. The time of textuality is not the linear, before-and-after, cause-and-effect time embedded in the logic of the archive but the time of a continuous analeptic and proleptic shaping. Its structure is that of any dynamic but closed system, where all moments of the system are co-present, and the end is given at the same time as the beginning. In such a model the past is a function of the system: rather than having a meaning and a truth determined once and for all by its status as event, its meaning and its truth are constituted retroactively and repeatedly; if time is reversible then alternative stories are always possible. Data are not stored in already constituted places but are arranged and rearranged at every point in time. Forgetting is thus an integral principle of this model, since the activity of compulsive interpretation that organizes it involves at once selection and rejection. Like a well-censored dream, and subject perhaps to similar mechanisms, memory has the orderliness and the teleological drive of narrative. Its relation to the past is not that of truth but of desire.

NOTES

1. Bryan S. Turner, 'A Note on Nostalgia', *Theory, Culture and Society*, 4: 1 (1987), 151; cf. Georg Stauth and Bryan Turner, 'Nostalgia, Postmodernism and the Critique of Mass Culture', *Theory, Culture and Society*, 5: 2–3 (1988), 509–26.
2. Walter Benjamin, 'On Some Motifs in Baudelaire', *Illuminations*, trans. Harry Zohn (New York: Schocken, 1969), 159; cf. Benjamin, 'The Storyteller', ibid. 98, on the splitting of epic *Erinnerung* into the storyteller's *Gedächtnis* and novelistic *Eingedenken*.
3. Benjamin, 'On Some Motifs in Baudelaire', ibid. 163; my terms are very loose renditions of the concepts by which Benjamin distinguishes between two modes of experience. The English translation of these pages, it should be noted, is somewhat inconsistent.
4. Benjamin, ibid. 159–61; Benjamin adapts Freud's thesis in *Beyond the Pleasure Principle* that 'becoming conscious and leaving behind a memory trace

(*Gedächtnisspur*) are processes incompatible with each other within one and the same system'.

5. Jonathan Boyarin suggests that 'it is all too easy to suspect that the slogan and the multivolume project on "places of memory" work to reinvent 'la France profonde' as a defense against the onslaught within France of Others making claims for their own collective rights and identities'. Jonathan Boyarin, 'Space, Time, and the Politics of Memory', in Jonathan Boyarin (ed.), *Remapping Memory: The Politics of Timespace* (Minneapolis: University of Minnesota Press, 1994), 19.

6. Walter J. Ong, SJ, *Ramus: Method, and the Decay of Dialogue* (Cambridge, Mass.: Harvard University Press, 1958), 308.

7. This is not, of course, to deny the profound changes in the organization of memory brought about by the advent of print; on this, cf. Lucien Febvre and Henri-Jean Martin, *The Coming of the Book: The Impact of Printing, 1450–1800*, trans. David Gerard (London: Verso, 1984); Elizabeth L. Eisenstein, *The Printing Press as an Agent of Change: Communications and Cultural Transformations in Early Modern Europe*, 2 vols (Cambridge: Cambridge University Press, 1979); and Paul Hirst and Penelope Woolley, *Social Relations and Human Attributes* (London: Tavistock, 1982), 37–8.

8. Mary Carruthers, *The Book of Memory: A Study of Memory in Medieval Culture*, Cambridge Studies in Medieval Literature 10 (Cambridge: Cambridge University Press, 1990), 30; further references will be given in the text.

9. Borges, 'The Library of Babel', *Fictions*, 74.

10. Ibid. 134.

11. Henry L. Roediger, 'Memory Metaphors in Cognitive Psychology', *Memory and Cognition*, 8: 3 (1980), 232.

12. Things are more complicated: to paraphrase very briefly a very difficult argument, the central problem posed for Aristotle by memory is the question of how being which has disappeared can persist in memory. The first stage of his solution to this enigma is to posit two figures of representation: the mental image (*phantasma*) inscribed 'in the soul', and the physical trace (*typos* or *graphé*) which supports it but to which it is not reducible, inscribed 'in that part of the body which contains the soul'. Since the question still remains whether what we remember is the past thing or event itself or the image that we have of it, Aristotle then proposes a second stage of his solution, which rests upon the intrinsic ambivalence of the *phantasma*: figured now as a portrait or pictorial representation (*zógraphéma*), it can be read either as an object of contemplation in its own right (*zoion*) or as a likeness or copy (*eikón*) of the thing remembered. For commentary, cf. Richard Sorabji, *Aristotle on Memory* (Providence, RI: Brown University Press, 1972); David Farrell Krell, *Of Memory, Reminiscence, and Writing: On the Verge* (Bloomington: Indiana University Press, 1990), esp. 13–23; Michael V. Wedin, *Mind and Imagination in Aristotle* (New Haven: Yale University Press, 1988).

13. Carruthers, *The Book of Memory*, 29.

14. The classic critique of the notion of recall as 'the re-excitement in some way of fixed and changeless "traces" ' was made by Frederick Bartlett, whose experiments led him to think instead in terms of a process of schematic construction organized by a complex play of interests. Frederick C. Bartlett, *Remembering: A Study in Experimental and Social Psychology* (1932; repr. Cambridge: Cambridge University Press, 1950).

15. Cf. C. W. Kaha, 'Memory as Conversation', *Communication*, 11: 2 (1989), 116–19.

16. Borges, 'Funes the Memorious', *Fictions*, 102; further citations will be given in the text.

17. A. R. Luria, *The Mind of a Mnemonist* (Harmondsworth: Penguin, 1975).

18. Jorge Luis Borges, 'Prologue' to Part Two, *Fictions*, 95.

19. I should distinguish my use of the concept of textuality from that of Fentress and Wickham, for whom a 'textual' model of memory is a model of storage and

retrieval; they contrast it with iconic memory-maps, which they take to be characteristic of pre-literate cultures. James Fentress and Chris Wickham, *Social Memory* (Oxford: Basil Blackwell, 1991), ch. 1.

20. I equate textuality with narrative here only to the extent that any system of inscription is governed by a temporal order which can be read both sequentially and counter-sequentially.

21. Borges, 'The Garden of Forking Paths', *Fictions*, 84.

SECTION 5
JEWISH MEMORY DISCOURSE

Edited by Anne Whitehead

INTRODUCTION

Anne Whitehead

A remarkable number of the leading thinkers of memory of the nineteenth and twentieth centuries were of Jewish origin: Karl Marx, Sigmund Freud, Walter Benjamin, Jacques Derrida, to name but a few. Although not religious in the traditional sense, these thinkers were nevertheless deeply influenced by Jewish beliefs and attitudes. There has been much critical attention paid, in particular, to Benjamin's Jewish Messianism, which is evident in late works such as 'Theses on the Philosophy of History'. Benjamin was a lifelong friend of the scholar Gershom Scholem, who influentially defined Messianism as follows: 'Jewish Messianism is in its origins and by its nature . . . a theory of catastrophe. This theory stresses the revolutionary, cataclysmic element in the transition from every historical present to the Messianic future' (Scholem, 1971: 7). For Benjamin, the Jewish faith in redemption at any moment was translated into a secular revolutionary impulse. In the 'Theses', he designates the moment of memory that 'flashes up at a moment of danger' as the 'sign of a Messianic cessation of happening, or, put differently, a revolutionary chance in the fight for the oppressed past' (Benjamin, 1973: 257, 265). He ends the 'Theses' with a reminder that for the Jews 'every second of time was the strait gate through which the Messiah might enter' (Benjamin, 1973: 266).

Judaism surfaced most forcefully in Freud's work in the late study *Moses and Monotheism*. Although not published until after his death in 1939, the piece was started in Vienna in 1934 and completed in exile in London. In turning to Jewish history, Freud did not provide a heroic account, but rather a fictional story of Moses as an Egyptian. For Freud, there was not one Moses but two; the first was murdered by his followers. This unassimilated traumatic event and its subsequent resurfacing assumed particular significance for Freud. Cathy Caruth elaborates as follows:

> After the murder the Jews repressed it and took on another leader, also named Moses, who was eventually assimilated to the first Moses, who had been murdered. The belated experience of the murder and the return of the repressed Mosaic religion through Jewish tradition, Freud argues, ultimately established Jewish monotheism and determined the subsequent history of the Jews. (Caruth, 1996: 67)

For Jacqueline Rose, *Moses and Monotheism* is significant for returning to and reviving the theory of the traumatic neurosis, while at the same time extending its significance beyond the individual:

> In terms of *history*, trauma reappears; the journey of the concept through Freud's opus thus beautifully imitates its content (trauma always returns). The story, and the analogy, are there to remind us of that part of historical being, passionate and traumatized, which runs backwards and forwards, never completely in the grasp of its subjects, through psychic time. (Rose, 1996: 11)

In a late work, Edward Said also returns to Freud's essay, drawing out its implications for contemporary Israeli politics. He emphasises that, in Freud's account, the founder of Judaism was an Egyptian, a non-Jew. For Said, Freud's insistence that identity is never 'pure', but always has its own inherent limitations, could potentially provide the basis of a new understanding between Palestinians and Israelis. He explains:

> Freud's meditations and insistence on the non-European from a Jewish point of view provide, I think, an admirable sketch of what it entails, by way of refusing to resolve identity into some of the nationalist or religious herds into which so many people want so desperately to run. More bold is Freud's profound exemplification of the insight that even for the most definable, the most identifiable, the most stubborn communal identity – for him, this was the Jewish identity – there are inherent limits that prevent it from being fully incorporated into one, and only one, Identity. (Said, 2003: 53–4)

The writing of Jacques Derrida is also imbricated in his Jewish origins. This is evident in his 1976 study of Edmond Jabès's *The Book of Questions*, but it can also be seen in his later work. In *Archive Fever* (1995), for example, Derrida reflects on Freud's ideas of remembrance in the context of an extended meditation on religion, inscription and the archive. Taking as his focus the notion of the archive, Derrida suggests that Freud's concept of the death drive 'not only incites forgetfulness, amnesia, the annihilation of memory' (Derrida, 1995: 11), but even commands the eradication of the supplementary aids to memory: the archive, the documentary or monumental apparatus for preserving memory. He explores the archivisation of psychoanalysis itself as an institution. In a particularly poignant passage, Derrida also analyses the significance of the inscription Freud's father made inside the gift of a rebound Bible, presented as a memorial and reminder of his Jewish roots. This provokes in Derrida a meditation on this most ancient of texts, the Hebrew Bible, the 'arch-archive', designed to preserve the memories of a whole people. Although the work of Derrida is inextricable from his Jewishness, it nevertheless remains important to resist too straightforward an identification between the two. Jonathan Boyarin rightfully urges us to engage with the complexity of the relation to Jewish origins in the work of Derrida and other thinkers, asking us to hesitate before 'relegat[ing] the[ir] Jewishness to a mere "biography effect"' (Boyarin, 1992: 81).

In seeking to answer the question 'what is a Jew?' Nicholas de Lange resists the notion that it is the Jewish religion that unites the Jewish people. Rather, he argues, what binds the Jews together is 'a strong sense of common origin, a shared past and a shared destiny' (de Lange, 2000: 26). Shared or collective memory has become predominantly associated with questions of space or territory; in the work of Pierre Nora, memory is closely connected to national identity and a uniquely shared land and language. For Jews, the desire for a shared territorial presence has predominantly been expressed in Zionism. As Boyarin acknowledges, 'the sense of a specific territorial origin and attachment to the Land of Israel is profoundly important to Jewish identity, even if it is not strictly "essential"' (Boyarin, 1992: 62). Carol B. Bardenstein (1999) has drawn on Nora's work in order to demonstrate how, in quite different and asymmetrical ways, both Israelis and Palestinians use trees and forests to articulate their collective memories, and to embody their connection to the land. Simon Schama has also commented on the significance of tree-planting as an implicit affirmation of Israel as the Jewish homeland. He describes sponsoring tree-planting in Israel as a schoolboy in London, arguing that the trees 'were our proxy immigrants' (Schama, 1996: 5). In ideological terms, he argues, the trees replaced a diaspora of 'drifting sand' with a firmly 'rooted forest' (Schama, 1996: 6).

Schama's experience reminds us, however, that if Jews ground their collective, 'national' existence in a specific territory, it is for the majority a territory (the Land of Israel) other than that in which they live. For Boyarin, the Jewish diaspora provides a challenge to the prevailing emphasis in memory studies on co-territorial presence. He argues that it is as important to conceptualise the Jews 'as a collective through continuity (coextension in time) at least as much as through contiguity (coextension in space)' (Boyarin, 1992: xvii). In different ways and from differing perspectives, each of the extracts in this section seeks to engage with ideas of collective memory and to explore the extent to which they relate to, or are challenged by, the Jewish historical experience. Much of the work in this section corresponds closely to the writing on diaspora (Part III, Section 9), in implicitly or explicitly questioning the interrelationship between collective memory and the nation.

The first extract in this section is taken from **Yosef Hayim Yerushalmi**'s *Zakhor: Jewish History and Jewish Memory* (1996). Yerushalmi strikingly places memory at the heart of Jewish faith and tradition: 'Only in Israel and nowhere else is the injunction to remember felt as a religious imperative to an entire people' (Yerushalmi, 1996: 9). In his volume, Yerushalmi traces the evolution of Jewish memory across four distinct historical periods: Biblical and rabbinical origins; the Middle Ages; after the Spanish expulsion; and in our own times. Throughout, he is concerned to emphasise the highly selective nature of Jewish memory, in which heroic individual and national deeds are subordinated to God's acts. The priest or prophet, rather than the historian, assumes the role of master of memory. In a key passage of the work, Yerushalmi points out: 'The meaning of history is explored more directly and more deeply in the prophets than in the actual historical narratives; the collective memory is transmitted more actively through ritual than through chronicle' (Yerushalmi, 1996: 15).

In this extract, Yerushalmi discusses the transmission of memory in the Middle Ages. Reading or writing history was dismissed by Maimonides as 'a waste of time', and accordingly Jewish memory was transmitted through ritual and liturgy and in rabbinic custom and law. Yerushalmi identifies four distinct modes or 'vessels' of Jewish memory: penitential prayers in the liturgy; memorial books in the community; 'second Purims' to create renewed deliverance; and special fast days. He uses the term 'collective memory' and, in the 'Prologue to the Original Edition', he acknowledges his debt to the pioneering work of Maurice Halbwachs. However, he also argues that Halbwachs's conception of 'collective memory' is not entirely adequate to describe the Jewish experience:

> What has been learned from the study of oral tradition, for example, will only partially apply to so literate and obstinately bookish a people. Notions of collective memory derived from the folklore and mythology of peasants or primitives are also of limited relevance when we consider how much of Jewish society and culture was molded, prior to modern times, by guiding elites. (Yerushalmi, 1996: xxxiv)

In the 'Preface to the 1989 Edition', Yerushalmi also points out that the 'vessels' and 'vehicles' of memory that he outlines 'correspond closely' with Nora's conception of *lieux de mémoire* (Yerushalmi, 1996: xxix). However, Yerushalmi's work has recently been criticised, alongside that of Nora, for constructing too rigid a division between memory and history. Both thinkers have a tendency to associate memory with an irrecoverable past and to adopt a nostalgic and elegiac tone. Thus Boyarin argues that Yerushalmi has 'retraced and reinscribed the break between "Jewish history" and "Jewish memory"' and that he separates himself as a 'critical, individualist historian' from the 'lulling tales of Jewish "memory"' that he describes (Boyarin, 1994: 148).

The second extract in this section is from **Jonathan Boyarin and Jack Kugelmass**'s *From a Ruined Garden: The Memorial Books of Polish Jewry*

(1983). Reflecting on this project, Boyarin argues that it represents his attempt to 'construct myself through contact with my own destroyed "ancestors", the Yiddish-speaking Jews of Eastern Europe' (Boyarin, 1992: xiv). Implicit in this comment is a sense of the Holocaust as a profound and catastrophic break in Jewish 'tradition'. Seeking contact with a 'destroyed world', Boyarin found it in the books that people had written about their lives (Boyarin, 1992: xiv). In the extract reproduced in this section, Kugelmass and Boyarin explore memorial books written by Polish-Jewish survivors of the Holocaust about their communities before and during the Nazi persecution. In so doing, they identify an often overlooked aspect of memorialising. The memorial books, embedded in a commemorative community, emerged as a spontaneous collective response to the Holocaust and many contributors, drawn to participate in this collective voice, wrote for the first time in their lives. The books record in as much detail as possible a world that had been lost. As Boyarin and Kugelmass point out, the memorial books were local in circulation: those reading the volumes most often knew the people and events commemorated. The memorial books draw on a long tradition of Jewish mourning literature, which provides a focus and form for the expression of grief: 'if there were no precedent for them in Jewish history and culture, they would not have appeared as a distinct genre so soon after the war nor taken hold in such a massive way' (this volume, p. 175). Reflecting on the value of these texts, Boyarin observes that, rather than seeing them as 'tainted by subjectivism or reified as first-hand, eyewitness representations', he and Kugelmass viewed them as having their own validity – which was neither overly subjective nor unproblematically realist – both for the survivors themselves and for those who came after (Boyarin, 1992: xiv).

The final extract in this section is taken from **James E. Young**'s *The Texture of Memory* (1993). In this work Young, like Boyarin and Kugelmass, pays tribute to the role of the memorial books in remembering the Holocaust:

> In keeping with the bookish, iconoclastic side of Jewish tradition, the first 'memorials' to the Holocaust period came not in stone, glass or steel – but in narrative. The Yizkor Bikher – memorial books – remembered both the lives and destruction of European Jewish communities according to the most ancient of Jewish memorial media: words on paper. For a murdered people without graves, without even corpses to inter, these memorial books often came to serve as symbolic tombstones. (This volume, p. 182)

Following the trauma of the Holocaust, the memorial books provided, through the act of reading, a shared space of witnessing and remembrance. The focus of Young's study extends beyond this, however, to explore the subsequent sites of memory that emerged; the various memorials that were erected to commemorate the victims of the Holocaust. Studying a range of Holocaust memorials across Europe, Israel and the United States, Young persuasively argues that there is not a single Holocaust, but numerous different Holocausts, which vary across distinct national memory communities. In the extract, taken from the 'Introduction' to the volume, Young positions himself in relation to Nora and Halbwachs, demonstrating that his work has a strong basis in their ideas on collective memory: 'memorials provide the sites where groups of people gather to create a common past for themselves, places where they tell the constitutive narratives, their "shared" stories of the past' (this volume, p. 182). Beyond their places in the constellations of national memory, however, Young is also concerned to explore the ways in which Holocaust memorials and monuments remain animate through the role that they play in individual lives. Young is concerned not simply with the genesis and contours of the memorials, but also with their reception; the ways in which they change, and are changed by, those who reflect on them and interact with them. For Young, then, collective memories are undeniably shaped by national interests and concerns, but they are also dependent on 'the conflation of private and public memory, in the memorial activity by which minds reflecting on the past inevitably precipitate in the present historical moment' (Young, 1993: 15).

REFERENCES AND FURTHER READING

Arendt, Hannah (1978) *The Jew as Pariah: Jewish Identity and Politics in the Modern Age*. New York: Grove.

Bardenstein, Carol B. (1999) 'Trees, Forests, and the Shaping of Palestinian and Israeli Collective Memory', in Mieke Bal, Jonathan Crewe and Leo Spitzer (eds), *Acts of Memory: Cultural Recall in the Present*. Hanover, NH, and London: University Press of New England, pp. 148–70.

Benjamin, Walter (1973) 'Theses on the Philosophy of History', in Hannah Arendt (ed.) *Illuminations*, trans. Harry Zohn. London: Fontana, pp. 255–66.

Blanchot, Maurice (1986) *The Writing of the Disaster*, trans. Ann Smock. Lincoln, NE: University of Nebraska Press.

Boyarin, Jonathan (1991) *Polish Jews in Paris: The Ethnography of Memory*. Bloomington, IN: Indiana University Press.

—— (1992) *Storm from Paradise: The Politics of Jewish Memory*. Minneapolis, MN: University of Minnesota Press.

—— (ed.) (1994) *Remapping Memory: The Politics of Timespace*. Minneapolis, MN and London: University of Minnesota Press, pp. 137–60.

—— and Jack Kugelmass (eds) (1983) *From a Ruined Garden: The Memorial Books of Polish Jewry*. New York: Schocken.

Caruth, Cathy (1996) *Unclaimed Experience: Trauma, Narrative, and History*. Baltimore, MD, and London: Johns Hopkins University Press.

De Lange, Nicholas (2000) *An Introduction to Judaism*. Cambridge: Cambridge University Press.

Derrida, Jacques (1976) 'The Question of the Book', in *Writing and Difference*, trans. Alan Bass. Chicago: University of Chicago Press, pp. 64–78.

—— (1995) *Archive Fever: A Freudian Impression*, trans. Eric Prenowitz. Chicago and London: University of Chicago Press.

Freud, Sigmund ([1939] 1990) 'Moses and Monotheism', in Albert Dickson (ed.), *The Origins of Religion*, Penguin Freud Library vol. 13, trans. James Strachey. Harmondsworth: Penguin, pp. 237–386.

Handelman, Susan (1982) *Slayers of Moses: The Emergence of Rabbinic Tradition in Modern Literary Theory*. Albany, NY: State University of New York Press.

Hartman, Geoffrey H. and Sanford Budick (eds) (1986) *Midrash and Literature*. New Haven, CT: Yale University Press.

Jabès, Edmond (1976) *The Book of Questions*. Middletown, CT: Wesleyan University Press.

Rose, Jacqueline (1996) *States of Fantasy*. Oxford: Clarendon Press.

Said, Edward W. (2003) *Freud and the Non-European*. London and New York: Verso.

Schama, Simon (1996) *Landscape and Memory*. London: Fontana.

Scholem, Gershom (1971) *The Messianic Idea in Judaism*. New York: Schocken.

Yerushalmi, Yosef Hayim (1991) *Freud's Moses: Judaism Terminable and Interminable*. New Haven, CT: Yale University Press.

—— (1996) *Zakhor: Jewish History and Jewish Memory*. Seattle, WA, and London: University of Washington Press.

Young, James E. (1993) *The Texture of Memory: Holocaust Memorials and Meaning*. New Haven, CT, and London: Yale University Press.

—— (ed.) (1994) *The Art of Memory: Holocaust Memorials in History*. Munich and New York: Prestel-Verlag.

—— (2000) *At Memory's Edge: After-Images of the Holocaust in Contemporary Art and Architecture*. New Haven, CT, and London: Yale University Press.

YOSEF HAYIM YERUSHALMI: *FROM* ZAKHOR: JEWISH HISTORY AND JEWISH MEMORY

It remains for us to inquire into the efforts made by Jews in the Middle Ages to preserve the remembrance of events that had been experienced, not by generations long past, but by themselves.

In this context I should like to identify four characteristic vehicles of medieval Jewish memory, each of which can tell us something about the mentality that created them.

The single most important religious and literary response to historical catastrophe in the Middle Ages was not a chronicle of the event but the composition of *selihot*, penitential prayers, and their insertion into the liturgy of the synagogue. Through such prayers the poet gave vent to the deepest emotions of the community, expressed its contrition in face of the divine wrath or its questions concerning divine justice, prayed for an end to suffering or vengeance against the oppressor, and, in effect, 'commemorated' the event. A very large number of medieval historical *selihot* have survived.[1] While some contain actual names and descriptions of events, most do not. The poetic forms themselves militated against too literal a concern with specific details, while in general the poet could take it for granted that the community knew the 'facts.' For later generations, however, it was different. Even modern scholars, with all the tools of research available to them, will sometimes have difficulty in determining to which particular event a certain *selihah* refers.

Source: Yosef Hayim Yerushalmi, *Zakhor: Jewish History and Jewish Memory* (Seattle, WA, and London: University of Washington Press, 1982), pp. 45–52.

Memorbücher – 'Memorial Books' – flourished especially, though not exclusively, among Ashkenazic Jews. Kept for centuries in the archives of the community, into such volumes were inscribed not only the names of famous rabbis and communal leaders, but records of persecutions and lists of martyrs to be read aloud periodically in the synagogue during memorial services for the dead. Most *Memorbücher* were confined to the past of the local community. Others were wider in scope. The famous *Memorbuch* of Nuremberg, begun in 1296 and running up to 1392, contains, in addition to a poem on the building and dedication of the synagogue and lists of communal benefactors with prayers in Hebrew and in Old French, a martyrology that summarizes persecutions in Germany and France from the First Crusade of 1096 to the Black Death of 1349.[2] Yet although *Memorbücher* may contain important historical information, they cannot be regarded as historiography. Typically, their major purpose was to preserve the names of those for whose souls communal prayers were to be offered in the house of worship.

'Second Purims' were instituted in Jewish communities the world over to commemorate a deliverance from some danger or persecution.[3] I will cite only a few random examples, merely to indicate their diffusion and the variety of circumstances that could give birth to them. Thus in Muslim Spain in the year 1038 a battle was fought near the village of El Fuente by the armies of Granada and Almeria. The vizier of the Kingdom of Granada was a Jew, the great Hebrew poet, scholar, and statesman, Samuel Ibn Nagrela, the only instance in the Middle Ages where a Jew occupied such a position of power. He had ample reason to fear that should Granada be defeated it would mean not only his personal downfall, but that of the entire Jewish community. Accordingly, when the Granadan forces were victorious he declared a Second Purim, and sent forth copies of a magnificent Hebrew poem he had composed for the occasion to Tunis, Palestine, and Babylonia, asking that the Purim be celebrated there as well.[4] The Purim of Narbonne in Southern France originated in the deliverance of the community in 1236 when an anti-Jewish riot, sparked after a Christian fisherman was killed by a Jew in a private quarrel, was subdued by the governor of the city.[5] In 'Saragossa' (actually Syracuse in Sicily), either in 1380 or 1420, a Jewish apostate named Marcus revealed that the Jews had removed the Torah scrolls from their cases before the latter, according to custom, were shown to the king during a royal procession. Regarding this as an insult, the king decided to have the cases inspected on the next occasion. Meanwhile, we are told, Elijah the prophet warned of the danger and the scrolls were put back. When the king returned, the scrolls were found to be present, the community was saved, and Marcus was hanged, thus giving rise to the 'Purim of Saragossa,' which was still celebrated centuries later in various communities of the Ottoman Empire.[6] In 1578 Dom Sebastian, the young king of Portugal, landed with a crusading army in Morocco. The Jews were forewarned by two Marranos that if he proved victorious he intended to baptize them all by force, just as had been done to the whole of Portuguese Jewry in 1497. When Sebastian was defeated and killed at the Battle of Alcazarquebir, the Jews of Morocco instituted a Second Purim called, variously, 'Purim Sebastiano' or 'Purim de los Cristianos.'[7] [. . .]

Just as they created Second Purims, so medieval Jewish communities instituted special fast-days which, like the *selihot* that accompanied them, recalled those more bitter occasions when there was no deliverance.[8] I should like now to focus closely upon the rather extraordinary career of just one such special fast.

In May of the year 1171, in the French town of Blois, a Christian servant alleged that he had seen a Jew throw the corpse of a child into the river Loire. No corpse was ever found, but the forty Jews residing in Blois were imprisoned. The affair was further complicated by the fact that the ruler Count Thibaut, was having an affair with a Jewess, Polcelina, which aroused the jealousy of the count's wife, while other Christians resented the lady's influence at court. All now conspired to bring about the destruction of the community. Attempts at bribery were ineffectual. The servant was put through a dubious ordeal by water, after which his testimony was declared to be true. Offered the choice of baptism, most of the Jews, including Polcelina, chose to die. On the 20th of Sivan, May 26, 1171, thirty-two Jews, seventeen of them women, were burned at the stake.[9]

These, then, are the bare outlines of the first ritual murder accusation in continental Europe. The martyrdom at Blois made an enormous impression on contemporaries. In addition to two Hebrew prose accounts a number of *selihot* were composed. Upon hearing the tragic news the greatest Jewish authority of the age, Rabbi Jacob Tam (known as Rabbenu Tam), declared the day of the burning a perpetual fast. At the end of a prose narrative of the event written by Ephraim of Bonn we read:

> Wednesday the 20th of Sivan 4931 [i.e., 1171 C.E.] was accepted by all the communities in France, England and the Rhineland as a day of mourning and fasting, of their own will, and at the behest of the illustrious scholar our master Jacob son of Rabbi Meir [Tam] who wrote letters to them and informed them that this day is worthy to be declared a fast-day for all our people, and this fast shall be greater than the Fast of Gedaliah ben Ahikam, for it is a day of atonement. These are the words that our master wrote, and thus is it proper, and thus did the Jews accept it.[10]

To appreciate the subsequent fate of this fast-day of the 20th of Sivan, we must now leap forward almost five centuries in time, from France to Eastern Europe.

In 1648, in Poland and the Ukraine, there erupted the great wave of Cossack pogroms led by Bogdan Chmielnitzky in which hundreds of Jewish communities were devastated, and thousands were killed, sold into captivity, or left destitute. For the Jews of Eastern Europe 1648 marked a blow whose scars were never healed.

As after the Crusades, so now, several chronicles were composed, as well as a considerable number of *selihot* and other liturgical poems. It has been pointed out that although the situation of Polish Jewry during the pogroms was quite different from that of the Jews of the Rhineland during the First Crusade, the two were homologized, and the writers depicted the slaughter of 1648 as a *repetition* of the martyrdom of the Crusades.[11]

This typological equation is significant in itself, but there is more to be said. In the *Megillat 'Efah* (the 'Scroll of Terror'), an account of the Cossack massacres by Rabbi Shabbetai Katz, we read:

> Therefore I have ordained for myself and for the coming generations of my descendants a day of fasting, sorrow, mourning and lamentations *on the twentieth day of the month of Sivan* . . . because this day has been the beginning of persecution and pain . . . and because (on this day) afflictions were doubled . . . *for the persecution of 4931 [1171] was on the same day* . . . and I have composed these *selihot* and laments with tears and supplications, so they may be recited on this day in each and every year . . . .[12]

What was apparently initiated by Shabbetai Katz as a private fast-day was quickly accepted as a general one. When the Council of Four Lands, the governing body over the whole of Polish Jewry, met in Lublin in 1650, 'they took it upon themselves and their posterity to fast throughout the Four Lands *on the twentieth day of the month Sivan*, each and every year . . . .'[13]

The *selihot* composed by Shabbetai Katz were recited in Lithuania. In Poland proper the communities began to follow the custom of another prominent rabbinic leader of the time, Yom Tob Lipmann Heller. Unlike Shabbetai Katz, Heller took old *selihot*, among them two that had been composed in the twelfth century after the burning in Blois, and ordained that these be recited on the 20th of Sivan for the pogroms of 1648. The reason he gave is of surpassing interest:

> What has occurred now is similar to the persecutions of old, and all that happened to the forefathers has happened to their descendants. Upon the former already the earlier generations composed *selihot* and narrated the events. *It is all one*. Therefore I said to myself – I shall go and glean among them, 'for the fingernail of the former generations is worth more than the belly of the later ones' [*Yoma* 9b]. Also because by reciting their prayers it will help our own to be accepted, since one cannot compare the words uttered by the small to those of the great. And thus the lips will move in the grave, and their words shall be like a ladder upon which our prayer will mount to heaven.[14]

Although, at the insistence of various persons, Yom Tob Lipmann Heller also wrote some new prayers of his own, his first view prevailed throughout Poland and spread beyond. Eventually, in most standard prayerbooks almost none of the *selihot* specially composed for the Cossack massacres remained.[15] For the 20th of Sivan which, to the eve of World War II, was still observed in Eastern

Europe as a commemoration of 1648, only the medieval *selihot* were recited, and thus the cycle was closed.

I have dwelt in some detail on the peregrinations of the fast-day of the 20th of Sivan because, as a case study, it affords several insights into the workings of Jewish collective memory in the Middle Ages. In retrospect we are struck by the following elements:

1. The longevity of the original fast of Blois, which had obviously been carried to Eastern Europe through the waves of Ashkenazic migration into the Polish expanse and which, though instituted in the twelfth century, was still observed in the seventeenth.
2. The primacy of liturgy and ritual over historical narrative. There is no real evidence that, over the centuries, the prose accounts of the Blois tragedy were known to any but isolated individuals.[16] The fast, by contrast, was observed by entire communities.
3. The power of a commemorative observance such as the fast of the 20th of Sivan to preserve the essential memory of an event, without necessarily preserving its historical details.
4. Resistance to novelty in history. The pronounced tendency, after 1648, to fit the recent catastrophe into the mold of past tragedies, so dramatically expressed in Yom Tob Lipmann Heller's conviction that the *selihot* composed almost five centuries earlier were quite sufficient to embrace the contemporary event as well, 'for it is all one.'
5. The almost fortuitous character of the commemoration of what happened at Blois. One can readily imagine what would have occurred had Rabbenu Tam not seen fit to call for a perpetual annual fast. The event might well have left no trace on posterity. The fact is that other major and cataclysmic events, including large-scale massacres or expulsions of entire Jewries, did not find their place in the calendar, and so did not survive in memory.

The features I have just enumerated are by no means exceptional. They are characteristic of medieval Jewish thinking [. . .]. In sum, memories of post-Talmudic events were partial and uneven at best, and there was no concerted effort to remember more.

There were three highways of religious and intellectual creativity among medieval Jews – halakhah (jurisprudence), philosophy, and Kabbalah – each of which offered an all-embracing orientation, and none of which required a knowledge of history in order to be cultivated or confirmed. These alone led to ultimate truths and to spiritual felicity. By comparison the study of history seemed at best a diversion, at worst – a 'waste of time.'

None of the other factors usually put forth to explain the relative indifference of medieval Jews to historical knowledge will suffice. It has been stated repeatedly that suffering and persecutions numbed their historical consciousness, or that they wrote little or no history because, lacking a state and political power, ordinarily the prime subjects of history, they had nothing to write about. It has even been suggested that there was little historiography because Jews had neither royal chroniclers nor monks who would devote themselves to such tasks. Such explanations, however, prove to be self-liquidating. All these factors remained equally true of the Jewish people in the sixteenth century. Yet in that time there was a sudden and unique flowering of Jewish historical writing that surpassed, in scope and in quality, almost anything that had appeared among the Jews since Graeco-Roman times.

NOTES

1. See M. Steinschneider, *Die Geschichtsliteratur der Juden* (Berlin, 1905), *passim*, and the texts published in such anthologies as Habermann, *Sefer gezerot Ashkenaz ve-Zarefat*, and S. Bernfeld, *Sefer ha-dema'ot* [The book of tears], 3 vols. (Berlin, 1924–26). A full corpus of medieval *selihot* and *qinot* ('laments') based on historical events remains a desideratum.

2. Edited with a German translation by S. Salfeld, *Das Martyrologium des Nürnberger Memorbuches* (Quellen zur Geschichte der Juden in Deutschland, vol. 3 [Berlin, 1898]). In the Introduction, pp. xvi–xxxix, there is a list of *Memorbücher* from fifty-five communities. Additional references in Steinschneider, *Geschichtsliteratur*, no. 24.

3. See M. Steinschneider, 'Purim und Parodie,' *MGWJ*, 47 (1903): 283–86. Another list, not complete, is given in *Encyclopedia Judaica* (English), vol. 13, s. v. 'Purim.' Second Purims were created well into modern times. See C. Roth, 'Some Revolutionary Purims (1790–1801),' *HUCA*, 10 (1935): 451–83 (mostly on deliverances during the turmoil of the Napoleonic invasions of Italy).

4. See the poem '*Eloha 'oz*, in *Divan Shemuel Ha-Nagid*, ed. D. Yarden (Jerusalem, 1966), pp. 4–14.

5. See the short account by Meir ben Isaac in Neubauer, *MJC*, 2: 251; D. Kaufmann, 'Le Pourim de Narbonne,' *REJ*, 32 (1896): 129–30.

6. The Hebrew text was published by M. Slatki, *Ner Mosheh* (Jerusalem, 1882) fols. 83–4. For the confusion of Syracuse as 'Saragossa,' see D. Simonsen, 'Le Pourim de Saragosse est un Pourim de Syracuse,' *REJ*, 59 (1910): 90–5.

7. For the events, see the account of Samuel ben Saadya Ibn Danan in *Siddur 'ahabat ha-qadmonim* [Prayerbook according to the rite of Fez] (Jerusalem, 1889), fols. 12b–13a. A Spanish translation of the scroll read annually in memory of this occasion is given by F. Cantera Burgos, 'El "Purim" del Rey Don Sebastián,' *Sefarad*, 6 (1945): 224ff., and another in French by A. I. Laredo in his study of 'Les Purim de Tanger,' *Hespéris*, 35 (1948): 193–203 (see 197–9, with facsimile). Cf. also G. Vajda, *Un recueil de textes historiques Judeo-Marocains* (reprinted from *Hespéris*, 25–6 [Paris, 1951]), pp. 15–17, with a French translation from a manuscript of Ibn Danan's account that contains some variations. The so-called 'Purim de las bombas,' sometimes confused with that of Sebastian, is entirely distinct and has a scroll of its own, relating the deliverance from the bombardment of Tangier by a French squadron in 1844 (see Laredo, pp. 199ff.).

8. For a list of such annual commemorative fasts, see L. Zunz, *Die Ritus des synagogalen Gottesdienstes* (Berlin, 1859), pp. 127–30, and the additions of D. Simonsen, 'Freud und Leid: Locale Fest- und Fasttage im Anschluss an Zunzens Fastenabelle,' *MGWJ*, 38 (1894): 524–7.

9. On the events and their aftermath, see S. Spiegel, 'Mi-pitgamey ha-'Akedah: Serufey Blois ve-hithadshut 'alilot ha-dam' [The martyrs of Blois and the renewal of ritual murder accusations], *Mordecai M. Kaplan Jubilee Volume* (New York, 1953), Hebrew section, pp. 267–87; R. Chazan, 'The Blois Incident of 1171: A Study in Jewish Intercommunal Organization," *PAAJR*, 36 (1968): 13–31.

10. Habermann, *Sefer gezerot Ashkenaz ve-Zarefat*, p. 126.

11. J. Katz, 'Beyn TaTNU le-TaH ve-TaT' [Between 1096 and 1648–49], *Sefer ha-yobel le-Yitzhak Baer* (Jerusalem, 1961), pp. 318–37.

12. Shabbetai Katz, *Megillat 'Efah*, printed as an appendix to M. Wiener's edition of Solomon Ibn Verga's *Shebet Yehudah* (Hannover, 1856; reprint, 1924), p. 139.

13. *Pinqas Va'ad Arba Arazot* (Acta Congressus Generalis Judaeorum Regni Poloniae, 1580–1764), ed. I. Halperin (Jerusalem, 1945), no. 207, pp. 77–8.

14. From the printer's preface to *Selihot le-yom ha-'esrim le-Sivan*, n.p., n.d. [Cracow, 1650]. The entire preface was reprinted, along with the extant poems of Heller, by A. M. Habermann, 'Piyyutav ve-shirav shel Rabbi Yom Tob Lipmann Heller,' in *Li-kebod Yom Tob*, ed. J. L. Hacohen Maimon (Jerusalem, 1956), pp. 125ff. It is significant that Heller had earlier composed special *selihot* for a fast-day of the 14th of Heshvan in Prague emanating from the troubles of 1618–21, when the populace revolted and elected a new king. The printer now asked him why he would not write new *selihot* for the Cossack massacres as well. Heller replied that the two events are to be differentiated. The danger in Prague emanated from a general state of war in which the 'destroyer does not distinguish between the righteous and the wicked' (citing TB *Baba Kama* 60a). The Cossack massacres were due to the same hatred of Jews as in all the calamities through the ages, and so the old *selihot* would suffice.

15. N. Wahrmann, *Meqorot le-toledot gezerot TaH ve-TaT: Tefillot u-selihot le-Kaf Sivan* [Sources for the history of the persecutions of 1648–49: prayers and selihot for the 20th of Sivan] (Jerusalem, 1949), p. 9.

16. Along with the Crusade chronicles they somehow came into the hands of Joseph Ha-Kohen in the sixteenth century (he quotes from them in his *Dibrey ha-Yamim* [Sabbionetta, 1554], fols. 57b–59a). None of the other sixteenth-century Jewish historians allude directly to what occurred at Blois. Although himself an Ashkenazic Jew, David Gans does not mention it, but states only that 'in the year 4,931 the Jews encountered many troubles, and by divine grace they were saved' *(Zemah David* [Prague, 1591], fol. 55b).

5.2

JACK KUGELMASS AND JONATHAN BOYARIN: *FROM* FROM A RUINED GARDEN: THE MEMORIAL BOOKS OF POLISH JEWRY

Completely overlooked in recent writing about the Holocaust is the single most important act of commemorating the dead on the part of Jewish survivors. These are the hundreds of *yizker-bikher*, memorial books devoted to the lives and deaths of entire Jewish communities in Eastern Europe. Four hundred such books have been written by survivors and émigrés from Polish-Jewish communities alone. These books range in size and format from now crumbling, thin paperbound volumes produced in D.P. camps shortly after World War II, to the four large-format volumes devoted to every aspect of the history and daily life of the Jews of Slonim. Even now, almost forty years after the end of the war, new memorial books are being published each year. [. . .]

The memorial-book writers were not constrained by the size of the Jewish community in their town. The town of Chorostkow (Khorostkov), with 350 Jewish families, was as likely to have a memorial book as Lodz, with its 200,000 Jews. As a result, the preponderance of memorial books are for *shtetlekh* rather than major cities, and cannot be taken to reflect accurately the demographics of prewar Polish Jewry, over one-third of whom lived in Poland's three largest cities.

The titles of the books reveal much about their origins and intent. Sometimes the name of the town alone suffices. Usually, however, it is preceded by words such *yizker-bukh*, indicating that the book is intended to serve as a substitute

Source: Jack Kugelmass and Jonathan Boyarin, 'Introduction', in *From a Ruined Garden: The Memorial Books of Polish Jewry*, eds Jack Kugelmass and Jonathan Boyarin (New York: Schocken, 1983), pp. 1–6.

for the traditional memorial service; *sefer*, suggesting that the book is to be regarded as a holy text; *pinkes*, meaning that the book is a substitute for the lost town chronicle, or *le-kedoshei*, marking its dedication to the town's Holocaust martyrs.

The inside covers of many books bear maps. Sometimes these are regional, showing the relation of the town to neighboring locations. Others are free-style, schematic representations of the town's layout. For smaller communities, these may show each house and be numerically coded to match a listing of each homeowner's name. Others show cows, crosses, gravestones and the like to represent the locations of pastures, churches, and cemeteries.

The volumes typically open with a frontispiece featuring symbols of mourning as well as symbols of life destroyed: a talis (prayer shawl) draped over a tombstone; a ghostly figure rising from the grave, his eyes covered by his hands and tears falling; a menorah overturned, its candle flames igniting the entire town; a tree cut down at the height of vitality, with a small green shoot growing from its stump.

The books' tables of contents reflect both thematic and chronological principles of organization. Given that the topics of most selections reflect the authors' choice rather than an editor's assignment, it is understandable that the chapter divisions are less than clear-cut. Whereas books are frequently divided into pre-World War I, interwar, and Holocaust sections, they also include chapters and individual selections on town characters, rabbis, or political parties that contain references to all three periods. For example, the story 'Dear God!' describes peaceful traditional life, the Russian revolution, and the Holocaust in the space of a few pages. Generally the constellations that exist in memory prevail, rather than a particular chronological or historical sequence. [. . .]

Most of the books [. . .] begin with a substantial account of the history of the town from the time of its first Jewish settlement. Frequently these accounts are largely based on articles found in general publications such as the Polish encyclopedia (Encyclopedia Powszechna.) Others are original works of value to contemporary scholars interested in the early history of Jews in Poland. These essays do not share the sense of immediacy so characteristic of memorial books. In contrast, articles such as 'The Court of the Plyaters,' detailing the dealings of successive generations of a Jewish community with successive generations of a noble Polish landowning family, are much more arresting. The world of secular historiography – from which academic historians writing in Yiddish drew their principles of analysis – has a Greek heritage, harking back to Thucydides' accounts of numbers and strategies. But there is a Biblical model for 'The Court of the Plyaters,' epitomized by Exodus 1:8, 'Now there arose a new king over Egypt, who knew not Joseph.' This attitude toward history views relations with non-Jewish rulers in the Diaspora in the context of paradigmatic events such as the sojourn in Egypt; and personal relations, individual morality, and memory are all pivotal.

Another type of material found in the yizker-bikher is folkloric and linguistic: collections of customs relating to particular holidays, sayings characteristic of the town, even lists of particular individuals' nicknames, and explanations of how they had acquired them:

> At the time for the Torah portion 'Shemini,' the stork comes flying from the warm countries. It was a sign for those who leased orchards to finish making arrangements with noblemen and priests. At the same time a Jew used to come from far away, from deep Russia, to lease fields in Zembrove. We called him 'the stork.'[1]

One book contains a description of the cryptic language used by a tavern owner's wife who would substitute Hebraicisms for common Yiddish terms when she didn't want a gentile customer to understand what she was saying to her husband. The book for Bendin (Bedzin) describes the different chronological strata of Yiddish phonology used in different parts of town.[2] One of the several books for Tshenstokhov (Czestochowa) contains a glossary of Yiddish slang of the Nazi era.[3] [. . .]

Soon after the war, memorial books became the major cultural focus of *landsmanshaftn*, mutual aid and fraternal societies of Jewish emigrants from East European towns now living in America, Israel, Argentina, and elsewhere. Before the war, the landsmanshaftn had been the immigrant's chief tie to the community he left behind. Landsmanshaftn collected money and sent representatives to distribute relief funds to destitute townspeople. After the war, the landsmanshaftn were still involved in relief work, providing funds for the emigration and resettlement of survivors and for the new State of Israel. Together with survivors who joined the landsmanshaftn, members looked for suitable ways to commemorate the dead, such as the annual memorial meetings generally held on the anniversary of the liquidation of the town's ghetto by the Nazis. Several landsmanshaftn set up communal tombstones for their towns' dead in local cemeteries – a phenomenon that began in Poland in the late 1940s and at Yad Vashem in Jerusalem, as well as in North America and Western Europe. The books, however, are an international effort, making it possible for the now widely dispersed survivors and émigrés to create an international memorial.[4]

The landsmanshaftn were remarkably suited to the task of creating these symbolic burials. By the time World War II ended, their provision of funeral benefits for their members was an integral part of immigrant life. They were the functional descendants of many of the shtetl's communal institutions, including the *khevre kedishe* – the burial society – one of the most prestigious of those institutions.[5]

Thus memorial books emerged as a genuinely collective response to the Holocaust.[6] So compelling was the urge to participate in this collective voice that many contributors wrote for the first time in their lives. The memorial-book literature for all of Eastern Europe consists of more than five hundred volumes, and individual volumes contain dozens of vignettes and articles written by different people.

Why this compulsion to write? Terrence Des Pres has argued convincingly that 'the need to bear witness' became a motivating force for many survivors.[7] Yet the events of the Holocaust are only part of the experience depicted in the memorial books. Survivors felt obligated not only to bear witness to the Nazi destruction, but to the world the Nazis sought to destroy. In response to this mandate, the circle of survivors grew in proportion to the size of the task, and came to include *landslayt* – townspeople – who had left Europe long before the Holocaust.

Most concentration camp survivors were young, and therefore had not been included in the initial selections for extermination. They looked healthier, were more able to survive the rigors of camp food and labor details, and had stood a better chance of foiling the Nazis' intent. The older townsfolk of their parents' age provided descriptions of a time too distant to comprise a well-defined region of their own memories. The collective voice that thus emerged blurred the line of demarcation between survivors and émigrés, ultimately imposing on all, as Lifton notes, 'a series of immersions into death which mark [even] our existence.'[8] [. . .]

The memorial books are the result of a spontaneous effort. They were produced by independent landsmanshaftn without the urging or financial support of a government or any other agency. Yet if there were no precedent for them in Jewish history and culture, they would never have appeared as a distinct genre so soon after the war nor taken hold in such a massive way. The consistency of structure from book to book demands explanation.

There are probably as many contributing elements in the shaping of memorial books as there are in the culture of East European Jews. Three elements which stand out, however, are the Nazi Holocaust; the emergence of modern Yiddish literature; and the long tradition of Jewish mourning literature, evident as early as the Book of Lamentations. Although the latter two shaped the overall form of the memorial books long before the Nazi rise to power, only the extent of the Holocaust and the nature of the experience imposed by its perpetrators could generate the massive response represented by the memorial books.

NOTES

1. Yom-tov Levinsky, *'Fun mayn kindhayt' Sefer Zembrove (Zambrow)*, p. 375.
2. Dovid Liver, *'Bendin dialekt,' Pinkas Bendin (Bedzin)*, pp. 156–7.
3. Dr. B. Orenshtayn, *'Tshenstokhover folklor in der Natsi-tsayt', Tshenstokhov (Czestochowa); Nayer tsugob tsum bukh 'Tshenstokhover Yidn,'* pp. 66–7.
4. It is worthwhile noting that when *landslayt* from the town of Zwolen set out to produce a memorial book, their expressed intention was 'to create a monument.'
5. In his study of Ashkenazic Jewry from the sixteenth to the eighteenth centuries, Jacob Katz indicates that members of the *khevre kedishe* 'formed something of an elite in the kehilla; they were so considered both by themselves and the general public'. *Tradition and Crisis: Jewish Society at the End of the Middle Ages* (New York: Schocken, 1971), p. 159.

6. In his study of Holocaust literature, Alvin Rosenfeld suggests that Holocaust literature in general has a fragmentary quality, 'more impressive in the sum of its parts than as a separate statement.' *A Double Dying: Reflections on Holocaust Literature* (Bloomington, IN: Indiana University Press, 1980), p. 34.

7. Terrence des Pres, *The Survivor: An Anatomy of Life in the Death Camps* (New York: Pocket Books, 1977).

8. Robert J. Lifton, *Death in Life: Survivors of Hiroshima* (New York: Random House, 1967), p. 479.

JAMES E. YOUNG: *FROM* THE TEXTURE OF MEMORY: HOLOCAUST MEMORIALS AND MEANING

Forgetting the extermination is part of the extermination itself.
 – Jean Baudrillard

No one can become what he cannot find in his memories.
 – Jean Améry

So this story will not finish with some tomb to be visited in pious memory. For the smoke that rises from crematoria obeys physical laws like any other: the particles come together and disperse according to the wind, which propels them. The only pilgrimage, dear reader, would be to look sadly at a stormy sky now and then.
 – André Schwartz-Bart[1]

The further events of World War II recede into time, the more prominent its memorials become. As the period of Holocaust is shaped in the survivors' diaries and memoirs, in their children's films and novels, public memory of this time is being molded in a proliferating number of memorial images and spaces. Depending on where and by whom these memorials are constructed, these sites remember the past according to a variety of national myths, ideals, and political needs. Some recall war dead, others resistance, and still others mass murder. All reflect both the past experiences and current lives of their communities, as well as the state's memory of itself. At a more specific level, these memorials also

Source: James E. Young, *The Texture of Memory: Holocaust Memorials and Meaning* (New Haven, CT, and London: Yale University Press, 1993), pp. 1–8.

reflect the temper of the memory-artists' time, their place in aesthetic discourse, their media and materials.

Memory is never shaped in a vacuum; the motives of memory are never pure. Both the reasons given for Holocaust memorials and the kinds of memory they generate are as various as the sites themselves. Some are built in response to traditional Jewish injunctions to remember, others according to a government's need to explain a nation's past to itself. Where the aim of some memorials is to educate the next generation and to inculcate in it a sense of shared experience and destiny, other memorials are conceived as expiations of guilt or as self-aggrandizement. Still others are intended to attract tourists. In addition to traditional Jewish memorial iconography, every state has its own institutional forms of remembrance. As a result, Holocaust memorials inevitably mix national and Jewish figures, political and religious imagery.

In Germany, for example, memorials to this time recall Jews by their absence, German victims by their political resistance. In Poland, countless memorials in former death camps and across the countryside commemorate the whole of Polish destruction through the figure of its murdered Jewish part. In Israel, martyrs and heroes are remembered side by side, both redeemed by the birth of the state. As the shape Holocaust memory takes in Europe and Israel is determined by political, aesthetic, and religious coordinates, that in America is guided no less by distinctly American ideals and experiences – such as liberty, pluralism, and immigration.

By themselves, monuments are of little value, mere stones in the landscape. But as part of a nation's rites or the objects of a people's national pilgrimage, they are invested with national soul and memory. For traditionally, the state-sponsored memory of a national past aims to affirm the righteousness of a nation's birth, even its divine election. The matrix of a nation's monuments emplots the story of ennobling events, of triumphs over barbarism, and recalls the martyrdom of those who gave their lives in the struggle for national existence – who, in the martyrological refrain, died so that a country might live. In assuming the idealized forms and meanings assigned this era by the state, memorials tend to concretize particular historical interpretations. They suggest themselves as indigenous, even geological outcroppings in a national landscape; in time, such idealized memory grows as natural to the eye as the landscape in which it stands. Indeed, for memorials to do otherwise would be to undermine the very foundations of national legitimacy, of the state's seemingly natural right to exist.

The relationship between a state and its memorials is not one-sided, however. On the one hand, official agencies are in position to shape memory explicitly as they see fit, memory that best serves a national interest. On the other hand, once created, memorials take on lives of their own, often stubbornly resistant to the state's original intentions. In some cases, memorials created in the image of a state's ideals actually turn around to recast these ideals in the memorial's own image. New generations visit memorials under new circumstances and invest them with new meanings. The result is an evolution in the memorial's significance, generated in the new times and company in which it finds itself.

The capacity for change in memorials has not always been so apparent, however. For, traditionally, the monument has been defined as that which by its seemingly land-anchored permanence could also guarantee the permanence of a particular idea or memory attached to it. In this conception, the monument would remain essentially impervious to time and change, a perpetual witness-relic to a person, event, or epoch. Hence, the first monuments mentioned in the Bible: a small pillar and a witness heap of stones (*gal-ed*) gathered to mark the agreement between Laban and Jacob (Gen. 31:45–48); the matzevah (tombstone) Jacob erected on Rachel's grave (Gen. 35:20). In both cases, the monuments would suggest themselves as everlasting remnant-witnesses by which subsequent generations would remember past events and people.

At this point, a clarification of terms may be in order. Many presume that 'memorials' recall only past deaths or tragic events and provide places to mourn, while 'monuments' remain essentially celebratory markers of triumphs and heroic individuals. In this vein, Arthur Danto has written that 'we erect monuments so that we shall always remember and build memorials so that we shall never forget. Thus, we have the Washington Monument but the Lincoln Memorial. Monuments commemorate the memorable and embody the myths of beginnings. Memorials ritualize remembrance and mark the reality of ends . . . Monuments make heroes and triumphs, victories and conquests, perpetually present and part of life. The memorial is a special precinct, extruded from life, a segregated enclave where we honor the dead. With monuments, we honor ourselves.'[2]

But in fact, the traditional monument (the tombstone) can also be used as a mourning site for lost loved ones, just as memorials have marked past victories. A statue can be a monument to heroism and a memorial to tragic loss; an obelisk can memorialize a nation's birth and monumentalize leaders fallen before their prime. Insofar as the same object can perform both functions, there may be nothing intrinsic to historical markers that makes them either a monument or a memorial.

[. . .] I prefer to distinguish a memorial from a monument only in a broader, more generic sense: there are memorial books, memorial activities, memorial days, memorial festivals, and memorial sculptures. Some of these are mournful, some celebratory: but all are memorials in a larger sense. Monuments, on the other hand, [. . .] refer [. . .] to a subset of memorials: the material objects, sculptures, and installations used to memorialize a person or thing. [. . .] I treat all memory-sites as memorials, the plastic objects within these sites as monuments. A memorial may be a day, a conference, or a space, but it need not be a monument. A monument, on the other hand, is always a kind of memorial.

In the last century, the very idea of the memorial-monument and its place in modern culture has grown no less contentious than its definition. Indeed, the traditional assumption of the monument's timelessness has nearly relegated it as a form to the margins of modem discourse. For once it was recognized that monuments necessarily mediate memory, even as they seek to inspire it, they came to be regarded as displacements of the memory they were supposed to embody. Even worse, by insisting that its memory was as fixed as its place in the landscape, the monument seemed to ignore the essential mutability in all cultural artifacts. 'What is the use to the modern man of this "monumental" contemplation of the past?' Nietzsche asked. 'Monumental' was, after all, Nietzsche's disdainful epithet for any version of history calling itself permanent and ever-lasting, a petrified history that buried the living.[3]

A few years later, Lewis Mumford echoed Nietzsche's scorn for the monumental when he pronounced the death of the monument insofar as it seemed hopelessly incompatible with his sense of modern architectural forms. 'The notion of a modern monument is veritably a contradiction in terms,' he wrote. 'If it is a monument, it is not modem, and if it is modern, it cannot be a monument.'[4] In Mumford's view, the monument defied the very essence of modern urban civilization: the capacity for renewal and rejuvenation. Where modern architecture invites the perpetuation of life itself, encourages renewal and change, and scorns the illusion of permanence, Mumford wrote, 'Stone gives a false sense of continuity, and a deceptive assurance of life' (p. 434).

Instead of changing and adapting to its environment, the monument remained static, a mummification of ancient, probably forgotten ideals. Instead of placing their faith in the powers of biological regeneration, fixing their images in their children, the eminent and powerful had traditionally sought in their vanity a petrified immortality. In Mumford's words, 'They write their boasts upon tombstones; they incorporate their deeds in obelisks; they place their hopes of remembrance in solid stones joined to other solid stones, dedicated to their subjects or their heirs forever, forgetful of the fact that stones that are deserted by the living are even more helpless than life that remains unprotected and preserved by stones' (p. 434). Indeed, after his mentor Patrick Geddes, Mumford suggests that it was usually the shakiest of regimes that installed the least movable monuments, a compensation for having accomplished nothing worthier by which to be remembered.

More recently, the late German historian Martin Broszat has suggested that in their references to the fascist era, monuments may not remember events so much as bury them altogether beneath layers of national myths and explanations.[5] As cultural reifications, in this view, monuments reduce or, in Broszat's words, 'coarsen' historical understanding as much as they generate it. In another vein, art historian Rosalind Krauss finds that the modernist period produces monuments unable to refer to anything beyond themselves as pure marker or base.[6] After Krauss, we might ask, in fact, whether an abstract, self-referential monument can ever commemorate events outside of itself. Or must it motion endlessly to its own gesture to the past, a commemoration of its essence as dislocated sign, forever trying to remember events it never actually saw?

Still others have argued that rather than embodying memory, the monument displaces it altogether, supplanting a community's memory-work with its own material form. 'The less memory is experienced from the inside,' Pierre Nora warns, 'the more it exists through its exterior scaffolding and outward signs.'[7] If the obverse of this is true as well, then perhaps the more memory comes to rest in its exteriorized forms, the less it is experienced internally. In this age of mass memory production and consumption, in fact, there seems to be an inverse proportion between the memorialization of the past and its contemplation and study. For once we assign monumental form to memory, we have to some degree divested ourselves of the obligation to remember. In shouldering the memory-work, monuments may relieve viewers of their memory burden.

As Nora concludes, 'Memory has been wholly absorbed by its meticulous reconstruction. Its new vocation is to record: delegating to the *lieu de mémoire* the responsibility of remembering, it sheds its signs upon depositing them there, as a snake sheds its skin' (p. 13). As a result, the memorial operation remains self-contained and detached from our daily lives. Under the illusion that our memorial edifices will always be there to remind us, we take leave of them and return only at our convenience. To the extent that we encourage monuments to do our memory-work for us, we become that much more forgetful. In effect, the initial impulse to memorialize events like the Holocaust may actually spring from an opposite and equal desire to forget them.

Added to this is a contemporary skepticism of the supposedly common values all bring to public spaces, one of the reasons for the uprising against so much public art. 'In the absence of shared belief and even common interests,' John Hallmark Neff writes, 'it should not be surprising that so much of the well-intentioned art acquired for public spaces has failed – failed as art and as art for a civic site.'[8] That is, Neff suggests, without a set of shared expectations, beliefs, or interests, artists and their prospective public audience have no grounds for engagement, no common cultural language in which they might even argue their respective views.

But this formulation may overlook one of the basic functions of all 'public art': to create shared spaces that lend a common spatial frame to otherwise disparate experiences and understanding. Rather than presuming a common set of ideals, the public monument attempts to create an architectonic ideal by which even competing memories may be figured. In this light, Neff's observation might be modified: in the absence of shared beliefs or common interests, art in public spaces may force an otherwise fragmented populace to frame diverse values and ideals in common spaces. By creating common spaces for memory, monuments propagate the illusion of common memory.

As in any state's official use of commemorative spaces, this function of monuments is clear most of all to the governments themselves. Though the utopian vision may hold that monuments are unnecessary as reminders when all can remember for themselves, Maurice Halbwachs has argued persuasively that it is primarily through membership in religious, national, or class groups that people are able to acquire and then recall their memories at all.[9] That is, both the reasons for memory and the forms memory takes are always socially mandated, part of a socializing system whereby fellow citizens gain common history through the vicarious memory of their forbears' experiences. If part of the state's aim, therefore, is to create a sense of shared values and ideals, then it will also be the state's aim to create the sense of common memory, as foundation for a unified polis. Public memorials, national days of commemoration, and shared calendars thus all work to create common loci around which national identity is forged.

To the extent that all societies depend on the assumption of shared experience and memory for the very basis of their common relations, a society's institutions are automatically geared toward creating a shared memory – or at least the illusion of it. By creating the sense of a shared past, such institutions as national memorial days, for example, foster the sense of a common present and future, even a sense of shared national destiny. In this way, memorials provide the sites where groups of people gather to create a common past for themselves, places where they tell the constitutive narratives, their 'shared' stories of the past. They become communities precisely by having shared (if only vicariously) the experiences of their neighbors. At some point, it may even be the activity of remembering together that becomes the shared memory; once ritualized, remembering together becomes an event in itself that is to be shared and remembered.

THE SITE OF MEMORY

In keeping with the bookish, iconoclastic side of Jewish tradition, the first 'memorials' to the Holocaust period came not in stone, glass, or steel – but in narrative. The Yizkor Bikher – memorial books – remembered both the lives and destruction of European Jewish communities according to the most ancient of Jewish memorial media: words on paper. For a murdered people without graves, without even corpses to inter, these memorial books often came to serve as symbolic tombstones: 'The memorial book which will immortalize the memories of our relatives and friends, the Jews of Pshaytsk, will also serve as a substitute grave. Whenever we pick up the book we will feel we are standing next to their grave, because even that the murderers denied them.'[10]

The scribes hoped that, when read, the Yizkor Bikher would turn the site of reading into memorial space. In need of cathartic ceremony, in response to what has been called 'the missing gravestone syndrome,' survivors thus created interior spaces, imagined grave sites, as the first sites for memory.[11] Only later were physical spaces created. While the function of place in mnemonic memory has been well examined, starting with Cicero, and re-examined through the brilliant studies of Yates and others, the reciprocal exchange between a monument and its space is still too little studied. For a monument necessarily transforms an otherwise benign site into part of its content, even as it is absorbed into the site and made part of a larger locale. This tension between site and memorial can be relieved by a seemingly natural extension of site by monument, or it can be aggravated by a perceived incongruity between site and monument. It is better in the view of many contemporary monument makers, in fact, to provoke the landscape with an obtrusive monument than to create a form so pleasingly balanced that it – and memory – recede into the landscape (and oblivion) altogether.

Taken further, a monument becomes a point of reference amid other parts of the landscape, one node among others in a topographical matrix that orients the rememberer and creates meaning in both the land and our recollections. For like narrative, which automatically locates events in linear sequence, the memorial also brings events into some cognitive order. In this sense, any memorial marker in the landscape, no matter how alien to its surroundings, is still perceived in the midst of its geography, in some relation to the other landmarks nearby.

A stainless steel obelisk situated in an empty field, for example, generates different meanings from that situated in a neighborhood shopping mall. Instead of being the only thing standing, it is one of several towers, barely noticed, surrounded by large buildings. American monuments, in particular, are placed often to maximize opportunities for symbolic meaning: the U.S. Holocaust Memorial Museum on the Mall in Washington, D.C., necessarily resonates to other nearby national monuments. The Museum of Jewish Heritage: A Living Memorial to the Holocaust, planned for the Battery in New York, will form part of an immigrant triad, with Ellis Island and the Statue of Liberty in sight. Likewise, the Liberation monument in Liberty Park in Jersey City, New Jersey, echoes the ideals and theme of the Statue of Liberty on the skyline in the background. A new Holocaust memorial in Boston, whatever shape it finally takes, will derive further American meaning from its place on the 'Freedom Trail.'

NOTES

1. Epigraphs: Jean Baudrillard, *The Evil Demon of Images* (Sidney, 1988), 23; Jean Améry, *At the Mind's Limits: Contemplations by a Survivor on Auschwitz and Its Realities*, trans. Sidney Rosenfeld and Stella P. Rosenfeld (Bloomington, 1980), 84; André Schwarz-Bart, *The Last of the Just*, trans. Stephen Becker (London, 1961), 409.
2. Arthur Danto, 'The Vietnam Veterans Memorial,' *The Nation*, 31 Aug. 1986: 152. This particular definition is repeated in an otherwise excellent analysis of the memorial by Marita Sturken, 'The Wall, the Screen, and the Image: The Vietnam Veterans Memorial,' *Representations* 35 (Summer 1991): 118–42.
3. Friedrich Nietzsche, *The Use and Abuse of History*, trans. Adrian Collins (New York, 1985), 14–17.
4. Lewis Mumford, *The Culture of Cities* (New York, 1938), 438.
5. For the full, much more complex, context of Broszat's remarks, see his series of letters to Saul Friedländer and Friedländer's excellent replies printed first in *Vierteljahreshefte für Zeitgeschichte* 36, no. 2 (April 1988): 339–72, subsequently translated and reprinted as 'Martin Broszat/Saul Friedländer: A Controversy about the Historicization of National Socialism,' in *Yad Vashem Studies* 19 (Fall 1988): 1–47; also reprinted in *New German Critique* 44 (Spring–Summer 1988): 85–126.

The exchange between Broszat and Friedländer was initially sparked by Friedländer's response to Broszat's 'Plädoyer für eine Historisierung des Nationalsozialismus' [Plea for a historicization of National Socialism], *Merkur* 39 (1985): 373–85.

Broszat's specific reference to monuments comes in his comments on 'mythical memory,' which he distinguishes from 'scientific insight' (*New German Critique* 44 [Spring–Summer 1988]: 90–1).

6. Rosalind Krauss, *The Originality of the Avant-Garde and Other Modernist Myths* (Cambridge, Mass., and London, 1988), 280.

7. Pierre Nora, 'Between Memory and History: *Les Lieux de Mémoire*,' trans. Marc Roudebush, *Representations* 26 (1989): 13. Reprinted from Pierre Nora, 'Entre mémoire et histoire,' *Les Lieux de mémoire*, vol. 1: *La République* (Paris, 1984), xxvi.

8. John Hallmark Neff, 'Introduction [to Public Art]: Daring to Dream,' *Critical Inquiry* 16 (Summer 1990): 857.

9. See Maurice Halbwachs, *Les Cadres sociaux de la mémoire* (Paris, 1952); also see his *La Mémoire collective* (Paris, 1950).

10. From 'Forwort,' in *Sefer Yizkor le-kedoshei ir (Przedecz) Pshaytask Khurbanot ha'shoah*, p. 130, as quoted in Jack Kugelmass and Jonathan Boyarin, eds., *From a Ruined Garden: The Memorial Books of Polish Jewry* (New York, 1983), 11.

11. On the missing grave syndrome, see Joost Merloo, 'Delayed Mourning in Victims of Extermination Camps,' in Henry Krystal, ed., *Massive Psychic Trauma* (New York, 1968), 74.

SECTION 6
TRAUMA

Edited by Anne Whitehead

INTRODUCTION

Anne Whitehead

The initial emergence of the concept of trauma seems inextricable from the advent of modernity. The phenomenon of trauma was closely linked to advances in industrialisation, which produced the machines that in turn gave rise to train and factory accidents. As E. Ann Kaplan points out, industrialisation led to the expansion of the bourgeois family which 'became the site for female hysteria' (Kaplan, 2005: 25). Industrialisation also underpinned the new, mechanised warfare of the First World War and made possible the totalitarian atrocity of the Holocaust. Trauma, then, is inherently linked to modernity and has been connected, in particular, with the groundbreaking work of Walter Benjamin. As Kevin Newmark emphasises, Benjamin conceives of modernity as a break in consciousness which, as we shall see in the extract below, is analogous to the conceptualisation of trauma. Newmark thus elaborates on Benjamin:

> When the formal patterns of continuity that are presumed to have been grounded in traditional experience by the assimilation of consciousness to memory are disturbed by the truly alien experience of modernity, the coherence of subjective experience is itself displaced in an unexpected way. Consciousness and memory, whatever their relationship in some more or less mythic past, are no longer able to function as associative elements within the same system of individual and collective identity. According to this model, then, modernity would itself be structured like a historical 'accident' that has at some prior moment befallen and disrupted the homogeneous structure of experience. (Newmark, 1995: 238)

Although there are potential problems in Benjamin's implied nostalgia for a mythologised, pre-modern past, it is nevertheless clear that his writing provides an important reference point for thinking through the complex relations between trauma and modernity.

The problem of trauma preoccupied Sigmund Freud from the time of his initial studies of hysterical patients in the 1890s. The topic became particularly acute for him, however, in his encounters with 'shell shocked' male soldiers during the First World War. Freud's attempt to clarify the theoretical under-pinnings of his approach to the problem of trauma resulted in his essay *Beyond the Pleasure Principle* (1921). Here, Freud removed the functions of awareness from consciousness and relocated them in the preconscious, an area between the unconscious and the conscious where censorship takes place. For Freud, then, memory became an effect of the impact of the outside world on the unconscious and preconscious; consciousness took on significance in providing a first line of defence against external stimuli. In Freud's model, trauma resulted from a rupture or breach in the protective shield of consciousness. This was less likely to occur when the subject was prepared for the onslaught of external stimuli, for example through anxiety or narcissism. The symptoms of the trauma victim, the nightmares of the shell-shocked soldier which returned him to the terrible event, acted as a means of trying to establish these mechanisms of preparedness after the fact. Freud's conceptualisation of trauma, like Benjamin's of modernity, thus figures the consciousness as besieged and disrupted by alien, external forces.

Late twentieth-century interest in trauma arose in the wake of the Vietnam War, as returning soldiers manifested the symptomatology of trauma. Post-traumatic stress disorder (PTSD) was officially recognised by the American Psychiatric Association in their *Diagnostic and Statistical Manual* in 1984. Following on from this, feminists such as Judith Lewis Herman critiqued the male bias that they discerned in the categories of PTSD. In her best-selling *Trauma and Recovery* (1992), Herman forcefully argued that women were also displaying the symptoms of PTSD, which resulted from childhood sexual abuse or domestic violence. Laura S. Brown similarly argued that the definition of PTSD as '*an event outside the range of human experience*' (Brown 1995: 100; original emphasis) implicitly discounted the routine encounters of many women with the traumatic experiences of rape, incest and violence.

Particular interest in trauma arose at Yale University out of the Fortunoff Video Archive project, led by Dori Laub and Geoffrey Hartman, which aimed to record the video-testimonies of Holocaust survivors. Through Laub, who was trained as a psychoanalyst and acted as an interviewer for some of the tes-timonies, a psychological dimension was introduced into the taped interviews. In addition to producing a remarkable archive, the project formed the basis for a number of publications, including Lawrence L. Langer's *Holocaust Testimonies* (1991), Shoshana Felman and Dori Laub's *Testimony* (1992) and Geoffrey Hartman's *The Longest Shadow* (1996). The first extract in this section is taken from **Lawrence L. Langer**'s *Admitting the Holocaust* (1995) and provides a reflection on the meaning and significance of testimony. Langer argues that traumatic memories of the Holocaust do not move forward or progress in a chronological fashion, but are characterised instead by what he terms 'durational time', in which the past disrupts the present and is re-experienced in the telling. Langer's distinction between 'chronology' and 'duration' owes a debt to Charlotte Delbo's elaboration of 'external' and 'deep' memory (Delbo, 1990: 1–4), which is discussed in the introduction to this Reader. Langer has argued elsewhere against the significance of gender in the context of trauma, arguing that in Holocaust testimonies 'the ultimate sense of loss unites former victims in a world beyond gender' (Langer, 1998: 362). Countering Langer, Sara R. Horowitz has claimed, on the contrary, that 'gender wounding emerges in literary texts by women – and, differently, in works by men' (Horowitz, 1998: 366). In the extract that follows, Langer discusses the testimony of Anna S. and it is worth considering whether her testimony articulates, in addition to the stumblings and hesitancies of an impossible story that resists conventional memory, a specifically gendered form of wounding.

Particularly influential in deepening and furthering trauma studies in the humanities, and extending their scope beyond the context of the Holocaust, was the publication of **Cathy Caruth**'s edited collection of essays, *Trauma: Explorations in Memory* (1995). In the second extract, taken from the 'Introduction' to the volume, Caruth returns to *Beyond the Pleasure Principle* in order to reflect on the surprising literality of the nightmares that afflicted the shell-shocked soldiers. For Caruth, these dreams and flashbacks take us to the enigmatic core of trauma; namely, that the very immediacy of the experience precludes its registration (in Freud's terms, it breaks through or breaches the defensive shield of consciousness), which means that there can be no 'simple knowledge and memory' (this volume, p. 202). In normative models of memory, there is a fundamental enigma at its heart. When the present was present, it could not be remembered; once it is past, its presence is only in recall. This is not the same presence that it had when it first occurred; in this sense, then, remembering involves the revival of a past that was never present. Caruth's formulation of trauma takes this one stage further. Here, the present was never present, not because it did not happen, but because its happening exceeded the individual's capacity for registration or understanding. If it has not been fully present, it cannot become past; it cannot even attain a presence in recall. Instead, Caruth suggests, the traumatic experience 'is fully evident only in connection with another place, and in another time' (this volume, p. 203); it is characterised by latency. Caruth provides a model of trauma that powerfully disrupts and revises our understanding of memory. Her work gives rise, in turn, to the question of whether the traumatic experience can belatedly become present, and so eventually be relegated to the past and consigned to memory. Although Caruth does not directly answer this question, the emphasis of her writing is on the elusiveness and incomprehensibility of trauma, which can only be represented or addressed in figurative terms. Trauma represents a 'fundamental dislocation', which challenges our received notions of memory, experience and even the event itself.

Following Caruth's volume, the study of trauma quickly extended beyond the Holocaust and became embedded into research in the humanities. In this context, concerns began to arise that trauma was becoming an all-encompassing term and that it was being too readily applied. The historian **Dominick LaCapra** has argued for a distinction between 'historical trauma' – which refers to specific, often human-made, historical occurrences and would include events such as the Holocaust, slavery, apartheid, child sexual abuse and rape – and 'structural trauma', which is LaCapra's term for originary, transhistorical losses, such as entry into language, separation from the mother or the inability to partake fully in a community (LaCapra, 2004: 112–17). Although LaCapra believes both of these categories to be traumatic, he argues that they are so in different ways. The final extract in this section is taken from LaCapra's *History in Transit* (2004). Here, he engages specifically with the work of Caruth and argues that in her writing there is an insufficient distinction between historical and structural trauma, which can result in a blurring of the two. For LaCapra, one of the crucial differences between these two modes of trauma is that, while historical trauma is susceptible to (at least partial) working through, structural trauma cannot be directly changed or healed. The blurring of boundaries that LaCapra distinguishes in Caruth therefore risks suggesting that *all* trauma is non-symbolisable and resistant to working-through. In a broader sense, LaCapra goes on to argue, this is suggestive of the ways in which conceptualisations of trauma, like those of Felman and Caruth, 'may, at least on one significant level, be read as a fascinatingly subtle, often disguised displacement of Paul de Man's variant of deconstruction in which the terminology changes (with unreadability becoming the incomprehensibility of trauma) but the aporetic and discursive strategies recur with some variation' (LaCapra, 2004: 123). LaCapra, then, discerns in the work of Felman and Caruth a tendency towards the traumatic sublime, which he positions as a belated effect of de Man's influence that has itself not been sufficiently worked through. A more positive interpretation of de Man's legacy to trauma studies is provided by Kaplan, who argues:

> By the late 1990s, critical theory had, indeed, through the influence of Lacan and poststructuralism more generally, become very abstract. Critics tended to be wary of falling back into an insufficiently theorized Marxism, on the one hand, or into an insufficiently theorized concept of the body and the subject, on the other. In addition, Felman and Caruth were at Yale where Laub and Hartman had begun to interview Holocaust victims in a climate where renewed interest in World War II and its socio-political meanings and personal sufferings was on the rise. Addressing the phenomena of trauma must have seemed one way for critics to begin to link high theory with specific material events that were both personal and

which implicated history, memory, and culture generally. To this extent, the turn was productive; suggesting reasons for it should not detract from the importance of the intervention. (Kaplan, 2005: 35)

In this light, then, trauma theory emerges as a mode of engaging theory with historical specificity. It can also be interpreted, as suggested in the introduction to the Reader, as a means of beginning to address, albeit belatedly, the troubling and as yet unresolved issue of theory's complicity with the Holocaust.

REFERENCES AND FURTHER READING

Alexander, Jeffrey, Ron Eyerman, Bernhard Giesen and Piotr Sztompka (eds) (2004) *Cultural Trauma and Collective Identity*. Berkeley, CA: University of California Press.

Belau, Linda and Peter Ramadanovic (eds) (2002) *Topologies of Trauma: Essays on the Limit of Knowledge and Memory*. New York: Other Press.

Brown, Laura S. (1995) 'Not Outside the Range: One Feminist Perspective on Psychic Trauma', in Cathy Caruth (ed.), *Trauma: Explorations in Memory*. Baltimore, MD, and London: Johns Hopkins University Press, pp. 100–12.

Caruth, Cathy (ed.) (1995) *Trauma: Explorations in Memory*. Baltimore, MD, and London: Johns Hopkins University Press.

—— (1996) *Unclaimed Experience: Trauma, Narrative, and History*. Baltimore, MD, and London: Johns Hopkins University Press.

—— (2000) 'Parting Words: Trauma, Silence and Survival', in Michael Rossington and Anne Whitehead (eds), *Between the Psyche and the Polis: Refiguring History in Literature and Theory*. Aldershot and Burlington, VT: Ashgate, pp. 77–96.

Delbo, Charlotte (1990) *Days and Memory*, trans. Rosette C. Lamont. Marlboro, VT: Marlboro Press.

Edkins, Jenny (2003) *Trauma and the Memory of Politics*. Cambridge: Cambridge University Press.

Felman, Shoshana and Dori Laub (1992) *Testimony: Crises of Witnessing in Literature, Psychoanalysis and History*. New York and London: Routledge.

Freud, Sigmund ([1921] 1991) 'Beyond the Pleasure Principle', in Angela Richards (ed.), *On Metapsychology: The Theory of Psychoanalysis*, trans. James Strachey, Penguin Freud Library, vol. 11. Harmondsworth: Penguin, pp. 269–338.

Hartman, Geoffrey (1996) *The Longest Shadow: In the Aftermath of the Holocaust*. Basingstoke: Palgrave Macmillan.

Herman, Judith Lewis (1992) *Trauma and Recovery: From Domestic Abuse to Political Terror*. London: Pandora.

Horowitz, Sara R. (1998) 'Women in Holocaust Literature: Engendering Trauma Memory', in Dalia Ofer and Lenore Weitzman (eds), *Women and the Holocaust*. New Haven, CT, and London: Yale University Press, 364–78.

Kaplan, E. Ann (2005) *Trauma Culture: The Politics of Terror and Loss in Media and Literature*. New Brunswick, NJ, and London: Rutgers University Press.

LaCapra, Dominick (2001) *Writing History, Writing Trauma*. Baltimore, MD, and London: Johns Hopkins University Press.

—— (2004) *History in Transit: Experience, Identity, Critical Theory*. Ithaca, NY, and London: Cornell University Press.

Langer, Lawrence L. (1991) *Holocaust Testimonies: The Ruins of Memory*. New Haven, CT, and London: Yale University Press.

—— (1995) *Admitting the Holocaust: Collected Essays*. New York and Oxford: Oxford University Press.

—— (1998) 'Gendered Suffering? Women in Holocaust Testimonies', in Dalia Ofer and Lenore J. Weitzman (eds), *Women and the Holocaust*. New Haven, CT, and London: Yale University Press, pp. 351–63.

Leys, Ruth (2003) *Trauma: A Genealogy*. Chicago: University of Chicago Press.

Miller, Nancy K. and Jason Tougaw (eds) (2002) *Extremities: Trauma, Testimony and Community*. Urbana and Chicago: University of Illinois Press.

Newmark, Kevin (1995) 'Traumatic Poetry: Charles Baudelaire and the Shock of Laughter', in Cathy Caruth (ed.), *Trauma: Explorations in Memory*. Baltimore, MD, and London: Johns Hopkins University Press, pp. 236–55.

Santner, Eric L. (1992) 'History Beyond the Pleasure Principle: Some Thoughts on the Representation of Trauma', in Saul Friedlander (ed.), *Probing the Limits of Representation: Nazism and the 'Final Solution'*. Cambridge, MA, and London: Harvard University Press, pp. 143–54.

LAWRENCE L. LANGER: *FROM* MEMORY'S TIME: CHRONOLOGY AND DURATION IN HOLOCAUST TESTIMONIES

One of the most striking events in Holocaust studies in recent years has been the proliferation of titles focusing on a single theme: memory. Saul Friedländer's *When Memory Comes* (1979), Pierre Vidal-Nacquet's *The Assassins of Memory* (1985), Charlotte Delbo's last work, *Days and Memory* (1985), Sybil Milton's *In Fitting Memory: The Art and Politics of Holocaust Memorials* (1991), my own *Holocaust Testimonies: The Ruins of Memory* (1991), a collection of essays on the convent controversy at Auschwitz called *Memory Offended* (1991), another set of essays on Elie Wiesel called *Between Memory and Hope* (1990). We also have James Young's study of Holocaust monuments called *The Texture of Memory* (1993), and Geoffrey Hartman's edited volume of Holocaust essays called *The Shapes of Memory* (1993). And I'm sure there are many others. Perhaps this means we have finally begun to enter the second stage of Holocaust response, moving from what we know of the event (the province of historians), to how to remember it, which shifts the responsibility to our own imaginations and what we are prepared to admit there.

If we are to trust the titles, memory itself is not neutral. *Between Memory and Hope* implies one agenda; *The Ruins of Memory*, another. One tries to edify; the other, to plunge us without life preservers into the maelstrom of the disaster. In the end, unlike Dante, the pilgrim of the Holocaust must learn to mistrust all guides, whether they lead us toward closure or not. Unlike history, memory can be a very *private* adventure, and when the Holocaust is its object, it can be a

Source: Lawrence L. Langer, *Admitting the Holocaust: Collected Essays* (Oxford and New York: Oxford University Press, 1995), pp. 13–9.

threatening one. Virgil could lead Dante through an Inferno ruled by external order: the consolations of Paradise lighten for the reader the harrowing experience of Hell. Surviving Holocaust victims, in one dimension of their testimonies, disclose an internal *dis*order void of consolations. Dante's pilgrim (and Dante's reader) moves from time to eternity; spatial and spiritual progress accompany each other. But as we shall see, in Holocaust testimony time itself divides, so that memory must contend with the paradox enshrined in Charlotte Delbo's statement 'I died in Auschwitz, but no one knows it,' or in the words of the former deathcamp inmate who said, 'One can be alive after Sobibor without having survived Sobibor.'

Sociologist-historian Pierre Vidal-Nacquet calls himself a 'memory-man,' and has confidence in the power of memory. Philosopher Jean-François Lyotard is not so sure, concerned as he is with what memory 'misses' through rejection or suppression. If there is a history of remembering, he argues, there is also a politics of forgetting. Holocaust memory entreats us to accept the destabilizing force of its content, even as traditional memory seeks ways to restore the balance. For example, there is no need to rehearse here the role of the funeral oration in allying grief to memory and celebrating the life which has just ended in death. Such commemorative moments foster communal unity and remembering. But funereal testimony differs from the funeral oration, since it rises not from the spring of chronological time but the tomb of what I call durational time: the one celebrating a life that has just ended in the sadness of death, transcended by a 'normal' future for those who remain; the other signifying a death that has not been preceded by a life connected to such an end, followed by a temporal void.

To illustrate these distinctions, let me turn to Abraham Lewin's description in *A Cup of Tears: A Diary of the Warsaw Ghetto* of the funeral in the ghetto of the distinguished Polish Jewish historian Majer Balaban, who in December 1942 died suddenly of a heart attack:

> He was 65 years old at his death [writes Lewin], but looked a lot older. The remains of the Jewish intelligentsia came to pay their last respects to the deceased. God! What a tragic and depressing sight the gathering at the funeral made. Firstly the small number who came. It was plain to see that very few of us are left, just a handful. And secondly: the appearance of the people! What impoverishment, what gloom, what weariness filled their faces! In this small gathering was expressed our total destruction in its most tragic and appalling form, the destruction of the greatest Jewish community in Europe. I was shaken to the core, looking at the extinguished and despairing eyes, and the lined faces and the torn and ragged clothes. Utter annihilation.[1]

We can remember in order to protect continuity or to verify disruption, to conceal or to flay. Both modes prevail in the figuration of the Holocaust, but only when we lapse into confusing the communal ritual of funeral orations with the estranging rite of funereal testimonies. Lewin was honest enough to recognize the difference, and left us a striking instance of how the threat of mass murder had slain an ancient tradition. Lyotard addresses this dilemma when he calls for 'an aesthetics of the memory of the forgotten, an anesthetics.'[2]

'Here,' says Lyotard, 'to fight against forgetting means to fight to remember that one forgets as soon as one believes, draws conclusions, and holds for certain. It means to fight against forgetting the precariousness of what has been established, of the reestablished past; it is a fight for the sickness whose recovery is simulated.'[3] Simulated recovery belongs to the realm of chronological time. In the realm of durational time, no one recovers because nothing is recovered, only uncovered and then re-covered, buried again beneath the fruitless struggle to expose 'the way it was.' Holocaust memory cannot be used to certify belief, establish closure, or achieve certainty. Hence chronological time is needed to intrude on this memory by those who insist on rescuing belief, closure, and certainty from testimonies about the disaster. Durational time resists and undermines this effort.

For Lyotard, Holocaust past is 'a past located this side of the forgotten, much closer to the present moment than any past, at the same time that it is incapable of being solicited by voluntary and conscious memory,'[4] and this is what I call duration, which exists *this side* of the forgotten, not to be dredged from memory because it is always, has always been there – an always-present past that in testimony becomes a presented past, for the witness more precisely a re-presented past, and then, in narrative forms other than testimony, a represented past. What is lost during the transitions?

How can written history, which began in the form of 'annals,' avoid chronology? When the annalist becomes an analyst, he also becomes a self-conscious servant to time. Do testimonies tell us about what precedes or dominates one's present life? Yes – and no. The duration of Holocaust time, which is a constantly *re*-experienced time, threatens the chronology of experienced time. It leaps out of chronology, establishing its own momentum, or fixation. Testimony may *appear* chronological to the auditor or audience, but the narrator who is a mental witness rather than a temporal one is 'out of time' as she tells her story. I as interviewer have the strange feeling that I am 'in' time as I listen, yet she is 'out' of time as she speaks. I try to enter her *mental* space, not her temporal or chronological one. Lyotard calls it the retrieval of a time that is lost 'because it has not had place and time in the psychic apparatus.' He speaks of a moment 'where the present is the past and the past is always presence,'[5] while at the same time admitting the unsuitability of the very terminology he uses.

But this is often the case in Holocaust discourse; we are led astray, or baffled by the lack of a language to confront the difference between the chronological current, which flows until we channel it between the permanent banks of historical narrative, and durational persistence, which cannot overflow the blocked reservoir of its own moment and hence never enters what we call the stream of time. Or at least not until I alter it by trying to write about it as if it had a before, a during, and an after, because most writing cannot exist without the temporal succession that violates the uniquely imprisoned persistence of the Holocaust event in the memory of its witnesses. The most successful artistic attempt I know to overcome these obstacles in narrative prose is Jorge Semprun's novel *The Long Voyage* (in which the narrator 'remembers' his future, a logical impossibility, but an artistic reality nonetheless).

To illustrate what I mean by the uniquely imprisoned persistence of a Holocaust event in a witness's memory, memory's time or more precisely durational time, let me turn to the testimony of Anna S. (not her real name). Anna married at eighteen because her parents thought that a husband might help her better to survive in the harsh conditions under Nazi rule. But after the Germans invaded their home one night and shot her father and brother – she, her husband, and her mother managed to hide or flee – husband and wife separated, she and her mother sleeping in barns and he leaving with his brothers for the forest. (She learned much later that they were captured, tortured, and executed by the Gestapo.) All this time Anna had been pregnant, and as she neared her term, her mother insisted that they find quarters in a nearby ghetto. Here Anna gives birth, while she is suffering from typhus, in a cold, tiny room where, as she tells us, she is sleeping in a *crib* (others are sleeping beneath it) because that is the only available bed. When she goes into labor, her mother rushes out to find a neighbor who had promised to help with the delivery. While she is gone, the baby is born. The testimonial moment begins:

ANNA	And I was burning up with typhus, and then – the baby came out.
INTERVIEWER	Stillborn?
ANNA	Hm?
INTERVIEWER	Stillborn.
ANNA	No.
INTERVIEWER	Alive?
ANNA	It was alive. It was alive.
INTERVIEWER	Was it a boy or a girl?
ANNA	Boy. Yes, he was born alive, and we didn't have a – doctor's no question – we didn't have a midwife to take the baby.

At this point she tells of her mother running out in search of the neighbor, returning just after the birth had occurred. Then she resumes (and note her *utter* inability to reconstruct these moments in any kind of chronological order):

ANNA	So finally, finally, I don't know how long it took, I was unconscious. I was like, I knew it happens something now, I couldn't, I don't know, I couldn't respond to anything. And then finally she came in, I don't know how long she

was there, I heard (she imitates choking sounds) he was choking, he was choking [whispering] and he died, he died, when she came he was dead already. [. . .] After a minute I woke up and gave a look. It was a beautiful boy, a beautiful boy. [. . .]

INTERVIEWER   So you were alone all that time?

ANNA   Yes. I was alone, and next to mine bed, mine crib, was a man dying, and I opened my eyes and I looked at him and he was dying – and I fall asleep.

Holocaust testimony enacts a resistance against the efforts of time to erase experience without a trace: what Lyotard calls 'time lost yet always there, a revelation that never reveals itself but remains there, a misery.'[6] For how could Anna's words reveal to us what that moment must have been for her, what it remains, not in conventional memory, since she is obviously not 'remembering' a forgotten moment? Her uttering of details, naming the unthinkable, her enactment for us of the truth that at the same time this self is *not* that self – she has remarried, and had a new family – and *is* that self, our difficulty in finding a familiar context or designation for what she describes, our inability to detect through a sequence of events the presence of a guilty agent somewhere in the obscurity of the past – all of these together are gathered in a cornucopia of diverse causes, which in the end paralyze our capacity to judge, evaluate, or perhaps even respond. We are confined, consumed by the moment of the narrative which is not a moment in sequential time, mesmerized by duration until chronology disappears from consciousness. These segments of testimony enable us to experience the effects of Holocaust duration as no other form of expression can.

Hearing testimony, we are in the presence of a past that has not been and cannot be effaced, a moment re-presented to us rather than represented, since, as Lyotard insists, only that which has been inscribed or represented (in word or image or form) can be forgotten. Such testimony disrupts chronology, where we are safely situated, and drags us into the menacing realm of duration, where nothing can shield us from this unpresented or never-before-presented rehearsal of inversion, where death replaces birth as the 'normal' course of events, only to have narrative restore the *illusion* of chronology. By this I mean that circumstances determine the baby's death before it is born, though chronology prompts us to hope that maybe it will be rescued. In describing the birth of her baby that is already doomed, Anna lures us into her own experience of duration, and for this instant, anyway, we escape what Lyotard calls 'the crude forgetting of the unforgettable secret.'[7] When, some minutes after this part of her testimony, Anna leans forward and whispers into the darkness beyond the cameras, 'I never told this story to no one before,' she is marking us with the scars of that hitherto undisclosed mystery of her ever-present past, which until now for us has been a never-present past. Where do we then fit it into the chronology of humanistic endeavor, of healing old wounds, of reconciliation, of redemption? Time as chronology does not and cannot heal the wounds of time as duration.

Chronology anticipates something. Duration anticipates nothing. Birth is a culmination of developing time. Its features are growth and nurture, expectation, the organization of various biological, chemical, and physical forces into life. Like history, it represents a gestation from the past in the service of the future. The disaster of the Holocaust violates such chronology in nature, and this moment sheds a glaring light on the reversal and disruption accompanying the disaster. The victim is powerless to prevent the disintegration of what for nine months has been integrating within her. What system of belief can we build from the debris of this testimony? I suppose I asked, 'And what happened next?' after this moment of narrative (since I was the interviewer), but what answer could I have expected? *Everything* happened afterward – and nothing. As Charlotte Delbo implied in the title for the trilogy of her Auschwitz memoirs, *Auschwitz et après*, there was an Auschwitz, and there was an afterward, and unless you understand that the two terms do not represent a chronology, you cannot begin to enter the abyss of the place we call Auschwitz. Such testimony *serves* nothing; it can only *pre*serve.

What else can it do? It can liberate the inaudible from the silence that insulates it from our ears *because* it is unbearable; testimony like the one we have been examining helps to make certain silences audible, creating the paradox of the audible silence. Unfortunately, we are still left with the burdensome legacy of the *in*audible silences, echoing from the inner walls of the gas chambers, whose text we will never hear. They will remain inaccessible and hence inaudible forever; we will have to make do with the fragments of audible silences like this one.

If we cannot find an aesthetics for Auschwitz, we must be content with what Lyotard calls an 'anesthetics.' Amnesia has been the comfortable stance of those disinclined to traffic with the threats of audible silence. As anesthesia is the medical means for making one insensible, anesthetics deals with the art of the insensible (and in a related way, with the non-sensible), plunges us into the non-sense (not the nonsense) of the disaster, reminds us that no ordinary feelings will make us sensitive to the appeal of such an unprecedented catastrophe. If art is concerned with the creation of beautiful forms, Holocaust testimony, and perhaps Holocaust art as well, deals with the creation of 'malforms,' though we may not yet have arrived at recognizing the legitimacy of this undertaking – to say nothing of the word itself. Birth-as-death makes the unnatural 'natural,' and though we resist the logic of this conjunction, it pursues us and persists through the duration of such testimonial evidence as the one we have just heard.

NOTES

1. Abraham Lewin, *A Cup of Tears: A Diary of the Warsaw Ghetto*, ed. Antony Polonsky, trans. Christopher Hutton (Oxford: Basil Blackwell, 1988), p. 228.

2. Jean-François Lyotard, *Heidegger and 'the jews'*, trans. Andreas Michel and Mark S. Roberts (Minneapolis, MN: University of Minnesota Press, 1990), p. xxii.
3. Ibid., p. 10.
4. Ibid., p. 12.
5. Ibid., p. 16.
6. Ibid., p. 23.
7. Ibid., pp. 26, 33.

CATHY CARUTH: *FROM* TRAUMA AND EXPERIENCE

In the years since Vietnam, the fields of psychiatry, psychoanalysis, and sociology have taken a renewed interest in the problem of trauma. In 1980, the American Psychiatric Association finally officially acknowledged the long-recognized but frequently ignored phenomenon under the title 'Post Traumatic Stress Disorder' (PTSD), which included the symptoms of what had previously been called shell shock, combat stress, delayed stress syndrome, and traumatic neurosis, and referred to responses to both human and natural catastrophes. On the one hand, this classification and its attendant official acknowledgment of a pathology has provided a category of diagnosis so powerful that it has seemed to engulf everything around it: suddenly responses not only to combat and to natural catastrophes but also to rape, child abuse, and a number of other violent occurrences have been understood in terms of PTSD, and diagnoses of some dissociative disorders have also been switched to that of trauma. On the other hand, this powerful new tool has provided anything but a solid explanation of disease: indeed, the impact of trauma as a concept and a category, if it has helped diagnosis, has done so only at the cost of a fundamental disruption in our received modes of understanding and of cure, and a challenge to our very comprehension of what constitutes pathology. This can be seen in the debates that surround 'category A' of the American Psychiatric Association's definition of PTSD (a response to an event 'outside the range of

Source: Cathy Caruth, 'Trauma and Experience: Introduction', in Cathy Caruth (ed.), *Trauma: Explorations in Memory* (Baltimore, MD, and London: Johns Hopkins University Press, 1995), pp. 3–12.

usual human experience'), concerning how closely PTSD must be tied to specific kinds of events;[1] or in the psychoanalytic problem of whether trauma is indeed pathological in the usual sense, in relation to distortions caused by desires, wishes, and repressions. Indeed, the more we satisfactorily locate and classify the symptoms of PTSD, the more we seem to have dislocated the boundaries of our modes of understanding – so that psychoanalysis and medically oriented psychiatry, sociology, history, and even literature all seem to be called upon to explain, to cure, or to show why it is that we can no longer simply explain or simply cure. The phenomenon of trauma has seemed to become all-inclusive, but it has done so precisely because it brings us to the limits of our understanding: if psychoanalysis, psychiatry, sociology, and even literature are beginning to hear each other anew in the study of trauma, it is because they are listening through the radical disruption and gaps of traumatic experience. [. . .]

While the precise definition of post-traumatic stress disorder is contested, most descriptions generally agree that there is a response, sometimes delayed, to an overwhelming event or events, which takes the form of repeated, intrusive hallucinations, dreams, thoughts or behaviors stemming from the event, along with numbing that may have begun during or after the experience, and possibly also increased arousal to (and avoidance of) stimuli recalling the event.[2] This simple definition belies a very peculiar fact: the pathology cannot be defined either by the event itself – which may or may not be catastrophic, and may not traumatize everyone equally – nor can it be defined in terms of a *distortion* of the event, achieving its haunting power as a result of distorting personal significances attached to it. The pathology consists, rather, solely in the *structure of its experience* or reception: the event is not assimilated or experienced fully at the time, but only belatedly, in its repeated *possession* of the one who experiences it. To be traumatized is precisely to be possessed by an image or event. And thus the traumatic symptom cannot be interpreted, simply, as a distortion of reality, nor as the lending of unconscious meaning to a reality it wishes to ignore, nor as the repression of what once was wished. Indeed, in 1920, faced with the onset of 'war neuroses' from World War I, Freud was astonished at their resistance to the whole field of wish and unconscious meaning, comparing them to another long-resistant phenomenon he had dealt with, the accident neurosis:

> Dreams occurring in traumatic neuroses have the characteristic of repeatedly bringing the patient back into the situation of his accident, a situation from which he wakes up in another fright. This astonishes people far too little . . . Anyone who accepts it as something self-evident that dreams should put them back at night into the situation that caused them to fall ill has misunderstood the nature of dreams. (*SE* 18: 13)

The returning traumatic dream startles Freud because it cannot be understood in terms of any wish or unconscious meaning, but is, purely and inexplicably, the literal return of the event against the will of the one it inhabits. Indeed, modern analysts as well have remarked on the surprising *literality* and non-symbolic nature of traumatic dreams and flashbacks, which resist cure to the extent that they remain, precisely, literal. It is this literality and its insistent return which thus constitutes trauma and points toward its enigmatic core: the delay or incompletion in knowing, or even in seeing, an overwhelming occurrence that then remains, in its insistent return, absolutely *true* to the event. It is indeed this truth of traumatic experience that forms the center of its pathology or symptoms; it is not a pathology, that is, of falsehood or displacement of meaning, but of history itself. If PTSD must be understood as a pathological symptom, then it is not so much a symptom of the unconscious, as it is a symptom of history. The traumatized, we might say, carry an impossible history within them, or they become themselves the symptom of a history that they cannot entirely possess.

Yet what can it mean that history occurs as a symptom? It is indeed this curious phenomenon that makes trauma, or PTSD, in its definition, and in the impact it has on the lives of those who live it, intimately bound up with a question of truth. The problem arises not only in regard to those who listen to the traumatized, not knowing how to establish the reality of their hallucinations and dreams; it occurs rather and most disturbingly often within the very knowledge and experience of the traumatized themselves. For on the one hand, the dreams, hallucinations and thoughts are absolutely literal, unassimilable to associative chains of meaning. It is this literality as we have said that possesses the receiver and resists psychoanalytic interpretation and cure.[3] Yet the fact that this scene or thought is not a possessed knowledge, but itself possesses, at will, the one it inhabits, often produces a deep uncertainty as to its very truth:

> A child survivor of the Holocaust who had been at Theresienstadt continually had flashbacks of trains, and didn't know where they came from; she thought she was going crazy. Until one day, in a group survivor meeting, a man says, 'Yes, at Theresienstadt you could see the trains through the bars of the children's barracks.' She was relieved to discover she was not mad. (Kinsler, 1990)

The survivors' uncertainty is not a simple amnesia; for the event returns, as Freud points out, insistently and against their will. Nor is it a matter of indirect access to an event, since the hallucinations are generally of events all too accessible in their horrible truth. It is not, that is, having too little or indirect access to an experience that places its truth in question, in this case, but paradoxically enough, its very overwhelming immediacy, that produces its belated uncertainty. Indeed, behind these local experiences of uncertainty, I would propose, is a larger question raised by the fact of trauma, what Shoshana Felman [. . .] calls the 'larger, more profound, less definable crisis of truth . . . proceeding from contemporary trauma.' Such a crisis of truth extends beyond the question of individual cure and asks how we in this era can have access to our own historical experience, to a history that is in its immediacy a crisis to whose truth there is no simple access.

I would suggest that it is this crisis of truth, the historical enigma betrayed by trauma, that poses the greatest challenge to psychoanalysis, and is being felt more broadly at the center of trauma research today. For the attempt to understand trauma brings one repeatedly to this peculiar paradox: that in trauma the greatest confrontation with reality may also occur as an absolute numbing to it, that immediacy, paradoxically enough, may take the form of belatedness. [. . .] Dori Laub has suggested that massive psychic trauma 'precludes its registration'; it is 'a record that has yet to be made' (Laub, 1991). [. . .] Central to the very immediacy of this experience, that is, is a gap that carries the force of the event and does so precisely at the expense of simple knowledge and memory. The force of this experience would appear to arise precisely, in other words, in the collapse of its understanding.

It is indeed the link between this inexplicable traumatic void and the nature of historical experience that is the focus of Freud's great study of Jewish history, *Moses and Monotheism*, in which he compares the history of the Jews with the structure of a trauma. What is striking, for Freud, is the return of the event after a period of delay:

> It may happen that someone gets away, apparently unharmed, from the spot where he has suffered a shocking accident, for instance a train collision. In the course of the following weeks, however, he develops a series of grave psychical and motor symptoms, which can be ascribed only to his shock or whatever else happened at the time of the accident. He has developed a 'traumatic neurosis.' This appears quite incomprehensible and is therefore a novel fact. The time that elapsed between the accident and the first appearance of the symptoms is called the 'incubation period,' a transparent allusion to the pathology of infectious disease . . . It is the feature one might term *latency*. (Freud, 1939, 84)

In the term 'latency,' the period during which the effects of the experience are not apparent, Freud seems to describe the trauma as the successive movement from an event to its repression to its return. Yet what is truly striking about the accident victim's experience of the event and what in fact constitutes the central enigma of Freud's example, is not so much the period of forgetting that occurs after the accident, but rather the fact that the victim of the crash was never fully conscious during the accident itself: the person gets away, Freud says, 'apparently unharmed.' The experience of trauma, the fact of latency, would thus seem to consist, not in the forgetting of a reality that can hence never be fully known, but in an inherent latency within the experience itself. The historical power of the trauma is not just that the experience is repeated after its forgetting, but that it is only in and through its inherent forgetting that it is first experienced at all. And it is this inherent latency of the event that paradoxically explains the peculiar, temporal structure, the belatedness, of historical experience: since the traumatic event is not experienced as it occurs, it is fully evident only in connection with another place, and in another time. If repression, in trauma, is replaced by latency, this is significant in so far as its blankness – the space of uncon-sciousness – is paradoxically what precisely preserves the event in its literality. For history to be a history of trauma means that it is referential precisely to the extent that it is not fully perceived as it occurs; or to put it somewhat differently, that a history can be grasped only in the very inaccessibility of its occurrence.[4]

Freud's late insight into this inextricable and paradoxical relation between history and trauma can tell us something about the challenge it presently poses for psychoanalysis; for it suggests that what trauma has to tell us – the historical and personal truth it transmits – is intricately bound up with its refusal of historical boundaries; that its truth is bound up with its crisis of truth. This is why, I would suggest, psychoanalysis has been beset by problems surrounding, precisely, the historical truth it accords to trauma, or whether it locates its ultimate origin inside or outside the psyche. On the one hand, many have noted in the debate surrounding the historical reality of trauma for Freud, that he was, from the beginning, always concerned with the relation between the occurrence of real traumatic events and the experience of pathology; many have pointed to the early *Studies on Hysteria* and 'Preliminary Communication,' but one could perhaps already see the beginnings of this interest in his first published book, *On Aphasia*, exploring physical trauma to the brain. On the other hand, many have suggested that Freud's apparent 'giving up' of the reality of childhood seduction served – for Freud's followers, if not entirely for Freud himself – to relocate the origins of trauma entirely inside the psyche, in the individual's fantasy life, and hence to disavow the historical reality of violence (see, for example, Masson, 1984). While the insistence on the reality of violence is a necessary and important task, particularly as a corrective to analytic therapies that would reduce trauma to fantasy life or adult trauma to the events of childhood, nonetheless the debate concerning the location of the origins of traumatic experience as inside or outside the psyche may also miss the central Freudian insight into trauma, that the impact of the traumatic event lies precisely in its belatedness, in its refusal to be simply located, in its insistent appearance outside the boundaries of any single place or time. From his early claims, in the *Project for a Scientific Psychology*, that a trauma consists of two scenes – the earlier (in childhood) having sexual content but no meaning, the later (after puberty) having no sexual content but sexual meaning[5] – to his later claims, in *Moses and Monotheism*, that the trauma occurs only after a latency period, Freud seems to have been concerned, as we have suggested, with the way in which trauma is not a simple or single experience of events but that events, insofar as they are traumatic, assume their force precisely in their temporal delay. The apparent split between external and internal trauma in psycho-analytic theory, and related problems in other psychiatric definitions of trauma – whether to define it in terms of events or of symptomatic responses to events, or the relative contribution of previous traumas to the present one – would all be a function, in Freud's definition, of the split within immediate experience that characterizes the traumatic occurrence itself. It is the fundamental dislocation implied by all traumatic experience that is both its testimony to the event and to the impossibility of its direct access. [. . .]

This historical conception of trauma can also be understood as conveying the urgent centrality for psychoanalytic thinking of the relation between crisis and survival. [. . .] Understood as an attempt to explain the experience of war trauma, Freud's difficult thought provides a deeply disturbing insight into the enigmatic relation between trauma and survival: the fact that, for those who undergo trauma, it is not only the moment of the event, but of the passing out of it that is traumatic; that *survival itself*, in other words, *can be a crisis*. [. . .]

The trauma is a repeated suffering of the event, but it is also a continual leaving of its site. The traumatic reexperiencing of the event thus *carries with it* what Dori Laub calls the 'collapse of witnessing,' the impossibility of knowing that first constituted it. And by carrying that impossibility of knowing out of the empirical event itself, trauma opens up and challenges us to a new kind of listening, the witnessing, precisely, *of impossibility*. [. . .]

The final import of the psychoanalytic and historical analysis of trauma is to suggest that the inherent departure, within trauma, from the moment of its first occurrence, is also a means of passing out of the isolation imposed by the event: that the history of a trauma, in its inherent belatedness, can only take place through the listening of another. The meaning of the trauma's address beyond itself concerns, indeed, not only individual isolation but a wider historical isolation that, in our time, is communicated on the level of our cultures. Such an address can be located, for example, in Freud's insisting, from his exile in England, on having his final book on trauma – *Moses and Monotheism* – translated into English before he died; or in the survivors of Hiroshima first communicating their stories to the United States through the narrative written by John Hersey, or more generally in the survivors of the catastrophes of one culture addressing the survivors of another.[6] This speaking and this listening – a speaking and a listening *from the site of trauma* – does not rely, I would suggest, on what we simply know of each other, but on what we don't yet know of our own traumatic pasts. In a catastrophic age, that is, trauma itself may provide the very link between cultures: not as a simple understanding of the pasts of others but rather, within the traumas of contemporary history, as our ability to listen through the departures we have all taken from ourselves.

NOTES

1. This definition was used through DSM III-R. The phrase was eliminated from category A in the DSM IV definition, which appeared in 1994 (after the original publication of this introduction). The debate concerning what kinds of events may be considered potentially traumatizing nonetheless continues.
2. See for example the definition of PTSD in American Psychiatric Association (1987) and the discussion of PTSD in the introduction to van der Kolk (1984).
3. See Cohen (1990a, 1990b).
4. See Caruth (1991).

5. See Laplanche (1970).

6. *Moses and Monotheism* tells not only about the ancient trauma of the Jews but about Freud's own unsettling departure from Vienna in 1938. On the circumstances of the book's translation, see Gay (1988), 637, 638, and 643. With regard to the Hiroshima survivors, the publication of Hersey's *Hiroshima* (1985), written in the third person but based on directly received first-person accounts, produced the first widespread reaction in the United States to the human effects of the bombing.

REFERENCES

American Psychiatric Association (1987) *Diagnostic and Statistical Manual of Mental Disorders*, 3rd edn rev. Washington, DC: APA.

Caruth, Cathy (1991) 'Unclaimed Experience: Trauma and the Possibility of History,' *Yale French Studies* 79.

Cohen, Jonathan (1990a) 'The Role of Interpretation in the Psychoanalytic Therapy of Traumatized Patients.' Paper prepared for the Sixth Annual Meeting of the International Society for Traumatic Stress Studies, New Orleans.

—— (1990b) 'The Trauma Paradigm in Psychoanalysis'. Paper prepared for the Sixth Annual Meeting of the International Society for Traumatic Stress Studies, New Orleans.

Freud, Sigmund (1939) *Moses and Monotheism*, trans. Katherine Jones. New York: Vintage.

—— ([1920] 1955) *The Standard Edition of the Complete Psychological Works of Sigmund Freud*, Vol. 18, trans. under the editorship of James Strachey in collaboration with Anna Freud, assisted by Alex Strachey and Alan Tyson. 24 vols (1953–74). London: Hogarth.

Gay, Peter (1988) *Freud: A Life for Our Time*. New York: Norton.

Hersey, John (1985) *Hiroshima*. New York: Bantam.

Kinsler, Florabel (1990) 'The Dynamics of Brief Group Therapy in Homogeneous Populations: Child Survivors of the Holocaust.' Paper prepared for the Sixth Annual Meeting of the International Society for Traumatic Stress Studies, New Orleans.

Laplanche, Jean (1970) *Life and Death in Psychoanalysis*, trans. Jeffrey Mehlman. Baltimore, MD: Johns Hopkins University Press.

Laub, Dori (1991) 'No One Bears Witness to the Witness,' in *Testimony: Crises of Witnessing in Literature, Psychoanalysis and History*, eds Shoshana Felman and Dori Laub. New York: Routledge.

Masson, Jeffrey (1984) *The Assault on Truth: Freud's Suppression of the Seduction Theory*. New York: Penguin.

van der Kolk, Bessel A. (ed.) (1984) *Post-Traumatic Stress Disorder: Psychological and Biological Sequelae*. Washington, DC: American Psychiatric Press.

DOMINICK LACAPRA: *FROM* HISTORY IN TRANSIT: EXPERIENCE, IDENTITY, CRITICAL THEORY

Trauma is itself a shattering experience that disrupts or even threatens to destroy experience in the sense of an integrated or at least viably articulated life. There is a sense in which trauma is an out-of-context experience that upsets expectations and unsettles one's very understanding of existing contexts. Moreover, the radically disorienting experience of trauma often involves a dissociation between cognition and affect. In brief, in traumatic experience one typically can represent numbly or with aloofness what one cannot feel, and one feels overwhelmingly what one is unable to represent, at least with any critical distance and cognitive control. Here one has an aporetic relation between representation and affect with the possibility of uncontrolled oscillation between poles of a double bind. Indeed one might postulate that an aporia marks a trauma that has not been viably worked through, hence inducing compulsive repetition of the aporetic relation. One might also maintain that, in the terms used by Walter Benjamin (at least as I am appropriating them), trauma as experience is *Erlebnis* rather than *Erfahrung*.[1] As *Erlebnis* trauma is a shock to the system and may be acted out or compulsively repeated in so-called traumatic memory. *Erfahrung* involves more viable articulations of experience allowing openings to possible futures.

The problem of working through trauma or, more precisely, its recurrent symptoms, is to move from *Erlebnis* to *Erfahrung* to the extent that this movement is possible. (Narration, including experimental narrative, plays an

Source: Dominick LaCapra, *History in Transit: Experience, Identity, Critical Theory* (Ithaca, NY, and London: Cornell University Press, 2004), pp. 117–23.

important role here, especially in engaging posttraumatic symptoms of limit events and experiences, but so may other forms such as the lyric or essay as well as performative modes including ritual, song, and dance.)[2] The experience of trauma is thus unlike the traumatizing event in that it is not punctual or datable. It is bound up with its belated effects or symptoms, which render it elusive.[3] Its elusiveness – or what Cathy Caruth terms its unclaimed quality – makes the historical experience of trauma distinguishable only with difficulty from structural or transhistorical trauma, hence facilitating in certain cases the confusion of the imaginary or vicarious experiential identification with certain events and the belief that one actually lived through them (so-called recovered memory).[4] Moreover, [. . .] working through trauma does not imply the possibility of attaining total integration of the self, including the retrospective feat of putting together seamlessly (for example, through a harmonizing or fetishistic narrative) the riven experience of the past trauma. Any such retrospective 'suturing' would itself be phantasmatic or illusory. *Working-through means work on posttraumatic symptoms* in order to mitigate the effects of trauma by generating counterforces to compulsive repetition (or acting-out), thereby enabling a more viable articulation of affect and cognition or representation, as well as ethical and sociopolitical agency, in the present and future. Hence, at least as I am using the term, working-through does not mean total redemption of the past or healing its traumatic wounds. Indeed there is a sense in which, while we may work on its symptoms, trauma, once it occurs, is a cause that we cannot directly change or heal. And any notion of full redemption or salvation with respect to it, however this-worldly or deferred, is dubious. But, at least in trauma's historical dimension, we can work to change the causes of this cause insofar as they are social, economic, and political and thereby attempt to prevent its recurrence as well as enable forms of renewal. Insofar as trauma is transhistorical, we can only learn how to live better with its attendant anxiety and not mystifyingly attribute it to an event as its putative cause or project responsibility for it onto a discrete group of scapegoats.

Traumatic memory (at least in Freud's account) may involve belated temporality and a period of latency between a real or fantasized early event and a later one that somehow recalls it and triggers renewed repression, dissociation, or foreclosure and intrusive behavior. But when the past is uncontrollably relived, it is as if there were no difference between it and the present. Whether or not the past is reenacted or repeated in its precise literality (which figures such as Cathy Caruth and Bessel van der Kolk at times maintain but that I doubt), one experientially feels as if one were back there reliving the event, and distance between here and there, then and now collapses. One may, as at times in Caruth, closely approximate or even conflate the event and the experience of trauma for a distinctive reason: a belief that traumatic recall or the posttraumatic symptom, for example the nightmare or flashback, is literal in the dual sense of being, or at least deriving from, a precise replication or repetition of the event and constituting something incomprehensible, nonsymbolizable, or unreadable. (Van der Kolk bases this belief on the questionable idea that the traumatic event leaves a neural pathway or imagistic imprint in the amygdala and that the problem of symbolization or verbalization is based on the lateral 'translation' of the dissociated image from the amygdala to the verbal centers of the brain.)[5] In a particularly intriguing statement, Caruth is led to indicate ways in which understanding and working-through entail what she sees as losses:

> The trauma thus requires integration, both for the sake of testimony and for the sake of cure. But on the other hand, the transformation of the trauma into a narrative memory that allows the story to be verbalized and communicated, to be integrated into one's own, and others', knowledge of the past, may lose both the precision and the force that characterizes traumatic recall . . . Yet beyond the loss of precision there is another, more profound, disappearance: the loss, precisely, of the event's essential incomprehensibility, the force of its *affront to understanding*. It is this dilemma that underlies many survivors' reluctance to translate their experience into speech . . . The possibility of integration into memory and the consciousness of history thus raises the question, van der Kolk and van der Hart ultimately observe, 'whether it is not a sacrilege of the traumatic experience to play with the reality of the past.'[6]

Caruth here seems dangerously close to conflating absence (of absolute foundations and total meaning or knowledge) with loss and even sacralizing, or making sublime, the compulsive repetition or acting-out of a traumatic past. I have already indicated that working-through need not be understood to imply the integration or transformation of past trauma into a seamless narrative memory and total meaning or knowledge.[7] Narrative at best helps one not to change the past through a dubious rewriting of history but to work through posttraumatic symptoms in the present in a manner that opens possible futures. It also enables one to recount events and perhaps to evoke experience, typically through nonlinear movements that allow trauma to register in language and its hesitations, indirections, pauses, and silences. And, particularly by bearing witness and giving testimony, narrative may help performatively to create openings in existence that did not exist before. But a more basic point may be that Caruth's argument represents a displacement of some long-standing religious views relating to a radically transcendent, inscrutable divinity and his mysterious, nonsymbolizable unreadable, or unrepresentable ways. In secular terms, one is in the vicinity of an aesthetic of the sublime. Caruth's views resonate in certain ways with those of others, such as Theodor Adorno, who at times believed that any mitigation, mediation, or modification of the utterly unacceptable and catastrophic was indicative of unmerited consolation and co-optation by the dominant system, indeed, that it amounted to joining in the SS-dictated music played at Auschwitz to accompany the suffering of victims.

Although there are significant countertendencies in Caruth (and in Adorno) that indicate the desirability of working-through,[8] views such as those in the above-quoted passage at times shade into a rather prevalent valorization, even a negative sacralization or rendering sublime, of trauma – a sublimation in a peculiar sense. There may also be a resistance to working-through – working-through often understood (I think mistakenly) in extreme terms both as total transcendence of trauma and as a betrayal of it.[9]

NOTES

1. On this distinction in Benjamin, see John McCole, *Walter Benjamin and the Antinomies of Tradition* (Ithaca, NY: Cornell University Press, 1993), esp. 2.
2. See, for example, the discussion of 'black music' in Paul Gilroy, *The Black Atlantic: Modernity and Double Consciousness* (Cambridge, MA: Harvard University Press, 1993), ch. 3.
3. Those living through limit events generally have limit experiences. But one may have a limit experience without living through a major limit event in history. One may even place oneself intentionally in a high-risk or near-death situation in order to undergo a limit experience with the attendant possibility of 'sublime' elation. Such activity may be defended insofar as it does not victimize others (including nonhuman animals) and is entered into with the consent of all participants. One may even see such activity as an attempt to confront structural or transhistorical trauma and provide a setting in which it may be engaged or played out. By contrast historical traumas involving victimization (such as genocides) may be understood in part as ways in which perpetrators avoid or deny such engagement in its relation to their own anxiety and vulnerability.
4. In one sense recovered memory might be seen as a localization and condensation of the transhistorical in the historical and of the general in the particular. Hence from the belief that the human condition is one of originary sinfulness or abjection, I conclude that I have been sinned against or rendered abject by a parent or a particular group. Or from the belief that child abuse is prevalent in my society, I conclude that I have been a victim of child abuse. Of course intermediary processes of imaginary identification or transposition, at times involving interaction with a therapist, might be necessary in the unfolding of such a practical syllogism. For example, in the complex, contested case of Binjamin Wilkomirski, he identified with Holocaust victims, reacted to a film seen early in life, transposed the loss of the mother, and participated in therapeutic sessions.
5. This literalized notion of lateral dissociation is the basis of van der Kolk's dubious rejection of repression and the Freudian unconscious at least with respect to trauma.
6. Cathy Caruth, 'Recapturing the Past: Introduction,' in Cathy Caruth (ed.), *Trauma: Explorations in Memory*, (Baltimore, MD and London: Johns Hopkins University Press, 1995), pp. 151–7, at p. 154. Tending to conflate historical trauma with, or simply subsume it under, a transhistorical notion of trauma (such as the Lacanian real), Slavoj Žižek, in *The Plague of Fantasies* (London: Verso, 1997), is close to Caruth (or even Felman and Agamben) when he writes of Lanzmann's *Shoah*: 'This example also brings home the *ethical* dimension of fidelity to the Real *qua* impossible: the point is not simply to "tell the entire truth about it," but, above all, to confront the way we ourselves, by means of our subjective position of enunciation, are always-already involved, engaged in it' (p. 215). Elaborating his 'example,' Žižek states: 'Let us clarify the key point apropos of trauma and the Real. Claude Lanzmann's film *Shoah* alludes to the trauma of the Holocaust as something beyond representation (it can be discerned only via its traces, surviving witnesses, remaining monuments); however, the reason for this impossibility of representing the Holocaust is not simply that it is "too traumatic," but, rather, that we, observing subjects, are still involved

in it, are still a part of the process which generated it (we need only recall a scene from *Shoah* in which Polish peasants from a village near the concentration camp, interviewed now, in our present time, continue to find Jews "strange," – that is, repeat the very logic that brought the Holocaust about . . .).' I would certainly agree that there is a strong, perhaps inevitable, tendency to repeat aspects of the traumatic past and that historical trauma is not squarely in the past but implicates 'us' to varying degrees depending on our relation to that past and our present practices or even possibilities – indeed that this 'transferential' implication is one of the most important considerations with which we have to come to terms in studying the past. I would also acknowledge the inclination of the traumatized to experience post-traumatic symptoms not simply as pathological traits to be transcended but as marks of devotion if not monuments to dead intimates. Along with this recognition, I would affirm the need to empathize with survivors such as Charlotte Delbo who did indeed experience a 'fidelity' to traumatic experience or to those who were consumed by the events related to it. But I would hesitate to affirm the indiscriminate identification Žižek enacts between 'us' and the Polish peasants or the related notion that historical trauma is simply the instantiation of the transhistorically traumatic real (Žižek does not observe that Lanzmann often distances himself radically from Polish peasants, whom he at times treats with disdainful irony, and enacts an identification between himself and victims, something I argue facilitates his tendency to pose obtrusive questions to survivors in a desire to have them relive – so that he too may 'relive' – the traumatic past that he did not directly experience.) [. . .] Moreover, as Žižek at times recognizes, the notion of an ethics of psychoanalysis in terms of a 'fidelity' to the traumatic real has the value of enjoining the acknowledgment of a transhistorical dimension of trauma that should not be converted into historical trauma, notably through the operation of a scapegoat mechanism. But, when this notion is hyperbolically made into the basis of ethics in general, it threatens to eventuate in a 'sublime' aestheticization of ethics that is dubious in its implications for social and political life in that it ignores or downplays the significance of working through problems and subordinates ethics to a tragic or posttragic vision without sufficiently elaborating the tense, intricate relations between the two. One would also think that a crucial dimension of an ethics of psychoanalysis would be directed at the problem of transference, its uses, and abuses.

7. Nor should belated recognitions, often associated with working through the past, be conflated with teleology. Belated recognitions, through which one is able to understand or read differently a past phenomenon because of the occurrence of intervening events, may be related both to a qualified sense of historical necessity and to the way a future anterior is active in the past. Without undermining all efforts at contextualization, such recognitions also bring out the illusoriness of attempts to understand something purely and simply in its own terms and its own time (as if the past were not as riven and problematic as the present or future). But the conflation of belatedness with teleology constitutes a dubious attempt to provide full meaning or explanation to a past in relation to the present and future, thereby giving rise to foregone conclusions or a notion of historical inevitability. For example, one may read Nietzsche differently and be attentive to certain dimensions of his thought (its elitism, its invocation of the *Übermensch*, its gestures in the direction of eugenics, its sometimes oracular, ecstatic style) because of Nazi uses and abuses of it. But the conclusion need not be that there is some inevitable link between Nietzsche and the Nazis. Indeed one may also belatedly be particularly aware of aspects of Nietzsche's thought that run counter to Nazi appropriations of it, for example, its self-directed playfulness, irony, and humor or its disdain for scapegoating in general and anti-semitism in particular.

8. See especially Adorno, 'What Does Coming to Terms with the Past Mean?' in *Bitburg in Moral and Political Perspective*, ed. Geoffrey Hartman (Bloomington, IN: Indiana University Press, 1986), 114–29. (Adorno's essay was first published in 1959.)

9. See, for example, Colin Davis, 'Levinas on Forgiveness; or, the Intransigence of Ray Hanina,' in *PMLA* 117 (2002): 299–302. Davis objects to Julia Kristeva's attempt to elaborate a notion of working-through with respect to forgiveness and opposes it to what he sees as the preferable approach of Levinas 'in his darkest and most uncompromising moments' (302). Invoking a particular exegesis to make an argument of a very general if not universal nature, Davis in effect insists on the sublimely intransigent nature of acting-out and, in the process, may even unselfconsciously act out or repeat in his own analysis the aggressive pattern he presents a younger rabbi enacting toward Rav Hanina. In the story Rav Hanina refuses to grant forgiveness to the younger rabbi who, after an act that Hanina, in classically Oedipal fashion, interprets as aggressive, requests it of him. Davis concludes: 'Rav Hanina's intransigence hints that to be human is to remain unforgiven' (ibid.). There are of course many ways to be human, and Davis elicits and affirms only one of them. One might also observe that Hanina would not even have been confronted with the problem of forgiveness had he interpreted the younger rabbi's supposed attempt to outshine him as a compliment to the effectiveness of his school's and his own teaching.

PART III
IDENTITIES

SECTION 7
GENDER

Edited by Kate Chedgzoy

INTRODUCTION

Kate Chedgzoy

In Western culture, Memory traditionally has a female form – that of the Greek goddess Mnemosyne. Yet women's contributions to cultural memory have scarcely been noted in the twentieth century's explosion of work on that subject: women are almost entirely absent from such key works in the field as Raphael Samuel's *Theatres of Memory* series and the *Lieux de mémoire* project directed by Pierre Nora. At the same time, though the words and deeds of men dominate such studies, their ubiquity and dominance remain taken-for-granted: in the scholarship on memory, masculinity is rarely subjected to critical analysis. Yet because memory is crucial to understanding oneself as a social subject, gender is inevitably at the heart of its workings. Informed by the increasingly important role of memory in feminist scholarship, this section traces some of the ways in which the interrelations of gender and memory are being explored. Here, the focus is on women's experience, but the sophisticated methodologies employed in these extracts point to ways that future scholarship can make good the lack of critical attention to the distinctive role of masculinity in shaping cultures of memory.

In an influential study of the politics of cultural memory in the contemporary US, Marita Sturken defines it as 'a field of cultural negotiation through which different stories vie for a place in history' (1997: 1). When women's stories – recorded and shared through oral transmission, manuscript or print, for men and women in their society and those who come after – are accorded their due place in cultural memory, what difference does it make to our understanding of the history they enter? Feminist scholarship is itself a work of memory that has retrieved many women from oblivion as historical actors and recorders. Its very existence bears witness to the gendered and power-laden dynamics of remembering and forgetting. Women's problematic and vulnerable place in cultural memory does not come down to a simple choice between being remembered or cast into oblivion. Rather, *how* a woman is remembered is critical.

The selections that follow focus primarily on women's relations to, and uses of, the practices and discourses of autobiographical and cultural memory. They are concerned both with how women record and make sense of their own memories, and how women are remembered. They share an insistence on the profound interimplication of these two modes of memory, exemplifying the continuing relevance of the feminist insight that 'the personal is political'. And in doing so, they reveal the formative role played by gender in shaping how people and societies remember.

The first selection in this chapter is from **Anna Reading**'s study of gender's role in cultural efforts to make sense of the social inheritance of the Holocaust. Reading's work typifies the interdisciplinarity characteristic of memory studies in its wide-ranging exploration of how gender is articulated within different media forms and environments. In this excerpt, she reveals the gendered nature of the most fundamental issues concerning the cultural nature of memory: who remembers? How are their memories communicated, to whom, and with what consequences? What authority do they have? In many societies, women's voices are harder to hear than men's and are listened to with less respect: consequently, women's accounts of their memories may be undervalued or distrusted. Though memory has often been symbolised as feminine, women's relations to the practices of memory have been vulnerable and uneasy.

Marianne Hirsch has been a key figure for two decades in both feminist literary criticism and theorising memory. She has been particularly influential through her development of the concept of postmemory, denoting the distinctive positioning in relation to the autobiographical and cultural memory of children – such as the descendants of Holocaust survivors, like Hirsch herself – who grow up dominated by traumatic narratives of a past that preceded their birth. **Valerie Smith** is best known for her contributions to the effort to remember African-American women's participation in the making of modern North America. The second excerpt comes from the introduction to the special issue of the feminist journal *Signs* which they co-edited on the subject of Gender and Memory. Analysing what they call the 'uneven developments' (Hirsch and Smith, 2002: 4) of feminist studies and memory studies, Hirsch and Smith address some of the key theoretical, methodological and political issues that can be located at the intersection of these fields. Addressing a public commemorative event, Princeton University's Martin Luther King Day Celebration 2004, Smith called up 'a vision of memory as a critical function' (Smith, 2004), rather than a matter merely of celebration, commemoration or mourning, insisting on the politics of what is forgotten as well as what is remembered. The extract here makes plain that this understanding of memory work as enabling a critical revision of the past is at the heart of the feminist engagement with it.

This questioning, critical emphasis is carried forward in the final selection, from the work of **Annette Kuhn**, who, with others, has been influential in developing methods for memory work as an undertaking, at once critical and personal, which 'takes an inquiring attitude toward the past and the activity of its (re)construction through memory' (2000: 186). Primarily a film scholar, Kuhn is interested above all in the ways in which looking at personal and cultural documents such as films and photographs enables people to develop a repertoire of ways to make sense of the world and their relation to it. The extract from *Family Secrets* both introduces key theoretical and methodological issues in the study of memory, and exemplifies memory work as a form of purposeful intellectual, political and emotional labour.

REFERENCES AND FURTHER READING

Brison, Susan J. (2002), *Aftermath: Violence and the Remaking of a Self*. Princeton, NJ, and Oxford: Princeton University Press.

Chambers, Ross (1998) *Facing It: AIDS Diaries and the Death of the Author*. Ann Arbor, MI: University of Michigan Press.

—— (2004) *Untimely Interventions: AIDS Writing, Testimonial, and the Rhetoric of Haunting*. Ann Arbor, MI: University of Michigan Press.

Cvetkovich, Ann (2003) *An Archive of Feelings: Trauma, Sexuality and Lesbian Public Cultures*. Durham, NC, and London: Duke University Press.

Haaken, Janice (1998) *Pillar of Salt: Gender, Memory and the Perils of Looking Back*. New Brunswick, NJ, and London: Rutgers University Press.

Herman, Judith Lewis (1992) *Trauma and Recovery: From Domestic Abuse to Political Terror*. London: Pandora.

Hirsch, Marianne (1997) *Family Frames: Photography, Narrative and Postmemory*. Cambridge, MA, and London: Harvard University Press.

—— and Valerie Smith (eds) (2002) *Signs: Journal of Women in Culture and Society*, Special Issue, Gender and Cultural Memory, 28: 1.

Horowitz, Sara (1998) 'Women in Holocaust Literature: Engendering Trauma Memory', in Dalia Ofer and Lenore J. Weitzman (eds), *Women in the Holocaust*. New Haven, CT, and London: Yale University Press, pp. 364–78.

Kuhn, Annette (1995) *Family Secrets: Acts of Memory and Imagination*. London: Verso.

—— (2000) 'A Journey through Memory', in Susannah Radstone (ed.), *Memory and Methodology*. Oxford: Berg, pp. 179–96.

Samuel, Raphael (1996) *Theatres of Memory Vol 1: Past and Present in Contemporary Culture*. London: Verso.

—— (1999) *Theatres of Memory Vol. 2: Island Stories: Unravelling Britain*. London: Verso.

Smith, Valerie (2004) 'Keynote Speech: Princeton University Martin Luther King Day', http://www.princeton.ed/pr/mlk/mlkspeech.html. Last accessed 20/05/06.

Steedman, Carolyn (1996) *Landscape for a Good Woman: A Story of Two Lives*. London: Virago.

Sturken, Marita (1997) *Tangled Memories: The Vietnam War, the AIDS Epidemic and the Politics of Remembering*. Berkeley: University of California Press.

7.1

ANNA READING: *FROM* THE SOCIAL INHERITANCE OF THE HOLOCAUST: GENDER, CULTURE AND MEMORY

Escape for thy life; look not behind thee . . . but his wife looked back from behind him, and she became a pillar of salt. (Genesis 20: 15, 23–4)

Salt. A white powder or colourless crystalline solid; consisting mainly of sodium chloride and used for seasoning and preserving food. (*Collins English Dictionary*, 1990: 1029)

REMEMBERING MEN, PETRIFYING WOMEN

The meaning of 'looking back', embedded in the story of Lot and his wife and handed down in Genesis in the Bible's Old Testament, is one that has been explored by several authors and poets. Janice Haaken (1998) describes the sadness that remained with her as a young girl from 'the woman with no name' (p. 1). The Russian poet Anna Akhmatova vows in her poem 'Lot's Wife' 'in my heart she will not be forgot / who, for a single glance, gave up her life.' (Cosman, Keefe and Weaver, 1984: 191). To me as a girl the story was petrifying: it was a warning. Lot's wife looks back, disobeying God's commandment not to do so while he destroys the cities and people of Sodom and Gomorrah. In looking back – in witnessing his act of mass destruction, she is literally petrified – transformed from living flesh to granules of sodium chloride; she becomes nothing but a voiceless, colourless pillar left amid the burning landscape to erode. Abraham, in contrast, watching from a distant hill, we are later told, is

Source: Anna Reading, *The Social Inheritance of the Holocaust: Gender, Culture and Memory* (Basingstoke: Palgrave Macmillan, 2002), pp. 1–2, 7–10.

the right person, in the right place, at the right time. He is able to witness the destruction and he is later remembered by God.

One reading of this culturally specific story, handed down within Christianity and Judaism, is that women should be wary of disobeying patriarchal authority: if they attempt to witness the destruction caused by it they may themselves be destroyed and forgotten. The story in this respect *is* petrifying. Yet, at the same time, Lot's wife is not entirely forgotten – the story of her looking back is embedded in the memories of some. And, she is here, the puzzle of her story told again. But why do we not know her name? Why, when she looked back, was she petrified? Is this particular story indicative of what happens in societies and cultures more broadly when it comes to women and men looking back at atrocities?

How memory works – who looks back, who has the authority to look back, who is believed when they look back, who is remembered as witnesses by those with authority, who is threatened with being forgotten – is complex. It is also, [. . .] as the story of Lot and his wife suggests, gendered. [. . .]

OLD LADY MENG'S SOUP

Despite the dearth of academic research, particularly within media and cultural studies, looking specifically at gender in relation to socially inherited memory, its significance is embedded not only in the culturally specific story of Lot and his wife but is also suggested by the iconography of memory in different cultures. In the Ancient Greeks' world, memory was understood to be the precursor to all human thinking and was represented in the form of the goddess, Mnemosyne. She was the mother of all nine muses and was, in the last analysis, 'the progenitor of all the arts and sciences, among them history' (Samuels, 1994: vii). History, in turn, was represented by another female figure, Clio, who was memory's daughter, and would not sing unless homage was first paid to her mother. Thus both memory and history were envisaged as female figures – not as gods, but as related goddesses. These views of memory, subsequently, became socially inherited and syncretised within Europe by the Romans, who, drawing on the beliefs of the Ancient Greeks, conceived of memory as the fountain of thought and the mother of all other pedagogies (Yates, 1999).

In elements of Hindu culture memory is also feminine. The tenth chapter of the Hindu *Bhagavadgita*, for example, describes the divine glories fit for meditation, including the feminine form of memory. 'I am death, the all-devouring and the origins of things that are yet to be; and of feminine beings, fame, prosperity, speech, memory, intelligence, firmness and patience' (cited in Bhandare, 1993: 3). Likewise, in Indian and Tibetan Buddhism, an important element in memorisation and mindfulness are the female matikas. The word, from the original Sanskrit for 'mother', is understood to be the seed from which the building blocks of Buddhist texts are remembered and recalled. [. . .]

In contrast, within Chinese lore, it was and is forgetting rather than remembering that was represented by a female icon: a person who would not forget the past was someone who was said to have not drunk Old Lady Meng's soup. The soup is believed to cast people into oblivion. The figure of Old Lady Meng in turn was syncretised originally from Buddhism in which the soup of oblivion was thought to be given to souls departing this world: after drinking the soup, the soul goes over the bridge of Pain and demons hurl the soul into waters for new life (Schwarcz, 1998: 40).

These icons of memory, though, are not necessarily indicative of the value of women and men or the authority given to their articulations of the past within these societies. Within Ancient Greek society a goddess did not denote the same qualities as those attributed to human females. Women in Athenian society were treated as minors, segregated from men, treated as the property of men, and largely denied educational and intellectual experience. Silence was seen as a woman's best virtue and being talked about as one of her sins (Okin, 1980: 18–20). In Chinese culture, girl babies are still less valued than boy babies, to the extent that each year thousands of girl babies are abandoned, neglected, given away or sent away to children's homes or made permanent residents at boarding schools (Yen Mah, 1997). Even in Chinese communities abroad the lesser value given to girls permeates their lives, with memory itself a key element in the social construction of femininity and masculinity.

> In China your father had a sister who killed herself. She jumped into the family well. We say that your father has all brothers because it is as if she had never been born . . . Don't humiliate us. You wouldn't like to be forgotten as if you had never been born. (Hong Kingston, 1981: 11, 13)

What this suggests, as with the earlier example of the story of Lot and his wife, is the manner in which cultural mediations involving memory and forgetting are used to articulate, disarticulate and rearticulate aspects of gender relations and sexuality to create and maintain social cohesion. This particular cultural mediation – the handed-down story, related by Maxine Hong Kingston in *The Woman Warrior*, about an aunt who became pregnant by another man while her husband was away – was often recollected by family members. The threat was that if the girl child went against the norm then family history would be rewritten and the girl symbolically annihilated and her selfhood forgotten – like Lot's wife, who was disobedient and looked back on the mass destruction of men, women and children in the cities of sin.

Not only are tales of the past important in gaining social consensus concerning aspects of gender, but studies of the role and construction of collective memory in earlier societies also suggest that the recording and recollection of the past is itself articulated in complex ways by different media in relation to gendered discourses and structures. Research on collective memory practices in Ancient Mesopotamia has shown that when memory was locally organised through offerings and ritual practice around statues at local temples, women and men participated equally, but with the shift to writing in Babylonian society, the names retained in cultural memory were decided by male scribes (Yonkers, 1995: 89). Increasing centralisation led to the gradual erasure of the memory of women and their role in the family and society (Yonkers, 1995: 237). Women were rarely used as witnesses in medieval Europe, so much so that male historiographers of the time usually felt it necessary to explain and justify why they had used a woman's testimony in a document (Van Hoots, 1999: 51). To some, the witch hunts in Europe, in which as many as nine million people were tortured and burnt as witches between the fourteenth and seventeenth centuries, as well as being virulently antisemitic, were also part of a process of discrediting the word of women as witnesses: only if they failed to burn at the stake was their word deemed truthful (Kramarae and Treichler, 1985). This distrust of a woman's word could be seen to have continued with the withdrawal of Sigmund's Freud's thesis of 1896 that his female patients' hysteria could be explained by abuse by fathers or male relatives (Schur, 1972: 104). Later, patients' stories of abuse were described as fantasies rather than actual memories (Masson, 1984).

Yet today, are women's testimonies still less accepted than men's? In cultural mediations of the past are women's accounts included equally in voice and image alongside men? Are gender-specific experiences articulated or silenced? Do men and women remember or forget different aspects of the past?

REFERENCES

Bhandare, Shaila (1993) *Memory in Indian Epistemology and Status*. Delhi: Sri Satguru Publications.

Cosman, Carol, Keefe, Joan and Weaver, Kathleen (1978) *The Penguin Book of Women Poets*. Harmondsworth: Penguin.

Haaken, Janice (1998) *Pillar of Salt: Gender, Memory and the Perils of Looking Back*. New Brunswick, NJ, and London: Rutgers University Press.

Kingston, Maxine Hong (1981) *The Woman Warrior: Memoirs of a Girlhood among Ghosts*. London: Picador.

Kramarae, Cheris and Treichler, Paula A. (1985) *A Feminist Dictionary*. London: Pandora Press.

Mah, Adeline Yen (1997) *Falling Leaves: The True Story of an Unwanted Chinese Daughter*. London: Penguin.

Masson, Jeffrey M. (1984) *The Assault on Truth: Freud's Suppression of the Seduction Theory*. London and Boston: Faber & Faber.

Okin, Susan M. (1980) *Women in Western Political Thought*. London: Virago.

Samuel, Raphael (1994) *Theatres of Memory: Volume 1*. London: Verso.

Schur, M. (1972) *Freud: Living and Dying*. New York: International Universities Press.

Schwarcz, Vera (1998) *Bridge across Broken Time: Chinese and Jewish Cultural Memory*. New Haven, CT, and London: Yale University Press.

Van Houts, Elizabeth (1999) *Memory and Gender in Medieval Europe 900–1200*. Basingstoke: Macmillan Press – now Palgrave Macmillan.

Yates, Frances A. (1999) *The Art of Memory*. London: Routledge & Kegan Paul.

Yonkers, Gerdien (1995) *The Topography of Remembrance: The Dead, Tradition and Collective Memory in Mesopotamia*. Leiden: E. J. Brill.

MARIANNE HIRSCH AND VALERIE SMITH: *FROM* FEMINISM AND CULTURAL MEMORY: AN INTRODUCTION

THE FIELD

For the last thirty years, feminist scholarship has been driven by the desire to redefine culture from the perspective of women through the retrieval and inclusion of women's work, stories, and artifacts. This period has also seen an explosion of literary and cultural production by women in numerous languages and cultures that in itself has shaped much of the cultural memory of the late twentieth century. Much of recent feminist scholarship touches directly or indirectly on questions of cultural memory. For instance, feminist writing on sexual abuse and violence against women has been intensely preoccupied with memory, trauma, and transmission in the family and in society.[1] Debates about recovered memory have divided feminists throughout the 1990s. Feminist readings of autobiography and memoir, and feminist practices of oral history, have struggled to define the gendered manifestations of these literary genres and have thus analyzed gender differentiations in acts of personal and cultural memory.[2] Preoccupations with the gendered politics of decolonization, exile, migration, and immigration have given rise to questions about the archive and about the transmission of memory across spatial and generational boundaries.[3] And historical and literary analyses of the institution of slavery and its legacy have provided an idiom for representing the difficulties inherent in the transmission of cultural trauma. Often vilified as divisive, numerous black

Source: Marianne Hirsch and Valerie Smith, 'Feminism and Cultural Memory': An Introduction, *Signs: Journal of Women in Culture and Society*, 28: 1 (Fall 2002), pp. 3–12.

feminists have nevertheless produced literary, cinematic, and critical texts that focus centrally on the gendered nature of the atrocities of enslavement and the ways in which that experience is bequeathed and recalled in the narratives and on the bodies of subsequent generations.[4]

Thus feminist studies of sexual abuse, autobiographical literature, migration, and slavery have either assumed gender to be relevant to cultural memory or have engaged it explicitly. But scholars working in other areas of cultural and collective memory – especially national memory and countermemory, nostalgia, memorialization, legal memory and testimony, and the memory and 'postmemory' of the Holocaust – have only recently begun to engage with feminist theoretical analyses of gender, sexuality, race, nation, and class. The unspeakable victimization of the Holocaust, like the dehumanization of slavery, has come to shape much recent thinking about trauma, memory, memorialization, and transmission. Yet, unlike scholars of slavery, many interpreters of the Holocaust have actively resisted making gender differentiations among witnesses and analyzing how representational paradigms might be gendered.[5] And the major recent theoretical work on trauma has yet to grapple fully with the mark of gender.[6] [. . .]

To date there have been very few sustained efforts to theorize in such general and comparative terms about memory from the perspective of feminism. To our knowledge, the first attempts occurred at a 1986 conference at the University of Michigan, published as a special issue of the *Michigan Quarterly Review* on 'Women and Memory' and edited by Margaret Lourie, Domna Stanton, and Martha Vicinus in 1987. These editors and authors use the concept of 'memory' to define the field of women's studies as a form of 'countermemory' and feminist scholarship, literature, and art as means of redressing the official 'forgetting' of women's histories. While some of the *MQR* essays do address gender differences in the act of remembering, most expose the psychological and political structures of forgetting or repression that have disempowered women or enabled them to veil their own painful past lives. Essays on history, literature, and psychoanalysis are supplemented by poems and visual texts that are in themselves acts of memory. The themes in this historic volume on women and memory are so consonant with the burgeoning theoretical work on cultural memory in such fields as Holocaust studies, memorialization, trauma, and testimony of the late 1980s and the 1990s that one can only wonder why memory studies and feminist studies developed on parallel but separate tracks.[7] [. . .]

CULTURAL MEMORY AND GENDER

Our own understanding of the term *cultural memory* is indebted to Paul Connerton's notion of an 'act of transfer' (1989, 39), an act in the present by which individuals and groups constitute their identities by recalling a shared past on the basis of common, and therefore often contested, norms, conventions, and practices.[8] These transactions emerge out of a complex dynamic between past and present, individual and collective, public and private, recall and forgetting, power and powerlessness, history and myth, trauma and nostalgia, conscious and unconscious fears or desires. Always mediated, cultural memory is the product of fragmentary personal and collective experiences articulated through technologies and media that shape even as they transmit memory. Acts of memory are thus acts of performance, representation, and interpretation. They require agents and specific contexts. They can be conscious and deliberate; at the same time, and this is certainly true in the case of trauma, they can be involuntary, repetitious, obsessive.

In a variety of ways, feminist theory can provide a valuable lens through which cultural memory may be studied. Indeed, gender, along with race and class, marks identities in specific ways and provides a means by which cultural memory is located in a specific context rather than subsumed into monolithic and essentialist categories. Moreover, gender is an inescapable dimension of differential power relations, and cultural memory is always about the distribution of and contested claims to power. What a culture remembers and what it chooses to forget are intricately bound up with issues of power and hegemony, and thus with gender. Finally, the cultural tropes and codes through which a culture represents its past are also marked by gender, race, and class. [. . .]

Cultural memory is most forcefully transmitted through the individual voice and body – through the testimony of a witness. This is not to say that the witness tells only of her own memory; as Maurice Halbwachs has made clear, 'it is in society that people normally acquire their memories. It is also in society that they recall, recognize, and localize their memories' (1992, 38). [. . .] Cultural memory [. . .] can best be understood at the juncture where the individual and the social come together, where the person is called on to illustrate the social formation in its heterogeneity and complexity. The individual story, whether told through oral narrative, fiction, film, testimony, or performance, also serves as a challenge and a countermemory to official hegemonic history. This is particularly poignant in Charlotte Salomon's fragmentary 'Postscript' to her visual autobiography *Life? or Theatre?* in which she suggests how one woman's life is shaped by the intersections between familial abuse and depression, on the one hand, and the historical catastrophe of World War II and the Holocaust, on the other hand.

Indeed, at this juncture of private and public, gender may be seen as a determining factor. Women's history as counterhistory that restores forgotten stories to the historical record certainly illustrates this point. But beyond this explicit instance, the technologies of memory, the frames of interpretation, and the acts of transfer they enable are in themselves gendered, inasmuch as they depend on conventional paradigms and received cultural models, on codes that are culturally shared and available. Furthermore, experience, as well as its recollection and transmission, is subject to gendered paradigms. But gender, like memory, must be grounded in context if it is not to remain an abstract binary structure. [. . .] Identity, whether individual or cultural, becomes a story that stretches from the past to the present and the future, that connects the individual to the group, and that is structured by gender and related identity markers. [. . .]

FEMINISM AND CULTURAL MEMORY

Feminist art and scholarship have worked to restore to hegemonic cultural memory the stories that have been forgotten or erased from the historical record. But feminism has done more. It has defamiliarized and thus reenvisioned traditional modes of knowing the past. Theorizing cultural memory through the lens of feminism does not merely foreground the dynamics of gender and power. It also applies feminist modes of questioning to the analysis of cultural recall and forgetting. [. . .]

Feminist studies and memory studies both presuppose that the present is defined by a past that is constructed and contested. Both fields assume that we do not study the past merely for its own sake; rather, we do so to meet the needs of the present. Both fields emphasize the situatedness of the individual in his or her social and historical context and are thus suspicious of universal categories of experience. Beyond these broad points of convergence, developments in feminism and work on cultural memory demonstrate that the content, sources, and experiences that are recalled, forgotten, or suppressed are of profound political significance. What we know about the past, and thus our understanding of the present, is shaped by the voices that speak to us out of history; relative degrees of power and powerlessness, privilege and disenfranchisement, determine the spaces where witnesses and testimony may be heard or ignored.

From feminist and other varieties of social history, we have learned that public media and official archives memorialize the experiences of the powerful, those who control hegemonic discursive spaces. To find the testimonies of the disenfranchised, we have turned to alternate archives such as visual images, music, ritual and performance, material and popular culture, oral history, and silence. We have recovered forgotten texts and have learned alternate reading strategies from them. From feminist literary and cultural criticism we have learned to be what Judith Fetterley (1978) has called 'resisting readers' who interrogate the ideological assumptions that structure and legitimate coherent linear narratives and who can decode narrative repetition, indirection, signifying, and figuration. We have learned to question claims to narrative reliability, seeking instead to understand alternative ways in which truthfulness might be assessed and used. Perhaps most important, we have learned how to analyze and document the practices of private everyday experience, recognizing that they are as politically revealing in their own way as any event played out in the public arena.

NOTES

1. See, e.g., Spillers (1987); Herman (1992); Culbertson (1995); Painter (1995); Haaken (1998); Sturken (1999); Brison (2002).
2. A selective, but by no means exhaustive, list might include the following: Benstock (1988); hooks (1989); Lionnet (1989); Nussbaum (1989); Miller (1991); Kuhn

(1995); Leydesdorff, Passerini, and Thompson (1996); Smith and Watson (1998); Gilmore (2001).

3. For example, Ganguly (1992); Pratt (1992); Sharpe (1993); McClintock (1995); Lee (1999); Saldivar-Hull (2000).

4. See, e.g., McDowell (1989); Smith (1993, 1998); Dubey (1995); Hartman (1997); Rody (2001).

5. Recent scholarship on gender, national memory, and countermemory includes Lowe (1996); Sturken (1997); Brear (2000); Yuhl (2000); McAllister (2001). Work on gender and legal memory includes Williams (1991, 1995) and Matsuda (1996). On gender, sexuality, and nostalgia, see, e.g., Greene (1991); Probyn (1996); and Rubenstein (2001). There is a substantial and contested literature on women's experiences in the Holocaust that distinguishes it from the experiences of men. See, e.g., Ringelheim (1984, 1990), Goldenberg (1990); Rittner and Roth (1993); Ofer and Weitzman (1998); and Kremer (1999). For feminist analyses of gender and the memory and memorialization of the Holocaust, see, e.g., Hirsch and Spitzer (1993); Horowitz (2001); and Kahane (2001).

6. Caruth (1996) and Leys (2000).

7. A more recent conference and book explicitly connect gender and memory in the much more specific context of the memorialization of World War II and Nazi crimes in the two Germanies as well as abroad. See Eschebach, Wenk, and Jacobeit (2002).

8. See also Bal, Crewe, and Spitzer (1999).

REFERENCES

Bal, Mieke, Jonathan Crewe, and Leo Spitzer (1999) *Acts of Memory: Cultural Recall in the Present.* Hanover, NH: University Press of New England.

Benstock, Shari, (ed.) (1988) *The Private Self: Theory and Practice of Women's Autobiographical Writings.* Chapel Hill: University of North Carolina Press.

Brear, Holly Beachley (2000) 'We Run the Alamo and You Don't: Alamo Battles of Ethnicity and Gender.' In *Where These Memories Grow: History, Memory, and Southern Identity*, ed. W. Fitzhugh Brundage. Chapel Hill, NC: University of North Carolina Press, pp. 299–317.

Brison, Susan J. (2002) *Aftermath: Violence and the Remaking of the Self.* Princeton, NJ: Princeton University Press.

Caruth, Cathy (1996) *Unclaimed Experience: Trauma, Narrative and History.* Baltimore, MD: Johns Hopkins University Press.

Connerton, Paul (1989) *How Societies Remember.* New York: Cambridge University Press.

Culbertson, Roberta (1995) 'Embodied Memory, Transcendence and Telling: Recounting Trauma, Re-establishing the Self,' *New Literary History*, 26 (1): 169–95.

Dubey, Madhu (1995) 'Gayl Jones and the Matrilineal Metaphor of Tradition,' *Signs: Journal of Women in Culture and Society*, 20 (2): 245–67.

Eschebach, Insa, Silke Wenk and Sigrid Jacobeit (eds) (2002) *Gedächtnis und Geschlecht: Deutungsmuster in Darstellungen des nationalsozialistischen Genozids.* Berlin: Campus.

Fetterley, Judith (1978) *The Resisting Reader: A Feminist Approach to American Fiction.* Bloomington, IN: Indiana University Press.

Ganguly, Keya (1992) 'Migrant Identities and the Constructions of Selfhood', *Cultural Studies*, 6 (1): 29–50.

Gilmore, Leigh (2001) *The Limits of Autobiography: Trauma and Testimony.* Ithaca, NY: Cornell University Press.

Goldenberg, Myrna (1990) 'Different Horrors, Same Hell: Women Remembering the Holocaust,' in *Thinking the Unthinkable: Meanings of the Holocaust*, ed. Roger S. Gottlieb. New York: Paulist Press, pp. 150–66.

Greene, Gayle (1991) 'Feminist Fiction and the Uses of Memory,' *Signs*, (16) 1: 290–321.

Haaken, Janice (1998) *Pillar of Salt: Gender, Memory, and the Perils of Looking Back*. New Brunswick, NJ: Rutgers University Press.

Halbwachs, Maurice (1992) *On Collective Memory*, trans. and ed. Lewis Coser. Chicago: University of Chicago Press.

Hartman, Saidiya V. (1997) *Scenes of Subjection: Terror, Slavery, and Self-Making in Nineteenth-Century America*. New York: Oxford University Press.

Herman, Judith Lewis (1992) *Trauma and Recovery: The Aftermath of Violence from Domestic Abuse to Political Terror*. New York: Basic.

Hirsch, Marianne and Leo Spitzer (1993) 'Gendered Translations: Claude Lanzmann's Shoah,' in *Gendering War Talk*, eds Miriam Cooke and Angela Woollacott. Princeton, NJ: Princeton University Press. pp. 3–19.

hooks, bell (1989) 'Writing Autobiography'. In her *Talking Back: Thinking Feminist, Thinking Black*, 155–9. Boston: South End Press.

Horowitz, Sarah (2001) 'The Wounded Tongue: Engendering Jewish Memory.' In *Shaping Losses: Cultural Memory and the Holocaust*, ed. Julia Epstein and Lori Hope Lefkowitz, 107–27. Urbana: University of Illinois Press.

Kahane, Claire (2001) 'Dark Mirrors: A Feminist Reflection on Holocaust Narrative and the Maternal Metaphor.' In *Feminist Consequences: Theory for the New Century*, ed. Elizabeth Bronfen and Misha Kavka, 161–88. New York: Columbia University Press.

Kremer, Lillian S. (1999) *Women's Holocaust Writing*. Lincoln: University of Nebraska Press.

Kuhn, Annette (1995) *Family Secrets: Acts of Memory and Imagination*. London: Verso.

Lee, Rachel C. (1999) *The Americas of Asian American Literature: Gendered Fictions of Nation and Transnation*. Princeton, NJ: Princeton University Press.

Leydesdorff, Selma, Luisa Passerini, and Paul Thompson (1996) *Gender and Memory*. Vol. 4, *International Yearbook of Oral History and Life Stories*. Oxford: Oxford University Press.

Leys, Ruth (2000) *Trauma: A Genealogy*. Chicago: University of Chicago Press.

Lionnet, Françoise (1989) *Autobiographical Voices: Race, Gender, Self-Portraiture*. Ithaca, NY: Cornell University Press.

Lourie, Margaret, Domna Stanton, and Martha Vicinus, (eds) (1987) 'Women and Memory,' special issue of *Michigan Quarterly Review*, 27 (1).

Lowe, Lisa (1996) *Immigrant Acts: On Asian American Cultural Politics*. Durham, NC: Duke University Press.

Matsuda, Mari J. (1996) *Where Is Your Body? and Other Essays on Race, Gender, and the Law*. Boston: Beacon.

McAllister, Kirsten Emiko (2001) 'Captivating Debris: Unearthing a World War Two Internment Camp,' *Cultural Values*, 5 (1): 97–114.

McClintock, Anne (1995) *Imperial Leather: Race, Gender and Sexuality in the Colonial Context*. New York: Routledge.

McDowell, Deborah E. (1989) 'Negotiating between Tenses: Witnessing Slavery after Freedom – Dessa Rose,' in *Slavery and the Literary Imagination*, eds Deborah E. McDowell and Arnold Rampersad. Baltimore, MD: Johns Hopkins University Press, pp. 144–63.

Miller, Nancy K. (1991) *Getting Personal: Feminist Occasions and Other Autobiographical Acts*. New York: Routledge.

Nussbaum, Felicity A. (1989) *The Autobiographical Subject*. Baltimore, MD: Johns Hopkins University Press.

Ofer, Dalia, and Lenore J. Weitzman (eds) (1998) *Women in the Holocaust*. New Haven, CT: Yale University Press.

Painter, Nell Irvin (1995) 'Soul Murder and Slavery: Toward a Fully Loaded Cost Accounting.' In *U.S. History as Women's History: New Feminist Essays*, eds Linda

Kerber, Alice Kessler-Harris, and Kathryn Kish Sklar. Chapel Hill, NC: University of North Carolina Press, pp. 125–46.

Pratt, Mary Louise (1992) *Imperial Eyes: Travel Writing and Transculturation*. New York: Routledge.

Probyn, Elspeth (1996) *Outside Belongings*. New York: Routledge.

Ringelheim, Joan (1984) 'The Unethical and the Unspeakable: Women and the Holocaust.' In *Simon Wiesenthal Center Annual*: 1983, ed. Alex Grobman. Chappaqua, NY: Rossel, pp. 64–87.

—— (1990) 'Thoughts about Women and the Holocaust,' in *Thinking the Unthinkable: Meanings of the Holocaust*, ed. Roger S. Gottleib. New York: Paulist Press, pp. 141–9.

Rittner, Carol, and John K. Roth, (eds) (1993) *Different Voices: Women and the Holocaust*. New York: Paragon House.

Rody, Caroline (2001) *The Daughter's Return: African-American and Caribbean Women's Fictions of History*. New York: Oxford University Press.

Rubenstein, Roberta (2001) *Home Matters: Longing and Belonging, Nostalgia and Mourning in Women's Fiction*. New York: Palgrave.

Saldivar-Hull, Sonia (2000) *Feminism on the Border: Chicana Gender Politics and Literature*. Berkeley, CA: University of California Press.

Salomon, Charlotte (1998) *Life? Or Theatre?* Zwolle: Waanders Publishers.

Sharpe, Jenny (1993) *Allegories of Empire: The Figure of Woman in the Colonial Text*. Minneapolis, MI: University of Minnesota Press.

Smith, Sidonie, and Julia Watson, (eds) (1998) *Women, Autobiography, Theory: A Reader*. Madison, WI: University of Wisconsin Press.

Smith, Valerie (1993) ' "Circling the Subject": History and Narrative in *Beloved*,' in *Toni Morrison: Critical Perspectives, Past and Present*, eds Henry Louis Gates, Jr., and K. Anthony Appiah. New York: Amistad Media Ltd, pp. 342–55.

Smith, Valerie (1998) *Not Just Gender: Black Feminist Readings*. New York: Routledge.

Spillers, Hortense (1987) 'Mama's Baby, Papa's Maybe: An American Grammar Book,' *Diacritics*, 17 (2): 65–81.

Sturken, Marita (1997) *Tangled Memories: The Vietnam War, the Aids Epidemic, and the Politics of Remembering*. Berkeley, CA: University of California Press.

—— (1999) 'Narratives of Recovery: Repressed Memory as Cultural Memory,' in Bal, Crewe, and Spitzer, op. cit., pp. 87–104.

Williams, Patricia (1991) *The Alchemy of Race and Rights: Diary of a Law Professor*. Cambridge, MA: Harvard University Press.

—— (1995) *The Rooster's Egg: On the Persistence of Prejudice*. Cambridge, MA: Harvard University Press.

Yuhl, Stephanie E. (2000) 'Rich and Tender Remembering: Elite White Women and an Aesthetic Sense of Place in Charleston, 1920s and 1930s,' in *Where These Memories Grow: History, Memory, and Southern Identity*, ed. W. Fitzhugh Brundage. Chapel Hill, NC: University of North Carolina Press, pp. 227–48.

ANNETTE KUHN: *FROM* FAMILY SECRETS: ACTS OF MEMORY AND IMAGINATION

Most of us imagine the family as a place of safety, closeness, intimacy; a place where we can comfortably belong and be accepted just as we are. If we think of family ties as given, not chosen, they have this much at least in common with our other attachments: nation, race, class, gender. And yet we know quite well that in real life matters are rarely quite so simple. Just as for many family life is precarious, so these other allegiances are as often as not uncertain and mutable. And if it is we who, by imagining them, bring into being our 'imagined communities', we are undoubtedly formed by them, too. For in a way they actually are 'out there', they do pre-exist us. Disputing the givenness of social categories like class, race, gender identity and sexual preference confers no exemption from the necessity of negotiating their social meanings in daily life. While fully aware that femininity is a fabrication, for example, as far as the world is concerned – and indeed as far as I, too, am concerned – I am still a woman, and live with the very real consequences of a particular gender label. So it is with the identity conferred by family.

A family without secrets is rare indeed. People who live in families make every effort to keep certain things concealed from the rest of the world, and at times from each other as well. Things will be lied about, or simply never mentioned. Sometimes family secrets are so deeply buried that they elude the conscious awareness even of those most closely involved. From the involuntary amnesias of repression to the wilful forgetting of matters it might be less

Source: Annette Kuhn, *Family Secrets: Acts of Memory and Imagination* (London: Verso, 1999), pp. 1–5, 55–8.

than convenient to recall, secrets inhabit the borderlands of memory. Secrets, perhaps, are a necessary condition of the stories we are prompted by memory to tell about our lives.

Telling stories about the past, our past, is a key moment in the making of our selves. To the extent that memory provides their raw material, such narratives of identity are shaped as much by what is left out of the account – whether forgotten or repressed – as by what is actually told. Secrets haunt our memory-stories, giving them pattern and shape. Family secrets are the other side of the family's public face, of the stories families tell themselves, and the world, about themselves. Characters and happenings that do not slot neatly into the flow of the family narrative are ruthlessly edited out.

But exactly what sort of family is at stake in this book, *Family Secrets?* A kinship group, a real-life one, the author's own, perhaps? Or the family as an *idea*, an abstraction that provides the model for so many forms of belonging? And what sort of secrets, for that matter? Each term – family, secrets – has so many meanings. If family secrets are to be disclosed, does this suggest some personal revelation, confession even (an alluring prospect, to be sure)? Or is it a question more of what goes into the act of bringing the secrets to light? Am I making public what I have consciously known but never before revealed, or am I seeking knowledge that is as new to me as it is to you?

The family secrets are indeed mine, in a manner of speaking; and like all such things, they have roots in the past and reverberations in the present. None of which can be understood until the memories behind the secrets are brought to light and looked at closely. This calls for a certain amount of delving into the past, and for a preparedness to meet the unexpected. What is required is an active and directed work of memory.

Since my family secrets are no doubt shaped by the same kinds of amnesias and repressions as other people's, their substance will very likely seem familiar, commonplace even. Few of my secrets are likely to be particularly out-of-the-ordinary. But if my family secrets are neither unique nor special, that is precisely the point. Neither, although they take an individual life as their starting point, are the stories that I have to tell autobiographical in any conventional sense of the word. I offer no life story organized as a linear narrative with a beginning, a middle and an end, in that order. Nor is the present the goal towards which my stories are inexorably directed. The present figures rather differently, in fact: indeed the memory work that makes the telling of my stories possible is probably more important, and certainly of greater practical use in the present, than their actual content. And yet, without any conscious intent on my part, these stories have a great deal in common – in the forms they assume, the ways they narrate themselves – with other memory texts which are neither con-fessions nor autobiographical writings.

If pressed to slot these pieces of memory work, my memory texts, into some sort of category, I would hazard first of all that they tread a line between cultural criticism and cultural production; or rather that they try to span the gulf between those who comment on the productions of culture and those who actually do the producing. As such, they are driven by two sets of concerns. The first has to do with the ways memory shapes the stories we tell, in the present, about the past – especially stories about our own lives. The second has to do with what it is that makes us remember: the prompts, the pretexts, of memory; the reminders of the past that remain in the present. If *Family Secrets* has a prime objective, it is to unravel the connections between memory, its traces, and the stories we tell about the past, especially – though not exclusively – about the past of living memory.

The past is gone for ever. We cannot return to it, nor can we reclaim it now as it was. But that does not mean it is lost to us. The past is like the scene of a crime: if the deed itself is unrecoverable, its traces may still remain. From these traces, markers that point towards a past presence, to something that has happened in this place, a (re)construction, if not a simulacrum, of the event can be pieced together. Memory work has a great deal in common with forms of inquiry which – like detective work and archaeology, say – involve working backwards – searching for clues, deciphering signs and traces, making deductions, patching together reconstructions out of fragments of evidence.

The clues that form the starting point of my excursions into memory work are traces of my own past: for the most part, images and the memories associated with them. The images are both 'private' (family photographs) and 'public' (films, news photographs, a painting): though, as far as memory at least is concerned, private and public turn out in practice less readily separable than conventional wisdom would have us believe. [. . .] If the memories are one individual's, their associations extend far beyond the personal. They spread into an extended network of meanings that bring together the personal with the familial, the cultural, the economic, the social, and the historical. Memory work makes it possible to explore connections between 'public' historical events, structures of feeling, family dramas, relations of class, national identity and gender, and 'personal' memory. In these case histories outer and inner, social and personal, historical and psychical, coalesce; and the web of inter-connections that binds them together is made visible.

In working on these case histories, I have made a number of discoveries. I have seen how memory shapes not just our inner worlds but also the outer world of public expression and circulation of memory-stories. I find, too, that 'memory texts' – cultural productions across a range of media which, like the fruits of my own memory work, are in effect secondary revisions of the source materials of memory – appear to be a cultural phenomenon, a genre even, in their own right. Memory, it turns out, has its own modes of expression: these are characterized by the fragmentary, non-linear quality of moments recalled out of time. Visual flashes, vignettes, a certain anecdotal quality, mark memory texts as diverse as oral history accounts, unrevised written memoirs, scholarly writings like *The Uses of Literacy*, and even a film like *Distant Voices, Still Lives*.

I observe, too, the unfolding in memory texts of connections between memory and the past, memory and time, memory and place, memory and experience, memory and images, memory and the Unconscious. And I note, finally, that in all memory texts, personal and collective remembering emerge again and again as continuous with one another. If these discoveries call to mind the liberationist and feminist slogan 'The personal is political', they offer a far more profound understanding of that statement than any sloganizing would grant. Clearly, if in a way my memories belong to me, I am certainly not their sole owner. All memory texts [. . .] constantly call to mind the collective nature of the activity of remembering.

In unearthing some of 'my' family secrets, I have learned in the most practical and immediate way that, with the proper motivation, memory work, especially when it draws on the readily available resource of the family album, is easy to do, offers methodological rigour, and can be fruitful in countless, and often unexpected, ways. As the veils of forgetfulness are drawn aside, layer upon layer of meaning and association peel away, revealing not ultimate truth, but greater knowledge. Memory work has about it the quality of pursuing the enigma in a mystery novel that turns on characters remembering things buried deep in their past and long forgotten: except that in a novel there is always an ending, and usually a resolution. Memory work, on the other hand, is potentially interminable: at every turn, as further questions are raised, there is always something else to look into. [. . .]

A photograph of me wearing the costume for what I believe to be the last fancy dress competition I entered shows me, aged about nine, wearing a long shift to which are attached empty cigarette packets, drinks cartons, ice-cream containers, drinking straws, matchboxes; with a head-dress comprised of one waxed Kia-Ora orange juice carton flanked by a pair of ice-cream tubs. On my right arm rests a placard explaining the costume – 'Cinema Litter'; and on my left a jigsaw puzzle, presumably my prize. It is difficult to put a precise date to this photograph, partly because, [. . .] it has been trimmed down: the background is consequently minimal, offering no clues as to location; and whatever had been written on the back of the picture has been almost completely cut away.

(I find myself extraordinarily, perhaps excessively, troubled by this habit of my mother's of cutting photographs down. The historian in me objects to the tampering with evidence; the critic to the lack of respect for image composition. But the strength of the feeling really has to do with the fact that these acts of my mother's seem to me to be crude gestures of power, at once both creating the evidence that fits in with her version of events and destroying what does not; and also negating the skills and aesthetic choices of the photographer, usually my father. This particular photograph certainly looks like one of my father's efforts: if so, it must be among the last pictures of me he made, for by this time he had more or less given up what was in any case by now no more than a hobby.)

In the context of my own memories, I see this photograph, which I find very painful to look at, as a 'cusp' image, marking a transition. It must have been made around the time of our move away from my first home in Chiswick to live in the house of my recently deceased Granny, my mother's mother. This move was highly traumatic for me, in large part (as I now construe it) because although they remained together, leaving Chiswick marked some decisive rift between my parents.

Our new home was very much my mother's territory: it had been lived in not only by her mother, but before that by one of her brothers. Over the following few years she saw to it that both her sons moved with their families into other houses on the same street. In all this, I believe my father must have felt increasingly marginalized: illness – he suffered from bronchitis which later became emphysema – by now dominated his life and isolated him from those closest to him. This, along with his abandonment of the hobby of photography, which had been a source of such pride and pleasure, must surely be symptomatic. I, too, felt displaced: in my new school, corporal punishment – completely alien and shocking to me – was practised; I was mocked by the other children for my 'posh' accent; I even caught head lice and had to have my plaits chopped off. Desperately unhappy, I started putting on weight.

It was around this time, too, that I started 'answering back', embarking on a lengthy and bitter struggle with my mother over issues of separation – issues which would never finally be resolved. I recall feeling unhappy about being put into this particular costume and into the fancy dress competition, and had doubtless let my objections be known in the various overt and covert ways of the uncompliant child – whining, sulks, refusal to smile and a general 'slouching on parade'. If the photograph itself reveals nothing of all this, neither, though, does it seem to me to present an entirely untroubled surface.

The girl looks neglected and slightly scruffy [. . .] Little effort seems to have been put into her hair, badly cut [. . .] and all over the place; her smile seems slightly doubtful; her eyes are closed. The costume is even more illuminating. In itself, it is certainly a clever idea: but more remarkable is the fact that the child wearing it is being displayed as a figure for the detritus, the discarded by-products, of a pursuit whose pleasures hold a distinctly erotic appeal. The implications scarcely need spelling out: it is fortunate, perhaps, that this was to be the last of my fancy dress costumes.

My mother's passion for fancy dress can be regarded in certain respects as an extension of her earlier investment in 'dressing up' her infant daughter: though there is undoubtedly more to it than that. As a cultural form, fancy dress gestures with some urgency towards the performance aspect of clothes. Indeed, it renders this aspect entirely overt: for the whole point of fancy dress is that the masquerade is there, self-evident, on the surface. Fancy dress partakes of the car-nivalesque, a turning upside-down of the everyday order of hierarchies of class, status, gender, ethnicity. A bus conductor's daughter can be queen for an hour – or even, indeed, king, for girls can be boys and boys girls, and either can be neither. A fracturing of the clothes/identity link is thus sanctioned – at once permitted and contained, that is – by the cultural conventions of fancy dress.

Also, and relatedly, there is clearly a fantasy component to fancy dress: indeed, the word 'fancy' itself derives from a contraction of 'fantasy'. But whose fantasy? In the case of 'Cinema Litter', as of the other fancy dress costumes my mother made for me, certainly not the little girl's, certainly not the daughter's. Costume which presents itself so unequivocally as performance or masquerade will often – and certainly in the case of 'Cinema Litter' – beg for a symptomatic reading. But while an interpretation of 'Cinema Litter' reveals meanings tied specifically to a particular costume and context, taken together with all the other fancy dress costumes my mother made for me (and certainly if it is accepted that one of the issues at stake here is a mother's identification with her daughter) this can be seen as expressive also of fantasies of a rather different nature: the desire of a working woman, no longer young, to be noticed – seen, applauded, rewarded – as someone special, different from the rest, out of the ordinary, precisely 'an original'. The daughter in fancy dress, attracting attention, winning prizes even, becomes a vehicle for the mother's desire to transcend the limitations, dissatisfactions and disappointments of her own daily life.

But given the 'conceptual' and/or the androgynous quality of the costumes she favoured, it seems to me that at this point my mother's fantasy had little to do with femininity as a site of redemption, and much to do with a wish to overcome the limitations femininity imposes. To this extent, the unconscious aspect of the fancy dress project either runs somewhat counter to the earlier project of producing a 'well turned out' little girl, or underscores the contradictions and ambivalences around femininity that were already, perhaps, lurking in the latter.

While all this might bespeak resistance, or signal the (limited?) liberatory potential of certain cultural practices for individuals and social groups who lack power in the public world, it should not be forgotten whose fantasy it was that drove these particular practices of dressing up and the fancy dress. For the little Annette, her mother was all-powerful; and it seems never to have occurred to her, the mother, that her daughter could possibly harbour genuine feelings or wishes or hopes or ambitions that in any way diverged from her own, the mother's.

What, then, of the daughter's story: the daughter put on display, exhibited to the public gaze in a quest for rewards from strangers for costumes, for outward appearances, that by nature and intent cloak, occlude and subvert – as well as create – identities? What if the daughter was not entirely comfortable with such identities, with being the site of another's investments, the vehicle of another's fantasies? What of the daughter who refused to smile prettily at the judges, refused to want to be picked out from all the others as a winner, and yet who found utterly unbearable the humiliation of losing? What of her? That little girl got fat, looked terrible in everything she wore, and answered back. What a disappointment to her mother.

SECTION 8
RACE/NATION

Edited by Pablo Mukherjee

INTRODUCTION

Pablo Mukherjee

The extracts included in this section are from works of seminal importance to studies of 'race' and nationalism. It is difficult to find any course on nationalism that does not include Benedict Anderson's *Imagined Communities* (1983; rev. edn 1991). Étienne Balibar's 'The Nation Form' (1991) significantly broadened the avenues opened up by Anderson and Paul Gilroy's *There Ain't No Black in the Union Jack* (1987) was a clarion call to reassess the role 'race' played in British nationalism of the 1980s. Understandably, perhaps, the formative role played by these texts in the field of race/nation studies has tended to obscure the pathways they could also open up in other adjacent and proliferating fields of enquiry. Of these latter, the rapidly expanding field of cultural memory/memory studies stands to reap especial benefit from the works of Anderson, Gilroy and Balibar.

Benedict Anderson's *Imagined Communities: Reflections on the Origins and Spread of Nationalism* (1983; rev. edn 1991) marked an important moment in the analysis and understanding of nationalism. Anderson examined the process by which communities 'nationalised' themselves and how this imagined idea of the nation was globalised. For Anderson, a variety of factors contributed to this universalisation of the nation form, the chief among which were territorialisation of the major religious faiths, the decline of kinship structures, the nexus between print and capitalism, the development of vernacular 'state' languages, and changing conceptions of time. He suggested that modern nationalism, as we know it, grew first in the Americas and from there was adopted by Europe, and eventually by tri-continental anti-imperialist movements in Asia, Africa and South America. This thesis has been contested on many grounds (among them, the model of nationalism as a 'derivative' discourse and Anderson's ignoring of the uneven development of imperial capital) but it has remained, it is safe to say, the touchstone for subsequent scholarship on nationalism.

A glance at Anderson's list of factors reveals how implicit, but nonetheless crucial, was the notion of collective cultural memory in his scheme. It is difficult to see how the shift in the conception of time, for instance, would not involve a corresponding way in which communities came to perceive their own pasts, presents and futures. Again, the rise of what he calls 'print capitalism' was bound to alter ways in which communities were able to remember or invent their 'origins'. In the 1983 edition of *Imagined Communities*, however, 'memory' remained a relatively undertheorised category in Anderson's reflections on nationalism.

This changed in a new edition of the book published in 1991, in which Anderson added a chapter entitled 'Memory and Forgetting'. Here, he showed how national communities came to think of themselves as 'old' and clearly positioned memory as an important category in his analysis. Anderson argued that in the 'new land' of the Americas, large bodies of European settlers were able to think of themselves as simultaneously sharing a space with 'old' Europe *and* creating a rupture in the conception of time/duration by declaring that they inhabited a revolutionary new chronology. Thus the formation of 'new nationalisms' depended on a reconfiguration of collective memory about 'old/original' European spaces as well as chronologies. But once this revolutionary moment had passed (exemplified by the American revolution and its European counterpart, the French Revolution), the second generation of American and European nationalists worked towards emplotting their communities within a narrative of historical memory whereby their 'nations' were continuously linked to the past generations, thus 'making sense' of their current social configurations. On the other hand, this act of memorialising 'origins' also demanded a forgetting of those episodes (usually traumatic) in the lives of the communities that disturbed this smooth, organic linkage of the 'past' with the 'present'. According to Anderson, then, 'nations' are called into being when communities with access to certain kinds of technologies and in certain kinds of relationship with other communities are able to produce a narrative of their pasts which depends on acts of both memorialising and forgetting.

Anderson's work enabled other scholars to ask a range of questions, including assessments of the modality of nationalist imaginations. Under what conditions, they began to ask, does this creation of a 'national' memory take place? How exactly do communities convert themselves into nations by using language? **Étienne Balibar**'s short but significant study, 'The Nation Form: History and Ideology', was first published in 1991, in a volume co-authored with Immanuel Wallerstein called *Race, Nation and Class: Ambiguous Identities*. By giving prominence to the two categories of 'race' and 'class', the authors sought to refine Anderson's thesis on nationalism. Balibar agreed that all national communities were imaginative constructs in that they rely on a particular use (and textualisation) of collective memory. But he went on to examine the conditions under which that process of memorialisation took place and suggested that in order to imagine a nation, a community has to first create a memory of being a 'people'. That is, social groups nationalise themselves by first constructing a memory of being a 'naturally homogeneous' community. This construction is done, Balibar shows, through specific uses of the notions of 'common language' and *common race*. While 'race' emerges in Balibar's analysis as a key element in the making of nations, what is again suggestive is the connection he draws between the social construction of memory and the very making of 'race' and 'nation'.

In some important ways, Balibar was responding not only to Anderson's key work, but also to such studies as **Paul Gilroy**'s *There Ain't No Black in the Union Jack* (1987) that had attracted a storm of popular and critical attention on its publication. Today, the text is remembered (it has recently been reprinted in the 'Routledge Classics' series) as a challenging appraisal of race relations in Thatcher's Britain. But in offering detailed case studies of the entanglements of race thinking and British nationalism, Gilroy further illuminated the *process* by which disparate social groups create a 'national' identity (British) precisely by racialising memory. He thus critiques Anderson's ignoring of 'race' as a crucial element in the making of nations and anticipates Balibar's arguments. In the extract below, Gilroy analyses the discourse on 'race' being produced by both the British Right and Left from the 1970s onward. He shows that the notions of Britain as a 'nation' and the 'British' as an ethnic group were created by a memorialising of Black slavery, of classless and homogeneous 'white' communities, of the imperial past of military invasions and conquests. The increasing presence of the peoples from the former colonies and imperial territories in 'post-imperial' Britain demanded a significant reimagining of the 'nation'. Gilroy shows that the textualisation of a racialised memory was the key process through which this was achieved.

While nation and race are the foregrounded subjects of these studies, all of them analyse and present the textualisation and collectivisation of socio-cultural memory as a crucial element in the construction of these categories. In so doing, they may be used as powerful resources in any pioneering assessment of the complex relationship between race, nation and memory.

REFERENCES AND FURTHER READING

Anderson, Benedict (1983; rev. edn 1991) *Imagined Communities: Reflections on the Origin and Spread of Nationalism*. London: Verso.
—— (1998) *The Spectre of Comparison: Nationalism, South-East Asia, and the World*. London: Verso.
Balibar, Étienne (1991) 'The Nation Form: History and Ideology', in Étienne Balibar and Immanuel Wallerstein, *Race, Nation and Class: Ambiguous Identities*. London: Verso.
Boym, Svetlana (2001) *The Future of Nostalgia*. New York: Basic Books.

Castro-Klaren, Sara and Charles Chasteen (eds) (2003) *Beyond Imagined Communities: Reading and Writing the Nation in Nineteenth-Century Latin America.* Washington, DC: Woodrow Wilson Center Press.

Chatterjee, Partha (1986) *Nationalist Thought and the Colonial World: A Derivative Discourse?* London and Totoya, NJ: Zed Books.

—— (1993) *The Nation and Its Fragments: Colonial and Postcolonial Histories.* Princeton, NJ: Princeton University Press.

Cheah, Pheng and Jonathan Culler (eds) (2003) *Grounds of Comparison: Around the Work of Benedict Anderson.* New York and London: Routledge.

Connerton, Paul (1989) *How Societies Remember.* Cambridge: Cambridge University Press.

Fentress, James (1992) *Social Memory.* Oxford: Blackwell.

Gilroy, Paul (1987) *There Ain't No Black in the Union Jack: The Cultural Politics of Race and Nation.* London: Hutchinson.

—— (2001) *Between Camps: Nations, Cultures and the Allure of Race.* London: Penguin.

—— (2004) *After Empire: Melancholia Or Convivial Culture?* London: Routledge.

Gramsci, Antonio (1985) *Selections from Cultural Writings*, eds David Forgacs and Geoffrey Nowell-Smith. London: Lawrence & Wishart.

—— (1971) *Selections from the Prison Notebooks*, eds Quintin Hoare and Geoffrey Nowell-Smith. London: Lawrence & Wishart.

Gross, David (2000) *Lost Time: On Remembering and Forgetting in Late Modern Culture.* Amherst, MA: University of Massachusetts Press.

Gruesser, John (2005) *Confluences: Postcolonialism, African American Literary Studies, and the Black Atlantic.* Athens, GA, and London: University of Georgia Press.

Nairn, Tom (1977) *The Break-Up of Britain: Crisis and Neo-Nationalism.* London: NLB.

—— (1997) *Faces of Nationalism: Janus Revisited.* London: Verso.

Weber, Max (1971) *The Interpretation of Social Reality*, ed. J. E. T. Eldridge. London: Nelson.

—— (1994) *Political Writings*, eds Peter Lassman and Ronald Speirs. Cambridge: Cambridge University Press.

White, Hayden (1975) *Metahistory: The Historical Imagination in Nineteenth-Century Europe.* Baltimore, MD, and London: Johns Hopkins University Press.

—— (1985) *Tropics of Discourse.* Baltimore, MD and London: Johns Hopkins University Press.

Williams, Raymond (1958) *Culture and Society, 1780–1950.* London: Harper & Row.

—— (1961) *The Long Revolution.* Harmondsworth: Penguin.

—— (1973) *The Country and the City.* New York: Oxford University Press.

—— (2003) *Who Speaks for Wales? Nation, Culture, Identity.* Cardiff: University of Wales Press.

Wright, Patrick (1985) *On Living in an Old Country.* London: Verso.

BENEDICT ANDERSON: *FROM* IMAGINED COMMUNITIES: REFLECTIONS ON THE ORIGIN AND SPREAD OF NATIONALISM

SPACE NEW AND OLD

New York, Nueva Leon, Nouvelle Orléans, Nova Lisboa, Nieuw Amsterdam. Already in the sixteenth century Europeans had begun the strange habit of naming remote places, first in the Americas and Africa, later in Asia, Australia, and Oceania, as 'new' versions of (thereby) 'old' toponyms in their lands of origin. Moreover, they retained the tradition even when such places passed to different imperial masters, so the Nouvelle Orléans calmly became New Orleans, and Nieuw Zeeland New Zealand.

It was not that, in general, the naming of political or religious sites as 'new' was in itself so new. In Southeast Asia, for example, one finds towns of reasonable antiquity whose names also include a term for novelty: Chiangmai (New City), Kota Bahru (New Town), Pekanbaru (New Market). But in these names 'new' invariably has the meaning of 'successor' to, or 'inheritor' of, something vanished. 'New' and 'old' are aligned diachronically, and the former appears always to invoke an ambiguous blessing from the dead. What is startling in the American namings of the sixteenth to eighteenth centuries is that 'new' and 'old' were understood synchronically, co-existing within homogeneous, empty time. Vizcaya is there *alongside* Nueva Vizcaya, New London *alongside* London: an idiom of sibling competition rather than of inheritance.

Source: Benedict Anderson, *Imagined Communities: Reflections on the Origins and Spread of Nationalism*, rev. edn. (London and New York: Verso, 1991), pp. 187–9, 191–7, 201–6.

This new synchronic novelty could arise historically only when substantial groups of people were in a position to think of themselves as living lives *parallel* to those of other substantial groups of people – if never meeting, yet certainly proceeding along the same trajectory. Between 1500 and 1800 an accumulation of technological innovations in the fields of shipbuilding, navigation, horology and cartography, mediated through print-capitalism, was making this type of imagining possible.[1] It became conceivable to dwell on the Peruvian altiplano, on the pampas of Argentina, or by the harbours of 'New' England, and yet feel connected to certain regions or communities, thousands of miles away, in England or the Iberian peninsula. One could be fully aware of sharing a language and a religious faith (to varying degrees), customs and traditions, without any great expectation of ever meeting one's partners.[2]

For this sense of parallelism or simultaneity not merely to arise, but also to have vast political consequences, it was necessary that the distance between the parallel groups be large, and that the newer of them be substantial in size and permanently settled, as well as firmly subordinated to the older. These conditions were met in the Americas as they had never been before. In the first place, the vast expanse of the Atlantic Ocean and the utterly different geographical conditions existing on each side of it, made impossible the sort of gradual absorption of populations into larger politico-cultural units that transformed Las Españas into España and submerged Scotland into the United Kingdom. Secondly, [. . .], European migration to the Americas took place on an astonishing scale. By the end of the eighteenth century there were no less than 3,200,000 'whites' (including no more than 150,000 *peninsulares*) within the 16,900,000 population of the Western empire of the Spanish Bourbons.[3] The sheer size of this immigrant community, no less than its overwhelming military, economic and technological power vis-à-vis the indigenous populations, ensured that it maintained its own cultural coherence and local political ascendancy.[4] Thirdly, the imperial metropole disposed of formidable bureaucratic and ideological apparatuses, which permitted them for many centuries to impose their will on the creoles. (When one thinks of the sheer logistical problems involved, the ability of London and Madrid to carry on long counter-revolutionary wars against rebel American colonists is quite impressive.) [. . .]

The doubleness of the Americas and the reasons for it, sketched out above, help to explain why nationalism emerged first in the New World, not the Old.[5] They also illuminate two peculiar features of the revolutionary wars that raged in the New World between 1776 and 1825. On the one hand, none of the creole revolutionaries dreamed of keeping the empire intact but rearranging its internal distribution of power, *reversing* the previous relationship of subjection by transferring the metropole from a European to an American site.[6] In other words, the aim was not to have New London succeed, overthrow, or destroy Old London, but rather to safeguard their continuing parallelism. (How new this style of thought was can be inferred from the history of earlier empires in decline, where there was often a dream of *replacing* the old centre.) On the other hand, although these wars caused a great deal of suffering and were marked by much barbarity, in an odd way the stakes were rather low. Neither in North nor in South America did the creoles have to fear physical extermination or reduction to servitude, as did so many other peoples who got in the way of the juggernaut of European imperialism. They were after all 'whites,' Christians, and Spanish- or English-speakers; they were also the intermediaries necessary to the metropoles if the economic wealth of the Western empires was to continue under Europe's control. Hence, they were the one significant extra-European group, subjected to Europe, that at the same time had no need to be desperately afraid of Europe. The revolutionary wars, bitter as they were, were still reassuring in that they were wars between kinsmen.[7] This family link ensured that, after a certain period of acrimony had passed, close cultural, and sometimes political and economic, ties could be reknit between the former metropoles and the new nations.

TIME NEW AND OLD

If for the creoles of the New World the strange toponyms discussed above represented figuratively their emerging capacity to imagine themselves as communities *parallel and comparable to* those in Europe, extraordinary events in the last quarter of the eighteenth century gave this novelty, quite suddenly, a completely new meaning. The first of these events was certainly the Declaration of (the Thirteen Colonies') Independence in 1776, and the successful military defence of that declaration in the years following. This independence, and the fact that it was a *republican* independence, was felt to be something absolutely unprecedented, yet at the same time, once in existence, absolutely reasonable. Hence, when history made it possible, in 1811, for Venezuelan revolutionaries to draw up a constitution for the First Venezuelan Republic, they saw nothing slavish in borrowing verbatim from the Constitution of the United States of America.[8] For what the men in Philadelphia had written was in the Venezuelans' eyes not something North American, but rather something of universal truth and value. Shortly thereafter, in 1789, the explosion in the New World was *paralleled* in the Old by the volcanic outbreak of the French Revolution.[9]

It is difficult today to recreate in the imagination a condition of life in which the nation was felt to be something utterly new. But so it was in that epoch. The Declaration of Independence of 1776 makes absolutely no reference to Christopher Columbus, Roanoke, or the Pilgrim Fathers, nor are the grounds put forward to justify independence in any way 'historical,' in the sense of highlighting the antiquity of the American people. Indeed, marvellously, the American nation is not even mentioned. A profound feeling that a radical break with the past was occurring – a 'blasting open of the continuum of history'? – spread rapidly. Nothing exemplifies this intuition better than the decision, taken by the Convention *Nationale* on 5 October 1793, to scrap the centuries-old Christian calendar and to inaugurate a new world-era with the Year One, starting from the abolition of the *ancien régime* and the proclamation of the Republic on 22 September 1792.[10] (No subsequent revolution has had quite this sublime confidence of novelty, not least because the French Revolution has always been seen as an ancestor.)

Out of this profound sense of newness came also *nuestra santa revolución*, the beautiful neologism created by José Maria Morelos y Pavón (proclaimer in 1813 of the Republic of Mexico), not long before his execution by the Spaniards.[11] Out of it too came San Martín's 1821 decree that '*in the future* the aborigines shall not be called Indians or natives; they are children and citizens of Peru and they shall be known as Peruvians.'[12] This sentence does for 'Indians' and/or 'natives' what the Convention in Paris had done for the Christian calendar – it abolished the old time-dishonoured naming and inaugurated a completely new epoch. 'Peruvians' and 'Year One' thus mark rhetorically a profound rupture with the existing world.

Yet things could not long remain this way – for precisely the same reasons that had precipitated the sense of rupture in the first place. In the last quarter of the eighteenth century, Britain alone was manufacturing between 150,000 and 200,000 watches a year, many of them for export. Total European manufacture is likely to have then been close to 500,000 items annually.[13] Serially published newspapers were by then a familiar part of urban civilization. So was the novel, with its spectacular possibilities for the representation of simultaneous actions in homogeneous empty time.[14] The cosmic clocking which had made intelligible our synchronic transoceanic pairings was increasingly felt to entail a wholly intramundane, *serial* view of social causality; and this sense of the world was now speedily deepening its grip on Western imaginations. It is thus understandable that less than two decades after the Proclamation of Year One came the establishment of the first academic chairs in History – in 1810 at the University of Berlin, and in 1812 at Napoléon's Sorbonne. By the second quarter of the nineteenth century History had become formally constituted as a 'discipline,' with its own elaborate array of professional journals.[15] Very quickly the Year One made way for 1792 A.D., and the revolutionary ruptures of 1776 and 1789 came to be figured as embedded in the historical series and *thus as historical precedents and models*.[16]

Hence, for the members of what we might call 'second generation' nationalist movements, those which developed in Europe between about 1815 to 1850, and also for the generation that inherited the independent national states of the Americas, it was no longer possible to 'recapture / The first fine careless rapture' of their revolutionary predecessors. For different reasons and with different consequences, the two groups thus began the process of reading nationalism *genealogically* – as the expression of an historical tradition of serial continuity.

In Europe, the new nationalisms almost immediately began to imagine themselves as 'awakening from sleep,' a trope wholly foreign to the Americas. Already in 1803 [. . .] the young Greek nationalist Adamantios Koraes was telling a sympathetic Parisian audience: '*For the first time* the [Greek] nation surveys the hideous spectacle of its ignorance and *trembles* in measuring with the eye the distance separating it from its ancestors' glory.' Here is perfectly exemplified the transition from New Time to Old. 'For the first time' still echoes the ruptures of 1776 and 1789, but Koraes's sweet eyes are turned, not ahead to San Martín's future, but back, in trembling, to ancestral glories. It would not take long for this exhilarating doubleness to fade, replaced by a modular, 'continuous' awakening from a chronologically gauged, A.D.-style slumber: a guaranteed return to an aboriginal essence.

Undoubtedly, many different elements contributed to the astonishing popularity of this trope.[17] For present purposes, I would mention only two. In the first place, the trope took into account the sense of parallelism out of which the American nationalisms had been born and which the success of the American nationalist revolutions had greatly reinforced in Europe. It seemed to explain why nationalist movements had bizarrely cropped up in the civilized Old World so obviously *later than in the barbarous New*.[18] Read as late awakening, even if an awakening stimulated from afar, it opened up an immense antiquity behind the epochal sleep. In the second place, the trope provided a crucial metaphorical link between the new European nationalisms and language. [. . .] [T]he major states of nineteenth-century Europe were vast polyglot polities, of which the boundaries almost never coincided with language-communities. Most of their literate members had inherited from mediaeval times the habit of thinking of certain languages – if no longer Latin, then French, English, Spanish or German – as languages of civilization. Rich eighteenth-century Dutch burghers were proud to speak only French at home; German was the language of cultivation in much of the western Czarist empire, no less than in 'Czech' Bohemia. Until late in the eighteenth century no one thought of these languages as belonging to any territorially defined group. But soon thereafter [. . .], 'uncivilized' vernaculars began to function politically in the same way as the Atlantic Ocean had earlier done: i.e. to 'separate' subjected national communities off from ancient dynastic realms. And since in the vanguard of most European popular nationalist movements were literate people often *unaccustomed* to using these vernaculars, this anomaly needed explanation. None seemed better than 'sleep,' for it permitted those intelligentsias and bourgeoisies who were becoming conscious of themselves as Czechs, Hungarians, or Finns to figure their study of Czech, Magyar, or Finnish languages, folklores, and musics as 'rediscovering' something deep-down always known. (Furthermore, once one starts thinking about nationality in terms of continuity, few things seem as historically deep-rooted as languages, for which no dated origins can ever be given.)[19]

In the Americas the problem was differently posed. On the one hand, national independence had almost everywhere been internationally acknowledged by the 1830s. It had thus become an inheritance, and, *as an inheritance*, it was compelled to enter a genealogical series. Yet the developing European instrumentalities were not readily available. Language had never been an issue in the American nationalist movements. [. . .] [I]t was precisely the sharing with the metropole of a common language (and common religion and common culture) that had made the first national imaginings possible. To be sure, there are some interesting cases where one detects a sort of 'European' thinking early at work. For example, Noah Webster's 1828 (i.e., 'second-generation') *American Dictionary of the English Language* was intended to give an official imprimatur to an American language whose lineage was distinct from that of English. In Paraguay, the eighteenth-century Jesuit tradition of using Guaraní made it possible for a radically non-Spanish 'native' language to become a *national* language, under the long, xenophobic dictatorship of José Gaspar Rodríguez de Francia (1814–40). But, on the whole, any attempt to give historical depth to nationality via linguistic means faced insuperable obstacles. Virtually all the creoles were institutionally committed (via schools, print media, administrative habits, and so on) to European rather than indigenous American tongues. Any excessive emphasis on linguistic lineages threatened to blur precisely that 'memory of independence' which it was essential to retain.

The solution, eventually applicable in both New and Old Worlds, was found in History, or rather History emplotted in particular ways. We have observed the speed with which Chairs in History succeeded the Year One. As Hayden White remarks, it is no less striking that the five presiding geniuses of European historiography were all born within the quarter century following the Convention's rupturing of time: Ranke in 1795, Michelet in 1798, Tocqueville in 1805, and Marx and Burckhardt in 1818.[20] Of the five, it is perhaps natural that Michelet, self-appointed historian of the Revolution, most clearly exemplifies the national imagining being born, for he was the first self-consciously to write *on behalf* of the dead.[21] [. . .]

A vast pedagogical industry works ceaselessly to oblige young Americans to remember/forget the hostilities of 1861–65 as a great 'civil' war between 'brothers' rather than between – as they briefly were – two sovereign nation-states. (We can be sure, however, that if the Confederacy had succeeded in maintaining its independence, this 'civil war' would have been replaced in memory by something quite unbrotherly.) English history textbooks offer the diverting spectacle of a great Founding Father whom every schoolchild is taught to call William the Conqueror. The same child is not informed that William spoke no English, indeed could not have done so, since the English language did not exist in his epoch; nor is he or she told 'Conqueror of what?'. For the only intelligible modern answer would have to be 'Conqueror of the English,' which would turn the old Norman predator into a more successful precursor of Napoléon and Hitler. Hence 'the Conqueror' operates as the same kind of ellipsis as 'la Saint-Barthélemy', to remind one of something which it is immediately obligatory to forget. Norman William and Saxon Harold thus meet on the battlefield of Hastings, if not as dancing partners, at least as brothers.

But it is surely too easy to attribute these reassuring ancient fratricides simply to the icy calculations of state functionaries. At another level they reflect a deep reshaping of the imagination of which the state was barely conscious, and over which it had, and still has, only exiguous control. In the 1930s people of many nationalities went to fight in the Iberian peninsula because they viewed it as the arena in which global historical forces and causes were at stake. When the long-lived Franco regime constructed the Valley of the Fallen, it restricted membership in the gloomy necropolis to those who, in its eyes, had died in the world-struggle against Bolshevism and atheism. But, at the state's margins, a 'memory' was already emerging of a 'Spanish' Civil War. Only after the crafty tyrant's death, and the subsequent, startlingly smooth transition to bourgeois democracy – in which it played a crucial role – did this 'memory' become official. In much the same way, the colossal class war that, from 1918 to 1920, raged between the Pamirs and the Vistula came to be remembered/forgotten in Soviet film and fiction as 'our' civil war, while the Soviet state, on the whole, held to an orthodox Marxist reading of the struggle.

In this regard the creole nationalisms of the Americas are especially instructive. For on the one hand, the American states were for many decades weak, effectively decentralized, and rather modest in their educational ambitions. On the other hand, the American societies, in which 'white' settlers were counterposed to 'black' slaves and half-exterminated 'natives,' were internally riven to a degree quite unmatched in Europe. Yet the imagining of that fraternity, without which the reassurance of fratricide cannot be born, shows up remarkably early, and not without a curious authentic popularity. In the United States of America this paradox is particularly well exemplified.

In 1840, in the midst of a brutal eight-year war against the Seminoles of Florida (and as Michelet was summoning his Oedipus), James Fenimore Cooper published *The Pathfinder*, the fourth of his five, hugely popular, Leatherstocking Tales. Central to this novel (and to all but the first of its companions) is what Leslie Fiedler called the 'austere, almost inarticulate, but unquestioned love' binding the 'white' woodsman Natty Bumppo and the noble Delaware chieftain Chingachgook ('Chicago'!).[22] Yet the Renanesque setting for their bloodbrotherhood is not the murderous 1830s but the last forgotten/remembered years of British imperial rule. Both men are figured as 'Americans,' fighting for survival – against the French, their 'native' allies (the 'devilish Mingos'), and treacherous agents of George III.

When, in 1851, Herman Melville depicted Ishmael and Queequeg cozily in bed together at the Spouter Inn ('there, then, in our hearts' honeymoon, lay I and Queequeg'), the noble Polynesian savage was sardonically Americanized as follows:[23]

> . . . certain it was that his head was phrenologically an excellent one. It may seem ridiculous, but it reminded me of George Washington's head, as seen in popular busts of him. It had the same long regularly graded

retreating slope above the brows, which were likewise very projecting, like two long promontories thickly wooded on top. Queequeg was George Washington cannibalistically developed.

It remained for Mark Twain to create in 1881, well after the 'Civil War' and Lincoln's Emancipation Proclamation, the first indelible image of black and white as American 'brothers': Jim and Huck companionably adrift on the wide Mississippi.[24] But the setting is a remembered/forgotten antebellum in which the black is still a slave.

These striking nineteenth-century imaginings of fraternity, emerging 'naturally' in a society fractured by the most violent racial, class and regional antagonisms, show as clearly as anything else that nationalism in the age of Michelet and Renan represented a new form of consciousness – a consciousness that arose when it was no longer possible to experience the nation as new, at the wave-top moment of rupture.

THE BIOGRAPHY OF NATIONS

All profound changes in consciousness, by their very nature, bring with them characteristic amnesias. Out of such oblivions, in specific historical circumstances, spring narratives. After experiencing the physiological and emotional changes produced by puberty, it is impossible to 'remember' the consciousness of childhood. How many thousands of days passed between infancy and early adulthood vanish beyond direct recall! How strange it is to need another's help to learn that this naked baby in the yellowed photograph, sprawled happily on rug or cot, is you. The photograph, fine child of the age of mechanical reproduction, is only the most peremptory of a huge modern accumulation of documentary evidence (birth certificates, diaries, report cards, letters, medical records, and the like) which simultaneously records a certain apparent continuity and emphasizes its loss from memory. Out of this estrangement comes a conception of personhood, *identity* (yes, you and that naked baby are identical) which, because it can not be 'remembered,' must be narrated. Against biology's demonstration that every single cell in a human body is replaced over seven years, the narratives of autobiography and biography flood print-capitalism's markets year by year.

These narratives [. . .] are set in homogeneous, empty time. Hence their frame is historical and their setting sociological. This is why so many autobiographies begin with the circumstances of parents and grandparents, for which the autobiographer can have only circumstantial, textual evidence; and why the biographer is at pains to record the calendrical, A.D. dates of two biographical events which his or her subject can never remember: birth-day and death-day. Nothing affords a sharper reminder of this narrative's modernity than the opening of the Gospel according to St. Matthew. For the Evangelist gives us an austere list of thirty males successively begetting one another, from the Patriarch Abraham down to Jesus Christ. (Only once is a woman mentioned, not because she is a begetter, but because she is a non-Jewish Moabite). No dates are given for any of Jesus's forebears, let alone sociological, cultural, physiological or political information about them. This narrative style (which also reflects the rupture-in-Bethlehem become memory) was entirely reasonable to the sainted genealogist because he did not conceive of Christ as an historical 'personality,' but only as the true Son of God.

As with modern persons, so it is with nations. Awareness of being imbedded in secular, serial time, with all its implications of continuity, yet of 'forgetting' the experience of this continuity – product of the ruptures of the late eighteenth century – engenders the need for a narrative of 'identity.' The task is set for Michelet's magistrate. Yet between narratives of person and nation there is a central difference of employment. In the secular story of the 'person' there is a beginning and an end. She emerges from parental genes and social circumstances onto a brief historical stage, there to play a role until her death. After that, nothing but the penumbra of lingering fame or influence. (Imagine how strange it would be, today, to end a life of Hitler by observing that on 30 April 1945 he proceeded straight to Hell). Nations, however, have no clearly identifiable births, and their deaths, if they ever happen, are never natural.[25] Because there is no Originator, the nation's biography can not be written evangelically, 'down time,' through a long procreative chain of begettings. The only alternative is to fashion it 'up time' – towards Peking Man, Java Man, King Arthur, wherever the lamp of archaeology casts its fitful gleam. This fashioning, however, is marked by deaths, which, in a curious inversion of conventional genealogy, start from an originary present. World War II begets World War I; out of Sedan comes Austerlitz; the ancestor of the Warsaw Uprising is the state of Israel.

Yet the deaths that structure the nation's biography are of a special kind. In all the 1,200 pages of his awesome *La Méditerranée et le Monde Méditerranéen à l'Époque de Philippe II* Fernand Braudel mentions Renan's 'la Saint-Barthélemy' only in passing, though it occurred exactly *nel mezzo del camino* of the Habsburg dynast's reign [. . .]. For Braudel, the deaths that matter are those myriad anonymous events, which, aggregated and averaged into secular mortality rates, permit him to chart the slow-changing conditions of life for millions of anonymous human beings of whom the last question asked is their nationality.

From Braudel's remorselessly accumulating cemeteries, however, the nation's biography snatches, against the going mortality rate, exemplary suicides, poignant martyrdoms, assassinations, executions, wars, and holocausts. But, to serve the narrative purpose, these violent deaths must be remembered/forgotten as 'our own.'

NOTES

1. The accumulation reached a frantic zenith in the 'international' (i.e., European) search for an accurate measure of longitude, amusingly recounted in Landes, *Revolution in Time*, chapter 9. In 1776, as the Thirteen Colonies declared their

independence, the *Gentleman's Magazine* included this brief obituary for John Harrison: 'He was a most ingenious mechanic, and received the 20,000 pounds reward [from Westminster] for the discovery of the longitude [sic].'

2. The late spreading of this consciousness to Asia is deftly alluded to in the opening pages of Pramoedya Ananta Toer's great historical novel *Bumi Manusia* [Earth of Mankind]. The young nationalist hero muses that he was born on the same date as the future Queen Wilhelmina – 31 August 1880. 'But while my island was wrapped in the darkness of night, her country was bathed in sun; and if her country was embraced by night's blackness, my island glittered in the equatorial noon.' p. 4.

3. Needless to say, 'whiteness' was a legal category which had a distinctly tangential relationship to complex social realities. As the Liberator himself put it, '*We* are the vile offspring of the predatory Spaniards who came to America to bleed her white and to breed with their victims. Later the illegitimate offspring of these unions joined with the offspring of slaves transported from Africa.' Italics added. Lynch, *The Spanish-American Revolutions*, p. 249. One should beware of assuming anything 'eternally European' in this *criollismo*. Remembering all those devoutly Buddhist-Singhalese Da Souzas, those piously Catholic-Florinese Da Silvas, and those cynically Catholic-Manileño Sorianos who play unproblematic social, economic, and political roles in contemporary Ceylon, Indonesia, and the Philippines, helps one to recognize that, under the right circumstances, Europeans could be gently absorbed into non-European cultures.

4. Compare the fate of the huge African immigrant population. The brutal mechanisms of slavery ensured not merely its political-cultural fragmentation, but also very rapidly removed the possibility of imagining black communities in Venezuela and West Africa moving in parallel trajectory.

5. It is an astonishing sign of the depth of Eurocentrism that so many European scholars persist, in the face of all the evidence, in regarding nationalism as a European invention.

6. But note the ironic case of Brazil. In 1808, King João VI fled to Rio de Janeiro to escape Napoléon's armies. Though Wellington had expelled the French by 1811, the emigrant monarch, fearing republican unrest at home, stayed on in South America until 1822, so that between 1808 and 1822 Rio was the centre of a world empire stretching to Angola, Mozambique, Macao, and East Timor. But this empire was ruled by a European, not an American.

7. Doubtless this was what permitted the Liberator to exclaim at one point that a Negro, i.e. slave, revolt would be 'a thousand times worse than a Spanish invasion.' [. . .]. A slave jacquerie, if successful, might mean the physical extermination of the creoles.

8. See Masur, *Bolívar*, p. 131.

9. The French Revolution was in turn *paralleled* in the New World by the outbreak of Toussaint L'Ouverture's insurrection in 1791, which by 1806 had resulted in Haiti's former slaves creating the second independent republic of the Western hemisphere.

10. The young Wordsworth was in France in 1791–1792, and later, in *The Prelude*, wrote these famous reminiscent lines:

> Bliss was it in that *dawn* to be alive,
> But to be young was very heaven!

Italics added.

11. Lynch, *The Spanish-American Revolutions*, pp. 314–15.

12. [Lynch, *The Spanish-American Revolutions*, p. 276].

13. Landes, *Revolution in Time*, pp. 230–31, 442–43.

14. [See Anderson, *Imagined Communities*, Chapter 2.]

15. See Hayden White, *Metahistory: The Historical Imagination in Nineteenth-Century Europe*, pp. 135–43, for a sophisticated discussion of this transformation.

16. But it was an A.D. with a difference. Before the rupture it still retained, however fragilely in enlightened quarters, a theological aura glowing from within its medieval Latin. Anno Domini recalled that irruption of eternity into mundane time which took place in Bethlehem. After the rupture, reduced monogrammatically to A.D., it joined an (English) vernacular B.C., Before Christ, that encompassed a serial cosmological history (to which the new science of geology was making signal contributions). We may judge how deep an abyss yawned between Anno Domini and A.D./B.C. by noting that neither the Buddhist nor the Islamic world, even today, imagines any epoch marked as 'Before the Gautama Buddha' or 'Before the Hegira.' Both make uneasy do with the alien monogram B.C.

17. As late as 1951, the intelligent Indonesian socialist Lintong Mulia Sitorus could still write that: 'Till the end of the nineteenth century, the coloured peoples still slept soundly, while the whites were busily at work in every field.' *Sedjarah Pergerakan Kebangsaan Indonesia* [History of the Indonesian Nationalist Movement], p. 5.

18. One could perhaps say that these revolutions were, in European eyes, the first really important *political* events that had ever occurred across the Atlantic.

19. Still, historical depth is not infinite. At some point English vanishes into Norman French and Anglo-Saxon; French into Latin and 'German' Frankish; and so on. [. . .]

20. *Metahistory*, p. 140. Hegel, born in 1770, was already in his late teens when the Revolution broke out, but his *Vorlesungen über die Philosophie der Weltgeschichte* were only published in 1837, six years after his death.

21. White, *Metahistory*, p. 159.

22. See his *Love and Death in the American Novel*, p. 192. Fiedler read this relationship psychologically, and ahistorically, as an instance of American fiction's failure to deal with adult heterosexual love and its obsession with death, incest, and innocent homoeroticism. Rather than a national eroticism, it is, I suspect, an eroticized nationalism that is at work. Male-male bondings in a Protestant society which from the start rigidly prohibited miscegenation are paralleled by male-female 'holy loves' in the nationalist fiction of Latin America, where Catholicism permitted the growth of a large mestizo population. (It is telling that English has had to borrow 'mestizo' from Spanish.)

23. Herman Melville, *Moby Dick*, p. 71. How the author must have savoured the malignant final phrase!

24. It is agreeable to note that the publication of *Huckleberry Finn* preceded by only a few months Renan's evocation of 'la Saint-Barthélemy'.

25. For such apocalypses the neologism 'genocide' was quite recently coined.

REFERENCES

Anderson, Benedict. *Imagined Communities: Reflections on the Origin and Spread of Nationalism*. Rev. ed. London: Verso. 1991.

Braudel, Fernand. *La Méditerranée et le Monde Méditerranéen à l' Époque de Philippe II*. Paris: Armand Colin. 1966.

Cooper, James Fenimore. *The Pathfinder*. New York: Signet Classics. 1961.

Fiedler, Leslie. *Love and Death in the American Novel*. New York: Stein & Day. 1966.

Landes, David S. *Revolution in Time: Clocks and the Making of the Modern World*. Cambridge, MA: Harvard University Press. 1983.

Lynch, John. *The Spanish-American Revolutions, 1808–1826*. New York: Norton. 1973.

Masur, Gerhard. *Simón Bolívar*. Albuquerque: University of New Mexico Press. 1948.

Melville, Herman. *Moby Dick*. London and Toronto: Cassell. 1930.

Pramoedya Ananta Toer. *Bumi Manusia*. Jakarta: Hasta Mitra. 1980.

Sitorus, Lintong Mulia. *Sedjarah Pergerakan Kebangsaan Indonesia*. Jakarta: Pustaka Rakjat. 1951.

White, Hayden. *Metahistory: The Historical Imagination in Nineteenth-Century Europe*. Baltimore: Johns Hopkins University Press. 1973.

8.2

ÉTIENNE BALIBAR: *FROM* THE NATION FORM: HISTORY AND IDEOLOGY

. . . a 'past' that has never been present, and which never will be.

Jacques Derrida, *Margins of Philosophy*

[. . .]

PRODUCING THE PEOPLE

A social formation only reproduces itself as a nation to the extent that, through a network of apparatuses and daily practices, the individual is instituted as *homo nationalis* from cradle to grave, at the same time as he or she is instituted as *homo oeconomicus*, *politicus*, *religiosus* . . . That is why the question of the nation form, if it is henceforth an open one, is, at bottom, the question of knowing under what historical conditions it is possible to institute such a thing: by virtue of what internal and external relations of force and also by virtue of what symbolic forms invested in elementary material practices? Asking this question is another way of asking oneself to what transition in civilization the nationalization of societies corresponds, and what are the figures of individuality between which nationality moves.

The crucial point is this: What makes the nation a 'community'? Or rather, in what way is the form of community instituted by the nation distinguished specifically from other historical communities?

Source: Étienne Balibar, 'The Nation Form: History and Ideology', in Philomena Essed and David Theo Goldberg, (eds), *Race Critical Theories* (London: Blackwell, 2002), pp. 220–30.

Let us dispense right away with the antitheses traditionally attached to that notion, the first of which is the antithesis between the 'real' and the 'imaginary' community. *Every social community reproduced by the functioning of institutions is imaginary*, that is to say, it is based on the projection of individual existence into the weft of a collective narrative, on the recognition of a common name and on traditions lived as the trace of an immemorial past (even when they have been fabricated and inculcated in the recent past). But this comes down to accepting that, under certain conditions, *only* imaginary communities are real.

In the case of national formations, the imaginary which inscribes itself in the real in this way is that of the 'people.' It is that of a community which recognizes itself in advance in the institution of the state, which recognizes that state as 'its own' in opposition to other states and, in particular, inscribes its political struggles within the horizon of that state – by, for example, formulating its aspirations for reform and social revolution as projects for the transformation of 'its national state.' Without this, there can be neither 'monopoly of organized violence' (Max Weber), nor 'national-popular will' (Gramsci). But such a people does not exist naturally, and even when it is tendentially constituted, it does not exist for all time. No modern nation possesses a given 'ethnic' basis, even when it arises out of a national independence struggle. And, moreover, no modern nation, however 'egalitarian' it may be, corresponds to the extinction of class conflicts. The fundamental problem is therefore to produce the people. More exactly, it is to make the people produce itself continually as national community. Or again, it is to produce the effect of unity by virtue of which the people will appear, in everyone's eyes, 'as a people,' that is, as the basis and origin of political power.

Rousseau was the first to have explicitly conceived the question in these terms, 'What makes a people a people?' Deep down, this question is no different from the one which arose a moment ago: How are individuals nationalized or, in other words, socialized in the dominant form of national belonging? Which enables us to put aside from the outset another artificial dilemma: it is not a question of setting a collective identity against individual identities. *All identity is individual*, but there is no individual identity that is not historical or, in other words, constructed within a field of social values, norms of behavior, and collective symbols. Individuals never identify with one another (not even in the 'fusional' practices of mass movements or the 'intimacy' of affective relations), nor, however, do they ever acquire an isolated identity, which is an intrinsically contradictory notion. The real question is how the dominant reference points of individual identity change over time and with the changing institutional environment.

To the question of the historical production of the people (or of national individuality) we cannot merely be content to rely with a description of conquests, population movements, and administrative practices of 'territorialization.' The individuals destined to perceive themselves as the members of a single nation are either gathered together externally from diverse geographical origins, as in the nations formed by immigration (France, the USA) or else are brought mutually to recognize one another within a historical frontier which contained them all. The people is constituted out of various populations subject to a common law. In every case, however, a model of their unity must 'anticipate' that constitution: the process of unification (the effectiveness of which can be measured, for example, in collective mobilization in wartime, that is, in the capacity to confront death collectively) presupposes the constitution of a specific ideological form. It must at one and the same time be a mass phenomenon and a phenomenon of individuation, must effect an 'interpellation of individuals as subjects' (Althusser) which is much more potent than the mere inculcation of political values or rather one that integrates this inculcation into a more elementary process (which we may term 'primary') of fixation of the affects of love and hate and representation of the 'self.' That ideological form must become an *a priori* condition of communication between individuals (the 'citizens') and between social groups – not by suppressing all differences, but by relativizing them and subordinating them to itself in such a way that it is the symbolic difference between 'ourselves' and 'foreigners' which wins out and which is lived as irreducible. In other words, to use the terminology proposed by Fichte in his *Reden an die deutsche Nation* of 1808, the 'external frontiers' of the state have to become 'internal frontiers' or – which amounts to the same thing – external frontiers have to be imagined constantly as a projection and protection of an internal collective personality, which each of us carries within ourselves and enables us to inhabit the space of the state as a place where we have always been – and always will be – 'at home.'

What might that ideological form be? Depending on the particular circumstances, it will be called patriotism or nationalism, the events which promote its formation or which reveal its potency will be recorded and its origin will be traced back to political methods – the combination of 'force' and 'education' (as Machiavelli and Gramsci put it) – which enable the state to some extent to fabricate public consciousness. But this fabrication is merely an external aspect. To grasp the deepest reasons for its effectiveness, attention will turn then, as the attention of political philosophy and sociology has turned for three centuries, towards the analogy of *religion*, making nationalism and patriotism out to be a religion – if not indeed *the* religion – of modern times.

Inevitably, there is some truth in this – and not only because religions, formally, in so far as they start out from 'souls' and individual identities, institute forms of community and prescribe a social 'morality'; but also because theological discourse has provided models for the idealization of the nation and the sacralization of the state, which make it possible for a bond of sacrifice to be created between individuals, and for the stamp of 'truth' and 'law' to be conferred upon the rules of the legal system.[1] Every national community must have been represented at some point or another as a 'chosen people.' Nevertheless, the political philosophies of the Classical Age had already recognized the inadequacy of this analogy, which is equally clearly demonstrated by the failure of the attempts to constitute 'civil religions,' by the fact that the 'state religion' ultimately only constituted a transitory form of national ideology (even when this transition lasted for a long time and produced important effects by superimposing religious on national struggles) and by the interminable conflict between theological universality and the universality of nationalism.

In reality, the opposite argument is correct. Incontestably, national ideology involves ideal signifiers (first and foremost the very *name* of the nation or 'fatherland') on to which may be transferred the sense of the sacred and the affects of love, respect, sacrifice, and fear which have cemented religious communities; but that transfer only takes place because *another type* of community is involved here. The analogy is itself based on a deeper difference. If it were not, it would be impossible to understand why national identity, more or less completely integrating the forms of religious identity, ends up tending to replace it, and forcing it itself to become 'nationalized.'

FICTIVE ETHNICITY AND IDEAL NATION

I apply the term 'fictive ethnicity' to the community instituted by the nation-state. This is an intentionally complex expression in which the term fiction, in keeping with my remarks above, should not be taken in the sense of a pure and simple illusion without historical effects, but must, on the contrary, be understood by analogy with the *persona ficta* of the juridical tradition in the sense of an institutional effect, a 'fabrication.' No nation possesses an ethnic base naturally, but as social formations are nationalized, the populations included within them, divided up among them or dominated by them are ethnicized – that is, represented in the past or in the future *as if* they formed a natural community, possessing of itself an identity of origins, culture, and interests which transcends individuals and social conditions.[2]

Fictive ethnicity is not purely and simply identical with the *ideal nation* which is the object of patriotism, but it is indispensable to it, for, without it, the nation would appear precisely only as an idea or an arbitrary abstraction; patriotism's appeal would be addressed to no one. It is fictive ethnicity which makes it possible for the expression of a preexisting unity to be seen in the state, and continually to measure the state against its 'historic mission' in the service of the nation and, as a consequence, to idealize politics. By constituting the people as a fictively ethnic unity against the background of a universalistic representation which attributes to each individual one – and only one – ethnic identity and which thus divides up the whole of humanity between different ethnic groups corresponding potentially to so many nations, national ideology does much more than justify the strategies employed by the state to control populations. It inscribes their demands in advance in a sense of belonging in the double sense of the term – both what it is that makes one belong to oneself and also what makes one belong to other fellow human beings. Which means that one can be interpellated, as an individual, *in the name of* the collectivity whose name one bears. The naturalization of belonging and the sublimation of the ideal nation are two aspects of the same process.

How can ethnicity be produced? And how can it be produced in such a way that it does not appear as fiction, but as the most natural of origins? History shows us that there are two great competing routes to this: language and race. Most often the two operate together, for only their complementarity makes it possible for the 'people' to be represented as an absolutely autonomous unit. Both express the idea that the national character (which might also be called its soul or its spirit) is immanent in the people. But both offer a means of transcending actual individuals and political relations. They constitute two ways of rooting historical populations in a fact of 'nature' (the diversity of languages and the diversity of races appearing predestined), but also two ways of giving a meaning to their continued existence, of transcending its contingency. By force of circumstance, however, at times one or the other is dominant, for they are not based on the development of the same institutions and do not appeal to the same symbols or the same idealizations of the national identity. The fact of these different articulations of, on the one hand, a predominantly linguistic ethnicity and, on the other, an ethnicity that is predominantly racial has obvious political consequences. For this reason, and for the sake of clarity of analysis, we must begin by examining the two separately.

The language community seems the more abstract notion, but in reality it is the more concrete since it connects individuals up with an origin which may at any moment be actualized and which has as its content the *common act* of their own exchanges, of their discursive communication, using the instruments of spoken language and the whole, constantly self-renewing mass of written and recorded texts. This is not to say that that community is an immediate one, without internal limits, any more than communication is in reality 'transparent' between all individuals. But these limits are always relative: even if it were the case that individuals whose social conditions were very distant from one another were never in direct communication, they would be bound together by an uninterrupted chain of intermediate discourses. They are not isolated – either *de jure* or *de facto*.

We should, however, certainly not allow ourselves to believe that this situation is as old as the worth itself. It is, on the contrary, remarkably recent. The old empires and the *Ancien Régime* societies were still based on the juxtaposition of linguistically separate populations, on the super-imposition of mutually incompatible 'languages' for the dominant and the dominated and for the sacred and profane spheres. Between these there had to be a whole system of translations.[3] In modern national formations, the translators are writers, journalists, and politicians, social actors who speak the language of the 'people' in a way that seems all the more natural for the very degree of distinction they thereby bring to it. The translation process has become primarily one of internal translation between different 'levels of language.' Social differences are expressed and relativized as different ways of speaking the national language, which supposes a common code and even a common norm.[4] This latter is, as we know, inculcated by universal schooling, whose primary function it is to perform precisely this task.

That is why there is a close historical correlation between the national formation and the development of schools as 'popular' institutions, not limited to specialized training or to elite culture, but serving to underpin the whole process of the socialization of individuals. That the school should also be the site of the inculcation of a nationalist ideology – and sometimes also the place where it is contested – is a secondary phenomenon, and is, strictly speaking, a less indispensable aspect. Let us simply say that schooling is the principal institution which produces ethnicity as linguistic community. It is not, however, the only one: the state, economic exchange, and family life are also schools in a sense, organs of the ideal nation recognizable by a common language which belongs to them 'as their own.' For what is decisive here is not only that the national language should be recognized as the official language, but, much more fundamentally, that it should be able to appear as the very element of the life of a people, the *reality* which each person may appropriate in his or her own way, without thereby destroying its identity. There is no contradiction between the instituting of *one* national language and the daily discrepancy between – and clash of – 'class languages' which precisely are not different languages. In fact, the two things are complementary. All linguistic practices feed into a single 'love of the language' which is addressed not to the textbook norm nor to particular usage, but to the 'mother tongue' – that is, to the ideal of a common origin projected back beyond learning processes and specialist forms of usage and which, by that very fact, becomes the metaphor for the love fellow nationals feel for one another.

One might then ask oneself, quite apart from the precise historical questions which the history of national languages poses – from the difficulties of their unification or imposition, and from their elaboration into an idiom that is both 'popular' and 'cultivated' (a process which we know to be far from complete today in all nation-states, in spite of the labors of their intellectuals with the aid of various international bodies) – *why the language community is not sufficient to produce ethnicity.*[5]

Perhaps this has to do with the paradoxical properties which, by virtue of its very structure, the linguistic signifier confers on individual identity. In a sense, it is always in the element of language that individuals are interpellated as subjects, for every interpellation is of the order of discourse. Every 'personality' is constructed with words, in which law, genealogy, history, political choices, professional qualifications, and psychology are set forth. But the linguistic construction of identity is by definition *open*. No individual 'chooses' his or her mother tongue or can 'change' it at will. Nevertheless, it is always possible to appropriate several languages and to turn oneself into a different kind of bearer of discourse and of the transformations of language. The linguistic community induces a terribly constraining ethnic memory (Roland Barthes once went so far as to call it 'fascist'), but it is one which none the less possesses a strange plasticity: it immediately naturalizes new acquisitions. It does so *too quickly* in a sense. It is a collective memory which perpetuates itself at the cost of an individual forgetting of 'origins.' The 'second generation' immigrant – a notion which in this context acquires a structural significance – inhabits the national language (and through it the nation itself) in a manner as spontaneous, as 'hereditary' and as imperious, so far as affectivity and the imaginary are concerned, as the son of one of those native heaths which we think of as so very French (and most of which not so long ago did not even have the national language as their daily parlance). One's 'mother' tongue is not necessarily the language of one's 'real' mother. The language community is a community *in the present*, which produces the feeling that it has always existed, but which lays down no destiny for the successive generations. Ideally, it 'assimilates' anyone, but holds no one. Finally, it affects all individuals in their innermost being (in the way in which they constitute themselves as subjects), but its historical particularity is bound only to interchangeable institutions. When circumstances permit, it may serve different nations (as English, Spanish, and even French do) or survive the 'physical' disappearance of the people who used it (like 'ancient' Greek and Latin or 'literary' Arabic). For it to be tied down to the frontiers of a particular people, it therefore needs an extra degree [*un supplément*] of particularity, or a principle of closure, of exclusion.

This principle is that of being part of a common race. But here we must be very careful not to give rise to misunderstandings. All kinds of somatic or psychological features, both visible and invisible, may lend themselves to creating the fiction of a racial identity and therefore to representing natural and hereditary differences between social groups either within the same nation or outside its frontiers. I have discussed elsewhere, as have others before me, the development of the marks of race and the relation they bear to different historical figures of social conflict. What we are solely concerned with here is the symbolic kernel which makes it possible to equate race and ethnicity ideally, and to represent unity of race to oneself as the origin or cause of the historical unity of a people. Now, unlike what applied in the case of the linguistic community, it cannot be a question here of a practice which is really common to *all* the individuals who form a political unit. We are not dealing with anything equivalent to communication. What we are speaking of is therefore a second-degree fiction. This fiction, however, also derives its effectiveness from everyday practices, relations which immediately structure the 'life' of individuals. And, most importantly, whereas the language community can only create equality between individuals by simultaneously 'naturalizing' the social inequality of linguistic practices, the race community dissolves social inequalities in an even more ambivalent 'similarity'; it ethnicizes the social difference which is an expression of irreconcilable antagonisms by lending it the form of a division between the 'genuinely' and the 'falsely' national.

I think we may cast some light on this paradox in the following way. The symbolic kernel of the idea of race (and of its demographic and cultural equivalents) is the schema of genealogy, that is, quite simply the idea that the filiation of individuals transmits from generation to generation a substance both biological and spiritual and thereby inscribes them in a temporal community known as 'kinship.' That way, *as soon as* national ideology enunciates the proposition that the individuals belonging to the same people are interrelated (or, in the prescriptive mode, that they should constitute a circle of extended kinship), we are in the presence of this second mode of ethnicization.

The objection will no doubt be raised here that such a representation characterizes societies and communities which have nothing national about them. But, it is precisely on this point that the particular innovation hinges by which the nation form is articulated to the modern idea of race. This idea is correlative with the tendency for 'private' genealogies, as (still) codified by traditional systems of preferential marriage and lineage, to disappear. The idea of a racial community makes its appearance when the frontiers of kinship dissolve at the level of the clan, the neighborhood community, and, theoretically at least, the social class, to be imaginarily transferred to the threshold of nationality: that is to say, when nothing prevents marriage with any of one's 'fellow citizens' whatever, and when, on the contrary, such a marriage seems the only one that is 'normal' or 'natural.' The racial community has a tendency to represent itself as one big family or as the common envelope of family relations (the community of 'French,' 'American,' or 'Algerian' families).[6] From that point onward, each individual has his/her family, whatever his/her social condition, but the family – like property – becomes a contingent relation between individuals. [. . .]

These historical differences in no sense impose any necessary outcome – they are rather the stuff of political struggles – but they deeply modify the conditions in which problems of assimilation, equality of rights, citizenship, nationalism, and internationalism are posed. One might seriously wonder whether in regard to the production of fictive ethnicity, the 'building of Europe' – to the extent that it will seek to transfer to the 'Community' level functions and symbols of the nation-state – will orientate itself *predominantly* towards the institution of a 'European co-lingualism' (and if so, adopting which language) or *predominantly* in the direction of the idealization of 'European demographic identity' conceived mainly in opposition to the 'southern populations' (Turks, Arabs, Blacks).[7] Every 'people,' which is the product of a national process of ethnicization, is forced today to find its own means of going beyond exclusivism or identitarian ideology in the world of transnational communications and global relations of force. Or rather: every individual is compelled to find in the transformation of the imaginary of 'his' or 'her' people the means to leave it, in order to communicate with the individuals of other peoples with which he or she shares the same interests and, to some extent, the same future.

NOTES

1. On all these points, the work of Kantorowicz is clearly of crucial significance: see *Mourir pour la patrie et autres textes* (Paris: PUF, 1985).
2. I say 'included within them,' but I should also add 'or excluded by them,' since the ethnicization of the 'others' occurs simultaneously with that of the 'nationals': there are no longer any historical differences other than ethnic ones (thus the Jews also have to be a 'people'). On the ethnicization of colonized populations, see J.-L. Amselle and E. M'Bokolo, *Au coeur de l'ethnie: ethnies, tribalisme et Etat en Afrique* (Paris: La Découverte, 1985).
3. Ernest Gellner, *Nations and Nationalism* (Oxford: Blackwell, 1983) and Benedict Anderson, *Imagined Communities* (London: Verso, 1983), whose analyses are as opposed as 'materialism' and 'idealism,' both rightly stress this point.
4. See Renée Balibar, *L'Institution du français. Essai sur le colingualisme des Carolingiens à la République* (Paris: PUF, 1985).
5. Jean-Claude Milner offers some very stimulating suggestions on this point, though more in *Les Noms indistincts* (Paris: Seuil, 1983), pp. 43 *et seq.* than in *L'Amour de la langue* (Paris: Seuil, 1978). On the 'class struggle'/ 'language struggle' alternative in the USSR at the point when the policy of 'socialism in one country' became dominant, see F. Gadet, J.-M. Gaymann, Y. Mignot, and E. Roudinesco, *Les Maîtres de la langue* (Paris: Maspero, 1979).
6. Let us add that we have here a sure *criterion* for the commutation between racism and nationalism: every discourse on the fatherland or nation which associates these notions with the 'defense of the family' – not to speak of the birth rate – is already ensconced in the universe of racism.
7. Right at the heart of this alternative lies the following truly crucial question: will the administrative and educational institutions of the future 'United Europe' accept Arabic, Turkish, or even certain Asian or African languages on an equal footing with French, German, and Portuguese, or will those languages be regarded as 'foreign'?

PAUL GILROY: *FROM* THERE AIN'T NO BLACK IN THE UNION JACK

'Race', Nation and the Rhetoric of Order

In his thoughtful study of nationalism, *Imagined Communities*, Benedict Anderson seeks to clarify the relationship between racism and nationalism by challenging Tom Nairn's (1977) argument that these two forms of ideology are fundamentally related in that the former derives from the latter. Anderson's conclusion is worth stating at length:

> The fact of the matter is that nationalism thinks in terms of historical destinies, while racism dreams of eternal contaminations transmitted from the origins of time through an endless sequence of loathsome copulations . . . The dreams of racism actually have their origins in the ideologies of class, rather than those of nation: above all in claims to divinity among rulers and to blue or white blood and breeding among aristocracies. No surprise then that . . . on the whole, racism and anti-semitism manifest themselves, not across national boundaries but within them. In other words they justify not so much foreign wars as domestic repression and domination. (Anderson, 1983, p. 136)

In support of this point, Anderson cites the fact that regardless of its internal 'race' politics, South Africa continues to enjoy amicable diplomatic relations with prominent black politicians from various African states. This is a curious

Source: Paul Gilroy, *There Ain't No Black in the Union Jack* (London: Routledge, 2002), pp. 43–6, 48–53, 62–5.

example because the formulation of the apartheid system, in particular the homelands policy, can be read as an attempt to externalize those 'internal' 'race' problems by representing them as the interaction of separate states which rest on distinct cultural and historical identities (Wolpe, 1980).

Anderson's theory claims that racism is essentially antithetical to nationalism because nations are made possible in and through print languages rather than notions of biological difference and kinship. Thus, he argues that anyone can in theory learn the language of the nation they seek to join and through the process of naturalization become a citizen enjoying formal equality under its laws. Whatever objections can be made to Anderson's general argument, his privileging of the written word over the spoken word for example, it simply does not apply in the English/British case. The politics of 'race' in this country is fired by conceptions of national belonging and homogeneity which not only blur the distinction between 'race' and nation, but rely on that very ambiguity for their effect. Phrases like 'the Island Race' and 'the Bulldog Breed' vividly convey the manner in which this nation is represented in terms which are simultaneously biological and cultural. It is important to recognize that the legal concept of patriality, introduced by the Immigration Act of 1968, codified this cultural biology of 'race' into statute law as part of a strategy for the exclusion of black settlers (WING, 1984). This act specified that immigration controls would not apply to any would-be settler who could claim national membership on the basis that one of their grandparents had been born in the UK. The Nationality Act of 1981 rationalized the legal vocabulary involved so that patrials are now known as British citizens.

A further objection to Anderson's position emerges from consideration of how the process of black settlement has been continually described in military metaphors which offer war and conquest as the central analogies for immigration. The enemy within, the unarmed invasion, alien encampments, alien territory and new commonwealth occupation have all been used to describe the black presence in this way. Enoch Powell, whose careful choice of symbols and metaphors suggests precise calculation, typifies this ideological strand:

> It is . . . truly when he looks into the eyes of Asia that the Englishman comes face to face with those who would dispute with him the possession of his native land.[1]

This language of war and invasion is the clearest illustration of the way in which the discourses which together constitute 'race' direct attention to national boundaries, focusing attention on the entry and exit of blacks. The new racism is primarily concerned with mechanisms of inclusion and exclusion. It specifies who may legitimately belong to the national community and simultaneously advances reasons for the segregation or banishment of those whose 'origin, sentiment or citizenship' assigns them elsewhere. The excluded are not always conceived as a cohesive rival nation. West Indians, for example, are seen as a bastard people occupying an indeterminate space between the Britishness which is their colonial legacy and an amorphous, ahistorical relationship with the dark continent and those parts of the new world where they have been able to reconstitute it. Asians on the other hand, as the Powell quote above suggests, are understood to be bound by cultural and biological ties which merit the status of a fully formed, alternative national identity. They pose a threat to the British way of life by virtue of their strength and cohesion. For different reasons, both groups are judged to be incompatible with authentic forms of Englishness (Lawrence, 1982). The obviousness of the differences they manifest in their cultural lives underlines the need to maintain strong and effective controls on who may enter Britain. The process of national decline is presented as coinciding with the dilution of once homogeneous and continuous national stock by alien strains. Alien cultures come to embody a threat which, in turn, invites the conclusion that national decline and weakness have been precipitated by the arrival of blacks. The operation of banishing blacks, repatriating them to the places which are congruent with their ethnicity and culture, becomes doubly desirable. It assists in the process of making Britain great again and restores an ethnic symmetry to a world distorted by imperial adventure and migration.

What must be explained, then, is how the limits of 'race' have come to coincide so precisely with national frontiers. This is a central achievement of the new racism. 'Race' is bounded on all sides by the sea. The effect of this ideological operation is visible in the way that the word 'immigrant' became synonymous with the word 'black' during the 1970s. It is still felt today as black settlers and their British-born children are denied authentic national membership on the basis of their 'race' and, at the same time, prevented from aligning themselves within the 'British race' on the grounds that their national allegiance inevitably lies elsewhere. This racist logic has pinpointed obstacles to genuine belonging in the culture and identity of the alien interlopers. Both are central to the theories of 'race' and nation which have emerged from the political and philosophical work of writers associated with Britain's 'new right' (Gamble, 1974; Levitas, 1986). [. . .]

Enoch Powell's superficially simple question 'what kind of people are we?' summoned those very images and axioms and answered itself powerfully in the negative. 'We' were not muggers, 'we' were not illegal immigrants, 'we' were not criminals, Rastafarians, aliens or purveyors of arranged marriages. 'We' were the lonely old lady taunted by 'wide-grinning piccaninnies'. 'We' were the only white child in a class full of blacks. 'We' were the white man, frightened that in fifteen to twenty years, 'the black man would have the whip hand over us'. The black presence is thus constructed as a problem or threat against which a homogeneous, white, national 'we' could be unified. To put this operation into perspective, it must be emphasized that these were not the only images and definitions of nationhood which were mobilized during this period. Other voices from the left and from the black communities themselves were to be heard. Even within the right there were alternative conceptualizations of the relationship between 'race' and nation which were more in keeping with a patrician reading of imperial history. On behalf of the populist new right, Powell has had to challenge these as well as the 'madness' of the liberal integrationists. His attack on the Queen's Christmas message of 1983 and by implication on the 'multi-racialist' stance of other members of the royal household is particularly revealing. It crystallizes some of the competing definitions of the nation which are even now in play.

Powell attacked the Queen's attachment to the Commonwealth and rebuked her advisers for not encouraging her to speak more as a 'British monarch to the British Nation'. She was, said Powell, 'more concerned for the susceptibilities and prejudices of a vociferous minority of newcomers than for the great mass of her subjects'. The racial message in this last sentence characteristically derives its full power from the absence of any overt reference to the black presence. The *Sun* picked up the inferred racial message and splashed the headlines 'Enoch Raps Queen. She must speak up more for whites' across its front page.[2] Powell censured the Queen further, for mouthing speeches which 'suggest that she has the interests and affairs of other countries, in other continents, as much or more at heart than those of her own people'. The *Sun* acknowledged the use of political 'code words' in Mr Powell's outburst and provided a summary of his 'basic message' in plain English. 'The Queen has allowed herself to be used as a mouthpiece for racial minorities, and ought to spend more time speaking out for the white majority.'

Powell's speech ended with a warning to those who were responsible for misleading the Crown and thereby disrupting the constitutional balance between monarch and people. It is a cogent if cryptic statement of his populism: 'The place of the crown in the affections of the people would be threatened if they began to sense that the crown was not in unique and exclusive sympathy with the people of the United Kingdom which their mutual dependence ought to imply.' The message in this last point is a little obscure but is similar to that which emerges from Powell's earlier comments on the relationship between formal (legal) citizenship and the substantive cultural identity which defines genuine membership of the British nation. Monarchs come and go, but the historic continuity which constructs the British people has a longer life span than any individual sovereign and, in Powell's view, a political privilege.

I have already introduced the idea that the new racism's newness can be gauged by its capacity to operate across the broad range of political opinion. This claim can be pursued further. The distinction which Powell and Worsthorne make between authentic and inauthentic types of national belonging, appears in an almost identical form in the work of Raymond Williams (Williams, 1983; Mulhern, 1984). It provides a striking example of the way in which the cultural dimensions of the new racism confound the left/right distinction.

Williams combines discussion of 'race' with comments on patriotism and nationalism. However, his understanding of 'race' is restricted to the social and cultural tensions surrounding the arrival of 'new peoples'. For him, as with the right, 'race' problems begin with immigration. Resentment of 'unfamiliar neighbours' is seen as the beginning of a process which ends in ideological specifications of 'race' and 'superiority'. Williams, working his way towards a 'new and substantial kind of socialism', draws precisely the same picture of the relationship between 'race', national identity and citizenship as Powell:

> . . . It is a serious misunderstanding . . . to suppose that the problems of social identity are resolved by formal (merely legal) definitions. For unevenly and at times precariously, but always through long experience substantially, an effective awareness of social identity depends on actual and sustained social relationships. To reduce social identity to formal legal definitions, at the level of the state, is to collude in the alienated superficialities of 'the nation' which are limited functional terms of the modern ruling class. (Williams, 1983, p. 195)

These remarks are part of Williams's response to anti-racists who would answer the denial that blacks can be British by saying 'They are as British as you are.' He dismisses this reply as 'the standard liberal' variety. His alternative conception stresses that social identity is a product of 'long experience'. But this prompts the question – how long is long enough to become a genuine Brit? His insistence that the origins of racial conflicts lie in the hostility between strangers in the city makes little sense given the effects of the 1971 Immigration Act in halting primary black settlement. More disturbingly, these arguments effectively deny that blacks can share a significant 'social identity' with their white neighbours who, in contrast to more recent arrivals, inhabit what Williams calls 'rooted settlements' articulated by 'lived and formed identities'. He describes the emergence of racial conflict where

> an English working man (English in the terms of sustained modern integration) protests at the arrival or presence of 'foreigners' or 'aliens' and now goes on to specify them as 'blacks'.

Williams does not appear to recognize black as anything other than the subordinate moment in an ideology of racial supremacy. His use of the term 'social identity' is both significant and misleading. It minimizes the specificities of nationalism and ideologies of national identity and diverts attention from analysis of the political processes by which national and social identities have been aligned. Several questions which are absolutely central to contemporary 'race' politics are thus obscured. Under what conditions is national identity able to displace or dominate the equally 'lived and formed' identities which are based on age, gender, region, neighbourhood or ethnicity? How has it come to be expressed in racially exclusive forms? What happens when 'social identities' become expressed in conflicting political organizations and movements and when they appeal to the authority of nature and biology to rationalize the relations of domination and subordination which exist between them? How these social identities relate to the conspicuous differences of language and culture is unclear except where Williams points out that the forms of identity fostered by the 'artificial order' of the nation state are incomplete and empty when compared to 'full social identities in their real diversity'. This does not, of course, make them any the less vicious. Where racism demands repatriation and pivots on the exclusion of certain groups from the imagined community of the nation, the contradictions around citizenship that Williams dismisses as 'alienated superficialities' remain important constituents of the political field. They provide an important point of entry into the nation's sense of itself. Where racial oppression is practised with the connivance of legal institutions – the police and the courts – national and legal subjectivity will also become the focus of political antagonism. Williams's discussion of 'race' and nation does not address these issues and is notable for its refusal to examine the concept of racism which has its own historic relationship with ideologies of Englishness, Britishness and national belonging.

Quite apart from Williams's apparent endorsement of the presuppositions of the new racism, the strategic silences in his work contribute directly to its strength and resiliance. The image Williams has chosen to convey his grasp of 'race' and nation, that of a resentful English working man, intimidated by the alterity of his alien neighbours is, [. . .] redolent of other aspects of modern Conservative racism and nationalism. [. . .]

I am not suggesting that the differences between Labour and Conservative languages of nation and patriotism are insignificant, but rather that these languages overlap significantly. In contemporary Britain, statements about nation are invariably also statements about 'race'. The Conservatives appear to recognize this and seek to play with the ambiguities which this situation creates. Their recent statements on the theme of Britishness betray a sophisticated grasp of the interface between 'race' and nation created in the post-'rivers of blood' era. During the coal dispute, for example, in a speech on the enduring power of the national constitution entitled 'Why Democracy Will Last', Mrs Thatcher invoked the memory of the Somerset case of 1772. Lord Mansfield's famous judgment in this case declared that British slaveholders could no longer compel their slaves to leave the country against their will ([. . .] Shyllon, 1977, 1974). It matters little that Mrs Thatcher quoted the case wrongly, suggesting that it brought slavery in this country to an end. With no trace of irony, her speech boldly articulates an apparently anti-racist position at the heart of a nationalist and authoritarian statement in which the mining communities were identified as 'enemies within'.[3]

The Conservatives' ethnic election poster of 1983 provides further insight into the right's grasp of these complexities [see Fig. 1]. The poster was presumably intended to exploit ambiguities between 'race' and nation and to salve the sense of exclusion experienced by the blacks who were its target. The poster appeared in the ethnic minority press during May 1983 and was attacked by black spokespeople for suggesting that the categories black and British were mutually exclusive. It set an image of a young black man, smartly

With the Conservatives, there are no 'blacks', no 'whites', just people.

Conservatives believe that treating minorities as equals encourages the majority to treat them as equals.

Yet the Labour Party aim to treat you as a 'special case', as a group all on your own.

Is setting you apart from the rest of society a sensible way to overcome racial prejudice and social inequality?

The question is, should we really divide the British people instead of uniting them?

WHOSE PROMISES ARE YOU TO BELIEVE?

When Labour were in government, they promised to repeal Immigration Acts passed in 1962 and 1971. Both promises were broken.

This time, they are promising to throw out the British Nationality Act, which gives full and equal citizenship to everyone permanently settled in Britain.

But how do the Conservatives' promises compare?

We said that we'd abolish the 'SUS' law.

We kept our promise.

We said we'd recruit more coloured policemen, get the police back into the community, and train them for a better understanding of your needs.

We kept our promise.

PUTTING THE ECONOMY BACK ON ITS FEET.

The Conservatives have always said that the only long term answer to our economic problems was to conquer inflation.

Inflation is now lower than it's been for over a decade, keeping all prices stable, with the price of food now hardly rising at all.

Meanwhile, many businesses throughout Britain are recovering, leading to thousands of new jobs.

Firstly, in our traditional industries, but just as importantly in new technology areas such as microelectronics.

In other words, the medicine is working.

Yet Labour want to change everything, and put us back to square one.

They intend to increase taxation. They intend to increase the National Debt.

They promise import and export controls.

Cast your mind back to the last Labour government. Labour's methods didn't work then.

They won't work now.

A BETTER BRITAIN FOR ALL OF US.

The Conservatives believe that everyone wants to work hard and be rewarded for it.

Those rewards will only come about by creating a mood of equal opportunity for everyone in Britain, regardless of their race, creed or colour.

The difference you're voting for is this:

To the Labour Party, you're a black person.

To the Conservatives, you're a British Citizen.

Vote Conservative, and you vote for a more equal, more prosperous Britain.

LABOUR SAYS HE'S BLACK. TORIES SAY HE'S BRITISH.

CONSERVATIVE ☒

Fig. 1   Conservative Party Election Poster, 1983.

dressed in a suit with wide lapels and flared trousers, above the caption 'Labour says he's black. Tories say he's British'. The text which followed set out to reassure readers that 'with Conservatives there are no "blacks" or "whites", just people'. A variant on the one nation theme emerged, entwined with criticism of Labour for treating blacks 'as a "special case", as a group all on your own'. At one level, the poster states that the category of citizen and the formal belonging which it bestows on its black holders are essentially colourless, or at least colour-blind. Yet as the writings of Powell and Worsthorne above illustrate, populist racism does not recognize the legal membership of the national community conferred by its legislation as a substantive guarantee of Britishness. 'Race' is, therefore, despite the text, being defined beyond these legal definitions in the sphere of culture. There is more to Britishness than a passport. Nationhood, as Alfred Sherman pointed out in 1976,

> remains . . . man's main focus of identity, his link with the wider world, with past and future, 'a partnership with those who are living, those who are dead and those who are to be born'. . . . It includes national character reflected in the way of life . . . a passport or residence permit does not automatically implant national values or patriotism.[4]

At this point the slightly too large suit worn by the young man, with its unfashionable cut and connotations of a job interview, becomes a key signifier. It conveys what is being asked of the black readers as the price of admission to the colour-blind form of citizenship promised by the text. Blacks are being invited to forsake all that marks them out as culturally distinct before real Britishness can be guaranteed. National culture is present in the young man's clothing. Isolated and shorn of the mugger's key icons – a tea-cosy hat and the dreadlocks of Rastafari – he is redeemed by his suit, the signifier of British civilization. The image of black youth as a problem is thus contained and rendered assimilable. The wolf is transformed by his sheep's clothing. The solitary maleness of the figure is also highly significant. It avoids the hidden threat of excessive fertility which is a constant presence in the representation of black women (Parmar, 1984). This lone young man is incapable of swamping 'us'. He is alone because the logics of racist discourse militate against the possibility of making British blackness visible in a family or an inter-generational group.[5] The black family is presented as incomplete, deviant and ruptured.

NOTES

1. Speech at Southall, 4.11.71.
2. *Sun*, 21.1.84.
3. Speech at the Carlton Club, 26.11.84.
4. *Sunday Telegraph*, 8.9.76.
5. The best example of this is the contrast between television situation comedies featuring blacks and whites. It is notable that none of the series featuring blacks seem able to portray inter-generational relations between black characters or show their experiences over time, in a diachronic dimension.

   The BBC series 'Frontline' (1985) about the relationship between two black brothers, one a 'Rasta', the other a policeman, began significantly with the death of their mother. An equivalent programme centred on a fractured white family in which notions of locality and 'ethnicity' play a similar role – 'Only Fools and Horses' – builds its humour out of the tension between generations.

REFERENCES

Anderson, B. (1983) *Imagined Communities: Reflections on the Origins and Spread of Nationalism*. London: Verso.

Gamble, A. (1974) *The Conservative Nation*. London: RKP.

Lawrence, E. (1982) 'In the abundance of water the fool is thirsty: sociology and Black pathology', in CCCS (eds), *The Empire Strikes Back*. London: Hutchinson.

Levitas, R. (1986) *The Ideology of the New Right*. Oxford: Polity Press.

Mulhern, F. (1984) 'Towards 2000: news from you know where', *New Left Review*, No. 148, November/December.

Nairn, T. (1977) *The Break Up of Britain*. London: New Left Books.

Parmar, P. (1984) 'Hateful contraries', *Ten 8*, No. 16.

Shyllon, F. (1974) *Black Slaves in Britain*. Oxford: IRR/Oxford University Press.

Shyllon, F. (1977) *Black People in Britain*. Oxford: IRR/Oxford University Press.

Williams, R. (1983) *Towards 2000*. Harmondsworth: Pelican.

WING (1985) *Worlds Apart: Women Under Immigration and Nationality Law*. London: Pluto Press.

Wolpe, H. (1980) 'Capitalism and cheap labour-power in South Africa: from segregation to apartheid', in H. Wolpe (ed.), *The Articulation of Modes of Production* London: Routledge & Kegan Paul.

SECTION 9
DIASPORA

Edited by Linda Anderson

INTRODUCTION

Linda Anderson

The term diaspora, used first of all, as seen in the introduction to Part II, Section 5, to denote the dispersal of the Jewish people, has become in contemporary theory a much more widespread term, applied not only to the great variety of global migrations and exiles of the twentieth century but more generally to describe a non-essentialist identity or culture, which is 'hybrid', made up of different 'crossings' and difficult to 'locate' in terms of territorial alignments. James Procter has drawn attention to the tendency of the word diaspora itself to migrate within critical discourse into an increasingly metaphorised version of itself, where its origins or precise philosophical place may become lost. Procter argues for the continued importance of 'dwelling' for diasporan communities and the important nuances of the word 'locale' (Procter, 2003: 13–14). For Mieke Bal the notion of 'travelling concepts', to which Procter refers, highlights the permeable boundaries of knowledge: concepts 'travel' between disciplinary fields, historical periods and geographically dispersed academic communities and as they do so their meanings change. What Bal wants to emphasise, however, is less the sense of the 'loss' which accompanies this than the rigidity of 'methodological dogma' to begin with and the way it can enforce and collude with a politics of exclusion (Bal, 2002: 6). A good example would be the changing definitions of 'place' within critical geography. Seen as a bounded space which is eternal and unchanging, 'place' implicitly supports territorialism. Alternatively, as Doreen Massey has argued, place itself can be seen as a dynamic concept, constructed out of a series of changing social relations, extending from the local to the global, which will always 'stretch beyond that "place" itself' (Massey, 1994: 115). In other words, place 'travels' discursively but it does so, it could be argued, because it has escaped a previous ideological framing which no longer fits the more fluid structures of contemporary experience. For Judith Butler the whole notion of borders has changed, making it difficult to think of them as delimiting or separating; instead they have become 'highly populated sites' which offer the possibility of encounters which may 'confound' identity in what could be 'a very auspicious direction' (Butler, 2004: 49). Like Paul Gilroy, for whom 'diasporan consciousness' provides new ways of theorizing identity by questioning any assumption about who 'naturally' belongs where (Gilroy, 2000: 127), Butler argues that 'shifting topographies' offer a positive impetus to think in new ways about both our own identities and our connections with others.

Contemporary discussions of diaspora, therefore, have tended to negotiate this complex terrain: acknowledging that there may be a personal dimension to exile or dislocation which involves a relation to a particular 'locale', while, at the same time, recognising the urgent need to interrogate the abstract terms such as 'origin', 'place' and 'nationhood' and the ideological weight they carry, in order to forge a political discourse capable of mapping new forms of identity. In the first extract **Victor Burgin** takes as his starting point Edward Said's influential essay 'Reflections on Exile' and his emphasis on the 'real', private pain of exile, which has 'torn millions of people from the nourishment of tradition, family and geography' and which is not easily assimilated to the use of exile as a literary motif (Said, 2001: 174). Said, however, according to Burgin, moves back and forward between private and public voices implicitly revealing how hard it is to 'place' the exile. Burgin is particularly interested in Said's use of the term 'paranoia' and the intermediate position it seems to occupy between the private and the public. Drawn from psychoanalysis, the term can be seen as having particular resonances as a way of understanding how space is figured through an interior relation to it. For Burgin nationalism and racism can both be seen as 'paranoid structures', and understood in terms of a 'paranoid' relation to territory which must be defended against others who are seen as invaders. For Burgin, we could say, a concept which 'travels' from psychoanalysis into political discourse provides a 'heuristic device' which allows us to 'reinscribe' the space between the personal and the political, between terms which have 'become frozen in opposition' (this volume, p. 284).

The extract by **Avtar Brah** brings together many of the preceding concerns with reconfiguring place through thinking through the relations between home, location, displacement and dislocation. What she adds, however, is a recognition of feminism's understanding of how spaces are gendered and how postionings, which can be multiple and contradictory, are always implicated in power and privilege. The same geographical space, therefore, can articulate different histories and meanings. '"[H]ome" ', as Brah points out, 'can simultaneously be a place of safety and terror' (this volume, p. 289). There are 'multiple semiotic spaces at diasporic borders' and a constant need to refine our strategies for reading them correctly (this volume, p. 289).

Brah also argues that autobiography has an important role to play in providing narratives which can hold various '"homes" and "identities" in perpetual suspension', even as the writer – in this case Minnie Bruce Pratt – may try 'to recapture them in re-memory' (this volume, p. 287). Paul Gilroy has also drawn attention to the importance of reconciling memory with the challenges represented by diaspora of movement and multiple positioning. In this context memory, he argues, does not mean reaching back to some unchanging core, but must offer itself as contingent, subject to continual modifying and reprocessing in the present (Gilroy, 2000: 28). Why we remember a place and how become therefore important questions for how we construct the places themselves and ourselves as subjects. Indeed what the memoir writer may encounter in relation to their past is a series of family 'stories' which complicate any direct access to the 'truth'. The writer, then, must place him or herself within a story which is already in existence, which has many versions, and which may have its roots in countries s/he has never visited and historical traumas s/he does not understand.

This is **Edward Said**'s dilemma in his moving memoir *Out of Place*. Being 'out of place' is a feeling strongly connected with childhood for him and illustrated through his reaction to his name which itself seems to pull him in different directions, a 'foolishly English' first name, Edward, 'yoked forcibly to the unmistakably Arabic family name Said' (this volume, p. 290). This ambiguity about his name is compounded for Said by the fact that he does not know which language he spoke first, Arabic or English. Language does not lead him back in any comfortable way, therefore, to his beginnings. His parents' origins also seem confused to him, with no 'simple dynastic sequence' (this volume, p. 292), but offered instead as a series of discontinuous narratives and revelations which he must try to 'order'. However his lack of information makes this difficult: 'There were never the right number of well-functioning connectives between the parts I knew about or was able somehow to excavate; the total picture was never quite right' (this volume, p. 292).

Yet if diaspora helps to underscore the discontinuous and fractured nature of modern memory, the significance of autobiography, to which Brah refers, as a form which can provide temporary 'dwellings' for the subject, which are simultaneously multiple and mobile, should not be underestimated. Said, himself, finds that through writing his memoir he can create a haven that becomes 'more generous and hospitable' (Said, 1999: 216) the more frequently he goes back and excavates it for his memoir. Writing and remembering – or remembering through writing – helps him, so Said believes, to overcome the bleak amnesia which he has used for much of his life to cope with his feeling of exile, his exclusion from places he cherishes. In this context, autobiography itself could be seen as a form of political intervention. For Hannah Arendt only someone's story – the story of which they are the hero – can truly reveal who they are or were. This connects, for her, with a failure of philosophical and political discourse which can deal only in universals (Arendt, 1985: 184). Recently Adriana Cavarero has extended this idea, suggesting that to be 'narratable' is a fundamental need for the subject, and the condition of our recognition of others' uniqueness. This is so despite the 'unmasterable process of intermittence and forgetting' which characterises the work of memory. Even before we know the other's story, even before we tell our own, we perceive each other as having a story to tell (Cavarero, 2000: 34).

This, of course, provides an interesting way of making that link between the personal and the political which has so preoccupied critics of diaspora. It is *because* we are aware of our own uniqueness, according to Cavarero, that we can recognise the same quality in others: 'The other always has a life-story and is a narratable identity whose uniqueness also consists, above all, in this story' (Cavarero, 2000: 34). It also takes us back to some of the important arguments laid out in this Reader and in particular the complicated connection between individual and collective memory. Ricoeur's contention, quoted in the Introduction, that 'we have nothing better than testimony' to give us access to the past, is echoed here (Ricoeur, 2004: 147). We have nothing better, we could say, than the perception of the unique story each of us has to tell – with its own burden of remembering and forgetting – to alert us not just to the past but to the current political necessity of our connection with others.

REFERENCES AND FURTHER READING

Agnew, Vijay (ed.) (2005) *Diaspora, Memory, and Identity: A Search for Home.* Toronto: University of Toronto Press.

Arendt, Hannah ([1958] 1985) *The Human Condition.* Chicago: University of Chicago Press.

Bal, Mieke (2002) *Travelling Concepts in the Humanities: A Rough Guide.* Toronto, Buffalo and London: University of Toronto Press.

Brah, Avtar (1996) *Cartographies of Diaspora: Contesting identities.* London and New York: Routledge.

Burgin, Victor (1996) *In/Different Spaces: Place and Memory in Visual Culture.* Berkeley, Los Angeles, and London: University of California Press.

Butler, Judith (2004) *Precarious Life: The Powers of Mourning and Violence.* London and New York: Verso.

Cavarero, Adriana (2000) *Relating Narratives: Storytelling and Selfhood*, trans. with intro. Paul A.Kottman. London: Routledge.

Gilroy, Paul (1993) *The Black Atlantic: Modernity and Double Consciousness.* London and New York: Verso.

—— (2000) *Between Camps: Race, Identity and Nationalism at the End of the Colour Line.* Harmondsworth: Penguin.

Massey, Doreen (1994) 'Double Articulation: A Place in the World', in Angelika Bammer (ed.), *Displacements: Cultural Identities in Question.* Bloomington, IN: Indiana University Press, pp. 110–22.

Procter, James (2003) *Dwelling Places: Postwar Black British Writing.* Manchester: Manchester University Press.

Ricoeur, Paul (2004) *Memory, History, Forgetting*, trans. Kathleen Blamey and David Pellauer. Chicago and London: University of Chicago Press.

Said, Edward W. (1999) *Out of Place: A Memoir.* London: Granta.

—— ([1985] 2001) 'Reflections on Exile', in *Reflections on Exile and Other Literary and Cultural Essays.* London: Granta, pp. 173–86.

—— (2003) *Freud and the Non-European.* London and New York: Verso.

VICTOR BURGIN: *FROM* IN/DIFFERENT SPACES: PLACE AND MEMORY IN VISUAL CULTURE

At the beginning of his essay 'Reflections on Exile,' Edward Said tells anecdotes about friends, mainly writers, who testify to their pain in being separated from their homeland and their mother tongue. He is quick to acknowledge not only that exile is suffered by a comparatively small number of writers and artists, but that it has 'torn millions of people from the nourishment of tradition, family and geography.' He speaks of the 'hopelessly large numbers, the compounded misery of "undocumented" people suddenly lost, without a tellable history.' Here, he says, we must 'leave the modest refuge provided by subjectivity and resort instead to the abstractions of mass politics.'[1] But this early interruption to his text, this irruption of a public voice, soon gives way to the privacy of another anecdote about a friend. The clash of private and public voices in Said's essay represents the difficulty of placing the exile. Said's anecdotes show the experience of exile as lived in irreducibly subjective isolation; at the same time, he observes, the exile exists only in relation to nationalism, the 'assertion of belonging in and to a place, a people, a heritage.'[2] But here Said asks, 'What is there worth saving and holding on to between the extremes of exile on the one hand, and the often bloody-minded affirmations of nationalism on the other? . . . Are they simply two conflicting varieties of paranoia?'[3] Said does not answer this question, but to ask it suggests that between the anecdotal expression of 'personal feelings' and the abstractions of political discourse we must interpellate the discursive space of that 'other locality' of which Freud

Source: Victor Burgin, *In/Different Spaces: Place and Memory in Visual Culture* (Berkeley, CA: University of California Press, 1996), pp. 117–21, 128–37.

spoke – that place, as Jacques Lacan put it, 'between perception and consciousness.' The term *paranoia* has of course passed from psychoanalysis into everyday use, but the 'ordinary language' sense of the word generates little of interest in answer to Said's question. In everyday use, 'paranoia' means 'a feeling of persecution unjustified in reality.' Insofar as the exile has, in Said's own words, been 'torn . . . from the nourishment of tradition, family and geography' then the feeling of persecution is surely justified. As for nationalism, it depends on the case, but there are instances where such a feeling would be equally justified. For example, the discourses of both Israeli and Palestinian nationalisms express feelings of persecution, for which both may legitimately argue a basis in reality. Some might judge one of these realities to be now past, while the other remains present. But at this point we encounter precisely the necessity of understanding the term *paranoia* in its psychoanalytic setting. There is no 'past reality' in the *psychical reality* that is the object of psychoanalysis. Freud puts it simply: 'There is no time in the unconscious': the past event, whether actual or fictional, produces real effects in the present.[4] Said recognizes this when he defines exile as a 'condition of terminal loss,' which also acknowledges that the space of exile is a psychical space as much as it is physical. Before considering this space in its unconscious dimensions, however, we should first fix its coordinates in the space of instrumental reason.

The opposition 'exile'/'nation' rests on a logic of exclusion/inclusion. According to this logic 'exile' is not the only term that may appear opposite 'nation.' Said, for example, distinguishes between 'exiles,' 'refugees,' 'expatriates,' and 'émigrés.' The origin of exile, he observes, is in the ancient practice of banishment, which stigmatizes the exile as rejected. Refugees, he finds, are a byproduct of the modern state, political innocents united in bewilderment. Expatriates share the condition of the exile in all respects but one: having chosen to leave their homeland they are therefore free to return. The status of the émigré, Said says, is 'ambiguous': the émigré may once have been an exile but, like the European settler in Africa, Asia, or Australia, may have constructed a new national identity away from national origins. As one category of displaced subject tumbles on the heels of another in Said's text the term *exile*, no longer connoting fixity, comes to indicate a contingent resting place in a world in which today's exile may be yesterday's tourist. The subject positions Said mentions are in differing relations to their homeland but in the same relation to their host country: they are all 'foreigners.' One of Julia Kristeva's more recent books, *Etrangers à nous-mêmes*, is a book about the foreigner. She writes:

> To live with the other, with the foreigner, confronts us with the possibility . . . of *being an other*. It is not simply a matter – humanistically – of our aptitude for accepting the other, but of *being in his or her place*, which amounts to thinking of oneself and making oneself other than oneself. Rimbaud's 'I is an other' was not only the avowal of the psychotic

phantom that haunts poetry. The word announced exile, the possibility or the necessity of being foreign [*être étranger*] and of living in the foreigner's country [*vivre à l'étranger*], thus prefiguring the art of living in a modern era, the cosmopolitanism of the excoriated [écorchés].[5]

Kristeva here makes a mirror of the foreigner: to encounter the other in one's own space is to confront one's own alterity to that other's space. The phrase by Rimbaud she invokes, 'I is an other,' moreover perfectly describes the alienated identification that the infant makes in the 'mirror stage,' as described by Lacan. In further presenting Rimbaud's phrase as haunted by psychosis, as announcing exile and as 'prefiguring the art of living in a modern era,' Kristeva echoes Said's assimilation of exile to paranoia, makes this the common condition of us all, and associates the condition with a changed global space.

It is now a familiar observation that our subjective sense of the spatial relations ordering our world has undergone a historical mutation. The unprecedented speed of the locomotives and airplanes of modernity had the effect on the popular imagination of causing geographical space to shrink; extensive contact with other cultures nevertheless still entailed actual bodily displacement and was available to comparatively few. The space engendered by the communication technologies of postmodernity, however, as Paul Virilio puts it, 'is not a geographical space, but a space of time.' Historical events no longer simply 'take place' in their immediate locality, but may be broadcast at the speed of light to simultaneously appear in a myriad other places. Jean Baudrillard has described the consequent tendency of historical reality to 'disappear behind the mediating hyperreality' of the 'simulacrum.' In the classical mimetic theories of representation which dominated Western thought before modernism, the image was a mirror of reality – not of any contingent reality but an ordered reality, the anticipation of a perfected reality. Today that mirror has shattered. Its fragments, perpetually in motion, reflect nothing reassuring. The psychoanalytic concept of the mirror stage, which I have already mentioned and to which I shall return, has alerted us to the importance of our relation to the image in the formation of a coherent identity out of pre-Oedipal fragmentation and disorganization. From a Western world in which images were once limited in number, circumscribed in meaning, and con-templated at length, we have today arrived at a society inundated with images consumed 'on the fly' – from glossy magazines, from photomats, video rental stores, broadcast and cable TV, communication satellites, and increasingly realistic computer simulations. Flipping and 'zapping' through avalanches of books and journals, TV channels and CD-ROM, we are in turn bombarded by pictures not only of hopelessly unattainable images of idealized identities but also images of past and present suffering, images of destruction, of bodies quite literally in pieces. We are ourselves 'torn' in the process, not only emotionally and morally but in the fragmentary structure of the act of looking itself. In an image-saturated environment that increasingly resembles the interior space of subjective fantasy turned inside out, the very subject–object distinction begins to break down, and the subject comes apart in the space of its own making. As Terry Eagleton has written, the postmodern subject is one 'whose body has been scattered to the winds, as so many bits and pieces of reified technique, appetite, mechanical operation or reflex of desire.' Such fragmentation, decentering, and loss of subject–object boundaries, is characteristic of paranoia. [. . .]

Paranoiacs do not clearly differentiate themselves from other people and things. Their speech does not coincide with their identity; they speak as if they were an other, or simply an object in a world of objects. They have lost the illusory but necessary sense of transcendence that would allow them to position themselves at the center of their own space. In her essay 'Space, Time, and Bodies,' Elizabeth Grosz writes: 'It is our positioning within space, both as the point of perspectival access to space, but also as an object for others in space, that gives the subject any coherent identity.' The matrix of space is the body. Grosz continues: 'The subject's relation to its own body provides it with basic spatial concepts and terms by which it can reflect on its own position. Form and size, direction, centredness (centricity), location, dimension and orientation are derived from the perceptual relation the subject has to and in space.'[6] Subjectivity 'takes place' in corporeal space. 'The ego,' says Freud, is 'a mental projection of the surface of the body.' The psychical representations of the body and the space it inhabits first form under the anarchic hegemony of the drives. The unitary body does not yet exist, there is only the borderless space of the body in fragments described by Klein. If we want a picture of this space, Lacan suggests: 'We must turn to the works of Hieronymous Bosch for an atlas of all the aggressive images that torment mankind.'[7] In the mirror stage the child anticipates its future coherence in an act of identification. However, as Edith Jacobson expresses it, such early identifications are founded on

> fusions of self and object images which disregard the realistic differences between the self and the object. They will find expression in illusory fantasies of the child that he is part of the object or can become the object by pretending to be or behaving as if he were it. Temporary and reversible in small children, such ideas in psychotics may turn into fixated, delusional convictions.[8]

In psychosis boundaries fail, frontiers are breached. In psychotic space an external object – a whole, a part, or an attribute of a person or thing – may be experienced as if it had invaded the subject. In his *Memoirs of My Nervous Illness*, Schreber writes: 'From the first beginnings of my contact with God . . . hardly a single limb or organ in my body escaped being temporarily damaged by miracles . . . my *lungs* were for a long time the object of violent and very threatening attacks . . . the *gullet* and the *intestines* . . . were torn or vanished repeatedly.'[9] The sense of being invaded may be projected onto some larger screen than that of the psychotic's own body; the threat may be seen as directed against some greater body with which the psychotic identifies: for example, the 'body-politic' of nation, or race. Psychosis, moreover, may be infectious. Speaking of the trial of the Papin sisters, Lacan remarks: 'One has heard in the course of the debates the astonishing affirmation that it was impossible that two beings should both be struck, together, by the same madness. . . . This is a completely false affirmation. Joint deliriums [*les délires à deux*] are amongst the most ancient of known forms of psychosis.'[10] In the age of the intimate address of the national imago to its counterpart before a television screen, the *folie à deux* may take on national proportions.

The same logic that generates the opposition 'exile'/'nation' across national frontiers may oppose one racial group to another within national borders. History has familiarized us with the insidious movement in which 'nation' is confused with 'race.' Institutionalized racism may ensure that racial minorities live in a condition of internal exile within the nation of which they are citizens – an exile that, if it is not legal, cannot be named. Roland Barthes once defined the bourgeoisie as 'the social class which does not want to be named.' He writes, 'Politically, the haemorrhage of the name "bourgeois" is effected through the idea of *nation* . . . today the bourgeoisie merges into the nation.'[11] By refusing to be named, the bourgeois class represents itself and its interests as a universal norm, from which anything else is a deviation. In the West the Caucasian race has in effect 'exnominated' itself in the word *White*. Whether or not there is any scientific justification for Johann Friedrich Blumenbach's term *Caucasian*, it does at least have the advantage of simply naming one racial category amongst others. *White* however has the strange property of directing our attention to color while in the very same movement it exnominates itself *as* a color. For evidence of this we need look no further than to the expression 'people of color,' for we know very well that this means 'not White.' We know equally well that the color white is the higher power to which all colors of the spectrum are subsumed when equally combined: white is the sum totality of light, while black is the total absence of light. In this way elementary optical physics is recruited to the psychotic metaphysics of racism, in which White is 'all' to Black's 'nothing' – as in the attitude of those white colonialists Hélène Cixous speaks of, who live in a country they have stolen 'as if the eyes of their souls had been put out.'[12] To speak of the color of skin is to speak of a body. 'People of color' are embodied people. To have no color is to have no body. The body denied here however is a very particular body, it is the abject body: the body that defecates, vomits, and bleeds; the entropic body that dies. In Kristeva's account, infantile abjection of the maternal body is the irreducible imperative that impels any subject whatsoever toward its necessary identity. Abjection, establishing the first line of demarcation, is the zero degree of identity; as inevitable as it is beyond reason, it cannot be explained. The paranoid racist subject, seeking to take its place on the 'clean and proper' side of abjection, has refused to symbolize the abject within itself. It has foreclosed its abject body only to have this body return to it in the form of the 'dirty Jew,' the 'dirty Italian,' and 'people of colour' – or as an American colleague once said to me about the English, 'They're a people who think their shit doesn't smell.'

I have noted the tendency for 'nation' to be confused with 'race.' Nazism is the most horrific example, but there are many others. At the end of the First World War, the armies of each of the allied nations marched in a victory parade in the Champs Elysées. The Harlem Hellfighters were a battalion of Black American soldiers. Highly decorated, they served longer than any other American unit and were the first allied unit to reach the Rhine. They were not allowed to march in the victory parade.[13] Clearly it was felt that there would be something wrong with the picture of America that this would present. In *The Four Fundamental Concepts of Psycho-Analysis*, Lacan tells an anecdote about a day when he, 'a young intellectual,' was out in a small boat with 'a few people from a family of fishermen.' As they were waiting for the moment to pull in the nets, one of the fishermen pointed out to Lacan something floating toward them on the waves. It was a sardine can, glittering in the sun. 'You see that can?,' said the fisherman, 'Well, it doesn't see you!' The fisherman found the incident highly amusing, Lacan 'less so.' Searching for the reason for his discomfort, it occurred to Lacan that 'in a sense' the can *was* looking at him, and that from the can's point of view – that is to say, from the position represented by the reflected point of light – Lacan 'looked like nothing on earth . . . rather out of place in the picture.'[14] A young bourgeois among workers, we might say, 'his face didn't fit.' On an afternoon in November of 1988, Karen Wood, a White woman from Binghamton, New York, was killed by a rifle bullet as she stood in the backyard of her new home in Bangor, Maine. The man who shot her was a local hunter, who said he believed he had seen a deer. According to an article in the *New York Times*[15] the man was obviously criminally negligent, in clear contravention of Maine laws governing hunting, and liable in Maine law to prosecution for manslaughter. However, he was not prosecuted. The *Bangor Daily News*, referring to the shooting as 'a double-tragedy,' reflected overwhelming local sympathy for the man. The newspaper criticized the victim for wearing white gloves in her garden, as these may have made the man think he saw a white-tailed deer. Another local journalist wrote that if Karen Wood 'had been wearing one piece of blaze-orange clothing, she'd be alive today.' The consensus expressed in readers' letters to local newspapers was that 'out-of-staters ought to learn a thing or two about Maine's traditional way of life.' On a night in August of 1989, Yusuf K. Hawkins, a Black teenager, was shot to death by White teenagers as he was on his way to look at a secondhand car in the Bensonhurst section of Brooklyn. Hawkins was from a mainly Black neighborhood of the East New York section of Brooklyn; Bensonhurst is predominantly White. *New York Times* journalists noted that many Bensonhurst residents expressed sympathy for the killers, reporting a White teenage girl on the scene as telling them, 'The black people don't belong here. This is our neighborhood.'[16] A racist decision by the military; an unkind joke; a tragic accident; a vicious murder. Certainly, it makes no sense in common sense to juxtapose these incidents. Nevertheless each incident may be seen as exemplifying the more or less aggressive defense of a space perceived as violated by an invader. Common sense, reason, is not at issue. What a situation may be in reality is quite simply disregarded by unconscious processes. Speaking of Aimée, Clément remarked, 'The forms taken by the fantasies derived from [her] hatred became increasingly remote from their original object.' Psychical space may have much the same relation to real space that the dream has. In another *New York Times* story I read of two communities in the town of Malverne, New York: one mostly Black, the other mainly White. The reporter writes, 'The two are divided by Ocean Avenue, and residents on both sides refer to the other as "over the ocean." '[17] In this example, and in the extreme case, the clinically paranoid person would quite simply *see* an ocean, in a less marked paranoid attitude the subject would behave exactly *as if* there were an ocean – with all the absolute territorial imperatives, all the patriotic moral fervor attached to the defense of the motherland, that this could invoke.

Moral fervor is frequently a characteristic of racism, and the morality is generally sexual. There has been no more strident call to White racist arms than that of the 'defense' of White women. The mobilizing fantasy image of this particular racist discourse is that of the sexual penetration of a body. The image seems to be one of invasion, the fantasy seems to be paranoid. We should however distinguish between two forms of the perceived threat: rape and seduction. One is invasive, the other is not. Even in the former case the structure seems neurotic rather than psychotic, seems more likely to involve repression rather than foreclosure. The White male racist who fantasizes a White woman's rape by a Black man might be seen as defending himself against his own aggressive sexual impulses. He represses the fantasy in which he himself is a rapist; the emotional investment in the unconscious fantasy forces it back into consciousness but now in an acceptable disguise: the rapist is identified as Black, absolving the subject of the fantasy of any culpability in the imaginary crime. Moreover the violence of the fantasy, as it may now lay claim to moral justification, can be unleashed in its full force ('projection' here may take on a deadly physical materiality). The racist's fear that the White woman may be seduced by the Black man however suggests delusional jealousy – a paranoid, rather than neurotic, symptom. It is the inverted form of his fear that the woman will actively seduce the man – which in turn is derived from the White's jealous envy of the Black, an unconscious envy untouched by statistics on unemployment or death rates. As a small child at school, in the late 1940s in the industrial North of England, I was told that there were three types of people in the world: those who lived in very cold climates, those who lived in very hot climates, and those like ourselves who lived in temperate climates. The people in cold climates had to work so hard just to stay alive that they never had time to create things, as a consequence they had no civilization. Those who lived in hot climates on the other hand were so well provided for by nature that they never had to work at all, they ate the fruits that fell into their laps and enjoyed their leisure. Needless to say, they had no civilization either. People in temperate climates however, people like us, had to work hard to feed themselves, but not so hard that they never had time to work at other things. That was why people like us had created civilization. I distinctly remember the envy I felt toward the people of the hot climates. It was a guilty feeling, as I knew I was supposed to feel proud to be a temperate and civilized person. Today I see that my teacher had communicated his own unconscious envy and guilt to me; it cannot have been much fun being a schoolteacher in a working class neighborhood of a bomb-ruined steel town in austere postwar Britain. The Garden of Eden my teacher created for the people of the hot climates, the people 'over the ocean,' was a Garden of Earthly Delights: a paradise where pleasure came as easily as the fruit on the trees, and one never lost one's appetite. Jealous envy is an unavoidable component of our relation to the other, the one who is different, who knows something we do not, who experiences things we shall never know. There is always something we want, and it is easy to believe that the other has it. In Spike Lee's film, *Do the Right Thing*, Mookie, the Black employee of 'Sal's Famous Pizzeria,' has the following exchange with Pino, Sal's White racist son:

Mookie: Who's your favorite basketball player?
Pino: Magic Johnson.
Mookie: And not Larry Bird? Who's your favorite movie star?
Pino: Eddie Murphy.
Mookie: Last question: Who's your favorite rock star?
(*Pino doesn't answer*)
Mookie: Barry Manilow?
(*Pino's brother Vito supplies the answer.*)
Vito: It's Prince. He's a Prince freak.
Mookie: Sounds funny to me. As much as you say nigger this and nigger that, all your favorite people are 'niggers.'
Pino: It's different. Magic, Eddie, Prince are not niggers, I mean, are not Black. I mean they're Black but not really Black. They're more than Black. It's different.
Mookie: Pino, I think secretly that you wish you were Black. That's what I think.[18]

Mookie has spotted Pino's envy. The exchange might have taken place in an analysis, albeit Mookie's technique would probably be judged overly interventionist. But if Pino has now accepted his admiration of Black achievements why is it that his racism remains intact? As already noted, from infancy onward the formation of an identity takes place through a series of identifications with others, alienated ideal models 'to which the subject attempts to conform.'[19] The mirror stage shows us the primacy of the visual image in this process. Our media-saturated environment provides an almost limitless choice of images that may serve to represent the ideal. Just as Aimée identified with a series of women celebrities, Pino identifies with a chain of literally spectacular Black men – 'magic' and 'princely' men who would not be found sweeping the sidewalk in front of a pizzeria (one of the unheroic tasks assigned to Pino by his father). As passive spectator to his Black heroes' media-amplified activity, Pino has adopted a 'feminine' attitude. In order to fully assimilate his self-image to the model of his ideals, and to regain the aggressively 'masculine' identity required of a young man of his class and ethnic background, he must foreclose their difference from him, of which Blackness is the privileged signifier. Blackness, foreclosed in the symbolic, returns in the real as the defining attribute of his persecutory bad object, the 'nigger.' Pino's racism then, far from being expunged by his love for Black entertainers will only intensify, for his hostility draws its strength from his jealous admiration.[20]

This is not to 'psychoanalyze' Pino – that would be preposterous (not least because he is a fictional character). By definition, a psychoanalysis entails a proper clinical setting in which an adequately experienced analyst gains access to a wide range of detailed materials over a long period of time. This is rather an instrumental use of psychoanalytic theory. I began with a now familiar situation in which someone writing in the area of critical theory of culture – 'cultural studies' – uses psychoanalytic terminology in a text from which psychoanalytic theory is, in any substantive sense, absent. The recourse to such terms is nevertheless meaningful. In Said's text I saw the use of the term *paranoia* as marking the place of a caesura between personal anecdote and political discourse. Taking Said at his word, I have begun to look at nationalism, at racism, *as if* they might indeed be paranoid structures. Psychoanalytic theory here functions as a heuristic device, a means to reinscribe a *space between* positions that have become frozen in opposition.[21] There are good reasons why debates over nationalism and racism are emotive, consequently they often generate more heat than light. We cannot afford to dispense with any source of illumination by which we may examine the images – real and fantasmatic – across which we construct our conflict-ridden identities. The conflict that flares into violence in Spike Lee's film is precisely over images, identities. On the walls of Sal's Famous Pizzeria are photographs of Italian American celebrities. Buggin' Out wants to see some Black faces on this wall of fame. Sal defends his own sovereign space. In this territorial dispute however neither party may claim original rights. When the sons of émigré Italians confront the descendants of abducted Africans in Sal's Pizzeria they do so in a Black and Hispanic district with a Dutch name, which was stolen from Native Americans. Most of us know the melancholy tension of separation from our origins. Said defines exile as a 'condition of terminal loss.' Kristeva chooses a more painful image to express this loss: she sees exile as the 'cosmopolitanism of the excoriated.' Excoriation, the loss of one's skin: violent image of the destruction of that first and last barrier between the ego and paranoiac space.

NOTES

1. Edward W. Said, 'Reflections on Exile,' *Granta*, 13 (Winter 1984), p. 161.
2. Ibid., 162.
3. Ibid., 162.
4. Indeed, in what Freud termed the 'compulsion to repeat' the subject repeats what it does not remember precisely in order to avoid bringing it to consciousness.
5. Julia Kristeva, *Etrangers à nous-mêmes*, Paris, Fayard, 1988, 25.
6. Elizabeth Grosz, 'Space, Time, and Bodies,' *On the Beach*, 13 April 1988 (Sydney).
7. Jacques Lacan, 'Aggressivity in Psychoanalysis,' in *Ecrits: A Selection*, New York, Norton, 1977, 11.
8. Edith Jacobson, *The Self and the Object World*, New York, International Universities Press, 1964, 47.
9. Daniel Paul Schreber, *Memoirs of My Nervous Illness*, Cambridge and London, Harvard University Press, 1988, 131–4.
10. Jacques Lacan, 'Motifs du crime paranoïaque (le crime des soeurs Papin),' *Minotaure*, no. 3 (15 December 1933), 27.
11. Roland Barthes, 'Myth Today,' in *Mythologies*, New York, Hill & Wang, 138.
12. Hélène Cixous, 'Sorties,' in Hélène Cixous and Catherine Clément, *The Newly Born Woman*, Minneapolis, University of Minnesota, 1986, 70. I offer the following as a depressingly typical example of the ordinary racism inscribed in everyday connotations of the black/white opposition: 'Black usually indicates death, misfortune or evil, or simply opposition to white's yielding and acceptance and purity.' See James Stockton, *Designer's Guide to Color*, San Fransisco, Chronicle Books, 1984, 34.
13. See Phyllis Rose, *Black Cleopatra: Josephine Baker in Her Time*, New York, Doubleday, 1989, 67.
14. Jacques Lacan, *The Four Fundamental Concepts of Psycho-Analysis*, London, Hogarth, 1977, 95–6.
15. *The New York Times Magazine*, 10 September 1989.
16. *The New York Times*, 25 August 1989.
17. Ibid., 19 December 1989.
18. See Spike Lee, 'Do the Right Thing' (script), in Spike Lee with Lisa Jones, *Do the Right Thing*, New York, Simon & Schuster, 1989, 184–5.
19. Jean Laplanche and Jean Bertrand Pontalis, *The Language of Psycho-Analysis*, London, Hogarth, 1973, 144.
20. We may recall that Schreber similarly 'split' his object: turning his doctor both into a God, in order that he might adopt a feminine attitude toward him without conflict, and also into a hated 'soul murderer', so that he might be protected from acknowledging the homosexual nature of his own feelings.
21. I have appropriated (or misappropriated) the idea of 'reinscription' in the space of the 'caesura' from Homi Bhaba. See 'Postcolonial authority and postmodern guilt,' unpublished paper, 1990.

9.2

AVTAR BRAH: *FROM* CARTOGRAPHIES OF DIASPORA: CONTESTING IDENTITIES

Together, the concepts of border and diaspora reference a politics of location. This point warrants emphasis, especially because the very strong association of notions of diaspora with displacement and dislocation means that the experience of *location* can easily dissolve out of focus. Indeed, it is the contradictions of and between location and dislocation that are a regular feature of diasporic positioning. Feminist politics have constituted an important site where issues of home, location, displacement and dislocation have long been a subject of contention and debate. Out of these debates emerges the notion of a 'politics of location' as *locationality in contradiction* – that is, a positionality of dispersal; of simultaneous situatedness within gendered spaces of class, racism, ethnicity, sexuality, age; of movement across shifting cultural, religious and linguistic boundaries; of journeys across geographical and psychic borders. [. . .] I would describe the politics of location as *a position of multi-axial locationality*. But politics is the operative word here, for multi-axial locationality does not predetermine what kind of subject positions will be constructed or assumed, and with what effects.

Self-reflexive autobiographical accounts often provide critical insights into political ramifications of border crossings across multiple positioning. One such account, an essay by Minnie Bruce Pratt entitled 'Identity: Skin, Blood, Heart' (Pratt 1984), has attracted attention in feminist analysis for its commitment to unravelling operations of power that naturalise identities inscribed in positions

Source: Avtar Brah, *Cartographies of Diaspora: Contesting Identities* (London and New York: Routledge, 1996), pp. 204–8.

of privilege, and the different costs involved in maintaining or relinquishing lived certainties attendant upon such positions. This text reveals what is to be gained when a narrative about identity continuously interrogates and problematises the very notion of a stable and essential identity by deconstructing the narrator's own position, in this case that of a white, middle-class, lesbian feminist raised as a Christian in the southern United States. Pratt is able to hold her various 'homes' and 'identities' in perpetual suspension even as she tries to recapture them in re-memory. She enacts her locationality from different subject positions, picking apart her position of racialised class privilege simultaneously as she works through her own experiences of coming out as a lesbian and confronting heterosexism in its many and varied manifestations. A critical strategy that enables this narrative to refuse reductive impulses is that it works at a number of different levels, addressing *the linked materiality of the social, the cultural, and the subjective*. As Biddy Martin and Chandra Talpade Mohanty point out:

> The narrative politicises the geography, demography, and architecture of these communities – Pratt's homes at various times of her history – by discovering local histories of exploitation and struggle. These histories are quite unlike the ones she is familiar with, the ones she grew up with. Pratt problematises her ideas about herself by juxtaposing the assumed histories of her family and childhood, predicated on the invisibility of the histories of people unlike her, to whom these geographical sites were also home. (Martin and Mohanty 1986: 195)

Pratt examines how her sense of safety in the world was largely related to her unquestioning acceptance of the normative codes of her social milieu, and the structures of legitimation that underpinned these norms. She is particularly attentive to the workings of racism as one of the central dynamics binding this Southern community together. The tenuous nature of her security and sense of belonging is revealed to her when, as a lesbian mother fighting for the custody of her children, she comes face-to-face with the heterosexism embedded not only in state structures but also in the everyday cultural practices taken for granted by her family, friends and the people she had considered as her 'community'. The withdrawal of emotional support by those whom she had previously loved throws into total disarray the concept of home and community which she had hitherto envisioned. Engulfed by a sense of dislocation and loss, Pratt 'moves home', and she chooses this moment of cultural and psychic journeying to learn about the processes which sustain social relations and subjectivities that had been at the centre of the world she had taken for granted.

While Pratt's narrative addresses the social universe of a white woman growing up in Alabama during the civil rights struggles, Angela Davis's autobiography articulates the positionality of a black woman growing up in Alabama at about the same time. A juxtaposition of these two narratives is helpful in offering related accounts of the operations of racism and class in the constitution of gendered forms of white and black subjectivity against the backdrop of a turbulent period in recent American history. Both women invoke the segregated South of their childhood, but their memories construct an experiential landscape charted from opposite sides of the racial divide. Pratt speaks of the terror endemic in the racist cultural formations of the South. Angela Davis recounts how this terror was unleashed on the black people in her hometown. She relates how she felt when, at the age of four, her family moved into an all-white area:

> Almost immediately after we moved there the white people got together and decided on a borderline between them and us. Center street became the line of demarcation. Provided we stayed on 'our' side of the line (the east side) they let it be known we would be left in peace. If we ever crossed over to their side, war would be declared. Guns were hidden in our house and vigilance was constant. (Davis 1974 [1990]: 78)

Racism was experienced by this four-year-old in the form of hostility from the white elderly couple who now became their neighbours:

> the way they stood a hundred feet away and glared at us, their refusal to speak when we said 'Good Afternoon' . . . sat on the porch all the time, their eyes heavy with belligerence . . . When a black minister and his wife transgressed the racial border and bought the house next door to the white elderly couple, the minister's house was bombed. As more black families continued to move in the bombings were such a constant response that soon our neighborhood became known as Dynamite Hill. (ibid.: 79)

Davis draws attention to class and gender differences both amongst and between black and white people, and to the conditions under which solidarities across these differentiations are made possible. One of the most poignant moments in the text is when, as a student in France, Davis reads a newspaper report about the racist bombing of a church in Birmingham, Alabama, and realises that the four girls named as killed are her friends. Her fellow students show sympathy but fail to grasp the systematic impact of racism as an institutional and cultural phenomenon underlying such violence, and instead treat the incident as one would a sudden 'accident' – 'as if my friends had just been killed in a crash'. Davis's account, quite rightly, does not ascribe this lack of understanding to their being white, but rather to the absence of an awareness on their part of the history of racism in the USA. Yet, awareness alone might still not have produced an understanding of this history. A deeper engagement with this history would inevitably call for a radical shift in subject position, of the kind that Pratt's narrative demonstrates. The point is that the issue is not simply one of acquiring knowledge but of deconstructing 'whiteness' as a social relation, as well as an experiential modality of subjectivity and identity (see [. . .] Breines, 1992; Ware 1992; Hall 1992; Frankenberg 1993).

What is especially important for the present discussion about these autobiographical accounts is the way in which they reveal how the same geographical space comes to articulate different histories and meanings, such that 'home' can simultaneously be a place of safety and terror. They also underscore [. . .] that diasporic or border positionality does not *in itself* assure a vantage point of privileged insight into and understanding of relations of power, although it does create a space in which experiential mediations may intersect in ways that render such understandings more readily accessible. It is essentially a question of politics. Diasporic identities cannot be read off in a one-to-one fashion straightforwardly from a border positionality, in the same way that a feminist subject position cannot be deduced from the category 'woman'. This point deserves emphasis especially because the proliferation of discourses about 'border crossings' and 'diasporic identities' might be taken to imply a common standpoint or a universalised notion of 'border consciousness'. Rather, there are multiple semiotic spaces at diasporic borders, and the probability of certain forms of consciousness emerging are subject to the play of political power and psychic investments in the maintenance or erosion of the status quo.

REFERENCES

Breines, W. (1992) *Young, White, and Miserable: Growing up Female in the Fifties.* Boston: Beacon Press.

Davis, A. (1990) *Angela Davis: An Autobiography*, first published 1974, London: Women's Press.

Frankenberg, R. (1993) *White Women, Race Maters: The Social Construction of Whiteness.* London: Routledge.

Frankenberg, R. and Mani, L. (1993) 'Crosscurrents, Crosstalk: Race, "Postcoloniality", and the Politics of Location', *Cultural Studies*, 7 (2): 292–310.

Hall, S. (1992) 'What is this "Black" in Black Popular Culture?', in G. Dent (ed.), *Black Popular Culture*, a project by Michelle Wallace. Seattle: Bay Press.

Martin, B. and Mohanty, C. T. (1986) 'Feminist Politics: What's Home Got to Do With It?', in T. de Lauretis (ed.), *Feminist Studies/Critical Studies.* Bloomington: Indiana University Press.

Pratt, M. B. (1984) 'Identity: Skin, Blood, Heart', in E. Bulkin, M. B. Pratt and B. Smith (eds), *Yours in Struggle: Feminist Perspectives on Racism and Anti-Semitism.* New York: Long Haul.

Ware, V. (1992) *Beyond the Pale: White Women, Racism, and History.* London: Verso.

EDWARD W. SAID: *FROM* OUT OF PLACE

All families invent their parents and children, give each of them a story, character, fate, and even a language. There was always something wrong with how I was invented and meant to fit in with the world of my parents and four sisters. Whether this was because I constantly misread my part or because of some deep flaw in my being I could not tell for most of my early life. Sometimes I was intransigent, and proud of it. At other times I seemed to myself to be nearly devoid of any character at all, timid, uncertain, without will. Yet the overriding sensation I had was of always being out of place. Thus it took me about fifty years to become accustomed to, or, more exactly, to feel less uncomfortable with, 'Edward,' a foolishly English name yoked forcibly to the unmistakably Arabic family name Said. True my mother told me that I had been named Edward after the Prince of Wales, who cut so fine a figure in 1935, the year of my birth, and Said was the name of various uncles and cousins. But the rationale of my name broke down both when I discovered no grandparents called Said and when I tried to connect my fancy English name with its Arabic partner. For years, and depending on the exact circumstances, I would rush past 'Edward' and emphasize 'Said'; at other times I would do the reverse, or connect these two to each other so quickly that neither would be clear. The one thing I could not tolerate, but very often would have to endure, was the disbelieving, and hence undermining, reaction: Edward? Said?

The travails of bearing such a name were compounded by an equally unsettling quandary when it came to language. I have never known what language I spoke

Source: Edward W. Said, *Out of Place: A Memoir* (London: Granta, 2000), pp. 3–12.

first, Arabic or English, or which one was really mine beyond any doubt. What I do know, however, is that the two have always been together in my life, one resonating in the other, sometimes ironically, sometimes nostalgically, most often each correcting, and commenting on, the other. Each *can* seem like my absolutely first language, but neither is. I trace this primal instability back to my mother, whom I remember speaking to me in both English and Arabic, although she always wrote to me in English – once a week, all her life, as did I, all of hers. Certain spoken phrases of hers like *tislamli* or *mish ʿarfa shu biddi ʿamal?* Or *rouhʿha* – dozens of them – were Arabic, and I was never conscious of having to translate them or, even in cases like *tislamli*, knowing exactly what they meant. They were a part of her infinitely maternal atmosphere, which in moments of great stress I found myself yearning for in the softly uttered phrase '*ya mama*,' an atmosphere dreamily seductive then suddenly snatched away, promising something in the end never given.

But woven into her Arabic speech were English words like 'naughty boy' and of course my name, pronounced 'Edwaad.' I am still haunted by the memory of the sound, at exactly the same time and place, of her voice calling me 'Edwaad,' the word wafting through the dusk air at closing time of the Fish Garden (a small Zamalek park with aquarium) and of myself, undecided whether to answer her back or to remain in hiding for just awhile longer, enjoying the pleasure of being called, being wanted, the non-Edward part of myself taking luxurious respite by not answering until the silence of my being became unendurable. Her English deployed a rhetoric of statement and norms that has never left me. Once my mother left Arabic and spoke English there was a more objective and serious tone that mostly banished the forgiving and musical intimacy of *her* first language, Arabic. At age five or six I knew that I was irremediably 'naughty' and at school was all manner of comparably disapproved-of things like 'fibber' and 'loiterer.' By the time I was fully conscious of speaking English fluently, if not always correctly, I regularly referred to myself not as 'me' but as 'you.' 'Mummy doesn't love you, naughty boy,' she would say, and I would respond, in half-plaintive echoing, half-defiant assertion, 'Mummy doesn't love you, but Auntie Melia loves you.' Auntie Melia was her elderly maiden aunt, who doted on me when I was a very young child. 'No she doesn't,' my mother persisted. 'All right. Saleh [Auntie Melia's Sudanese driver] loves you,' I would conclude, rescuing something from the enveloping gloom.

I hadn't then any idea where my mother's English came from or who, in the national sense of the phrase, she was: this strange state of ignorance continued until relatively late in my life, when I was in graduate school. In Cairo, one of the places where I grew up, her spoken Arabic was fluent Egyptian, but to my keener ears, and to those of the many Egyptians she knew, it was if not outright Shami, then perceptibly inflected by it. 'Shami' (Damascene) is the collective adjective and noun used by Egyptians to describe both an Arabic speaker who is not Egyptian and someone who is from Greater Syria, i.e., Syria itself, Lebanon, Palestine, Jordan; but 'Shami' is also used to designate the Arabic dialect spoken by a Shami. Much more than my father, whose linguistic ability was primitive compared to hers, my mother had an excellent command of classical Arabic as well as the demotic. Not enough of the latter to disguise her as Egyptian, however, which of course she was not. Born in Nazareth, then sent to boarding school and junior college in Beirut, she was Palestinian, even though her mother, Munira, was Lebanese. I never knew her father, but he, I discovered, was the Baptist minister in Nazareth, although he originally came from Safad, via a sojourn in Texas.

Not only could I not absorb, much less master, all the meanderings and interruptions of these details as they broke up a simple dynastic sequence, but I could not grasp why she was not a straight English mummy. I have retained this unsettled sense of many identities – mostly in conflict with each other – all of my life, together with an acute memory of the despairing feeling that I wish we could have been all-Arab, or all-European and American, or all-Orthodox Christian, or all-Muslim, or all-Egyptian, and so on. I found I had two alternatives with which to counter what in effect was the process of challenge, recognition, and exposure, questions and remarks like 'What are you?'; 'But Said is an Arab name'; 'You're American?'; 'You're American without an American name, and you've never been to America'; 'You don't look American!'; 'How come you were born in Jerusalem and you live *here*?'; 'You're an Arab after all, but what kind are you? A Protestant?'

I do not remember that any of the answers I gave out loud to such probings were satisfactory or even memorable. My alternatives were hatched entirely on my own: one might work, say, in school, but not in church or on the street with my friends. The first was to adopt my father's brashly assertive tone and say to myself 'I'm an American citizen,' and that's it. He was American by dint of having lived in the United States followed by service in the army during World War I. Partly because this alternative meant his making of me something incredible, I found it the least convincing. To say 'I am an American citizen' in an English school in wartime Cairo dominated by British troops and with what seemed to me a totally homogeneous Egyptian populace was a foolhardy venture, to be risked in public only when I was challenged officially to name my citizenship; in private I could not maintain it for long, so quickly did the affirmation wither away under existential scrutiny.

The second of my alternatives was even less successful than the first. It was to open myself to the deeply disorganized state of my real history and origins as I gleaned them in bits, and then to try to construct them into order. But I never had enough information; there were never the right number of well-functioning connectives between the parts I knew about or was able somehow to excavate; the total picture was never quite right. The trouble seemed to begin with my parents, their pasts, and names. My father, Wadie, was later called William (an early discrepancy that I assumed for a long time was only an Anglicization of his Arabic name but that soon appeared to me suspiciously like a case of assumed identity, with the name Wadie cast aside except by his wife and sister for not very creditable reasons). Born in Jerusalem in 1895 – my mother said it was more likely 1893 – he never told me more than ten or eleven things about his past, a series of unchanging pat phrases that hardly conveyed anything at all. He was at least forty at the time of my birth.

He hated Jerusalem, and although I was born and we spent long periods of time there, the only thing he ever said about it was that it reminded him of death. At some point in his life his father was a dragoman who because he knew German had, it was said, shown Palestine to Kaiser Wilhelm. And my grandfather – never referred to by name except when my mother, who never knew him, called him Abu Asaad – bore the surname Ibrahim. In school, therefore, my father was known as Wadie Ibrahim. I still do not know where 'Said' came from, and no one seems able to explain it. The only relevant detail about his father that my father thought fit to convey to me was that Abu-Asaad's whippings were much severer than his of me. 'How did you endure it?' I asked, to which he replied with a chuckle, 'Most of the time I ran away.' I was never able to do this, and never even considered it.

As for my paternal grandmother, she was equally shadowy. A Shammas by birth, her name was Hanné; according to my father, she persuaded him – he had left Palestine in 1911 – to return from the States in 1920 because she wanted him near her. My father always said he regretted his return home, although just as frequently he averred that the secret of his astonishing business successes was that he 'took care' of his mother, and she in return constantly prayed that the streets beneath his feet would turn into gold. I was never shown her likeness in any photograph, but in my father's regimen for bringing me up she represented two contradictory adages that I could never reconcile: mothers are to be loved, he said, and taken care of unconditionally. Yet because by virtue of selfish love they can deflect children from their chosen career (my father wanted to remain in the United States and practice law), so mothers should not be allowed to get too close. And that was, is, all I ever knew about my paternal grandmother

I assumed the existence of a longish family history in Jerusalem. I based this on the way my paternal aunt, Nabiha, and her children inhabited the place, as if they, and especially she, embodied the city's rather peculiar, not to say austere and constricted, spirit. Later I heard my father speak of us as Khleifawis, which I was informed was our real clan origin; but the Khleifawis originated in Nazareth. In the mid-1980s I was sent some extracts from a published history of Nazareth, and in them was a family tree of one Khleifi, probably my great-grandfather. Because it corresponded to no lived, even hinted-at, experience of mine, this startlingly unexpected bit of information – which suddenly gave me a whole new set of cousins – means very little to me.

My father, I know, did attend St. George's School in Jerusalem and excelled at football and cricket, making the First Eleven in both sports over successive years, as center forward and wicket keeper, respectively. He never spoke of learning anything at St. George's, nor of much else about the place, except that he was famous for dribbling a ball from one end of the field to the other, and then scoring. His father seems to have urged him to leave Palestine to escape conscription into the Ottoman army. Later I read somewhere that a war had broken out in Bulgaria around 1911 for which troops were needed; I imagined him running away from the morbid fate of becoming Palestinian cannon fodder for the Ottoman army in Bulgaria.

None of this was ever presented to me in sequence, as if his pre-American years were discarded by my father as irrelevant to his present identity as my father, Hilda's husband, U.S. citizen. One of the great set stories, told and retold many times while I was growing up, was his narrative of coming to the United States. It was a sort of official version, and was intended, in Horatio Alger fashion, to instruct and inform his listeners, who were mostly his children and wife. But it also collected and put solidly in place both what he wanted known about himself before he married my mother and what thereafter was allowed into public view. It still impresses me that he stuck to the story in its few episodes and details for the thirty-six years he was my father until his death in 1971, and that he was so successful in keeping at bay all the other either forgotten or denied aspects of his story. Not until twenty years after his death did it occur to me that he and I were almost exactly the same age when we, precisely forty years apart, came to the United States, he to make his life, I to be directed by his script for me, until I broke away and started trying to live and write my own.

My father and a friend called Balloura (no first name ever given) went first from Haifa to Port Said in 1911, where they boarded a British freighter to Liverpool. They were in Liverpool for six months before they got jobs as stewards on a passenger liner to New York. Their first chore on board was to clean portholes, but since neither of them knew what a porthole was, despite having pretended to 'great sea-going experience' in order to get the jobs, they cleaned everything but the portholes. Their supervisor was 'nervous' (a word my father used regularly to signify anger and general bother) about them, overturned a pail of water, and set them to floor swabbing. Wadie was then switched to waiting on tables, the only memorable aspect of which was his description of serving one course, then rushing out to vomit as the ship heaved and pitched, then staggering back to serve the next. Arriving in New York without valid papers, Wadie and the shadowy Balloura bided their time, until, on the pretext of leaving the ship temporarily to visit a nearby bar, they boarded a passing streetcar 'going they had no idea where,' and rode it to the end of the line.

Another of my father's much repeated stories concerned a YMCA swimming race at an upstate New York lake. This provided him with an engaging moral: he was the last to finish, but persisted to the end ('Never give up' was the motto) – in fact until the next race had already begun. I never questioned, and was duly submissive to, the packaged homily 'Never give up.' Then, when I was in my early thirties, it dawned on me that Wadie was so slow and stubborn he had in fact *delayed* all the other events, not a commendable thing. 'Never giving up,' I told my father – with the uppitiness of a recently franchised but still powerless citizen – could also mean a social nuisance, obstructing others, delaying the program, maybe even giving impatient spectators an opportunity to hoot and boo the offendingly slow and heedlessly stubborn swimmer. My father shot me a surprised, even slightly uncomfortable, smile, as if I had finally cornered him in a small way, and then he turned away without a word. The story was not repeated again.

He became a salesman for ARCO, a Cleveland paint company, and he studied at Western Reserve University. Hearing the Canadians were sending a battalion 'to fight the Turks in Palestine,' he crossed the border and enlisted. When he discovered that there was to be no such battalion he simply deserted. He then signed up for the American Expeditionary Force and was consigned to the rigors of Camp Gordon, Georgia, where his reaction to a battery of inoculations meant that he spent most of basic training ill and in bed. The scene then shifts to France, where he did time in the trenches; my mother had two photographs of him in the military dress of that time, a Cross of Lorraine hung round his neck in one of them, attesting to his French service. He used to speak of being gassed and wounded, then quarantined and interned in Mentone (he always used the Italian pronunciation). Once when I asked him what it was like to be in a war I recall him telling me about a German soldier whom he had killed at close range, 'raising up his hands in a great cry before I shot him;' he said that he had recurring nightmares about the episode over several years of tormented sleep. After his death, when we had some reason to recover his army discharge papers (lost for half a century) I was stunned to discover that as a member of the quartermaster's corps he was recorded as having participated in no known military campaigns. This was probably a mistake, since I still believe my father's version.

He returned to Cleveland after the war and set up his own paint company. His older brother, Asaad ('Al'), was then working as a sailor on the Great Lakes. Even back then it was the younger brother, 'Bill' – the name change occurred in the army – who supplied the older one with money and also sent his parents half his salary. Asaad once threatened to attack Bill with a knife: he needed more money from his prosperous younger brother in order to marry a Jewish woman whom my father guessed that he abandoned but did not divorce when he suddenly also came back to Palestine in the twenties.

Curiously, nothing of my father's American decade survived except his extremely lean retellings of it, and such odd fragments as a love of apple pie à la mode and a few often repeated expressions, like 'hunky-dory,' and 'big boy.' Over time I have found that what his stint in the United States really expressed in relation to his subsequent life was the practice of self-making with a purpose, which he exploited in what he did and what he made others around him, chiefly me, do. He always averred that America was his country, and when we strenuously disagreed about Vietnam, he would fall back comfortably on 'My country, right or wrong.' But I never met or heard about friends or acquaintances from that time; there was one tiny photograph of Wadie at a YMCA camp plus a few laconic and uninformative entries in a soldier's log from the war year, 1917–18. And that was it. After he died I wondered whether, like Asaad, he hadn't had a wife and perhaps even a family that he too had left behind. Yet so powerfully instructive was his story for the shape my youth took under his direction that I cannot recall ever asking anything like a critical question.

After America the story gathers immediacy and somehow loses even a suggestion of Horatio Alger romance: it was as if, having returned to Palestine in 1920 armed with U.S. citizenship, William A. Said (formerly Wadie Ibrahim) had quite abruptly turned sober pioneer, hard-working and successful businessman, and Protestant, a resident first of Jerusalem then of Cairo. This was the man I knew. The nature of the early relationship with his older cousin Boulos Said – who was also his sister Nabiha's husband – was never completely given, though clearly it was Boulos who founded the Palestine Educational Company, which Wadie entered (and invested in) on his return home. The two men became equal partners, although it was Wadie who in 1929 branched off from Palestine into Egypt, where, in a matter of no more than three years, he established the successful Standard Stationery Company, with two retail stores in Cairo, one in Alexandria, and various agencies and subdealerships in the Suez Canal Zone. There was a flourishing Syrian (Shami) community in Cairo, but he seems to have stayed clear of it, choosing instead to work long hours and play an occasional game of tennis with his friend Halim Abu Fadil; he told me that they played at two p.m., the hottest time of day, from which I was to conclude that an iron discipline, punishing in its rigors, ruled his efforts in everything he did, even sports.

My father alluded infrequently to those years before his marriage in 1932, but it seemed that fleshly temptations – Cairo's rococo nightlife, its brothels, sex shows, and opportunities for general profligacy offered to prosperous foreigners – were of little interest to him; his celibacy was virtuous and without a whiff of debauchery. My mother – who of course didn't know him then – used to tell how he would come home to his modest Bab el Louk flat, eat a solitary dinner, then spend the evening listening to classical records, reading his Home Library and Everyman's Library classics, which included many of the Waverley novels as well as the *Ethics* of G. E. Moore and Aristotle (during my adolescence and after, however, he confined his reading to works on war, politics, and diplomacy). He was well-off enough in 1932 to get married, and to take his much younger wife – she was eighteen and he was thirty-seven – for a three-month honeymoon in Europe. The marriage was brokered by my aunt Nabiha through her contacts in Nazareth and, to some degree, by my mother's aunt in Cairo, Melia Badr (Auntie Melia), a formidable spinster who with her amiable chauffeur, Saleh, became an important part of my childhood landscape. All these details came from my mother, who must have heard them as a sort of preparation for entering the state of matrimony with an older man she had not met, who lived in a place she knew virtually nothing about. And then he turned into the model husband and father whose ideas, values, and of course methods were to shape me.

Whatever the actual historical facts were, my father came to represent a devastating combination of power and authority, rationalistic discipline, and repressed emotions; and all this, I later realized, has impinged on me my whole life, with some good, but also some inhibiting and even debilitating effects. As I have grown older I have found a balance between these effects, but from my childhood through my twenties I was very much controlled by him. With the help of my mother, he tried to create a world very much like a gigantic cocoon, into which I was introduced and maintained at, as I look back over it half century later, exorbitant cost. What impresses me now is not that I survived it, but that by biding my time within his regime I somehow managed to connect the strengths of his basic lessons to my own abilities, which he seemed unable to affect, perhaps even to reach. What also remained of him in me, unfortunately, was his relentless insistence on doing something useful, getting things done, 'never giving up,' more or less all the time. I have no concept of leisure or relaxation and, more particularly, no sense of cumulative achievement. Every day for me is like beginning a new term at school, with a vast and empty summer behind it, and an uncertain tomorrow before it. Over time 'Edward' became a demanding taskmaster, registering lists of flaws and failures with as much energy as accumulated obligations and commitments, the two lists balancing and in a sense cancelling each other. 'Edward' still has to begin every day anew and by the end of it normally feels that very little has gone right.

BIOGRAPHICAL DETAILS OF EDITORS AND CONTRIBUTING EDITORS

EDITORS

Michael Rossington has research interests in the field of Romantic literature. He is currently working on a monograph entitled *Shelley's Europe* and co-editing volume 3 of the Longman edition of *The Poems of Shelley*.

Anne Whitehead has recently published *Trauma Fiction* (Edinburgh University Press, 2004) and co-edited a collection of essays entitled *W. G. Sebald: A Critical Companion* (Edinburgh University Press, 2004). She is currently working on *Memory* for the Routledge New Critical Idioms series.

Michael Rossington and Anne Whitehead have co-edited a collection of essays, *Between the Psyche and the Polis: Refiguring History in Literature and Theory* (Burlington, VT and Aldershot: Ashgate, 2000).

CONTRIBUTING EDITORS

Linda Anderson works in the fields of autobiography, feminism and gender studies. She has published *Remembered Futures: Women and Autobiography in the Twentieth Century* (Prentice Hall, 1997) and *Autobiography* (Routledge, 2001)

Kate Chedgzoy specialises in feminist, queer and postcolonial approaches to Renaissance literature. She has published *Shakespeare's Queer Children: Sexual Politics and Contemporary Culture* (Manchester University Press, 1996).

Pablo Mukherjee researches into nineteenth-century and contemporary imperial and popular cultures, and postcolonial and cultural theory. His monograph *Crime and Empire: Representing India in the Nineteenth Century* was published by Oxford University Press in 2003.

Jennifer Richards works in the Early Modern period. She has recently published *Civil Conversation and the Meaning of 'Honesty'* (Cambridge University Press, 2003) and is currently working on *Rhetoric* for the Routledge New Critical Idioms series.

INDEX

Note: page numbers in bold denote the texts of the readings